POLARISING SEXUALITIES AND GENDERS

POLARISING SEXUALITIES AND GENDERS

Divisions, Differences and LGBTQIA+ Equalities

Edited by
Kath Browne and Emily Kazyak

BLOOMSBURY ACADEMIC
LONDON • NEW YORK • OXFORD • NEW DELHI • SYDNEY

BLOOMSBURY ACADEMIC

Bloomsbury Publishing Plc, 50 Bedford Square, London, WC1B 3DP, UK
Bloomsbury Publishing Inc, 1359 Broadway, New York, NY 10018, USA
Bloomsbury Publishing Ireland, 29 Earlsfort Terrace, Dublin 2, D02 AY28, Ireland

BLOOMSBURY, BLOOMSBURY ACADEMIC and the Diana logo are trademarks of Bloomsbury Publishing Plc

First published in Great Britain 2025

Copyright © Kath Browne and Emily Kazyak, 2025

Kath Browne and Emily Kazyak have asserted their right under the Copyright, Designs and Patents Act, 1988, to be identified as Authors of this work.

For legal purposes the Acknowledgements on p. viii constitute an extension of this copyright page.

Cover design: Adriana Brioso

This work is published open access subject to a Creative Commons Attribution-NonCommercial-NoDerivatives 4.0 International licence (CC BY-NC-ND 4.0, https://creativecommons.org/licenses/by-nc-nd/4.0/). You may re-use, distribute, and reproduce this work in any medium for non-commercial purposes, provided you give attribution to the copyright holder and the publisher and provide a link to the Creative Commons licence.

Bloomsbury Publishing Plc does not have any control over, or responsibility for, any third-party websites referred to or in this book. All internet addresses given in this book were correct at the time of going to press. The author and publisher regret any inconvenience caused if addresses have changed or sites have ceased to exist, but can accept no responsibility for any such changes.

A catalogue record for this book is available from the British Library.

A catalog record for this book is available from the Library of Congress.

ISBN: HB: 978-1-3504-4986-2
PB: 978-1-3504-4985-5
ePDF: 978-1-3504-4988-6
eBook: 978-1-3504-4987-9

Typeset by Deanta Global Publishing Services, Chennai, India
Printed and bound in Great Britain

For product safety related questions contact productsafety@bloomsbury.com

To find out more about our authors and books visit www.bloomsbury.com and sign up for our newsletters.

CONTENTS

List of Illustrations vii
Acknowledgements viii
About the Authors ix

Chapter 1
INTRODUCTION 1
    Kath Browne and Emily Kazyak

Chapter 2
TALKING PAST EACH OTHER: POLITICAL POLARIZATION AND
TRANSGENDER ATHLETE BANS 17
    Elizabeth Rahilly and Kimberly Martin

Chapter 3
INCOMMENSURABLE REALITIES: LGBTQ BODIES AND THE
CONSTRUCTION OF RELIGION, SEXUALITY AND DISCRIMINATION IN
US FEDERAL RELIGIOUS EXEMPTION LITIGATION 33
    Emily Kazyak

Chapter 4
CLAIMING SPACE IN THE MARGINS: COMMUNITY ORGANIZATIONS
AS LIMINAL SPACES FOR BLACK TRANSGENDER WOMEN NAVIGATING
POLITICAL POLARIZATION IN THE US SOUTH 49
    Kimya Loder

Chapter 5
WE ARE JUST LIKE EVERYBODY ELSE: POLARISATION AND QUEER
ACTIVISM IN LITHUANIA 61
    Rasa Kamarauskaitė

Chapter 6
QUEER LEGAL GEOGRAPHIES OF POLARISATION IN INTERNATIONAL
LGBTQ RIGHTS LAW 75
    Kay Lalor

Chapter 7
UNEASY ALLIANCES: ORGANIZING ACROSS DIFFERENCE TO RESIST
ANTI-TRANS LEGISLATION 89
    Erika Slaymaker

Chapter 8
IDENTITY WORK IN THE HUBRISTIC PRESENT: HOW GENERATIONS
AS GROUPISM CREATE POLARIZATION 105
    S. L. Crawley

Chapter 9
'GENDER DEBATE' DISCOURSE: POLARISING, BIGOTED AND VALIDATING 119
    Elizabeth Peel

Chapter 10
MISINFORMATION IN THE 'GENDER WARS' IN BRITAIN: AFFECTIVE
ATTACHMENTS IN THE USE AND MISUSE OF EVIDENCE 137
    Sarah Lamble

Chapter 11
NAVIGATING THE TENSIONS OF CREATIVITY AND DIVISION:
LANNING AN ARTIST-LED WORKSHOP TO ADDRESS POLARISATIONS
AROUND SEXUALITIES/GENDERS/ABORTION 157
    Carol Ballantine, Leah Hilliard and Kath Browne

Chapter 12
CRUMBLED WORLDS OR IMPERFECT UTOPIAS: DISCUSSING OUR
POLARISED SEXUAL AND GENDERED LIVES 175
    Andrew McCartan, Jody Moore-Ponce, Ann Burke, Sarah Foudy and
    Eliza Thor

References 191
Index 225

ILLUSTRATIONS

Figures

8.1	Timeframe of reference on the timeline of (US) feminist/queer lexicon	113
11.1	The concentric circles with objects	164
11.2	Drawing using the extended sharpie pen	165
11.3	A placemat moving through the laminator	167
11.4	Diagram of a tablecloth with concentric circles, divided into three wedges	168

Tables

7.1	List of Participants by Race, Age and Gender	92
11.1	Timetable for Artist-Led Workshop	163

ACKNOWLEDGEMENTS

We, the editors, would like to thank all of those who participated in the symposium in Dublin that led to this book. It was an exciting and engaging journey, and we are delighted to see your work in print. Thanks to all who contributed to the research that made these chapters possible.

We would like to thank Seán Pender for his help in pulling the book together, including finding the many, many missing references! We would also like to thank Eliza Thor for her help organising the symposium, for her integral part in bringing us together and for developing ideas with us.

Thanks go to Olivia Dellow and all at Bloomsbury for commissioning the book and supporting us through its production.

This book and the symposium are supported by the European Union under the Horizon 2020 programme, Grant no. 817897, the National Science Foundation, Division of Social and Economic Sciences, award #2230882 and the University of Nebraska-Lincoln College of Arts & Sciences Research Impact and Engagement Grant.

Kath would like to thank Emily for the exciting opportunity she came to me with. Working with you was a pleasure and a privilege, and I hope it will continue! I would also like to thank Denise Twomey, Cara, Taidgh and Callie, who I promised would be named in my next book!

Emily would like to thank Kath for the opportunity to collaborate and for your generosity while I was in Dublin. I look forward to our continued conversations! Thanks also to James Brunton, Roz and Julie for bringing so much joy into my days.

ABOUT THE AUTHORS

Ann Burke:
Ann Burke is a PhD researcher and President's Scholar at South East Technological University (SETU) in Ireland. Her doctoral focus is on morality in social movements, with particular interest in gendered critiques.

Andrew McCartan:
Andrew McCartan is a postdoctoral researcher in the School of Geography at University College Dublin, Ireland. His research interests focus on the spatiotemporalities of queer activisms in 'post-equality' landscapes, resistances to and contestations around and within LGBT equalities and communities, and the sense of belonging among diverse undergraduate students. He teaches critical social geographies and fieldwork methodologies.

Carol Ballantine:
Carol Ballantine is a postdoctoral research fellow at University College Dublin, Ireland. Her research to date has focused on gender, violence and migration, using feminist, narrative and creative approaches.

Emily Kazyak:
Emily Kazyak is a professor of sociology and women's and gender studies at the University of Nebraska-Lincoln, United States. She has published widely on the topic of sexuality in American culture, politics and law. In addition to her research on religious freedom laws in the United States, her scholarship has addressed the intersection of geographies and sexualities, American public opinion of LGBTQ rights and the family relationships of LGBTQ people.

Elizabeth Peel:
Elizabeth Peel is a professor of communication and social interaction in the Department of Communication and Media, School of Social Sciences and Humanities at Loughborough University, UK, and a fellow of the British Psychological Society. She has published widely in critical social and health psychology. She is on the editorial board of four journals and co-edits the Routledge *Gender and Sexualities in Psychology* book series. Her co-authored award-winning textbook *Lesbian, Gay, Bisexual, Trans, Intersex and Queer Psychology* is published by Cambridge University Press. Email: e.peel@lboro.ac.uk; X/twitter: @profpeel.

Elizabeth Rahilly:
Elizabeth Rahilly is an assistant professor of sociology at Georgia Southern University, United States. Her research and teaching interests include gender, sexuality, LGBTQ+ studies, parenting, qualitative methods and political discourse. Her work has been published in many journal outlets, including *Gender & Society*, *Sexuality & Culture*, *LGBTQ+ Family*, *Journal of Family Studies*, *Discourse & Society* and *Sociological Inquiry*, and she has published a book regarding parents who support transgender children, *Trans-Affirmative Parenting: Raising Kids Across the Gender Spectrum*.

Erika Slaymaker:
Erika Slaymaker earned her PhD in sociology from the University of Texas at Austin. Her research focuses on social movements, transgender politics and the sociology of gender. Her dissertation investigates organising against anti-trans legislation and policies in Texas.

Eliza Thor:
Eliza Thor is a queer family scholar, earning their PhD in sociology from the University of Nebraska-Lincoln, United States. Their research interests are in queer- and trans-led families, household labour and how couples support one another's identities. They have taught queer studies, families, sociological theory and criminology.

Jody Moore-Ponce:
Jody Moore-Ponce is a PhD researcher in the sociology department of University College Cork (UCC), Ireland. Her research focuses on political and social polarisation, the new authority of 'lived experience', the rise of the far-right and deployments of 'lived experience' in social justice activism. She has worked as a part-time lecturer at UCC. Her work has been published in the *European Journal of Social Theory* and in *Transforming Society*. She currently holds a tutor of sociology position in University College Cork.

Kath Browne:
Kath Browne is a geography professor at University College Dublin, Ireland. Her research has focused on social justice and inequalities, specifically around gender and sexualities. She has worked with those marginalised because of their sexual and gender identities, exploring how lives can be made liveable, including with Niharika Banerjea. She has also developed the concept of heteroactivism, conceptualising the activisms of those who are opposed to sexual and gender equalities, with Catherine Nash and Andrew Gorman-Murray. She leads the Beyond Opposition research, an ERC consolidator project that seeks to explore new ways of engaging difference, differently. She is the project co-ordinator for the RESIST research project.

Kay Lalor:
Kay Lalor is a reader in human rights law at Manchester Metropolitan University, UK. Her work explores the growth of LGBTQI+ rights activism in international legal arenas, focusing in particular on the spatio-legal dimensions of how legally informed activism is translated into non- and quasi-legal projects and what this means for the development of human rights theory, law and practice. She is the co-director of the Sylvia Pankhurst Centre for Gender and Diversity Research at Manchester Met and the production editor for *Feminist Legal Studies*.

Kimya Loder:
Kimya Loder is an assistant professor of sociology at the Georgia Institute of Technology, United States. Her research draws upon theories of race, gender and sexuality-based inequality offered by feminist and race scholars to understand the political behaviour of marginalised groups.

Kimberly Martin:
Kimberly Martin is an assistant professor of political science at Georgia Southern University, United States. She teaches courses in American government, research methods, public policy and leadership. Her research interests include political leadership, state politics and LGBTQ+ policy.

Leah Hilliard:
Leah Hilliard is an artist, educator, researcher and cultural programmer whose art practice is based on joyful performance and the power of conversation. She regularly exhibits and participates in research projects in Ireland and internationally. Using conversation, colour, materials and texture, she explores society, technology and connection in a technology-focused world. Leah lectures in the media department in the School of Fine Art at the National College of Art and Design, Dublin, Ireland.

Rasa Kamarauskaitė:
Rasa Kamarauskaitė is a former PhD student at SSEES, UCL, UK. She has recently submitted her thesis on 'Everyday (in)visibility of Lithuanian LGBQ+ people'.

S. L. Crawley:
S. L. Crawley is a professor of sociology and affiliated faculty in women's, gender and sexuality studies at the University of South Florida in Tampa, Florida, United States, and currently editor (with V. Patil, Z. Magubane and O. Lizardo) of the journal *Sociological Theory*. They have published in such journals as *Gender & Society, Journal of Lesbian Studies, Symbolic Interaction, Sexualities, Journal of Contemporary Ethnography, Sociological Theory, The Sociological Quarterly* and *Hypatia* and co-authored the book *Gendering Bodies* with Lara J. Foley and Constance L. Shehan. Some of their work has been translated into Ukrainian and Russian.

Sarah Foudy:
Sarah Foudy worked on the Beyond Opposition research project at UCD.

Sarah Lamble:
Sarah Lamble is a professor of criminology and queer theory at Birkbeck, University of London, UK. Lamble's research addresses questions of gender, sexuality and the criminal legal system and explores queer feminist alternatives to imprisonment, policing and punishment.

Chapter 1

INTRODUCTION

Kath Browne and Emily Kazyak

Introduction

Divisions around sexual and gendered lives, loves, politics and activisms are not new. There is nothing new in the vilification of lesbian, gay, bisexual, trans, queer, intersex and asexual plus (LGBTQIA+) people or the creation of homo/bi/trans/queerphobic legislations and social norms and the resistances to these. Contemporary LGBTQ+ polarisations build on and develop from previous and ongoing tensions, both in terms of pro/anti-LGBTQIA+ divides and differentiation among LGBTQIA+ people in ways that create good/bad gays (Bell & Binnie, 2004; Duggan, 2003; Warner, 2000) and/or tensions around gender/trans recognition (Stryker & Whittle, 2013). Thus, we face a contemporary moment where polarisations are seemingly increasing, modifying and defining ways of life, political systems and for some our very existence.

In this collection, we are centralising sexualities and genders and focusing on polarisations around LGBTQIA+ equalities that create contemporary lives and politics. This does not negate the ways LGBTQ arenas can be co-opted, used and reworked to serve a variety of political agendas; it is, however, to refuse to reduce contestations and divisions around LGBTQ lives to only 'wedge issues' that are deployed for various political gains. Our focus is on recent shifts in LGBTQ equalities legislations, and social acceptances in certain places, such as same-sex marriage, employment equalities and gender recognition (Week, 2007). These are countered by legal challenges, resistances and reactions to these, (Nash & Browne, 2020; Patternote & Kuhar, 2018; Kazyak & Stange, 2018; Kazyak et al., 2023a, 2023b; Burke et al, 2022), including distancing the nation from these 'Western' imports and state repressions and resistances (Weiss & Bosia, 2013; Rao, 2020). The 'progress' they entail alters the terms of local, national and global debates around sexualities and genders. These manifest in people's lives, as well as political and geopolitical assertions and expectations of localities, states and nations (Browne & Bakshi, 2013; Nash & Browne, 2020; Banerjea & Browne, 2023). The intra-community LGBTQIA+ tensions and divisions that have long divided supposedly coherent communities (Hemmings, 2005; Stryker & Whittle, 2013; Ward, 2008) also emerge in new, and often more visible, ways in contemporary mainstream landscapes (Pearce et al., 2020). These previously intra-community divisions can now be seen as being created to be mainstream, including in media and policy debates (Rahilly and Martin, Peel, Lamble).

This book emerged from an in-person one-day symposium in Dublin in June 2023. Chapter authors wrote drafts and came together to discuss polarisations around LGBTQIA+ equalities.[1] This chapter sets the scene for the resulting chapters from this symposium and the discussions therein. It initially and briefly examines the predominant mode of engaging with the concept of polarisation – political polarisations. We then examine these in relation to the supposed 'wedge issue' of LGBTQ/anti-LGBTQ, questioning this framing. It then turns to the divisions and schisms within LGBTQIA+ and feminist activisms and academic writing since the late twentieth century, noting that these divisions are not new, but different. In doing so, we do not (indeed cannot) offer an in-depth literature review of polarisations within and beyond LGBTQIA+ equalities. Instead, we use this chapter to highlight some key discussions of polarisations. We move to bring together an overview of how authors defined polarisations across this collection, recognising the place of both exploring the entrenched sides that form polarised debates, and also the shaping of action and the creation of polarisations through practices of opposition. These offer different considerations for addressing polarisations through empowerment of marginalised people and considering opposition itself. We then outline each chapter and their articulations and empirical research on polarisation between those who hold fundamental differences around sexualities/genders from outside and within LGBTQIA+ communities.

Political polarisations: Electoral divides and allegiances

Considerations of polarisation often circulate around politics and social issues, where complex social relations are perceived and presented as 'black and white' based on a conflict between two entrenched social groups (McNeil-Wilson et al., 2019, p. 6) and a multiplicity of differences are reduced to 'them and us' (McCoy, Rhaman, & Sommer, 2018). This creates in/out groups and loyalties (Zeller & Vidra, 2021). Researchers have discussed the existence of 'ideological polarization', or the ideological differences that exist between people on certain social issues (see, e.g. Abramowitz & Saunders, 2008). More recently, exploring in-group/out-group creations, Gidron and Horne (2020) coined the term 'affective polarization' to describe the heightened emotional responses wherein one's own political party is highly regarded whereas other political parties are seen as the enemy. Such affective polarisation relies on negative emotions and animosity towards and about the political party out-group (Hahm et al., 2022). Affective polarisation, it is argued, is important for populist radical right (PRR)/far-right groups to legitimise their policies (Harteveld, Mendoza, & Rooduijn, 2022). Although much of this literature is focused on the United States and the polarisation of left-right politics, there are increasingly considerations of Europe in ways that adhere to and challenge these framings (Borbáth et al., 2023) and comparative cross-national studies (Boxell, Gentzkow, & Shapiro, 2024; Gidron, Adams, & Horne, 2020).

Focused on divisions, scholars have studied polarisation around a host of economic and social issues, including US electoral politics (e.g. Hetherington, 2009), Brexit (e.g. Hobolt et al., 2021), immigration (e.g. Baker & Edmonds, 2021) and climate change (e.g. Bliuc et al., 2015). Polarisations in these terms refer to intense schisms that are related to political, social, economic and cultural divergences. These are seen to result in specific ideological stances that influence electoral allegiances and political choices in the partisan politics of the United States (e.g. Baumer & Gold, 2010; Abramowitz & Saunders, 2008), the multiplicities of the European system (see Borbáth et al., 2023) as well as the creation of political power in authoritarian and 'illiberal' regimes to shore up power (e.g. Zeller & Vidra, 2021).

Studies of political polarisation often focus on identifying the factors that drive polarisation. In this framing, polarisation is seen as existing across all societies and is understood as problematic both nationally and globally at extreme levels, where divisive rhetoric and policy drives polarisations that create marginalised others and social divisions for political ends (e.g. Carothers & O'Donohue, 2019; Zeller & Vidra, 2021; McCoy & Sommer, 2019; McCarthy, 2019). Research questions in this framework pertain to how to measure and predict polarisations, whether it is increasing, what factors are associated with polarisation and what the consequences of polarisation are for democratic societies (McCoy et al., 2018; Zeller & Vira, 2021). In assessing what factors contribute to political polarisation, scholars point to broad sociodemographic changes like mass migration and generational divides in ageing societies (Ford & Jennings, 2020) or rising economic inequality (Stewart, McCarty, & Bryson, 2020). Documenting the polarisation in political attitudes seeks to assess the degree to which these divides are growing larger over time. In their analyses, Abramowitz and Saunders (2008) find that the US public has become increasingly ideologically divided since the 1970s, with stark divides between perspectives among Democrats and Republicans.

Despite somewhat of a consensus that political polarisation exists and both creates and is created by social polarisations, there are some critiques of polarisation itself and its social manifestations. There has been a querying of the degree to which perceptions about polarisation between groups are larger than the reality, for instance, if a focus on the polarisation of political elites in the United States obscures how everyday citizens have not become more polarised in their attitudes towards social issues (see Fiorina, Abrams, & Pope, 2008, 2010; Fiorina & Abrams, 2008; Hetherington, 2009).

This section has examined some of the key discussions of polarisation within political polarisation predominantly based in or on US partisan politics. This underpins the next section, which questions the framing of LGBTQ/anti-LGBTQ politics as only being an aspect of the political, ideological and affective divisions that drive broader political agendas and goals. In doing so, we negate the influence of the United States, particularly around the Christian Right, recognising that research in this collection from US partisan politics can create and are created through LGBTQ ideological divergences.

LGBTQIA+/anti-LGBTQIA+ polarisations beyond a 'wedge issue' for other political ends

Gender and sexuality can be seen as secondary to the 'main issue' of political polarisation, acting predominantly as a useful tool in the creation of ideological divisions that drive access to power and the continuing control of nation states. Rather than being intersectional, these tools are used to drive agendas in 'bigger' 'more important' arenas and, in turn, may be discarded where they are less useful. This assumes that LGBTQIA+ issues are not as important as other areas, such that catalysing social debates and polarisations around gender and sexuality can be dismissed in favour of the 'real issues': political power, authoritarianism and money. Yet, gender/sexuality have long been fiercely contested and hotly debated, creating oppositions and oppressions particularly of LGBTQIA+ people, but also more broadly of those who contest sexual and gendered 'moralities' (Stychin, 2003; Binnie et al., 2006). Conversely those who seek to promote sexual and gender moralities can be heavily invested in the maintenance of moral social orders for the 'good' of civilisation (Nash & Browne, 2020; Kazyak et al., 2021).

Bringing together issues of sexual/gendered moralities, contestations of equalities legislations and inclusions, and political polarisations—the US Christian Right has long been associated with the polarisations that have defined the US political landscape (Burak, 2008; Burke, 2016; Herman, 1997), as well as more recent manifestations and 'new frontiers' in the culture wars (Stein, 2022; Castle, 2019). More recent US public opinion research consistently shows how religiosity (being more religious) and being Evangelical Protestant, in particular, are both associated with being less supportive of LGBTQ+ rights (Beyerlein & Eberle, 2014; Kazyak et al., 2021). In the United States, conservative religious political activists can use strategies that seek to demonise LGBTQ people and restrict LGBTQ+ rights (Stone, 2012, 2017) driving social movement responses and creation (Fetner, 2008). Although it is clear that religiosity does not preclude LGBTQIA+ identification or inclusion (Yip, 2012; Hunt, 2009; Browne et al., 2010), intersectional issues can and do at times align, as Kazyak notes, around religion, gender and sexualities (re)constituting specific forms of polarisations. Thus, rather than a one-sided relationship, conservative religious ideology and more traditional beliefs about gender, sexuality and family have been shown to be co-constitutive (Burak, 2008; Burke, 2016, 2023; Hermann, 1997; Fetner, 2008; Whitehead & Perry, 2019). In this reconstitution, politics and the lives in the United States are shaped and reformed in ways that work across sexualities, genders and religion.

The US Christian Right has been seen as 'globalizing' and creating schisms through supporting anti-LGBTQIA+ oppressions across the globe (Butler, 2006). Beyond the US Christian Right, the Catholic Church is understood as having a transnational effect across Europe and beyond through its condemnation of 'gender ideology' and being 'anti-gender' (Patternote & Kuhar, 2018; Corrêa, 2017). Beyond religion, contestations of LGBTQIA+ inclusion, feminism and trans inclusion can be seen to align with 'illiberal regimes' and/or 'populist' right-wing parties, often termed the 'far right'. Alongside the use of LGBTQIA+ inclusions to argue for anti-immigrant politics (e.g. Haritaworn, 2015), these movements can use anti-LGBTQ, anti-feminism and anti-gender rhetoric and legislation to bolster authoritarian regimes and act as a threat to democracy itself (Yermakova, 2021; Edenborg, 2022; Zeller & Vidra, 2021; Korolczuk, 2023; Rasmussen, 2023). There can be little doubt then that schisms around sexualities and genders play a part in broader politics, but they are not reducible to these alignments or political agendas.

Geopolitically, anti-Western and anti-colonialism rhetoric can be aligned with anti-LGBTQIA+ policies and discourses (Tucker, 2009; Rao, 2020, Kamarauskaitė, this volume). This has produced specific geographies around sexual/gendered equalities that seemingly map Global North nations to 'progress' and 'liberal democracies' (Kulpa, 2016; Kondakov, 2023). These are contrasted with 'homophobic' nations that are 'oppressive' (Bosia & Weiss, 2012). These judgements are made on global indexes that use legal changes and inclusions to speak to the progress of the Global North, in contrast to the backwardness of the Global South (Banerjea & Browne, 2018; Lalor & Browne, 2023). Without negating the importance of inclusions and legislative equalities, explorations beyond progress/backward binaries point to how lives can be created and oppressions continue within and across these national legal landscapes (Banerjea & Browne, 2023; Kondakov, 2022). The assumptions of geographical homogeneity are queried when, for example, exploring Slovenia and Poland, Ayoub (2018) identifies that challenges to LGBT equalities endure in some Eastern European states and not in others. Moreover, the continued power of the Christian Right in the United States, and activism that seeks to reinforce heteronormativity (heteroactivism) in 'progressive' places such as Ireland, Great Britain, Canada, Sweden and Israel (Lagerman, 2023; Liiason, 2023; Nash & Browne, 2020; Rothschild, 2023) indicate that 'liberal democracies' continue to be divided. Polarisations around sexualities and genders play a critical role in redefining nation states, their geopolitical standings, and transnational movements and relationships.

Using religion in the United States, populism and geopolitical divides, we use this section to contest a reduction of gender/sexualities to solely 'wedge issues'. In this book, centralising LGBTQIA+ lives and politics, sexualities and genders create arenas for politicised divisions and polarisations, including through partisan and populist politics (Loder, Kazyak, Kamarauskaite, Rahilly and Martin, Slaymaker). However, sexual and gendered polarisations cannot be reduced to or subsumed within discussions of electoral politics where political parties utilise LGBTQIA+ issues to secure political power and stoke socio-economic divisions. This does not deny or overlook the ways these can be, and are, deployed to further political aims. Instead, it purports that genders and sexualities are core issues around which people are invested and that recreate their lives. Polarised divisions around LGBTQIA+ lives then are important within and beyond political, electoral and geopolitical arenas.

Intra-community LGBTQIA+/feminist divisions between 'us'

Polarisation around sexualities and genders is more than looking at the divisions that polarise LGBTQIA+/anti-LGBTQIA+. Divisions between 'us'[2] are a key characteristic of twentieth- and twenty-first-century Feminist and Queer activisms and writing. While some might reject feminists, queers and others who espouse racist ideals, anti-trans or anti-sex work politics (see, for example, Rogers, 2023), we see these divisions as worthy of exploration and engagement in discussions of intra-community polarisations. Alongside those who opposed feminist/queer inclusions in any form or who saw anything that deviated from patriarchal heterosexual orders as a threat in ways that were often supported by the state and legislation in the twentieth century, there were intra-community divisions concerning identities, politics, political aims and modes of contesting systems of oppression. These included divisions and disagreements around sex (including sex between men and women, kink, BDSM), sex work, activisms (queer/gay, transgressive/assimilationist), trans inclusions and intersectionalities (race/class/gender/disabilities) as we further outline below. The intra-community debates and indeed intense arguments that caused schisms around these areas were held in feminist/queer spaces, magazines, journals and books. This is no longer the case. Intra-community tensions and arguments once held as 'ours' now feature in mainstream media, politics and debates as social acceptances and legislative changes blur the boundaries of LGBTQIA+/anti-LGBTQIA+ polarisations. This section points to dis/continuities in these divisions between the late twentieth and early twenty-first centuries, highlighting key points of feminist/queer divisions and polarisations that offer short and limited insights into the dis/continuities of the chapters in this book. While there is a longer project in tracing lineages, connections and genealogies, this is beyond the scope of this section, which serves instead to remind, or start the process of noting, the histories of sexual and gendered polarisations that did not begin in the contemporary period.

Within queer activisms and politics in the late twentieth century, there were significant disagreements around what was seen as 'selling out' through assimilation in contrast to 'radical' queer contestations (Warner, 2000; Bell & Binnie, 2000). Queerness was often contrasted with seeking gay rights through state support and slow 'progress' through legal and social change. These changes were understood as 'selling out' and 'buying into' an oppressive capitalist, neoliberal and cis-heteronormative system that depoliticised and desexualised queerness, leaving many 'out in the cold' (Sears, 2005; Duggan, 2003). The focus of these debates varied, but a central feature was same-sex marriage, where lesbians and others contested the imperative to fight for a heteropatriarchal institution that was built on female oppression and subjectification (Auchmuty, 2004). In contrast, these theorists and activists sought for an end of marriage as a central kinship configuration that was supported in material and ideological ways by the state. In contrast, same-sex marriage and other equalities were seen as affording lesbians and gay men, in particular, rights and obligations and enabling people to live lives that were less subject to state violation and discrimination. They were, for some, a stepping stone to greater liberations (see Clarke & Finaly, 2004 and Bernstein & Taylor, 2013 for insights around these debates). The advent of civil partnerships and same-sex marriage in the twenty-first century called for nuance (Peel & Harding, 2008), alongside explorations of their place in reconstituting homonormativity (Duggan, 2003). Discussions of equalities have shown that these debates have continued moving in and around issues such as same-sex marriage (e.g. Conrad, 2014) and Pride commercialisations versus Pride as a protest (Di Feliciantonio, 2016; Browne & Bakshi, 2013). Thus, queer/LGBTQIA+ academia/activism has long been divided about focus, goals and means of achieving social change, as well as gender and sexual liberation. These have been understood in various ways, including as oppressive and exclusionary for those who do not (or cannot) 'fit' into the normalisations that state, kinship, societies demand.

Like queer activisms, any cursory glance at the histories of feminisms, often written through US/UK lenses, points to the extensive debates, divides and arguments that pervaded the twentieth/twenty-first century. The writing of these histories through 'waves' can homogenise and ignore the multiplicities of specific time periods and the feminists and feminisms that created them (Hemmings, 2011). Instead of reiterating these temporal divisions, we want to point to the divisions and contestations of 'respectable', middle-class, white, heterosexual feminisms that have often sought to gain social change and traction through the dismissal and silencing of others. It is now well-recognised that social differences, including racism, classism, ableism, colonialism and heteropatriarchy, are key to histories of feminisms and their reconstitution. Indeed, even those which sought to challenge these intersectional, often 'internal', oppressions have been contested in the move from the United States to Europe. In 'post-racial Europe', intersectionalities have been moved from Black origins, intersectionalities and other 'diversities', which can mean that race is downplayed as a social issue (Boulila, 2019).

Divisions and inequities within feminisms are not therefore new, and conversely, using women's rights and gay (and lesbian) rights to further anti-immigration rhetorics and politics contests the neat alignments of political polarisations around religion/liberal equalities/political affiliations. Femonationalism that supports women's rights and gender equalities through reinforcing nativist national boundaries (Farris, 2017) and homonationalism that offers racist readings of 'dangerous others' in contrast to 'queer lovers' (Haritaworn, 2015; Puar, 2007), (re)create and reinforce divisions around race/migration through the pursuit and maintenance of specific forms of sexual and gender equalities. Both portray lesbians, gay men and women as being under threat by increased immigration of non-white, often Muslim immigrants to legitimise politics that are anti-immigrant and anti-Islam while also deflecting accusations of being queerphobic / misogynistic (Haritaworn, 2015). In doing so, they shift the alignments of schisms around gender/sexualities and race/nationalisms to deploy inclusions of some (white, cisgendered, middle class, able-bodied) people. This does not negate or address polarisations, but it does realign intersectional differences and solidarities, creating the 'good gay' and the women who need protection from these 'dangerous others'.

Further highlighting the internal divisions and debates that raged in feminist activisms, the sex wars can be seen as defining late twentieth-century feminisms and included a range of issues such as trans inclusions within Radical Feminisms, sex with men, pornography and sex work (Duggan & Hunter, 2006; Burke, 2023; Banerjea et al., 2019). Debates regarding aspects such as sex work raged, with scholars/activists including those who use the frame of prostitution, claiming sex work is abuse and a perpetuation of (hetero)patriarchy (MacKinnon, 1982), and those who see sex work as complex around choice, capitalism and commodification (Hubbard, 2006; Chapkis, 1997; Jones, 2020). The latter recognise that division and polarisation around sex work harms sex workers, as the infighting and lack of agreement can stall policymaking and increase the safety and protection of engaging in safe work (Comte, 2014).

Debates regarding assimilation/transgression, intersectionalities and sex have not gone away. Yet, there has been a shift, particularly evident in places where 'equalities' have gained social traction and legal recognition in the past three decades (Weeks, 2007; Nash & Browne, 2020). Reacting to, and being reconstituted by, these changes has meant that challenging women's rights, abortion, and gender and sexual equalities has taken a different form, often outside of state support and dominant social narratives (Browne & Nash, 2018). The (re)emergence of debates around trans inclusions and recognitions within LGBTQIA+ communities has focused, particularly in the UK, around 'gender wars'. This can be seen as a shift from previous 'culture wars' such as abortion and LGB acceptance, as they have become less polarising in places such as the UK but continue to rage in the United States, across Europe and elsewhere. The mainstream UK 'trans debates' often counterpose and presume the incompatibility of 'women's' and trans people's (usually trans women) rights/spaces, further discussed in the Lamble and Peel chapters. Media has been core to framing these debates (see the Lamble chapter) that can draw on emotional reactions including to the perceived loss of lesbian space to speak and be heard (Thurlow, 2024). In contrast to the late twentieth century, these trans polarisations and contestations regarding LGBTQIA+ lives and politics are no longer contained within gay/queer community spaces.

While the full complexity and detail of the debates cannot be covered here, and these are a fraction of those that raged, it is important to note that schisms around feminisms/queer politics, activisms and lives are not new. These debates have long-standing, and at times can feel repetitious, historical roots. Yet what were once intra-community debates in community spaces in a world where legislations and cultures oppressed us all, shifts in the recognition and welcome for some of us, meaning that these debates can now have mainstream audiences and be part of broader political landscapes. Sexual and gendered polarisations emerging in the twenty-first century thus need to be seen as both emergent, context-specific and critical to explore. They also need to be recognised as rooted historically in ways that refuse a forgetting of key elements of feminist/queer histories. This rejects a romanticisation of a united and coherent past, but also requires urgent investigations of contemporary alignments and schisms.

What is polarisation around LGBTQIA+ equalities?

There is a dearth of conceptualisations of sexual and gendered polarisations. The divisions and schisms highlighted around feminism/queer communities are not theorised within this concept, and there are limitations to theorisations of political polarisations that rely heavily on US contexts and concepts. To develop these conceptual interrogations, for this collection, we, as editors, asked authors to consider how they were using polarisations. In doing so, we refused a presumption that there is a common sense understanding of polarisation that is shared across places, disciplines or people. We sought to make the term strange to get to grips with a concept that circulates in various ways across academia, activism and politics.

Chapter authors have articulated their understanding in multiple ways, some of which align with the political polarisations based on US electoral politics. Others used understandings that drew on schisms, divisions, binaries and wars to place polarisations as central to their chapters' focus on LGBTQIA+ lives and politics. In this section, we demonstrate these conceptual moves not to create a 'working definition' or a coherence that is applicable across all chapters or for all who read this book. Instead, we bring together the authors to explicitly articulate the different ways in which the concept and term polarisation is used. This furthers our understanding of the multiplicities of how polarisation around gender/sexualities can be conceptualised and enables new insights into how they manifest and create real effects, offering new conceptual and practical possibilities.

Polarisations around sexualities and genders are conceptualised by some authors as based in binary oppositions that are linked to broader political formations. Authors in this vein based in the United States read polarisations through ideologies, attitudes and politics that separated Republican (Conservative, anti-LGBTQIA+) and Democratic (Liberal pro-LGBTQIA+) political parties. These were conceptualised as existing political and ideological extremes that related directly to 'diametrically opposed' political parties, which are key to sustaining both the parties and the polarisations around LGBTQIA+ legislations and rhetorics (see Rahilly and Martin chapter). Attitudes towards gender and sexualities aligning with these divisions and Republican/Democratic allegiances are directly related but not fully defined by positions on LGBTQ+ laws, and particularly the passing and enactment of anti-trans bills (see Kazyak, Martin and Rahilly, Kazyak, Slaymaker chapters). Reading the push for binary biological definitions of gender through Democrat/Republican political polarisations, Rahilly and Martin see this as marking 'a larger trend in *political polarisation* in U.S. politics' (emphasis in original). Chapters in this collection then conceptualise political polarisations through US partisan contexts as it is created and lived through trans lives and resistances (Loder, Slaymaker) and anti-trans/LGBTQ mobilisations, bills and court cases (Rahilly and Martin, Kazyak).

Engaging polarisations but questioning 'sides', other authors in this collection point to the possibilities and limitations of *only* considering the sides, the associated choices and the presumed political alignments implied in some versions of polarisations (Lamble, Peel, Ballantine et al.). In two UK chapters (Peel and Lamble), the divisions between internal/external polarisations are blurred. In contrast to the United States, this is not easily based on political party divisions and does not align with left/right factions. These are created by gender-critical actors and organisations, including those who are defined as LGB, as well as mainstream 'external' actors. Peel and Lamble see British politicians, media, social media and politicians as stoking polarisations around trans lives but not within frames that apply to the partisan US political polarisations. Crawley, in the US context, also contests the coherence of sides in their consideration of the queer temporal case for challenging the counting of identity categories in order to count for political movements.

Lalor's conceptualisation of polarisation as 'shap[ing] and restrict[ing] the possibility of action' argues for a consideration of opposition and oppositional practices as creating polarisations and sides, rather than assuming, studying or debating their existence. While the shaping of action is somewhat established through social movement theorisations (e.g. Fetner, 2008) that see each side constructing the other relationally, this concept extends this by focusing on the processes and practices of opposition. This allows for a consideration not only of their relational reconstitution (indeed as Crawley notes, a critical consideration of the 'groupism' inherent to the formation of sides, similarities and disparities), but also the institutional productivities of polarisations.

Considering polarisation as continually (re)produced also allows for a consideration of it as productive. This includes analyses that push for a consideration of the problematic of opposition itself and how it creates polarisation (Rahilly and Martin, Kazyak). Questioning the binary upon which polarisation relies, both Peel and Lamble see polarisation as enacted through 'culture wars' and 'gender wars'. These create binaries of, in Lamble's terms, entrenched and 'starkly opposed' camps. Lalor names the fluidity of polarisations that underpin the chapters that see these as created 'not simply as political choices, or of different sides of an argument, but as spatio-legal mechanisms that shape and restrict the possibility of action'.

Understanding polarisation as productive rather than pre-existing, and as more than choice or sides, the practices, discourses and politics of polarisation can be seen as critical for shaping fields of action and inaction. Kazyak's exploration of court cases shows how political alignments create, and are created by, 'two competing and incompatible world views regarding sexuality, gender, and LGBTQ bodies' (Kazyak). Thus, polarisation is understood as 'processes that construct deep, oppositional and/or fundamental division around sexuality, gender, and/or abortion' (Ballantine et al.). This creates a 'them' versus 'us' that results in conflict between the 'opposite' groups (Kamarauskaitė). This extends social movement considerations that Slaymaker adeptly demonstrates reconstitutes empowering politics through divisions and opposition. Thus, the focus on the opposition itself sees polarisation as both continually reproduced through rhetorics, discourses, practices, politics and productive of these and their effects.

Addressing polarisations can depend on conceptualisations of the phenomenon. Polarisations can be understood as being driven by those opposed to LGBTQ/trans lives and rights, creating marginalised vulnerable 'out groups' (or, as Crawley notes, polarisation may be internal to LGBTQ+ communities), thus driving increasingly 'polarised times'. Loder, in this framing, names 'agency, self-determination, and innovation' as key to contesting these power relations, with Slaymaker pointing to the possibilities of polarisations for creating and consolidating coalitions to fight key political battles. Alongside Slaymaker's consideration of complex coalitions, Kamarauskaitė demonstrates the importance of strategies for resisting the separation of LGBTQ+ and the Central European Nationhood of Lithuania. Kamarauskaitė argues for recognition of respectability and multiplicities of queer activisms to offer belonging beyond 'them' and 'us'. Loder and Kamarauskaitė note that resistant strategies are not a 'complete response' in places where what is needed to do, is to 'dismantle the systems' that oppress (Loder).

Addressing polarisations where oppositionality is in question, and seen as problematic, calls for a different (but not conflicting) response. Since this conceptualisation sees polarisation as reconstituted through oppositions and sides, responses here can seek to move outside of partisan political approaches. Such a framing necessitates not just agency and resistance, but considerations of addressing oppositionality itself. Peel, in this vein, asks for a consideration 'at least theoretically' for a 'both/and' stance that allows for 'more fluidity and arguably could become an antidote to polarisation or extremism'. This understands divisions are not inevitable, 'static and enduring'.

Crawley asks for care in our 're-memberings' to work towards reducing intra-community polarisations and Rahilly and Martin, Peel and Lamble argue for considerations of dialogue that are based on contesting opposition itself. Lamble, in seeking the latter, demonstrates the stripping and loss of 'common understanding, dialogue, or shifting perspective' in creating the culture/gender wars in the UK based on entrenched divisions. This loss points not only to the recreation of binaries of them/us, enemy/ally, but the loss of possibilities (and even the possibility of considering) working against entrenchment and division itself. This is supported by Rahilly and Martin and Kazyak in their consideration of the entrenchment of sides that are structurally embedded in US courts and lawmaking, which offer little time for 'genuine cross dialogue' (Rahilly and Martin). Ballantine et al. take an experimental approach to working beyond opposition through detailing a workshop that brings 'all sides' together to consider how we might live together where we don't agree. These strategies rely on what Peel calls for 'taking a stance of principled hopefulness' where 'there *is* potential for growth and change if divergent perspectives are heard'.

Outline of chapters

The previous section has sought to begin conceptualisations of polarisations from the chapters in this collection. In this section, we outline each chapter in turn, where authors focus on a range of gender and sexuality issues in a range of geographical contexts. The book, similar to this chapter, initially explores divisions and schisms around LGBTQIA+/non-LGBTQIA+, starting in the United States, before moving on to explore polarisations within and between queer/feminist communities.

Rahilly and Martin's chapter centres on political debates in state legislatures in the United States regarding transgender sports policies. Their work shows how stark divisions between Republicans and Democrats emerge in these debates such that both sides are ultimately talking past each other. As such, they argue that 'political debates *perform* and *construct* a culture of polarization as much as they reflect it'. Arguing for spaces outside of political hearings and working towards more citizen participation, they contend, offers possibilities for less polarising and more effective social policies and democratic legislation.

Kazyak's chapter focuses on religiously motivated lawsuits opposing LGBTQ rights in the United States. By analysing the discourses that emerge in court opinions on public schools, she highlights the deeply held and felt divisions and oppositions related to the existence of LGBTQ people in public space. In part, the chapter highlights the processes by which Christian individuals who are anti-LGBTQ position themselves within the courts as marginalised victims vis-à-vis sociopolitical changes that advance LGBTQ inclusion. The 'multiple and contradictory logics that emerge from the judges' in the three cases considered are used to contend that the law can further polarise, as views are presented both to the court and in the adjudications as fundamentally incompatible. This allows insights into polarisations around LGBTQ politics that extend beyond presumed disembodied 'wedge issues' into the politics, lives and emotions that are created and affected by them.

Loder also focuses on polarisation in the United States regarding transgender lives. This chapter explores how Black transgender women in the Southern United States navigate space, find refuge from inequality/oppression/discrimination/polarisation, build community and thrive. Using liminality to explore the boundaries between inclusion and exclusion, Loder offers insights into how the organisation T.A.K.E offers refuge from a broader polarised sociopolitical context in which Black transgender women's lives and rights are debated, legislated and restricted. In this way, the chapter shows how political and court discourse are resisted to enable lives to be lived in and through the effects of polarisation.

Breaking away from US focus, Kamarauskaitė considers the polarising forces in Lithuania that position LGBTQ+ people as enemies of the nation. In the chapter, she asks how activists respond to such a context and highlights the strategies that individuals and groups utilise to legitimise and provide more nuanced understandings of LGBTQ+ Lithuanians. This serves to counter the oppositions that set Lithuanian LGBTQ+ people in contradistinction to the nation. Challenging the necessary normalisations of 'relatable queerness' as solely falling within homonormativities, this chapter pushes considerations of shared fun, vulnerabilities and empathy as 'strategies to foster connection with society', moving imaginings of LGBTQ+ people beyond being solely constructed through 'uncontrollable sexuality'.

Lalor brings an international focus to her chapter by theorising how polarisations around sexuality, gender and LGBTQ rights are deployed by state and diplomatic actors. By synthesising literature in legal geography and feminist legal geography, Lalor develops a queer legal geographic approach that draws attention to what she calls the 'structural elements of LGBTQ polarisations'. Specifically, her analysis theorises how structures of international law and state sovereignty are built on polarised foundations, which are then affirmed as state actors seek to regulate gendered and sexualised bodies and lives. This does not deny the agency, or materialities, of those on 'sides', seeing them as both 'materially situated' and 'discursively stretched across space and time'. It does explicitly consider the formations of polarisations as performatively reconstituted through actions that might be otherwise considered through a spatio-legal lens.

Other chapters in the volume focus on internal polarisations Slaymaker returns us to the US context and examines how a diverse coalition organised to contest anti-trans legislation in the state of Texas. The chapter addresses the tensions that arose between the three groups that were active in protesting the anti-trans legislation – transgender people, mostly cisgender parents of transgender children and LGBQ people. Slaymaker's analysis considers the complicated, and at times conflictual, dynamics and processes that exist even among those 'on the same side'. These intra-coalitions are shown not only to be complex, but also these challenges as formed through 'increasingly polarized times'.

Crawley's chapter offers theoretical considerations of internal divisions within and between LGBTQ communities through a turn to consider time in relation to lives. They provide an analysis of how internal polarisations within LGBTQ communities can develop and be sustained temporally. Specifically, Crawley theorises how as we narrate our identities and our communities, we reconstitute renderings of time that favour certain periods. This can mean that while some generations posit the present as 'the smartest, sexiest, happiest, most revolutionary, most politically-astute moment', others engage in 'mythical nostalgic re-memberings'. Challenging groupism, upon which social movements are based, Crawley argues that it creates a unity that is not present in everyday lives, and a disparity from others who are then seen as 'out group'. These constitutive narratives can work to further conflict and 'polarizations across our diverse temporal experiences'.

Peel and Lamble both foreground the 'culture/gender wars' in the UK. Analysing survey data from *the Future of Legal Gender* (FLAG) project, Peel examines how respondents understand and articulate the role of media in shaping their views about gender and transgender issues. She also outlines the divisive reaction in mainstream media and social media to a FLAG report. In this way, her chapter speaks to how divisions around genders and sexualities emerge and become entrenched through social media coverage and engagement.

As Peel notes, media is particularly important to address in terms of its role in making what were once intra-community disagreements (e.g. within queer and feminist communities) visible and manifest in the mainstream. She points to the hopefulness of considering divergent positions and the possibilities of moving beyond the binaries of polarisations.

Lamble's chapter speaks to how polarisation between supporters and opponents of trans rights in the UK has been escalated by fears of harm on both sides, speaking to emotion, and the role of media and misinformation matters in processes of polarisation. This creates a perception of a zero-sum game, where gains for one side are seen as losses for the other. Seeing the culture war debate as creating factions that then 'wrestle over social norms and values', Lamble shows how the 'gender wars' now exist in its own right because of their scale and power in pushing polarising agendas. Lamble's focus on the gender wars in the UK demonstrates how these have become prevalent in their own right beyond the 'culture wars'. Focusing on misinformation, Lamble contends that strategies based on left-right do not account for the UK context, that the emotional investment means 'factual corrections' can be ineffective, and that the place of institutions needs to be addressed, rather than the targeting of individuals. In this way, and along with Peel, Rahilly and Martin and Kazyak, her work shows how considerations of the opposition itself can create more meaningful engagements that can contest polarisations.

Working across LGBTQIA+ as polarising and 'internal' polarisations Ballantine, Hilliard and Browne take as a starting point the deeply held differing positions around sexuality, gender, and abortion. Rather than speak to the processes by which these divisions occur, or how they might be overcome, they ask how we all may creatively and productively co-exist with one another alongside these divisions. In their chapter, they outline the method and reasoning behind the one-day artist-led Irish workshop they hosted as part of the Beyond Opposition project. The workshop brought together participants with fundamentally different positions about feminism, LGBTQIA+ rights and abortion. Rather than engage in dialogue about these different positions explicitly, participants were asked to participate in different art activities to consider how worlds might be created where agreement can't be found. The authors reflect on the promise and limitations for bringing people together to work and live creatively alongside divergent positions.

Finishing this collection is a chapter written by PhD students and early career scholars who attended the symposium as discussants. Offering theoretical insights and complexities, McCartan, Moore-Ponce, Burke, Foudy and Thor provide a dialogue that engages with tensions and divergences. Using the chapters and discussions from the symposium, they open up questions of progress, us versus them and (im)possible futures that emerge from their conversations on these works. They address the ways in which the symposium chapters challenge narratives about progress and attend to the 'socio-political contexts which foster and are shaped by polarisation'. They discuss how polarisation belies nuance, contradictions and complexity as it reduces thinking to either/or or people to competing 'sides'. Finally, McCartan, Moore-Ponce, Burke, Foudy and Thor pose the question, 'will there ever be a time after polarisation?' and grapple with questions about what utopian futures may entail.

Overall, these chapters offer new considerations of polarisations and how they manifest and create LGBTQIA+ lives and politics. Readers may well see different linkages and thematic connections than the ones we describe as they move through the book. This is not only to be expected but to be welcomed as it can offer new possibilities and innovations that create different futures.

Conclusion

Social polarisations continue to rage, emerge, develop and be remade in different places. Polarisations around LGBTQIA+ equalities that are the focus of this book have their own purposes, aims, trajectories and 'lives' and can also feed into political agendas being used for electoral and political purposes (including the 'Far Right' in Europe and the US Christian Right). Including LGBTQIA+/anti-LGBTQIA+ polarisations, and considering how once internal LGBTQIA+ divides are reconstituting political landscapes and everyday lives, the chapters in this collection offer explorations of the partisan, entrenched and shifting boundaries between us/them. From this chapter and the chapters that follow, it is clear that the 'airing our queer laundry' around areas that used to be reserved for feminist, queer and LGBTQIA+ spaces takes new forms through the raging of debates and battles on mainstream national and international stages. We see sexual and gendered polarisations around LGBTQIA+ equalities in the twenty-first century as both offering continuity with the past and established thinking and research *and* as emerging and emergent, offering other ways of thinking and other possibilities for action. We see diverse and expansive considerations of sexual and gender polarisations as critical to opening up insights as we approach the middle of the third decade of a century.

Despite its strength in offering a start in opening up dialogue about contemporary polarisations around LGBTQIA+ equalities, we do want to note the book's limitations, including that it is limited in the geographical scope of the countries covered. It is anglophone-focused and cannot adequately cover a full discussion of polarisations around LGBTQIA+ lives and experiences. There are key contexts missing, including Latin America, Africa, many European contexts and Scandinavia. The book is also dominated by nationally and even locally based work and contexts, rather than exploring transnational movements and connectivities. There is much to be done to address these gaps and other gaps the readers will undoubtedly note. Moreover, it was written in 2023–4 and the contexts discussed have and will shift significantly. We hope this book provides a catalyst and a useful reference for those who see the imperatives of engaging in this work and of addressing the ongoing and reformulated challenges. It has been amazing to work with the people who chose to participate to create this collection. Our hope now is that this book will spark further conversations, research and hopeful possibilities.

Notes

1. We did not define 'equalities' and recognise its contestation as a term and political goal (see Conrad, 2014). We use it as a catch-all term to enable a focus on polarisations around LGBTQIA+ lives, politics, activisms and legislations to recognise the changes and continuities that create contemporary oppositions, division, schisms and poles – which are the focus of this collection.
2. We would like to thank Elizabeth Peel for making this thought explicit during the workshop.

Chapter 2

TALKING PAST EACH OTHER

POLITICAL POLARIZATION AND TRANSGENDER ATHLETE BANS

Elizabeth Rahilly and Kimberly Martin

Introduction

Despite important gains in transgender rights in recent years, the US political landscape has seen a reactionary anti-trans backlash, which is manifest in proliferating legislation that restricts trans liberties across states. These laws target multiple areas of social and institutional life, including schools, the family and medical care. At least twenty-six states, for example, have banned or restricted gender-affirming care for trans youth (HRC, 2023), and an additional nine states censor LGBTQ-inclusive curricula in schools (MAPS, 2023). Another prime target of these laws is school sports: since 2020, twenty-five states have passed legislation that bars transgender girls from competing on their schools' female sports teams in both legislative chambers (i.e. the Senate and the House), and another four states have passed this legislation in one chamber. Many regard these efforts as part of a concerted anti-trans agenda, which reinforces natal sexual biology and the traditional gender binary as the determinant of one's legal and social identity (Murib, 2022; Sharrow, 2021).

This conservative push for binary, biological understandings of gender marks a larger trend in *political polarization* in US politics, or a 'divergence of political attitudes to ideological extremes' (ECPS). The division concerns the two main parties, Republicans and Democrats, loosely known as 'conservatives' and 'liberals' in the United States, whose platforms have become diametrically opposed. Several studies show that Republicans and Democrats are more ideologically divided today than prior generations, and more so than parties in comparable Western democratic nations (Boxell, Gentzkow, & Shapiro, 2024; DeSilver, 2022). Indeed, the states that advanced trans-exclusive bills to the governor's desk were all Republican-majority legislatures (though some were vetoed by both Democratic and Republican governors) (Martin, 2022). Conversely, bills were typically 'dead-on-arrival' in committees in Democratic-majority states, where they rarely received a roll-call vote.

Such heightened polarization functions as a 'totalizing system, as it aims to dominate the existing systems of differences and identities', and the two camps sustain themselves more through their *opposition* than through their *content* (Palonen, 2009). Differences over who or what counts as 'male' or 'female' are particularly polarizing, as these social categories are fundamental to law and policy. Conservatives have seized on these differences for defining party lines. For conservatives, sex equals gender, and there are clear differences between men and women that cannot be denied. Liberals allow for more complexity when defining sex and gender, and believe the government has a duty to protect transgender rights. Such polarization in the political sphere has implications for broader public attitudes and divisions, as polarization among political elites is known to 'trickle down' to the populace (ECPS).

In this chapter, we perform a qualitative analysis of transcripts from committee hearings and chamber debates from eighteen states that passed transgender athlete bans. The legislative hearings these bans entail offer an illuminating laboratory for studying today's political polarization and its cultural effects. As we will show, political debates *perform* and *construct* a culture of polarization as much as they reflect it. This occurs through several different factors and dynamics. One is legislators' commitment to their party's position, which becomes a mantra in the proceedings, thwarting genuine engagement with contrasting perspectives. Another regards the rules and conventions of legislative debate itself, which limit opportunities for real cross-dialogue. A third element concerns legislators' gaps in knowledge, where appealing to voters through partisan signalling seems to trump more rigorous investigation of the subject, leaving misunderstandings unchecked. All of these factors work to create stark polarization between sides, which has implications for broader public engagement with the issues.

We begin with a review of the literature on sports, gender, political polarization and legislative debate. We proceed with a thematic analysis of each side's main arguments, to contextualize the overall discussion. In the name of 'fairness in women's sports', proponents reinforce traditional, binary beliefs about sex and gender. Opponents, in contrast, assert the bans are a 'solution without a problem' and economically wasteful. In effect, both parties are 'talking past each other', levying wholly different concerns and terms of understanding. We then examine the rarer moments, less than 10 per cent of the coded dataset, when legislators explicitly debated the bans' premise, 'male biological advantage', revealing the limits of those exchanges. This dialogue is important because it has the potential to influence broader public opinions about transgender rights. At the same rate, elected officials have the power to establish laws regardless of public opinion. These factors motivate our interest in studying legislative debate: it represents one key site where polarization is enacted and reproduced, constructing and fuelling ideologically extreme views on transgender issues.

Polarizing rhetoric and legislative debate

The literature on political communication is rife with studies concluding that people prefer political messages that reinforce their existing attitudes (Knobloch-

Westerwick & Meng, 2011). This is when partisan signalling is most effective. When it comes to Democrats and Republicans in the United States, the two main political parties, these attitudes could not be more distinct. Conover et al. (2011), for example, found that political messages on Twitter are highly segregated by party, with 'limited connectivity between left- and right-leaning' voters. Those on the political 'left' (Democrats) prioritize equality and social justice (Jost, 2006), benevolence and universalism (Jones et al., 2018), while the political 'right' (Republicans) prioritizes traditional family values and conformity and is more sensitive to threats from out-groups (Jost, 2006). These are the ideologically extreme viewpoints, tradition versus progress, that exemplify polarization and give rise to sharp divisions between the parties.

The Democratic Party's platform directly addresses transgender rights by pledging to ensure that 'transgender and gender non-conforming people receive fair and equitable treatment' in a variety of areas, including housing, education and criminal justice. The Democratic Party also pledges to 'protect the rights of transgender students' (DNC, 2020). Conversely, the Republican Party platform does not use the term 'transgender' anywhere, but does state that the party is against efforts to 'wrongly redefine sex discrimination to include sexual orientation or other categories', which they argue will 'reshape our schools – and our entire society – to fit the mold of an ideology alien to America's history and traditions' (RNC, 2016). Elsewhere in the platform, Republicans vow to protect religious liberty, traditional marriage and the family. These views are reiterated during legislative debate (Hemphill & Shapiro, 2019), and as we will show, are reflected in the debates on transgender athlete bans.

For some, legislative debates are meant to sway or convince an opposing side of one's position, but increasingly, debate is seen as an opportunity to rally one's political allies, as well as to signal their platform and values to voters for future elections (Brewer, 2003; Bächtiger, 2014; Proksch & Slapin, 2012). Partisan signalling patterns are often employed when lawmakers are attempting to increase their visibility for electoral purposes (Levendusky, 2010), so it is no surprise that parties' disparate values resurface as contrasting views during committee hearings and chamber debates. As we will show, both supporters and opponents of the bills are constrained by the polarizing rhetoric and value systems of their party. Party leaders counsel fellow partisan lawmakers on the 'right' opinion to have about a given issue, voters hear the party's preference and then adjust their opinions to match. The more ideologically homogeneous the rhetoric becomes, the more effective its message (Levendusky, 2010).

Beyond partisan speech patterns, the rules of the hearings themselves hinder more nuanced discussion and debate. Debate rules set by each chamber vary by state, but all follow some form of parliamentary procedure or Mason's Manual where the speaker must be recognized before speaking. An opposing speaker cannot interrupt, and any questions must be permitted before cross-dialogue can occur. Depending on the state and the chamber, there are limitations on the number of times that a legislator can speak and on the ability of legislators to respond to one another (Reilly, 2009).

Committee proceedings follow similar rules but are generally more flexible, allowing for cross-dialogue and time for questions and comments. Here, in-depth dialogue challenging the biological premise of the bills often occurred in committee hearings. However, it is important to note that committee hearings are attended by a small number of legislators (usually those assigned to the committee) and the public. The wider chamber is not exposed to these arguments, reducing their knowledge of the issues.

Much of the discussion in legislative debates, including those examined here, entails planned speeches and statements that incorporate party positions. Legislators are more likely to use their time to commit to policy positions on the official record than to 'debate' in any meaningful sense of the word (Laver, 2021). This fuels a level of polarization that other modes of public discourse may not, such as community workshops or town halls, which are more focused on citizen preferences.

Sports and (trans)gender

Transgender girls and women competing against cisgender female athletes marks a long-standing controversy (Jones, 2021). For transgender and non-binary youth, sports present some of the most compromising systems they encounter in schools (Travers, 2018; Witcomb & Peel, 2022). Unlike most other spheres of Western society, the world of sports still adheres to a staunch sex-segregated model, rooted in the premise that male athletes carry an inherent 'biological advantage'.

This 'biological advantage' refers to several physiological factors, where persons assigned male at birth are shown to have greater measures in lean body mass, muscle area and strength, and bone density, on average, than their cisgender female counterparts (Harper et al., 2021; Hilton & Lundberg, 2021). Some research suggests that these differences are moderated in trans women following hormonal transition, including speed, strength and haemoglobin levels, but not necessarily to cisgender women's levels (Harper et al., 2021; Roberts et al., 2021; Wiik et al., 2020; cf. Harper, 2015).

However, assessing just how and whether these sex differences translate into actual athletic performance advantages remains complicated (Vilain & Martinez-Patino, 2019), and can vary by sport (Berman & Garnier, 2017). For many, this raises questions about the validity of blanket bans on transgender athletes. Moreover, none of this research includes transgender athletes who have taken puberty blockers in their youth, a relatively recent medical approach that has emerged over the last 20–30 years (Diaz & Figueredo, 2022) that has major implications for 'athletic advantage'. Even researchers who conclude that there is some biological advantage in athletes assigned male at birth argue that we should abandon a sex-segregated model (Knox, Anderson, & Heather, 2019, p. 402). Some scholars advocate for a 'continuum' model instead, where actual ability is the classifying principle across athletes, not sex or gender (Kane, 1995). This model would recognize those skills and sports where stereotypically 'female' attributes hold the advantage, such as agility and flexibility, and would be especially pertinent to youth, who are actively developing their different athletic aptitudes.

Nevertheless, multiple world sports agencies have recently restricted transgender access to elite competitions (De La Cretaz, 2022; Futterman, 2022; Morse, 2023; Ortega, 2023). Such policies among the global elites of sports governance add validity to the bans being pursued by US conservative legislators and fuel feelings on both sides of the controversy. As we will discuss, little of opponents' efforts in hearings include data that would challenge athlete bans; their focus on transgender athletes is a matter of social justice and inclusion. Supporters, in contrast, have seized on the 'science' of male and female differences. The growing divide between Republicans and Democrats further amplifies these differing perspectives on sports policy, with political affiliations shaping the rhetoric that legislators use to describe the legislation. As discussions around transgender athlete bans unfold, it is increasingly evident that they are not just isolated policy debates, but deeply entwined with broader ideological schisms that characterize contemporary American politics.

Methodology

We conducted a qualitative analysis of committee testimony and chamber debates to identify dominant rhetorical patterns among supporters and opponents of transgender athlete bans from eighteen US states, including Arizona, Arkansas, Florida, Indiana, Iowa, Kansas, Kentucky, Louisiana, Mississippi, Montana, North Dakota, Oklahoma, Pennsylvania, South Carolina, South Dakota, Tennessee, Texas and Utah. These bills affect children from primary through secondary school levels (5–18 years of age). While there are slight differences between each bill, all explicitly ban transgender girls from participation on sports teams and all concern at least the secondary education level.

Raw video and audio footage from legislative hearings were captured from publicly available recordings on government websites and then sent to professional transcriptionists. Multiple sessions were collected from each state, ranging from ten minutes to several hours each. In total, we gathered over sixty hours of footage. Unfortunately, the quality and availability of transcripts were not consistent across states, and we were unable to include all states or sessions where athlete bans passed in at least one chamber. For example, Alabama passed a transgender athlete ban in 2021, but the state legislature is not required to maintain recordings of their proceedings and was therefore not included in this analysis.

Once footage was located and transcribed, transcripts were loaded into a qualitative analysis software program (Atlas.ti). Using thematic analysis methods (Braun & Clarke, 2006; Saldana, 2021), both authors reviewed transcripts for recurring themes and patterns in legislators' speech. While we started with a preliminary list of expected codes (e.g. 'biology', 'fairness'), we kept the coding inductive and noted additional themes as they emerged, such as 'economic boycotts'. We noted themes that were explicitly stated (e.g. 'discrimination', 'vulnerable'), as well as those that were subtle and/or implicit (e.g. declining to use or name 'transgender' signifiers where appropriate). We paid attention to specific wording, phrasing, metaphors, as well as common tropes or genres.

We populated a shared memo of analytic insights, flagging major thematic observations and sources of overlap between states, as well as notable variations, to corroborate our findings and develop our analysis. After an initial round of coding, codes were grouped into 'anti-trans' and 'pro-trans' positions to track when and how certain themes were used (e.g. 'Title IX', defined below). In addition, we iteratively consolidated codes into larger thematic clusters. Ultimately, we identified 3–4 dominant, opposing themes for each side, which speak to the polarizing dynamics of the debate. Some quotes were edited for clarity to remove filler words, stuttering or longer portions of the exchange.

Proponents

Sponsors and supporters of the bills focused predominantly on matters of sex and gender. The dominant themes we identified speak to their efforts to maintain consistency in their partisan messaging, which include *gender simplicity*, *male advantage*, *protecting women* and *preventing change*. These themes connect to broader value frames commonly used in conservative messaging, including tradition, fairness and simplicity, and were part of the polarizing rhetoric marshalled in hearings (Martin & Rahilly, 2023).

The notion of inherent differences between the sexes, and males' athletic superiority in those differences, was heavily reiterated by proponents in hearings. Through this refrain, males and females were constructed as diametric opposites, with no consideration for biological overlap or similarity, let alone for sports where stereotypical 'female' attributes would be advantageous. As seen below, legislators framed these differences as 'simple', 'common sense' and a matter of 'science', thwarting any regard for the complexity that sexual biology and gender identity may entail:

> Very simple today. I think it's sad that we have to pass legislation to acknowledge the reality of the biological differences between male and female, but I stand here to support female athletics and say that this is no more than common sense. (Senator Daniels, Oklahoma Senate, 24 March 2022)

> Science is all about this bill. As representative Casada said, we stand here physically different men and women from each other, skeletal muscle, the way our bones are put together, our ligaments are attached. When you look at the . . . fastest man in the world, Usain Bolt, if you put Usain Bolt against the fastest woman in the world, it wouldn't even be close, so all we're doing here is trying to make sure that we maintain . . . the competitive balance. (Representative Cepicky, Tennessee K12 Subcommittee, 9 February 2021)

Linking these themes in arguments presumes that both 'science' and 'common sense' can be known fully and shared by all, further obscuring the complexity of the topic.

As part of these presumed genetic differences, proponents stressed that 'no amount of' hormone therapy could alter or suppress males' inherent athletic advantage: 'Even given hormone replacement therapy, a female can never make up the ground from birth that a male has with regard to testosterone. Did you know that that was the position of a Harvard biologist?' (Senator Kimbrell, South Carolina Senate, 3 May 2022).

Proponents' refusal to use correct transgender terminology or to honor the gender identifications of trans athletes further enforced an unshakable, sex-based, binary logic in their arguments. Trans girls and women were routinely labeled as 'boys', 'male' and 'men' throughout the proceedings, including youth and young children. Sex and gender terms were used interchangeably as well, muddying important distinctions between 'males' and 'boys' and 'females' and 'girls'. We coded this tactic as '*refusal to name trans*' in the dataset, a position clearly represented here:

> The foundational argument against the bill is that trans girls are girls and trans women are women. However, this argument is not true. Trans girls are boys, not girls, trans women are men, not women. No matter how many times we hear two plus two equals five, two plus two does not equal five and will never equal five. (Senator Taylor, Iowa Senate, 2 March 2022)

Male biological superiority laid the foundation for another key theme of supporters: *protecting women*. Proponents frequently invoked the legacy of Title IX as an imperative to protect women from 'men' in sports. Title IX was landmark legislation passed in 1972 in the United States, which prohibits sex-based discrimination in any school programme that receives funding from the federal government. The statute was considered a major win for the second-wave feminist movement, historically regarded as a liberal cause. Ironically, conservative legislators marshaled 'women's rights' here as a cornerstone of US history and a 'tradition' that must be preserved.

'Protecting women' often meant ensuring their fair access to interscholastic opportunities and scholarships, which 'boys' and 'men' would 'steal' from them if they were allowed to compete. Sometimes, however, 'protecting women' was a matter of physical safety. Here, the image of the large 'male' physique harming the petite 'female' frame was conjured as a powerful rhetorical device in the hearings:

> You take a 16-year-old adolescent male that is just starting a transition that shows up on a soccer field of a girl's athletic team, they have an advantage most of the time in bone density, and body mass, and [the] threat or potential safety issues with respect to running over those girls is real. So talk to the parents that had that situation come up. There's more of them than you think going on in the

state, you just haven't heard about him yet. (Senator Perry, Texas, Senate State Affairs Committee, 26 March 2021)

Moreover, as Senator Perry's quote indicates, proponents hinted at matters beyond specific injuries on the field, to growing gender changes in society at large, which must be stopped. This forged the fourth major theme in their arguments: *preventing change*. This is where the athlete bans appeared as part of a broader anti-trans agenda, aimed at curtailing the threat of gender variance: 'The rates of transgender identity are on the rise. Whether it's due to increased social acceptance or changes in our society, this issue will not go away' (Senator Dwyer, North Dakota Senate, 22 April 2021).

In short, proponents of the bans promoted a staunch gender binary, rooted in 'biology and science', that must be maintained for the sake of women's safety and for traditional US values more broadly.

Opponents

Contrary to proponents, opponents did not focus on biology, sex or gender. Instead, they levied different thematic concerns, starting with the notion that transgender athletes are actually *not a problem* since so few participate in the first place. They also focused on the *economic and legal repercussions* the state could face should the legislation pass and the *mental health vulnerabilities of transgender youth*.

A dominant refrain from opponents was the idea that the athlete bans were addressing a problem that did not in fact exist. They often termed the bills a '*solution without a problem*', citing the limited number of cases where a transgender athlete was trying to compete. Senator Dossett of Oklahoma typified the retort: 'This is frivolous legislation that addresses a problem that simply doesn't exist' (Oklahoma Senate Chamber, 24 March 2022). Opponents frequently pushed sponsors to give a concrete number of transgender athletes in the state, which sponsors could not provide, per this typical exchange in Texas:

Senator Whitmire: Could I ask you, how many instances probably today in Texas are we dealing with? And, obviously, [the] direction of my question is, is it a wide enough concern of yours to justify proposed legislation? . . . I just don't see a significant incidence of what you're addressing.
Senator Perry: So, I'll answer it this way. Transgenders can still compete in competitive athletics under UIL [University Interscholastic League] under their biological sex. So, we're not prohibiting them from staying out of competitive sports . . .. But . . . to your question, as we see this trend and these issues become more and more prevalent—
Senator Whitmire: So you see a movement coming this direction from, you just mentioned, Connecticut.

In terms of the debate, it is worth noting Perry doesn't attempt to give a number in his response, but speaks to a general growing 'prevalence'.

Beyond the rarity of the problem, opponents leaned heavily on pragmatic matters of *state finances and the economy*, which, they argued, would be negatively impacted by the bans, either due to loss of business and boycotts to the state or from the inevitable litigation that would arise. For example, Senator Bennett in Montana remarked, '[D]o you wanna gamble on something so bizarrely petty and cruel, that could lose our state millions of dollars? I mean, there are so many big companies out there that just flatly refused to come into states that have policies like this' (Montana Senate Judiciary Committee, 18 March 2021).

Apart from these pragmatic concerns, however, opponents also appealed to the moral and emotional concerns of *the vulnerability of trans youth*, framing trans kids as a marginalized population whose existing psycho-social challenges would only be exacerbated by such discriminatory legislation. This line of argument was where traditional Democratic values like fairness, equality and social justice most clearly surfaced in the hearings. Opponents repeated notorious mental health statistics about trans youth, including high suicidality, and argued that the legislation would leave these youth that much more at risk. As Representative Schneider of North Dakota said, '[I]t's unfortunate that we will harm a very vulnerable group of children, those with the highest rates of depression and suicide, while we send a message to other kids that it's okay to discriminate, to hate, and to exclude' (North Dakota, Senate Session, 15 April 2021).

Altogether, and perhaps surprisingly, very little of the opponents' speech directly countered the bans' premise – 'male biological advantage' and an immutable sex/gender binary. This marked one key element of the polarizing dynamic of the forum, where each side's arguments were largely unrelated to the other. Much of the sessions amounted to the parties 'talking past each other', attempting to appeal to a broad base of voters versus tackling the foundational logics of the legislation.

Complicating sex and gender?

As noted in the introduction, the rules of the proceedings allowed for limited cross-dialogue between sides, especially during chamber debate. In the rare instances where cross-dialogue did occur, opponents occasionally attempted to complicate simplistic understandings of sex and gender, but the arguments were not fully developed or articulated and/or were often deflected by supporters. Below, we excerpt several illustrative examples of these exchanges. These stunted interchanges help develop our understanding of the ways political forums create polarization between political parties, perhaps more than merely reflecting existing opposition.

Failing to agree on basic terms and definitions is one key ingredient of polarization. In North Dakota, for example, Senator Bakke tried to assert a trans-inclusive understanding of sex classification, one that is not solely determined by assigned sex at birth. Her opponent, however, refuses to entertain the possibility of 'sex reassignment'. This exchange also fails to clarify the Chair's use of the term 'sexuality' for 'assigned sex', potentially confusing two distinct parts of identity for listeners:

> Senator Bakke: I take some offense at the definition of sex being, what you're born with, because transgender females are girls. They're not boys, they're girls.
> Madam Chair: That's not the definition we'll be using when it comes to exclusive sports.
> Senator Bakke: I take offense at that.
> Madam Chair: Well, that's, I guess that's your opinion but when it comes to biological functionality, there is a clear, defined difference between the physicality of a female and the physicality of a male and the clearest way to define that is by assigned sexuality at birth. So that's what we are going by in this legislation.
> Senator Bakke: So Madam Chair, you're saying that you don't acknowledge the fact that there is such a thing as transgender or there is such a thing as sex reassignment?
> Madam Chair: I'm not making a statement about that. What I'm making a statement about is that when we are having competition on athletic events in especially high school sports, that the clearest way of identifying whether they should play on a female – exclusively female sports team or an exclusively male sports team is by the definition of sexuality assigned at birth. Is there any further discussion? Yes, Senator Dwyer. [*Discussion follows regarding economic boycotts.*] (North Dakota, Conference Committee, 12 April 2021)

Here, there is a lack of shared agreement regarding the very terms and definitions at issue in the legislation, where one side's understanding of 'sex' is quite different from the other's, with no redress for closing the gap. This extract exposes several other aspects of polarization as well. Despite the assertions of Bakke, the Chair repeats her party's line, almost robotically. Additionally, the exchange is cut short by the rules of the debate, where there is pressure to move to the next question. In short, politicians use the limited time they do have for each exchange to simply recite party values.

Similar tactics are observed in the next exchange, even after a supporter *concedes* some level of complexity to the issue. Senator Stargel of Florida admits that sponsors of the ban did first consider the role of hormones in trans athletes' potential advantage, but since they could 'not settle on the science', they ultimately deferred to something more 'simplistic'. Senator Farmer counters, raising the possibility that some trans athletes might actually be smaller or slower than some cisgender female players, but Stargel simply repeats the position:

> Sen. Stargel: Thank you Mr. President. I think it's common sense that we would all agree that . . . men are generally stronger than women. That is the

reason why we had Title IX to begin with. So women could be competitive in women's sports. Now this issue of transgender . . . like I said, we tried to initially come up with a way of determining if someone possibly had had enough hormone therapy to be weaker to allow that opportunity to play. We could not settle on the science, so we went to what was the most simplistic way, which is to say that if you're a male at birth you may not play in women's sports and . . . I'm holding to that standard as making sure that women are safe. I think it would be agreed upon that . . . men are generally stronger than women.

Mr. President: Senator Farmer, you're recognized.

Sen. Farmer: Uh, why then did we not put language in here, or would you put language in here now, that would establish some sort of strength criteria or some sort of measurement which would determine [that], because it could be that maybe the trans athlete is smaller than the other female athletes against whom they would be participating.

Mr. President: Senator Stargel, you're recognized.

Sen. Stargel: Thank you, Mr. President. That was the original approach of the bill. We couldn't settle on how to exactly do that. So we've gone to what is the most simple . . . when you're talking about sports, is that men are generally stronger than women and we're going to settle on, women's sports are played by women and men's sports are played by men. (Florida, Senate Session, 28 April 2021)

This exchange clearly demonstrates politicians' commitment to party values during political debates – here, the conservative values of 'simplicity' and 'common sense' – over and above investigation of the factors involved. That these values were deployed as a valid conclusion among Stargel's party members, despite the complexity of the 'science' in question, exemplifies the degree to which partisan messaging dominates the discussion. This also fosters polarization: legislators adhere to their side's 'script' versus earnestly engaging with the questions.

Several key exchanges in Oklahoma regarding intersex athletes further aid our understanding of the polarization fostered in political debate. Intersex persons refer to those who are not conventionally classified as male or female due to having a combination of biological sexual attributes, which can include hormones, chromosomes, genitalia and/or reproductive organs. Raising the question of intersex students was a common way opponents sought to challenge supporters' notions of 'biological sex'. At every turn, however, supporters deflected such queries to the hypothetical decisions of doctors and schools, who would be the official arbiters of such cases, limiting any real discussion of what intersex might mean for the proposed legislation. Note here, for example, Representative Walke's questions about Castor Semenya, a renowned intersex athlete with XY chromosomes who identifies and competes as a female:

Representative Walke: Thank you, Mr. Speaker. Representative, could you define biological sex for me?

> Representative Dills: The sex that you are born at birth.
> Chair: You're recognized for a follow-up.
> Representative Walke: Thank you, Mr. Speaker. Well, so I'm going to give you an example, and I'd like for you to tell me the answer in your infinite wisdom. Castor Semenya, two-time Olympic gold athlete from South Africa, is chromosomally male, competed as a female, presents as a female, is a female, and won the female Olympics. So do tell this chamber what biological sex means.
> Representative Dills: Thank you for your question, but I believe in this bill, the school would be making those decisions. (Oklahoma House Session, 19 April 2021)

Representative Dills' cursory response stunts a more rigorous dialogue about the case of intersex athletes, let alone the implications of intersex traits for binaristic understandings of sex. This reveals another ingredient of polarization: potential caveats or outliers that don't fit within one side's schema get limited traction in the discourse, even when they pose a bona-fide category worthy of consideration. As such, alternative viewpoints, and the social groups they may represent, get sidelined and erased in the discussion.

In a separate Senate session in Oklahoma, a compelling exchange occurs between Senators Kirt and Daniels regarding the 'science' that would indicate 'male advantage' – or as Kirt puts it, 'the implication that women need to be protected from trans girls.' Kirt indicates that the science she has consulted renders a more complicated portrait of sexual biology than simple gendered hierarchies suggest. Her opponent, however, takes offense at the 'idea' that the science is any more complicated than 'males and females are different', a 'fact' that doesn't warrant further explanation:

> Senator Kirt: And what is the evidence for a categorical difference for trans women participating, or trans girls? [. . .] Based on the science I've read, the idea of biological sex is actually far less clear than this bill implies.
> Senator Daniels: Thank you for the question. I disagree with the premise of the 'idea' of biological sex. We all know the physiological differences between male and female. We know that the distinction between the sexes began at the time of fertilization, that we were born male or female, then through puberty, develop the physiological features and strengths that make us completely male or completely female. I do not see it as an *idea*, I see it as a fact that sadly, I must present legislation to have us reaffirm a fact.
> Mr. President: Senator Dossett, J.A., you are recognized for a question.
> (*Discussion continues regarding number of trans athletes in the state*; Oklahoma, Senate Chamber, 24 March 2022)

Several scholars have shown that scientific discourse reproduces cultural tropes about gender to interpret matters of sexual biology (Fausto-Sterling,

2000; Richardson, 2012), but Kirt does not fully articulate those perspectives, posing poignant but limited questions instead. Daniels, meanwhile, refutes any complicating arguments in the face of what she constructs as basic 'facts' allegedly 'known to everyone', no evidence needed. One side's understandings are presented as objective truths, where questions about them get dismissed as frivolous and irrational. In addition, the opposing side fails to fully explicate the intervening argument (e.g. the actual complexities of sexual biology). The exchange amounts to a rhetorical performance versus a deep dive into the topic. Again, all of this occurs within a limited timeframe, and members must move to an entirely different question within minutes. These dynamics foster polarization between parties.

Other key factors are observed in another instance, when Representative Clemmons raises the role of pre-pubertal hormone blockers in Tennessee, a critical intervention that otherwise rarely appeared in hearings. Here, Clemmons uses Usain Bolt as a hypothetical example. His opponent, Representative Cepicky, at first questions the validity of the interrogation, stating, 'there's no way for me to determine that', and then returns to the alleged futility of 'hormone treatment'. But Cepicky's response references cross-sex hormones, *not* the puberty blockers Clemmons first cited:

> Clemmons: If you gave Usain Bolt puberty blockers or hormone treatment when he was a teenager, how would he compete against women? Do you know the answer to that? [. . .] Would he have as much testosterone if he had received puberty blockers or hormone treatments?
> Haston: Chairman Cepicky.
> Cepicky: Are you asking me, would he be slower?
> Clemmons: Yeah, that's a fair question. If he was receiving those, that's a fair question.
> Cepicky: Well, I don't personally know Usain Bolt and there's no way for me to determine that, but if you look at the scientific data, the hormone treatment doesn't change the bone structure, doesn't change the muscle structure, doesn't change the ligament structure, so you are trying to suppress something that is there . . . it doesn't go away, and when you look across what's happening in athletics, with these athletes that are participating, they're changing the female sport, and all we're here to do today is maintain – once again, Mr. Chairman, I don't know where to go with this – maintain the competitive balance, the safety and the opportunity for advancement for our girls in our sports.
> Haston: Thank you, chairman Cepicky. Does anyone else have any further questions?
> Clemmons: Just one more.
> Haston: Representative Clemmons, one more question.
> Clemmons: Thank you, Chairman. I appreciate why you're out there. . . . [T]his bill really involves a lot of science that hasn't been addressed and, or because of a refusal to address it, I think there's a lack of understanding . . . I spent a lot of hours studying this issue last year and this year to better

understand this gender dysphoria, trans-male versus trans-female, all these types of things . . . I think we really need to be careful. We are looking at this from a perspective of 50 years ago, boy versus girl. That science has evolved, our understanding has evolved . . . it's not black and white . . . I had to educate myself. I was raised that same way, but there's a lot of science involved here. (Tennessee, K12 Subcommittee, 9 February 2021)

In this critical moment, Clemmons asserts that the 'science has evolved' from outdated notions of 'boys versus girls', but he does not explicitly correct Cepicky's response: we do not yet know the effects of blockers on long-term athletic advantage. Cepicky conflates two very different kinds of hormonal interventions, pre-pubertal suppressants with cross-sex hormones. This would be an important distinction to unpack because it potentially undermines the 'science' behind athletic advantage. However, detailed understanding is not the goal of polarized messaging. The misconception remains part of the discourse unchecked.

Altogether, these exchanges reveal the ways in which polarization is created and fuelled by political debates. Legislators often disagreed over the very terms and definitions at issue, and when alternative understandings were raised, these received limited explication or air time. Conservative legislators often repeated their party positions like a mantra, deflecting recognition of the caveats and questions posed. Meanwhile, the opposition often failed to carry their interventions through to fuller clarity. Both sides showed limited, sometimes fully incorrect, understandings of the issues, leaving misconceptions hanging in the discourse and ideological gaps unbridged.

Conclusion

In recent years, the United States has seen a swell in legislation targeting transgender rights, and school sports policies are a prime instrument in those efforts. Dozens of states have passed bills banning transgender girls, and sometimes transgender boys, from participating on the sports teams aligned with their gender identity. The legislative hearings that debate these policies are important because they are one of the major public forums addressing cultural understandings of sex, gender and identity, and they are where transgender rights are being determined. However, our analysis reveals that these hearings do not advance rigorous discussion of a complicated issue, but rather erect and perpetuate a polarizing divide, eclipsing opportunities for real engagement and understanding.

A review of the hearings shows that these two sides are often 'talking past each other', focusing on entirely different issues and concerns. Proponents of the bills assert an unfair 'biological advantage' in persons assigned male and invoke the legacy of women's rights to protect women's sports. Opponents, in contrast, claim the bans address a problem that 'doesn't exist'. In pragmatic appeals to a wide voting audience, opponents focus on the economy, taxpayer dollars and better uses of government oversight.

The polarization these hearings generate is exacerbated by the rules of the debate floor itself and the conventions of partisan messaging (Brewer, 2003; Bächtiger, 2014; Proksch & Slapin, 2012). Much of the discussion entails one-sided speeches and statements, with little time for genuine cross-dialogue or follow-up between members. Moreover, politicians increasingly use debate as a chance to signal party values to a future electorate, beholding speakers to established partisan rhetorics rather than engaging in real debate that generates greater understanding. Indeed, our coding was dominated by repeated and divergent refrains from each side, almost like a broken record; they were talking to their own party members and future voters, not with each other. Interestingly, several of these themes indicate a surprising reversal of traditional party values – Republicans held up 'women's rights' and the triumphs of the feminist movement while Democrats emphasized fiscal responsibility. However, this dynamic just testifies to the polarization at work in the forum: each party defines itself as much through its *opposition* to the other as through its actual *content* (Palonen, 2009).

In rare instances, the two sides explicitly debated the bio-essentialist premise of the bills – 'male biological advantage' and a staunch sex/gender binary. These exchanges indicate the potential of the hearings to expand the discourse on gender, but as our analysis demonstrates, they often played out in limited ways, stultifying robust inquiry into the issues. Opponents clearly sought to trouble straightforward definitions of 'biological sex'. But they often failed to carry the intervention through to its logical conclusion, cite contrasting findings from the research, or explicitly correct misconceptions from their colleagues. No one, for example, mentioned researchers' calls for a 'continuum' model in sports that categorizes by ability, not sex or gender (Kane, 1995; Knox et al., 2019) or specific data that contradict claims of universal 'male' advantage (e.g. Harper, 2015).

Supporters, conversely, refused to entertain queries or cases their opponents raised (*'I'm not making a statement about that'*), and sometimes did not know enough to respond, defaulting to partisan mantras about 'male and female differences', even when these bordered on non-sequitur. In one instance, a legislator asked about the implications of puberty suppressants for the bans, and the response he received concerned cross-sex hormones, an entirely different hormonal intervention. Questions about intersex cases were deflected to the hypothetical decisions of doctors and schools. Overall, interlocutors often seemed locked in an ideological impasse, where critical interventions were raised but not fully addressed or considered.

While these excerpts highlight the ways the forum raises and exacerbates differences between sides, it is important to recognize the productive potential they *do* carry for public discourse. Though opponents' interventions were not always fully developed, supporters' inability to fully address them exposed flaws in the legislation and could signal to voters that questions of sex and gender are indeed more complicated than a simple binary model permits. These moments of the debates, however limited, disrupt simplistic, binary narratives about men and women and signal the potential for more nuanced approaches to sports policy. As such, while legislators' tactics help to reproduce polarizing discourses, they also have the potential to give voice to diverse, competing perspectives on an issue at the center of US culture and democracy.

Altogether, these hearings mark an important site of political polarization and the transgender rights they debate. Our analysis indicates that other venues may be more effective at productive dialogue, which are less encumbered by debate rules and party politics. This could include open community forums, expert lectures, messaging boards or advertising campaigns, especially by actors and organizations outside state legislatures. The 'living libraries' discussed in Kamarauskaitė's chapter are one example. The findings also indicate the need for robust citizen participation in the legislative process and the important role they play in advancing the discussion, including expert testimonies, public advocates and community members, as Slaymaker's chapter reveals. These actors may be able to offer more nuanced understandings and interventions than legislators' partisan performances allow.

Chapter 3

INCOMMENSURABLE REALITIES

LGBTQ BODIES AND THE CONSTRUCTION OF RELIGION, SEXUALITY AND DISCRIMINATION IN US FEDERAL RELIGIOUS EXEMPTION LITIGATION

Emily Kazyak

Introduction

In June 2023, the United States Supreme Court announced its ruling in *303 Creative LLC v. Elenis*. The case involved Lorie Smith, a graphic designer who sought a religious exemption from adhering to the state of Colorado's nondiscrimination law in order to not create wedding websites for same-sex couples. The court ruled in Smith's favor, arguing that to not grant an exemption would violate the Free Speech Clause of the First Amendment. US courts have considered other cases involving religious freedom and LGBTQ rights, and the decision in *303 Creative* reflects the fact that, in recent years, religious litigants have faced success in the US Supreme Court, including a baker refusing to make a wedding cake for a same-sex couple (*Masterpiece Cakeshop v. Colorado Civil Rights Commission*) and an adoption agency refusing to work with same-sex couples (*Fulton v. City of Philadelphia*).

Yet at the same time, the court also recently expanded nondiscrimination protections for LGBTQ people in ruling in *Bostock v. Clayton County*, which expanded Title VII employment nondiscrimination protections to include sexual orientation and gender identity. Also, despite ruling in favor of religious litigants in recent years, the US Supreme Court has not overturned the precedent set in *Employment Division v. Smith* in relation to the Free Exercise Clause of the First Amendment. In the 1990 *Smith* decision, the Court ruled that so long as a law is neutral and generally applied, it does not violate the Free Exercise Clause, even if it burdens religion. In other words, the *Smith* precedent sets parameters for religious freedom such that people's religious beliefs and ability to practice those beliefs cannot be restricted, but their actions in public life may be curtailed, even if those actions are motivated by religious beliefs (Hamilton, 2009; Marshall, 2018). Indeed, these parameters have meant that religious litigants opposed to LGBTQ rights have in fact not faced that much success in the courts in the past three decades, despite recent victories like *Creative, Masterpiece* and *Fulton* (Kazyak et al., 2023b).

In this chapter, I analyze three US federal court cases involving religious litigants opposed to LGBTQ rights that federal courts have adjudicated since the Smith decision in 1990. Each case involves a public school that, in one way or another, affirmed the presence of LGBTQ bodies in the school by sponsoring a Gay-Straight Alliance's 'Day of Silence' (*Harper v. Poway*), reading books featuring LGBTQ families (*Parker v. Hurley*) or adopting a policy that permits transgender students to use facilities that align with their gender identity (*Parents v. Privacy*). In each instance, the public school's actions were met with opposition from Christian students and parents, which culminated in the lawsuits. By foregrounding the conflict or 'social drama' (Cooper, 2019, p. 17) that led to the lawsuits and the perspectives of litigants as articulated within the courts, this chapter points to how polarization related to sexuality and gender is constituted and experienced in interpersonal interactions in public spaces, public schools in particular (see Nash & Browne, 2020). In doing so, I aim to lay bare the incommensurable ways in which a particular event or action as it relates to LGBTQ people is experienced or interpreted, and argue for the importance of foregrounding attention to these polarized and emotionally heightened experiences and interpretations. Additionally, I aim to analyze the multiple and contradictory logics that emerge from the judges as a way to point to how institutions like the law may further create and reflect polarized interpretations about discrimination, religion, sexuality and gender.

Literature review

Law and public opinion of LGBTQ rights in the United States: Progressing and polarizing?

The sociopolitical landscape in the United States has changed dramatically in the past several decades with regard to increasing recognition of LGBTQ identities and civil rights for LGBTQ people. Several landmark Supreme Court decisions have furthered legal protections for LGBTQ people, from the 2003 *Lawrence v. Texas* decision, which declared sodomy laws unconstitutional, to the 2015 *Obergefell v. Hodges* decision, which legalized same-sex marriage, to the 2020 *Bostock v. Clayton County* decision, which extended federal employment nondiscrimination protections to include the basis of gender identity and sexual orientation. Likewise, much public opinion scholarship has documented the degree to which Americans have become more accepting and supportive in their attitudes towards same-sex sexuality and LGBTQ rights over the past several decades. For instance, a majority of Americans (64%) in 2023 assert that gay and lesbian relations are morally acceptable, whereas only a minority did (44%) in 2003 (Gallup, 2023). Public opinion on a range of LGBTQ rights, including same-sex marriage and employment nondiscrimination protections, has demonstrated a similar trend towards increasing acceptance (Flores, 2014).

Yet at the same time, recent years have witnessed an onslaught of anti-LGBTQ legislation, particularly legislation targeting and restricting transgender people (see Loder chapter, Rahilly and Martin chapter, and Slaymaker chapter), as well as Supreme Court rulings that have ruled in favor of litigants seeking religious exemptions from adhering to sexual orientation nondiscrimination laws (Kazyak & Burke, 2022). Moreover, when it comes to public opinion of LGBTQ rights, Americans tend to be more ambivalent and opposed to family-related rights compared to nondiscrimination protections (Stange & Kazyak, 2016) – as well as to transgender rights compared to LGBQ rights (Burke et al., 2023). Likewise, public opinion illustrates that despite majority support for a range of LGBTQ rights, American attitudes remain polarized in some ways. For instance, unlike in the UK (see Lamble chapter and Peel chapter), there are stark partisan divides, insofar as political conservatives express lower levels of support for LGBTQ rights compared to political liberals (Public Religion Research Institute, 2023). Similar divides exist when examining religion, insofar as religiously affiliated Americans tend to hold less favorable attitudes towards LGBTQ rights compared to those who are not affiliated with a religion (Public Religion Research Institute, 2023). Additionally, attitudes vary among religious groups as well. Specifically, white Evangelical Protestants consistently emerge as a religious group who is more opposed to LGBTQ rights compared to any other religious group. For instance, whereas the majority of Americans support nondiscrimination protections for LGBTQ people (83 percent), including those who are religiously affiliated (anywhere from 81 to 88 percent), only 59 percent of white Evangelical Protestants do (Public Religion Research Institute, 2020). Importantly, political and religious affiliation are not the only factors influencing public opinion on LGBTQ rights and religious affirmation of LGBTQ identities exists, even among conservative Protestants (Moon, Tobin, & Sumerau, 2019).

Nonetheless, numerous scholars have focused on the role of religious conservatives in the United States in opposing a wide range of gender, sexuality and family-related issues, including LGBTQ rights (Burke, 2016, 2022; Fetner, 2008; Herman, 2000). In her analysis of Christian Right activism, Herman (2000) underscores how its anti-gay agenda relates to its wider and underlying theological vision. Namely, she outlines how conservative Christians view gays and lesbians as one of many 'anti-Christian forces' and part of a 'wider Satanic conspiracy', both of which are 'intent on using the state to achieve the complete removal of Christianity from the public sphere' (p. 141). From this perspective, 'the gay agenda is the secular agenda is the liberal agenda is the devil's agenda' (p. 147). The Christian Right thus sees the state as 'too big' and as 'hijacked' by liberals and seeks to 'restore and rebuild America as a Christian nation' (p. 151). Such findings resonate with what Whitehead and Perry (2022, p. xx) refer to more broadly as 'Christian nationalism', a framework that seeks to fuse Evangelical Protestantism with American civic life. Public schools in the United States in particular are sites where conflicts over religion, politics and sexuality have been rife (Biegel, 2018; Fields, 2008). An Evangelical emphasis on 'working to lead others to Christ' arguably informs the perspective that one's religious beliefs and actions should work in tandem and has undergirded social movement activism in the United States (FitzGerald, 2017; Pew Research, 2011). Building on this literature, my analysis in this chapter centers not on social movement activists or activist groups per se but rather on people who have experienced a conflict between religion and sexuality in their everyday life and who have determined the courts an appropriate avenue through which to resolve said conflict. In doing so, I hope to illustrate the importance of scholars analysing how polarizations around sexuality emerge in interpersonal interactions, alongside other arenas like legislation (see Slaymaker chapter; Rahilly and Martin chapter), social media (see Peel chapter) or social movement activist campaigns (see Lamble chapter). In other words, this chapter foregrounds how interpersonal interactions in public space between religious conservatives and LGBTQ individuals, as articulated in court opinions, become a site through which polarizing experiences and interpretations are constituted.

Religious freedom, civil liberties and analogies to minoritized groups

In examining court opinions, my analyses in this chapter are also informed by socio-legal scholarship which underscores how definitions of discrimination, religious freedom and civil rights are not static or settled in the law but rather are open to debate and continually negotiated by judges (Richman, 2010). Work by legal scholar Janet Halley (1997, p. 40), for instance, highlights how advocates for LGBTQ rights have often sought to advance arguments for the importance of rights for LGBTQ people by making 'like-race' analogies and positing that rights for sexual and gender minorities are 'just like rights already established for racial minorities . . . by the black civil rights movement'. The 'like race' argument may be especially salient in religious exemption cases related to LGBTQ rights, given that the courts have rejected arguments that religious exemptions to adhering to race nondiscrimination laws are required (Minow, 2007). Indeed, the courts have considered questions of whether religious exemptions must be granted in the context of nondiscrimination laws protecting race, gender and sexual orientation for several decades (Cooper, 2019; Minow, 2007; Velte, 2021). In her analysis of these cases, Minow (2007) illustrates how religious exemptions for nondiscrimination laws protecting race, gender and sexual orientation have been treated differently by the courts. Specifically, courts have more uniformly responded that religious exemptions should *not* be granted for discrimination laws related to race, but court decisions related to gender and sexual orientation nondiscrimination laws have been more mixed. In further analyses of these cases, my collaborators and I have found variation in how courts construct the meaning of religious freedom in relation to LGBTQ rights (Kazyak et al., 2023a). We found, for instance, that distinctions between public and private inform how courts assess harm and whether a court grants a religious exemption.

In this chapter, I aim to extend these analyses by looking at how litigants construct arguments about facing discrimination on the basis of religion. In making these arguments, litigants not only outline the specific details of their experiences but also make specific legal claims and seek to draw parallels to other cases and legal precedents, which judges then address in their opinions. In other words, litigants try to position themselves as being similar to other individuals or groups who have faced discrimination and who have found success in the courts. In this way, rather than analyze judicial decisions only as they relate to the unfolding of legal precedent, I aim to shed light on the processes by which mostly Christian litigants experience and position themselves as facing discrimination and hostility by virtue of having to interact with LGBTQ people in public spaces. Public opinion polls show that white Evangelical Protestants in the United States see themselves as a minoritized, discriminated-against group (Public Religion Research Institute, 2021). Indeed, 59 percent believe that there is a lot of discrimination against Christians, and 71 percent believe that religious liberty is threatened (compared to only 36 and 39 percent of Americans who hold these beliefs, respectively). My analysis in this chapter sheds light on how sexuality and gender are central to the ways in which these polarized interpretations about discrimination are lived out in everyday life.

Methods

In this chapter, I provide an in-depth analysis of three cases that are connected to a larger project focused on all US federal court cases in the past three decades that involve a claim of religious exemption and discrimination litigation (see Burke, Kazyak, & Behrendt, 2023; Kazyak et al., 2023a, 2023b). The research team identified the cases using the following search terms in Nexis Uni: 'religious exemption', 'religious discrimination', 'free exercise' and 'RFRA' (n = 1,281) and then identified the LGBTQ-related cases (n = 63) by using the search terms: 'gay', 'homosexual', 'lesbian', 'transgender', 'bisexual', 'sexual orientation' and 'gender identity'. The case summaries, which include both majority opinions that reflect the decision of the court and any dissenting opinions that reflect disagreements a judge had about that decision, were then quantitatively and qualitatively analyzed by the research team (for more details about methodology, see Burke, Kazyak, & Behrendt, 2023; Kazyak et al., 2023a, 2023b).

For the analysis in this chapter, I chose three exemplar cases. The three cases have similar characteristics to the sixty-three cases in the larger sample (see Kazyak et al., 2023b), including the fact that the plaintiffs are Christians who bring religion-based claims to oppose LGBTQ rights. The plaintiffs are individuals, and the defendants are government agencies and/or parties representing the government in their official capacities; all the cases involve defendants that are public schools and public school administrators. Finally, in all three cases, the court ruled against the religious litigants, which again reflects the trend in the broader sample of cases (Kazyak et al., 2023a, 2023b).

I qualitatively analyzed the narratives and discourses in these three cases using the lens of polarization. Specifically, I was interested in exploring the drastically different ways that meanings about religion, sexuality and discrimination were constructed in the court opinions. I aimed to foreground litigants' lived experiences, as articulated in the court, as a way to capture their perspectives and to ultimately shed light on how polarization is lived out in people's daily lives. Rather than critique or endorse any one perspective, my goal is to outline the construction of the incommensurable realities. In other words, I am less interested in critiquing the religious litigants' perspectives for how they marginalize LGBTQ identities (which is an important but ultimately different analysis than the one I take up here). Rather, I am more interested in laying bare the fundamental disagreements related to gender and sexuality as experienced in everyday life, which raises questions about how we might engage and interact with one another amid polarized perspectives (see Ballantine, Hilliard and Browne chapter). Additionally, I aimed to analyze judges' opinions as a way to shed light on how the institution of law 'both reflects and contributes to a broader cultural and political landscape' (Burke & Kazyak, 2021). As Davina Cooper (2019, p. 16–18) notes, legal narratives as reflected in court opinions depict a social drama and ultimately tell a particular story about power, victimization and equality. Thus, the court is not a neutral actor but plays a role in constructing and maintaining incommensurable realities.

Findings

My analysis illustrates how incommensurable worldviews regarding LGBTQ existence in public space, particularly public schools, animate lawsuits involving religious exemption and sexuality. In doing so, I aim to illustrate how polarized experiences around sexuality and gender are constituted in everyday life. I analyze three cases as exemplars. These cases raise questions about the degree to which the presence of LGBTQ people necessitates opposition, as well as questions about how people who fundamentally oppose LGBTQ identities might co-exist with LGBTQ people in public life (see Ballantine, Hilliard and Browne chapter).

Harper v. Poway

The first case, *Harper v. Poway*, involves a public high school in California that the court opinion noted has had 'a history of conflict over issues of sexual orientation'. The court opinion narrated that the school had faced other litigation wherein gay students were successful in winning a lawsuit against the school for its failure to protect them from harassment. Additionally, in 2003, when the school's Gay-Straight Alliance (GSA) held a 'Day of Silence', some students made 'anti-homosexual comments' and wore 'Straight Pride Day' shirts with 'derogatory remarks about homosexuals', both of which resulted in fights on school grounds and some students receiving suspensions. The following year, when the GSA held another 'Day of Silence', Tyler Chase Harper, a Christian student, wore a shirt to school that read: 'Be ashamed, our school embraced what God has condemned' on the front and 'Homosexuality is shameful Romans 1:27' on the back. One of Harper's teachers sent him to the principal's office for a dress code violation, saying that the shirt was 'inflammatory' and 'created a negative and hostile working environment for others'. School administrators, as well as a school resource officer whose presence had been requested that day due to safety concerns, all tried to convince Harper to remove his shirt. Harper would not remove his shirt. Although Harper asked two times to be suspended, the school administrators did not suspend him, nor place any disciplinary record in his file. They did have him remain in the main office that day rather than attend classes. In response, Harper brought a lawsuit against the school and administrators that included claims of violation of the First Amendment Free Speech Clause, Establishment Clause and the Free Exercise Clause, among others. The court ruled against him. This case underscores several ways in which polarizing experiences of sexuality are lived out in public life.

First, the discourse in the court opinion reveals incommensurable interpretations of the Day of Silence event itself and Harper's T-shirt. The Day of Silence entailed a number of activities, including students wearing duct tape over their mouths as a way to symbolize the silencing effect of intolerance on gays and lesbians, students wearing T-shirts that said 'National Day of Silence' and students hanging up posters to promote awareness of harassment on the basis of sexual orientation. As the school administrators expressed in court, they understood that the purpose of the Day of Silence was to 'teach tolerance of others, particularly those of a different sexual orientation'. Thus, from the articulated perspective of the school, the shirt reflected 'inflammatory' rhetoric that is harmful to gay and lesbian students and to the learning environment of all students. In stark contrast, Harper expressed in court that 'the true purpose' of the Day of Silence was to 'endorse, promote, and encourage homosexual activity'. Thus, Harper understood his shirt to reflect his opposition to such a purpose given his sincerely held religious belief that 'homosexuality is harmful to both those who practice it and the community at large'. Like Harper, some parents were also concerned about the Day of Silence and voiced opposition to the school. In fact, the principal had requested the presence of the school safety officer during the Day of Silence after receiving a call from a parent who complained about the event and said 'he and several other parents had "had it" and "would be doing something about it."' Both the parent's and Harper's interpretations underscore the degree to which the event signified a significant, dangerous and harmful action that necessitated opposition and prompted emotional reactions of anger (the parent who had 'had it') and shame (Harper's shirt that referenced the need for students to be ashamed).

The meaning and purpose of the Day of Silence and Harper's shirt is similarly constituted in incommensurable ways by the majority judicial opinion and dissenting opinion. The judge writing the majority opinion emphasizes the degree to which Harper's shirt had a 'demeaning' effect on gay and lesbian students in particular. In doing so, the judge utilizes 'like race' analogies (Halley, 1997) to draw parallels between gay and lesbian students and racial minorities in public schools. For instance, the judge refers to sexual orientation as a 'core identifying characteristic', similar to 'race'. He also refers to gays and lesbians as 'members of minority groups that have historically been oppressed'. He reasons thus that gay and lesbian students 'have a right to be free from [verbal assaults on the basis of a core identifying characteristic] while on school campuses'.

Whereas the judge writing the dissenting opinion questions whether Harper's shirt actually caused harm as I'll outline in a moment, the judge writing the majority opinion draws a parallel to race in order to argue the negative and harmful effects of the shirt. The judge writes:

> As long ago as in *Brown v. Board of Education*, the Supreme Court recognized that '[a] sense of inferiority affects the motivation of a child to learn.' If a school permitted its students to wear shirts reading, 'Negroes: Go Back To Africa,' no one would doubt that the message would be harmful to young black students. So, too, in the case of gay students, with regard to messages such as those written on Harper's T-shirt (*Harper v. Poway*).

Here again, Black students and gay students are analogized as being similarly positioned as members of minority groups. Moreover, Harper's shirt is constituted as 'injurious to gay and lesbian students', as something that 'interfered with their right to learn', and as a 'verbal assault'.

In contrast, the discourse from the dissenting judge constitutes the Day of Silence and Harper's t-shirt in a drastically different manner. Here, rather than construct gays and lesbians as a historically oppressed, minoritized group, the dissenting judge emphasizes the degree to which 'acceptance of homosexuality is a political disagreement and debate'. The Day of Silence, the judge thus reasons, reflects a 'political activity that was sponsored or at the very least tolerated by school authorities' and a 'visible and highly politicized action'. The school, therefore, should have expected and tolerated students like Harper to be able to express their opposition. The judge writes:

> tolerance toward homosexuality and homosexual conduct is anathema to those who believe that intimate relations among people of the same sex are immoral or sinful. So long as the subject is kept out of the school environment, these differences of opinion need not clash. But a visible and highly publicized political action by those on one side of the issue will provoke those on the other side to express a different point of view, if only to avoid the implication that they agree (*Harper v. Poway*).

In this view, the existence of the Day of Silence 'provoked' opposition is seen as legitimate. In fact, to not allow opposition to be expressed is viewed as intolerant. In other words, the school should have either not allowed the Day of Silence to occur or allowed both the day and Harper's shirt to co-exist.

Further, the dissenting judge speculates that allowing Harper and other students to voice opposition to homosexuality may actually, ultimately and positively impact gay and lesbian students. The judge writes: 'Supporters of the Day of Silence may prefer to see views such as Harper's channeled into public discourse rather than officially suppressed but whispered behind backs or scribbled on bathroom walls. Confronting – and refuting – such views in a public forum may well empower homosexual students, contributing to their sense of self-esteem.' In this reasoning, by 'officially suppress[ing]' Harper's T-shirt, the school is constructed as potentially actually hurting and undermining support for gay and lesbian students. Rather than interpret Harper's T-shirt as a 'verbal assault', the dissenting judge posits that the shirt may actually empower gay and lesbian students and raise their self-esteem.

Finally, the dissenting judge questions the logic of which identities and statuses are seen as minority or majority. Here, the judge also draws parallels between race and sexual orientation (Haley, 1997), but to a very different effect. The dissenting judge offers that 'the school authorities may have been justified in banning the subject altogether by denying both sides permission to express their views during the school day' and provides the example of 'upholding ban on items that give rise to racial tension such as Confederate flags and Malcolm X t-shirts'. Here, rather than liken sexual minorities to racial minorities and draw a parallel between struggles for civil rights for gays and lesbians and African Americans, as the judge's majority opinion did, the discourse constructs Confederate flags and Malcolm X T-shirts as equally giving rise to racial tensions. Further, the dissenting judge references hypothetical scenarios involving white students and Christian students, which reinforce his questioning of which groups are viewed as in minority or marginalized in public schools. The judge writes:

> Students may well have their self-esteem bruised by being demeaned for being white or Christian, or having bad acne or weight problems, or being poor or stupid or any one of the infinite number of characteristics that will not qualify them for minority status. Under the rule the majority announces today, schools would be able to ban t-shirts with pictures of Mohammed wearing a bomb turban but not those with pictures of a Crucifix dipped in urine – yet Muslim and Christian children, respectively, may have their learning equally disrupted (*Harper v. Poway*).

Here again, the discourse flattens historical and contemporary inequalities between groups. The parallel to race is made in order to position being white as a potentially marginalized, minority status. Later, the dissenting judge asks: 'May a student wear a Black Pride t-shirt, or does this denigrate white and Asian students?' Unlike the majority opinion, which delineated clear boundaries between majority/minoritized identities and groups, and historicized existing inequities, here the discourse from the dissenting judge yet again flattens such distinctions. Likewise, the discourse questions why Christians cannot be considered a minority group. In sum, the majority and dissenting opinions construct, reflect and reinforce two incommensurable, polarized social realities concerning sexuality and the existence of LGBTQ students in public schools.

The differing ways that Harper and school administrators, along with the majority opinion judge, interpreted the school's actions in relation to the freedom of religion further illustrate the degree to which social reality can become polarized when lived out through the existence of LGBTQ sexuality. As part of his reasoning alleging a violation of his First Amendment Free Exercise rights, Harper argued that the school punished him for his religious views and attempted to change his religious views. He points to conversations with the school administrators and the school resource officers as evidence of these attempts. Specifically, the school resource officer talked with Harper about 'the content of the shirt . . . the Bible and [the] scripture reference on the shirt', which Harper characterized as an 'interrogation' and the deputy characterized as a 'casual conversation'. In their exchange, the school resource officer asserted that 'Christianity was based on love, not hate, and that [Harper] should not be offensive to others'. The court ultimately viewed that discussion as one directed toward changing Harper's behavior, not his beliefs. Additionally, the Assistant Principal, who went to the same church as Harper, also talked with him. In that conversation, the Assistant Principal stated that he 'shared the same Christian faith' as Harper and 'understood where he was coming from' but wished that he could 'express himself in a more positive way'. The Assistant Principal suggested that Harper, for instance, consider 'more positive and non-confrontational' ways of expressing his religious beliefs, like 'sponsoring activities through the campus Bible Club'. Again, the court ultimately viewed this conversation as also one that was directed towards changing Harper's behavior, not changing his religious views. Yet arguably Harper's perspective would be that his religious beliefs are not as easily disentangled from his actions. Although not explicitly noted in the court opinion, the sentiment that religious beliefs and actions are not, and should not, be separated is one shared by many religious people, particularly Evangelical Christians who emphasize the importance of evangelizing and 'taking a stand on social and political issues' as central to their faith (Pew Research Center, 2011).

Parker v. Hurley

The second exemplar case, *Parker v. Hurley*, centers on two sets of parents, the Parkers and the Wirthlins, who brought a lawsuit against a public school district and school officials in Massachusetts in 2006. The court opinion described the parents as 'devout Judeo-Christians' and noted that 'a core belief of their religion is that homosexual behavior and gay marriage are immoral and violate God's law'. Both sets of parents objected to books that their children's elementary school, Estabrook Elementary School, utilized as part of a 'nondiscrimination curriculum'. Specifically, in kindergarten, the Parkers' son, Jacob, received a 'Diversity Book Bag' which included the picture book *Who's in a Family?* As the court opinion outlines, the book 'depicted different families, including single-parent families, an extended family, interracial families, animal families, a family without children, and – to the concern of the Parkers – a family with two dads and a family with two moms'. The Parkers objected to their son receiving this book and were concerned that 'this book was part of an effort by the public schools "to indoctrinate young children into the concept that homosexuality and homosexual relationships or marriage are moral and acceptable behavior."' They feared that by doing so, the elementary school 'would require their sons [sic] to affirm a belief inconsistent with their religion'. The next year, their son's first grade classroom included the book *Who's in a Family*, as well as the picture book *Molly's Family*, a book that centers on the story of a girl with two moms. In a similar vein, the Wirthlins objected to their second-grade son being read aloud the picture book *King and King* by his teacher. The book depicts a prince falling in love with and getting married to another prince and includes a wedding scene and a scene of the two princes kissing. The parents described that their son told them about the book that evening and was 'agitated' and called the book 'silly'. Like the Parkers, the Wirthlins objected to the book being read to their son on the grounds that they considered it to be 'indoctrination of their son about gay marriage in contravention of their religious beliefs'.

Both parents met with the teacher and school administrators on multiple occasions to voice their objections to these books being utilized, as well as to request that they be notified in advance if any further 'discussions of homosexuality' were going to occur so that they may 'opt out' of their children being exposed to 'any materials or discussions featuring sexual orientation, same-sex unions, or homosexuality'. The parents pointed to a Massachusetts statute that stipulated school districts notify parents and provide them with the opportunity to exempt their children from 'curriculum which primarily involves human sexual education or human sexuality issues' and thus believed they were entitled to the option to 'opt out' per this state law. In those meetings, the school officials stated they disagreed that the statute was applicable to the types of class material and discussions the Parker and Wirthlin children received in their classrooms and responded that they thus would not be notifying the parents or allowing them to 'opt out' of such material or discussions. One of the meetings ended with one of the parents getting arrested after he 'refused to leave the school until his demands were met'. In response to the school's position, the Parkers and Wirthlins brought a lawsuit.

Their lawsuit alleged violations of the First Amendment Free Exercise Clause, of the Fourteenth Amendment due process right to have parental autonomy in raising their children, and of the Massachusetts 'opt-out' law. Importantly, the parents argued that the elementary school was 'systematically indoctrinating' their children 'contrary to the parents' religious beliefs'. Here, the presence of LGBTQ people, in this case via the form of fictional same-sex parent family characters and a depiction of marriage between two men in children's picture books, is constituted as antithetical to their religious beliefs. As such, the parents want to be able to exempt their children from 'classroom presentations or discussions the intent of which is to have children *accept the validity of*, embrace, affirm, or celebrate views of human sexuality, gender identity, and marriage constructs (my emphasis added)'. Again, this court case underscores the degree to which the existence of LGBTQ people in public space, or a public stance in which LGBTQ identities are accepted as valid, is met with opposition. It highlights the degree to which polarization emerges in relation to gender and sexuality in everyday public life: as school officials seemingly view the books as relatively innocuous, insofar as they did not think the state opt-out law was applicable, and the parents see the books as dangerous and evidence of indoctrination.

Moreover, the parents also argued that the school and school officials held a 'specific intention to denigrate the [families'] sincere and deeply-held faith'. The parents attempt to draw a comparison to families in a different case, *Yoder*, which involved Amish families successfully challenging a state public school's mandatory attendance policy that conflicted with the families' belief that education beyond eighth grade undermined their religiously focused way of life. The Parkers and Wirthlins liken themselves to those families insofar as 'the state is threatening their very "way of life."' Again, the court case illustrates the stakes involved from the perspectives of the religious litigants insofar as the public school's use of children's books depicting LGBTQ people is understood to be not only directly antithetical to their religious beliefs and tantamount to denigrating those beliefs but also as threatening to their entire way of life.

As such, not allowing parents to exempt their children from engaging with such materials is construed as intolerant of religious beliefs. The parents called it 'ironic . . . for a public school system to show such intolerance towards their own religious beliefs in the name of tolerance'. Also, they argue that the school district allowing parents to opt out 'would teach other students tolerance of different religious beliefs'. In contrast, in amici briefs submitted in support of the school district, groups asserted that allowing parents to opt out 'would send a message that children of same-sex parents are inferior'. These cases lay bare how competing, incommensurable worldviews co-exist and lead to tensions, conflicts and polarization related to gender and sexuality. The cases also further illustrate how both groups, LGBTQ people and religious litigants, are positioned as experiencing marginalization and intolerance.

Although the First Circuit court noted that 'we accept as true plaintiffs's assertion that their sincerely held religious beliefs were deeply offended', they ultimately ruled against the parents and in favor of the school district and officials. The court rejects the attempt to draw a parallel to the case involving the Amish community. In rejecting that parallel, the court reasons that the books 'will not automatically and irreversibly prevent the parents from raising [their children] in the religious belief that gay marriage is immoral' and because no criminal statute or punishment is imposed on the parents if they teach their children this religious viewpoint (unlike the Amish parents who faced such punishment for not sending their children to school past eighth grade). The court also rejects the argument that the plaintiffs' free exercise rights are violated. The court is particularly skeptical of Jacob's claim:

> we cannot see how Jacob's free exercize right was burdened at all: two books were made available to him, but he was never required to read them or have them read to him. Further, these books do not endorse gay marriage or homosexuality, or even address these topics explicitly, but merely describe how other children might come from families that look different from one's own. There is no free exercise right to be free from any reference in public elementary schools to the existence of families in which the parents are of different gender combinations (*Parker v. Hurley*).

Here we can see how the court and families are perhaps speaking past each other, akin to the legislators in Rahilly and Martin's chapter. The court views the books as relatively innocuous, merely depicting LGBTQ people, or 'families in which parents are of different gender combinations, including two mom and two dad families'.

Yet such depictions are precisely what the family finds so offensive and antithetical to their religious beliefs. In other words, the existence of LGBTQ people in public space is experienced, understood and constructed in radically different ways.

The court spends more time in their opinion discussing Joey's claim, which they refer to as 'more significant' in comparison to Jacob's claims. The court finds Joey's claim more significant because 'he was required to sit through a classroom reading of *King and King* and because that book affirmatively endorses homosexuality and gay marriage'. The court notes that the book was 'precisely *intended* to influence the listening children toward tolerance of gay marriage'. From the parents' perspectives as articulated in court, the reading of the book reflects 'indoctrination' and 'that the state has put pressure on their children to endorse an affirmative view of gay marriage'. However, the court rejects this argument in ruling against the parents. The court emphasized that the book was used in an attempt to influence students to be more tolerant, not in an attempt to indoctrinate. The judge stressed that 'there is no evidence of systemic indoctrination', pointing to the fact that the 'plaintiff's children were not forced to read the books on pain of suspension. Nor were they subject to a constant stream of like materials'. Unlike the parents' reactions, the judge's reasoning minimizes the impact of the books and construes its intent and impact in an entirely different manner (tolerance versus indoctrination).

Parents for Privacy v. Barr

The third case, *Parents for Privacy v. Barr*, centers on a public high school in Oregon and its policy to allow transgender students to use school facilities that align with their gender identity rather than the biological sex they were assigned at birth. Specifically, the high school developed a 'Student Safety Plan' in 2015 in relation to a student 'who had been born and who remained biologically female [and] publicly identified as a boy', who the school acknowledged as a 'transgender male' and the court acknowledged as a 'transgender boy'. The student had requested to be able to use the boys' bathroom and locker room for physical education class. In response, the school developed the Plan, which permitted him and any other transgender student to use school facilities that aligned with their gender identity. Students and parents who were concerned about the school's policy voiced opposition at school board meetings and circulated a petition to stop the public school from implementing the policy. Despite opposition, the school district continued to allow the transgender student to use the bathroom and locker room that aligned with the gender with which he identified. In response, several individuals, including students and parents with children in the school district, an association of former and current students and their parents and a non-profit, brought a lawsuit against the school district. Among other legal claims, they argued that the school's policy violated the First Amendment Free Exercise Clause, the Fourteenth Amendment right to privacy and right to direct the education and upbringing of one's children, and Title IX.

In the court opinion, the specific religion of the plaintiffs is not explicitly specified. Rather, the plaintiffs assert that they have the 'sincere religious belief' that 'children must not undress, or use the restroom, in the presence of a member of the opposite biological sex, and also that they must not be in the presence of the opposite biological sex while the opposite biological sex is undressing or using the restroom'. The plaintiffs thus argue that the school's policy interferes with the parents' and children's ability to fully practice 'traditional modesty' which their faith requires of them. In fact, the plaintiffs alleged that when a student started using the boys' locker room, several 'cisgender boys' felt 'embarrassment, humiliation, anxiety, intimidation, fear, apprehension, and stress' because of having to change clothes 'while someone who had been assigned the opposite sex at birth was present'. Such discourse underscores the degree to which the experiences of cisgender people are foregrounded and the degree to which appeals to emotions are central. Additionally, similar to *Parker v. Hurley*, the religious litigants who brought the lawsuit expressed concern about maintaining control over raising their children. Drawing on the Fourteenth Amendment, the plaintiffs assert the right to 'instill moral standards and values in their children' and to protect their children from having to 'risk exposing their own undressed or partially unclothed bodies to members of the opposite sex'. Again, the religious identity of the plaintiffs is not explicitly marked, nor is a transgender identity.

In this way, the discussion of the plaintiff's religious beliefs that appear in the court opinion does not explicitly mark transgender bodies as transgender. In fact, throughout the court opinion, the judge refers to the plaintiff's assertion about members of the 'opposite biological sex', but nowhere do the plaintiffs make explicit reference to the existence of a transgender identity or gender identity. In contrast, the school district, as reinforced by the judge's opinion, foregrounds the transgender student and the school's policy 'in seeking to create a safe, non-discriminatory school environment for transgender students'. Thus, the two sides appear to be speaking past each other to some degree (see Rahilly and Martin chapter). Here, the religious litigants' opposition to transgender rights is constituted via silence around transgender identities or the concept of gender identity, thus negating transgender existence (see Slaymaker chapter). The starting point of the debate reflects two incommensurate realities, one in which transgender people exist and public identification with a gender is paramount (school district and court) and one where biological sex is paramount (religious litigants) and thus, transgender people as such do not exist.

In this case, we see religious litigants position themselves as persecuted via other lawsuits involving violations of privacy. Although the court resoundingly rejects the comparisons, it is nonetheless telling to see how groups attempt to position themselves vis-à-vis others in making the case for how their rights have been violated akin to other groups. In this case, no 'like-race' analogies, or analogies to other religious groups like the Amish, emerge in these constructions. Rather, the religious litigants draw a parallel to their experiences sharing public facilities with transgender individuals with other cases involving what they view as a fundamental right to 'bodily privacy' and an 'elementary self-respect and personal dignity' that compels a 'desire to shield one's unclothed figure from . . . strangers of the opposite sex'. In making this argument, the plaintiffs referenced and attempted to draw a parallel between their case and cases which involved male law enforcement officers either viewing, touching or taking and distributing photographs of female assault victims against their will. In making such comparisons, the religious litigants position themselves as similarly in violation. The court rejected the comparison, referring to those cases as examples of 'an egregious privacy violation'. In contrast to those cases, the court noted: 'a transgender student's presence in the restroom provides no more of a risk to other students' privacy rights than the presence of... any other student who used the bathroom at the same time'. Again, as seen in the other two cases as well, whereas the discourse from the religious litigants sought to heighten the implications of the school's policy, the court discourse rejects that attempt.

Conclusion

In analysing three federal US cases related to a religious exemption claim in the context of LGBTQ rights, I aim to think through how polarization around sexuality and gender emerges in interpersonal interactions in public spaces in the contemporary United States. The conflicts that gave rise to these lawsuits underscore the degree to which individuals occupy drastically different social realities, which inform their interpretations and the conflicts that occur as a result. As expressed in the courtroom, the religious litigants in these three cases assert that they are acting in accordance with a sincerely held religious belief. Being opposed to same-sex sexuality, same-sex marriage or LGBTQ identities is experienced as central and fundamental to their faith. They seek to either minimize their interactions with LGBTQ people in public spaces (*Parker*, *Parents for Privacy*) or to vocalize their opposition to LGBTQ identities in public spaces (*Harper*). From the perspectives of the public school litigants articulated in court, with which most judges in these three cases ultimately aligned, such actions run counter to an interest in promoting awareness and tolerance and minimizing discrimination against LGBTQ people. The arguments brought forth in these cases demonstrate two competing and incompatible world views regarding sexuality, gender and LGBTQ bodies. Although the focus here is on religious, mainly Christian, groups and LGBTQ people in the United States, other scholarship and chapters in the volume demonstrate how these polarizations extend beyond religious or political lines in different geographical contexts (Lamble chapter, Nash & Browne, 2020; Peel chapter). Future work should continue to assess how certain discourses or claims gain resonance across groups and in different contexts; for instance, Nash and Browne (2020) demonstrate how the discourse of 'parental rights' has animated a diverse constituency of heteroactivists in Canada (Nash & Browne, 2020). In the case of the three cases analyzed here, it is worth noting that religion is less explicitly referenced (indeed, the actual religion of the plaintiffs is not identified) in *Parents for Privacy*, which involved a public school's affirmative policy for transgender students. The degree to which polarization related to transgender people and rights, in particular, beyond religious-based opposition, warrants attention in future research.

Additionally, this chapter highlights the processes by which Christian individuals who are anti-LGBTQ position themselves within the courts as marginalized victims vis-à-vis sociopolitical changes that advance LGBTQ inclusion. The judge writing the majority opinion in *Harper* rejects the idea that Christians can be minoritized and rather emphasizes the degree to which LGBTQ people are akin to racial minorities in facing discrimination that the law and courts can and should help remedy. Yet, the dissenting judge in *Harper*, for instance, questions the boundaries between majority/minority and leaves open the possibility for Christian Americans to be construed as a minority, potentially oppressed group. Some of the court discourse also foregrounds the logic that the existence of LGBTQ people necessitates opposition. The opinion from the dissenting judge in *Harper* serves as the most striking exemplar. Here, the judge argues that the public school allowing a Day of Silence in support of LGBTQ students 'will provoke those on the other side to express a different point of view'. To not expect or not allow for such expression is thus seen as intolerance. The parents in *Parker* likewise argue that the school is not willing to be tolerant towards their religious viewpoints. Finally, the discourse of religious litigants as articulated within the courts underscores the heightened emotional resonance of issues of sexuality and gender. Centering their presumably heterosexual, cisgender and Christian positions, the religious litigants attempt to stress the harm and risk that LGBTQ people pose (see also Lamble and Kamarauskaitė chapters). Viewing sexuality and gender as merely 'wedge issues' obscures how the presence of LGBTQ bodies in public spaces evokes deeply felt reactions (see McCartan, Moore-Ponce, Burke, Foudy and Thor chapter). Future work should examine how these reactions and emotions might manifest differently across different spaces (see Ballantine, Hilliard and Browne chapter). In a related vein, future work can also continue to grapple with how we might engage with one another amid polarized perspectives (see Ballantine, Hilliard and Browne chapter).[1]

Note

1 This chapter is based on research conducted as part of a project funded by the National Science Foundation (award #1918020), Religious Exemption Laws and Minority Rights. I'd like to thank Kelsy Burke (Co-PI on the grant) for our collaborative work and many fruitful conversations, and Matt Adams for furthering my thoughts on polarization. Finally, thanks to Carol Ballantine and Andrew McCartan who provided helpful feedback on this chapter.

Chapter 4

CLAIMING SPACE IN THE MARGINS

COMMUNITY ORGANIZATIONS AS LIMINAL SPACES FOR BLACK TRANSGENDER WOMEN NAVIGATING POLITICAL POLARIZATION IN THE US SOUTH

Kimya Loder

Introduction

Studies of polarization have sought to understand group identity formation (Iyengar et al., 2012; Iyengar & Westwood, 2015; Suhay, 2015; Tajfel & Turner, 1986), the behaviors of political elites (Druckman et al., 2013; Feinberg & Willer, 2015) and significant trends in public opinion (Bail et al., 2018; Boxell, Gentzkow, & Shapiro, 2017; Fiorina & Abrams, 2008). I advance existing literature by considering how polarization, which in this chapter is conceptualized as firmly held differences in value systems and ideological orientations, impacts the livelihoods of those whose identities are at the center of debate. More specifically, I contribute to studies of polarization by considering how the polarizing ideologies, discourses and practices of those who oppose trans inclusion impact the lived experiences of transgender people. Thus, this chapter examines data documenting the experiences of Black transgender women navigating the Southern United States to understand how individuals from multiply marginalized, highly stigmatized groups navigate the precarity of living in geographies where polarization has shaped interpersonal interactions and institutional environments.

The US South has historically been positioned as a critical terrain upon which the rights of marginalized groups have been stripped, contested and demanded. From entrenched systems of chattel slavery and Jim Crow to more recent waves of voter disenfranchisement and legislation targeting LGBTQ+ communities, the US South remains at the center of polarizing ideological and moral debates (Alijore, 2019; Grimsley, 2001; Frey et al., 2021; Perry, 2022; Stone, 2018; Woodell et al., 2015). Although the US South is certainly not the only region that has promulgated repressive policies and propaganda, it has undoubtedly played a central role in shaping race, gender and class-based inequality in the United States (Baker, 2022; Davis, 1981; Hogan, 2001). Seeing the repressive policies as directly affecting trans lives, this chapter asks where have individuals at the margins of social, economic and political life found refuge in highly polarized sociopolitical environments?

Due to religious indoctrination, anti-LGBTQ+ legislations and other exclusionary practices, the US South serves as an ideal geography for understanding how Black transgender women who experience the impacts of sexism, racism and transphobia navigate highly polarized sociopolitical environments. Between 2017 and 2021, the southern region of the United States proposed more exclusionary bills targeting transgender persons than any other region (Kline et al., 2021). Furthermore, the US South has the fewest states by percentage that offer legislative protections against discrimination in employment, housing and public accommodations based on sexual orientation (Cramer et al., 2017). Nearly 50 per cent of the 490 anti-LGBTQ bills introduced across the United States in 2023 have been introduced in southern states (ACLU, 2023). In addition to fuelling legislation restricting the rights of LGBTQ+ communities, polarizing ideological debates have also influenced public discourse. Repressive policies have been accompanied by mass public discourse on topics ranging from healthcare provisions for transgender youth to adoption by same-sex parents (the *Guardian*, 2022). Moreover, anti-transgender legislations that rely on identity-based criteria have incited what Westbrook and Schilt (2013, p. 34) refer to as 'gender panics', or 'situations where people react to disruptions to biology-based gender ideology by frantically reasserting the naturalness of a male-female binary'. Subsequently, political polarization in the US South among political elites and in public discourse on LGBTQ+ rights create unique challenges for race and gender-marginalized communities.

Still, despite its central role in perpetuating polarizing ideology, discourse and policies impacting sex and gender-marginalized communities, the Southern United States is home to nearly 3.5 million LGBTQ+ adults, making it the region with the largest population of LGBTQ+ adults in the country (35 per cent) (The Williams Institute, 2019). Furthermore, more Black transgender adults live in the South than in any other region in the United States (Herman et al., 2022). This means that it is important that we understand the strategies that groups at the margins adopt to survive and thrive amid political polarization.

To achieve this, this chapter leverages theories of liminality to understand how groups experiencing marginalization navigate the social, political and economic precarity that emerges in polarized terrain. Liminality has been conceptualized as a transitory state of being and/or space where individuals undergo processes of identity formation and develop a sense of belonging (Turner, 1969; Van Gennep, 1960). In this study, I look to the case of Black transgender women to explore how the organizations they develop function as liminal safe havens amid polarization, where identity formation, contestation and innovation can emerge. As a 'minority within and between larger queer and Black communities', (Washington, 2013, p. 73) Black transgender women living in the US South must identify ways to navigate some of the most intense manifestations of sociopolitical polarization in the United States, including political attack, charged discourse and social stigma. Thus, the stories of Black trans women allow us to consider strategies that can be adopted to combat institutional and interpersonal gender-based violence resulting from polarization.

In the following section, I introduce the case of Transgender Advocates Knowledgeable Empowering (T.A.K.E.), an organization in Birmingham, Alabama, dedicated to providing resources and support to Black transgender women. I bring into focus existing literature on liminality to consider how organizations like T.A.K.E. might function as liminal spaces or sites of identity formation and political contestation for marginalized groups. Finally, I introduce ethnographic data from my fieldwork at T.A.K.E. to reveal how Black transgender women living in the US South have cultivated spaces to thrive and build community in polarized terrain. The laws and doctrines that social, political and religious institutions in the South deploy to perpetuate sexuality and gender-based normativity have rendered gender-marginalized communities inferior and invisible in the southern imaginary (Herek, 2007). By bringing these narratives to the forefront of analyses, this project advances our understanding of polarization, inequality and queer placemaking.

The case of T.A.K.E.

Responding to the immense needs of Black transgender women in the United States, T.A.K.E. was created in 2013 as a peer support group where Black transgender women living in Birmingham met twice each month to eat, fellowship and discuss the challenges that they faced. Recognizing that more work needed to be done to provide support to its members who experienced vast inequality, the organization shifted its focus to providing direct services, including legal aid, health support, housing and weekly activity programming. I selected T.A.K.E. for this ethnographic study because it is the only organization in Alabama and one of the very few organizations in the United States that is led by a Black transgender woman.

From 2021 to 2022, I engaged in participant observation, gathering field notes from over 300 hours spent attending the organization's daily programming, meetings, community events, in addition to staff retreats, regional conferences and trainings for Black transgender-led organizations across the US South. During observations, I kept jottings of critical conversations and interactions that occurred and documented important pieces of dialogue. After each session, I referred to these jottings, spending several hours expanding them into detailed field notes that described the interactions I observed and the context in which they occurred.

Additionally, I conducted thirty oral histories with Black transgender women connected to T.A.K.E.; though some of the women were engaged in political organizing work, many of the women in the sample came to T.A.K.E to simply find resources and build community. In addition to the formal oral history interviews, I had countless conversations with staff, clients and community members that allowed me to clarify observations. Spending time at T.A.K.E. as both an observer and participant, volunteering at events, laughing alongside community members and documenting the organization's work allowed me to gain a holistic understanding of the challenges and triumphs of Black transgender women living in the South and the role that organizations like T.A.K.E. play in meeting their needs. In the spirit of memorializing the work of the organization, I received permission to use the organization's legal name. However, all participant names and details have been anonymized.

Polarization, liminality and resistance

Studies of polarization have been concerned with understanding how distance is created between groups due to strongly held differences in identity and ideological beliefs. In many cases, polarization emerges as individuals organize themselves along the lines of opposing poles, creating distance between 'in-group' and 'out-group' identities and beliefs (Suhay, 2015; Tajfel & Turner, 1986). As Suhay (2015, p. 226) writes, 'When people learn of a norm held by an out-group, particularly a derogated one, they tend to shift their attitudes or actions in the opposite direction.' Subsequently, the social stratification of groups emerging from the unequal distribution of resources (i.e. power, prestige, wealth) can lead to heightened animosity and antagonism (Tajfel & Turner, 1986, p. 371). Thus, polarization can harm the self-concept and social conditions of subjugated groups, especially when they lack the power, status and resources needed to transform their environment drastically.

While studies of polarization have been concerned with understanding how physical and ideological distance is created between groups, conceptualizations of liminality have examined the processes that emerge within opposing identities, states of being and locations. Liminal is derived from the Latin term *limen*, which refers to a threshold between two places. Liminality as a state of being or transitory experience emerging within rites of passage was initially conceptualized by Van Gennep (1960). Van Gennep (1960) proposed three phases within these rituals: (1) separation, or symbolic detachment; (2) liminality, or an ambiguous state distinct from the before and after period and (3) the consummation of passage, or adoption of the new identity/state of being. The concept of liminality has since been leveraged to explain a variety of social experiences characterized by temporary disorientation and ambiguity as individuals move 'betwixt and between' two states of being (Turner, 1969).

Expanding liminality to describe experiences of social precarity more broadly has helped explain how groups navigate marginality and social exclusion. Wynter (1992, p. 19) referred to groups on the margins of social life as 'liminal or boundary-category outcasts'. However, in addition to being spaces characterized by marginality and often subjugation, these 'liminal spaces of alterity' also function as sites where identities and experiences are constructed and reconstructed (Ladson-Billings & Donner, 2005; Rollock, 2012). Within this liminal positioning at the boundary of inclusion and exclusion, groups can engage in identity formation and develop an oppositional world view that allows them to critique and resist social norms.

Liminality, thus, serves as a valuable framework for understanding how marginalized groups can develop a positive self-concept, resist inequality and build community amid polarization. First, liminal spaces allow groups operating at the margins of social life to securely experience identity formation and development processes amid social exclusion. As Beech (2011, p. 287) maintains, 'Liminality can be defined as a reconstruction of identity (in which the sense of self is significantly disrupted) in such a way that the new identity is meaningful for the individual and their community.' In their seminal text *The Souls of Black Folk*, W. E. B. Du Bois (1903) describes the in-between space experienced by Black Americans whose citizenship status is complicated by a subjugated racial identity, stating, 'One ever feels his two-ness, – an American, a Negro; two souls, two thoughts, two unreconciled strivings.' Furthermore, in their analysis of the identity formation of gender-marginalized groups, Dentice and Dietart (2015) maintain, 'Transgender individuals are often in-between traditional binary gender labels, or they may inhabit "outside boundaries" of what is defined as male and female in Western culture.' For marginalized groups who hold both insider and outsider status, liminality fosters the development of both a personal and political consciousness.

Liminal spaces also function as obscured sites of contestation where individuals can deconstruct ideas and practices in ways that alter and advance their social conditions. Scott (1990, p. 183) referred to forms of political activity emerging from the margins as *infrapolitics*, stating, 'the circumspect struggle waged daily by subordinate groups is, like infrared rays, beyond the visible end of the spectrum. That it should be invisible . . . is in large part by design – a tactical choice born of a prudent awareness of the balance of power.' Although systems of social power including race, class and gender have relegated some groups to perpetual liminal statuses, scholars have argued that within these spaces groups exert agency by developing political consciousness and contesting dominant norms. In their study of the activism of undocumented persons, Swerts (2017, p. 379) argued that urban interstices, or the spaces between 'legality and illegality, visibility and invisibility, and formality and informality', served as strategic sites for political engagement. In this study, Swerts (2017) advances a theory of liminal politics which they define as the process by which precarious groups 'constitute themselves as political subjects by creating, using, and appropriating in-between spaces'. Where polarization has subdued some groups' influence and political power, liminal spaces can foster the development of political consciousness, encouraging individuals to challenge the dominant norms and ideologies that have sought to erase their existence.

These studies urge us to examine how liminal spaces foster identity formation and political consciousness among marginalized groups. Polarization has placed the marginalized identities and livelihoods of transgender communities in the US South at the center of public scrutiny, discourse and debate. Within the liminal spaces that they have constructed, Black transgender women can affirm identities that have been subjugated in their broader environment. Furthermore, liminal spaces allow Black transgender women to contest normative ideologies and practices related to race, gender and sexuality that have been leveraged to bolster polarizing ideologies. As Kelley (1996, p. 19) notes, 'some of the most dynamic struggles take place outside – indeed, sometimes in spite of – established organizations and institutions.' In the following sections, I illuminate and analyze the liminal spaces that have been forged by Southern Black transgender women at T.A.K.E. to provide refuge, social support and critical resources to the community.

'Who else am I going to talk to?': Community organizations as liminal spaces in polarized terrain

> It was just I didn't have nobody to talk to, anybody who I can trust to talk to and spend time with. It just felt like the world was going and taking people every day (Katrina, 48). I never thought I would befriend any other trans people because of what I heard (Diamond, 32). When you do good by one of the girls, and they just accept you and love you for who you are and what you went through, that means more than anything. (Mya, 33)

As the only organization dedicated to serving Black transgender women in Alabama, T.A.K.E. created a space where community members could feel affirmed and supported. In doing so, the organization functioned as a liminal space or a physical haven for Black trans women in the US South navigating the interpersonal and institutional violence emerging from polarization. Although in some ways the organization operated like any other direct service provider, offering housing assistance, legal aid and other forms of support, the space felt different in other ways. The organization held daily support groups ranging from art therapy to group wellness sessions with social workers where the women could discuss the challenges they faced. I sat in on many of these sessions and watched as the women laughed, cried, bickered and offered advice to new women who came through the center's doors as they navigated each day's challenges together. Adiah (28) offered a rich description of what spaces like T.A.K.E. meant to her and the community, stating:

> At the end of the day, there's nothing like it, to walk into a room full of beautiful black bodies and just feel the energy of so many backgrounds of people that have been counted out, counted down, cast away. And so many things that were supposed to have defined them, but they didn't, and we're here and we're happy.
> We're not being judged for being and identifying as who we are. We're not being persecuted for it. This is the one space where you can come and be loved for being you and no one's going to look at you sideways for it. So, we're free in this space. You can feed your belly and you can feed your mind at the same time. So it's a space created for the betterment of trans, black trans individuals to be able to thrive and survive in society.

It is a place that gives us all of the basic living necessities that we need to go on in the world and carry on valuable, important, meaningful lives. And it's a place where you can come and get your gas filled back up, when you're low and you're on 'E' and you just need community.

Adiah's description of T.A.K.E. stands in direct opposition to the sociopolitical reality that Black transgender women must navigate living in a politically polarized environment where their identities are dissected and condemned. Instead, T.A.K.E. is a space where Black transgender women are not 'judged for being and identifying as who [they] are'. At T.A.K.E., *'life as usual* is suspended' (March, 2021, p. 457) as Black transgender women find refuge from persecution in a space where they are affirmed and supported. Liminal spaces do not wholly ameliorate the impacts of polarization. However, they do hold the capacity to illuminate the radical possibilities of solidarity, liberation and abundance for transgender communities. As Adiah described, community organizations like T.A.K.E. provide a safe space for Black transgender women to gain support and resources without fear of persecution. These spaces are affirming, liberating, unbound by time and place; spaces of movement, development and becoming (Grosz, 2001, p. 93).

Liminal spaces also function as important sites of social support where polarization has facilitated the political exclusion and social isolation of Black transgender women. In their analysis of transgender non-profits, Greene (2021) defines kinship organizations as incorporating norms and resources from kinship systems into their formal structure. They write, 'At their best, kinship organizations mobilize a robust network of supporters, using personal and organizational resources to solve client problems' (Greene, 2021, p. 931). This was certainly the case at T.A.K.E., where the community provided social and emotional support to any woman who walked through its doors. The women learnt from one another, gaining the confidence and knowledge needed to survive and thrive at T.A.K.E. and beyond. Lakeyah (37) states:

I have learned that this is a great organization for a person who can't find themself and don't know what to do. I feel like this is a great program that lets you express who you are and it lets you open up and lets you talk about what's bothering you.

Lakeyah describes how the organization creates a space where Black transgender women can foster a positive self-concept and process feelings tied to their experiences. The rigid boundaries and expectations associated with hegemonic masculinity make the transition process particularly challenging and socially stigmatizing for transgender women (Melendez & Pinto, 2007; Graham et al., 2014). For Black transgender women living in the South, there were not many spaces where they could be affirmed in their identity or receive support in the process of identity development. T.A.K.E. functioned as a safe space where women could often engage in these dialogues without fear of ridicule or persecution.

In an excerpt from fieldnotes that I wrote after a visit to the organization, I recount witnessing the space that was created for women to work through tensions around identity and family in a safe and constructive manner:

> Today in our unpacking group session the women talked about respect and family dynamics. Morgan began to discuss her relationship with her family. Recently her mom had said 'I'm ok with you being gay, but this is a little bit extra,' when it came to her embodiment as a transgender woman. She also explains that while she'd received little support from her mother, her sister, who is pregnant, told her to do whatever would make her happy. I can tell from Morgan's tone and demeanor that opening up to the group makes her slightly uncomfortable. Her relationship with her family is something that she seems to struggle with on this journey. She makes it known that she really wants to have their support.
>
> Another woman in the group, Daphne responds to Morgan's concerns by stating that she is so hard on Morgan because she wants to push her to express who she is. She states 'Sometimes I tell you, you need to present as a woman. You can't be a trans woman and then go back to being a man. You can't jump back and forth. But that's not me throwing shade . . . . I just don't want for you to be offended when I tell you that you need to present as a woman, if you're going to come into this space, because it's just me trying to push you and give you tough love.'
>
> Morgan responds 'I understand that. And I don't find it offensive in any way.' She continues by describing how it doesn't bother her because when she comes into this space, she feels like she can be herself. She finishes her thought stating, 'When I come into this space I know I can get painted [referring to her makeup and presentation]. But in terms of my journey, that's just not where I'm at right now, and I'm trying to grow to that point and get to that point.'

In this excerpt, Morgan begins by describing the challenges that she has faced in discussing her gender identity with her family. Scholars have argued that racism and stereotypes of deviant sexuality among Black Americans pushed this group to refute these stereotypes by conforming to sexual norms and vigorously policing gender boundaries (Clarke, 1983; Brooks, 2016). Many of the women had experienced gender policing, exclusion and vitriolic attacks from family members and others in their communities who sought to correct or ignore what they perceived as deviant behavior. For Morgan, T.A.K.E. is a space where she can process these challenges in a community of individuals navigating similar challenges. It is also a space where she can safely engage in the process of self-definition, determining the parameters of her transition, as revealed through her dialogue with Daphne on gender presentation. Although this discussion involves difficult conversations around family dynamics and gender expression, the women find solace in knowing that T.A.K.E. is a space to work through their questions without fear of judgement or ridicule. This data also reveals that although community organizations are sites of refuge for Black transgender women, they are not fortresses immune to broader debates around gender identity and presentation. The polarizing ideology and discourse on transgender identities that emerge in their lives outside of T.A.K.E. are still present. However, T.A.K.E. serves as a liminal space where Black transgender women can unpack these topics within a secure, affirming environment.

In addition to affirming and supporting Black transgender women, T.A.K.E. also provided them with tangible resources. Political polarization in the US South has been characterized by legislative attacks that seek to restrict the rights of transgender people (Westbrook & Schilt, 2013). This has ranged from denying gender-affirming healthcare to making it more difficult for trans people to receive legal document changes. Furthermore, as polarizing ideologies increasingly permeate public discourse, transgender communities face discrimination and violence as they navigate various institutional spaces. For example, according to the 2022 US Trans Survey, more than one in ten (11 per cent) survey respondents reported being fired, forced to resign or laid off due to their gender identity (James et al., 2024). Subsequently, T.A.K.E. was a liminal space where Black trans women could consolidate resources and share helpful knowledge. At one group meeting, the women discussed the importance of T.A.K.E. as a space to gain knowledge and resources:

> We sat around the rectangular tables that had been pushed together to form a 'conference-like' set up and listened as Jenna discussed how important it was for her to be a model for other trans women. Just as Jenna finished her statement, Ayanna flung open the door and walked into the small room with a sense of urgency, still wearing her scrubs from work. 'Sorry I'm late y'all,' she said, as the woman all greeted Ayanna. Mya, who was leading the discussion, put the spotlight on her by congratulating her on a new job that she'd just received as a technical assistant at a local hospital. Ayanna began by thanking Jenna who had given her the information about the job and supported her through the process.
>
> Ayanna then went on to discuss how this was the first stable job that she had held in three years. She described how securing this job wasn't just about the money but was also about her dignity knowing that she didn't want to work as an escort anymore. 'I come from a strong, powerful family,' she then proceeded to discuss her grandmother who had been a retired nurse of 50 years and her grandfather, who was in the military.
>
> The women then began recounting moments of transition in their lives, where they wanted to do something different or be better. Mya then concluded the group discussion by saying 'The biggest thing I want to stress is how this group isn't just a space for people to vent, but it's truly a space where you can come and gain information that'll help you achieve goals and avoid the obstacles other people had to go through.'

In this interaction, Ayanna learns about a stable job opportunity from relationships she has built at T.A.K.E. This connection to resources occurred through informal mechanisms, as the previous field note shows, and through formal interactions.

T.A.K.E. provided resources to Black transgender women that were difficult for them to obtain in other institutional settings.

One evening at T.A.K.E., I watched Charletta, the organization's executive director, respond to a phone call from a client who had unsuccessfully attempted to stay at a local shelter. Charletta arranged for the client to be transported to T.A.K.E. and continued working to secure their housing. Describing the role that community organizations like T.A.K.E. played in meeting these types of needs for Black transgender women, Charletta stated, 'White folks they don't bend their rules. They close at five, and then after that, you're just out on your own. A lot of people end up coming to T.A.K.E. because we're open after five, and people can still get a meal as they need.' Though several direct service providers in the state offered support to members of the LGBTQ+ community, these organizations were not always willing and/or able to reach Black transgender women. According to Charletta, many white-led organizations did not 'bend their rules' to meet the unique needs of this group. Although T.A.K.E. was regularly open during non-traditional business hours, when many women needed assistance the most, many other direct service organizations were not. Thus, where political polarization created barriers to resource access for Black trans women, T.A.K.E. operated as a liminal space by taking a uniquely intersectional approach to serving this community and providing them with the resources necessary for survival.

Conclusion

Ideological and political polarization in the US South have required individuals from race- and gender-marginalized groups to exist in a perpetual state of precarity (Cramer et al., 2017; Frey et al., 2021; Herman et al., 2022; Kline et al., 2021; The Williams Institute, 2019). Liminality has been conceptualized as experiences of social precarity tied to marginality and social exclusion. Within liminal spaces at the boundary of inclusion and exclusion, groups can engage in identity formation and develop an oppositional world view that allows them to critique and resist social norms. Thus, liminality is a critical point of departure for understanding how marginalized groups might find refuge within highly contentious environments where they are the targets of political pundits, the center of popular debate and the topics of interpersonal dialogues. Narratives offered by the women in this study reveal how unity and solidarity can blossom even in the most sociopolitically polarized geographies. Within the ruptures created by the transmission of transphobic, homophobic, sexist, classist and racialized beliefs and practices, Black transgender women have curated joy and co-created community.

Organizations like T.A.K.E. function as liminal spaces by offering refuge from the detrimental effects of political polarization. Although this study highlights moments of solidarity building and resource consolidation among Black transgender women, not every person who encountered the organization had the same experience. As previously mentioned, the community organization was not immune to the challenges outside of its walls. In this work, however, I have chosen to introduce data highlighting instances of strategic community building, offering an alternative to the existing literature on the experiences of transgender women of color that primarily focuses on their struggles. While acknowledging that the spaces I examine in the study have been birthed out of extremely salient struggles, I also hope that this work will expand our analysis to consider demonstrations of agency, self-determination and innovation among this group. Specifically, this case study of T.A.K.E. also adds an essential dimension to our analysis of polarization by considering how the experiences of Black transgender communities in the US South might illuminate ways that communities globally have developed liminal spaces amid social and political polarization.

Finally, we must also consider the fact that liminal spaces are transitional and impermanent. 'Neither wholly revolutionary or reformist' (Cloke et al., 2017), these spaces, while necessary, are not a complete response to the structures that sustain political polarization. Nevertheless, though the goal of our praxis must ultimately be to dismantle the systems that continue to create barriers to access for the most unprotected groups, the sites of liminality derived by Black transgender women offer solidarities to communities globally seeking to experience moments of liberation while navigating increasingly polarized sociopolitical landscapes.[1]

Note

1 This chapter is derived from research conducted for a dissertation project entitled 'Owning Our Power: The Individual and Collective Politics of Black Transgender Women in the Southern United States'. I would like to thank all the participants who shared narratives of struggle, solidarity and hope that animated this work. I would also like to thank the editors and members of the Polarising Sexual and Gendered Lives symposium at University College Dublin for their thoughtful feedback and support.

Chapter 5

WE ARE JUST LIKE EVERYBODY ELSE

POLARISATION AND QUEER ACTIVISM IN LITHUANIA

Rasa Kamarauskaitė

Introduction

The chapter discusses the Lithuanian queer activist initiatives to counteract polarising anti-LGBTQ+ discourses that deem same-sex sexualities and the Lithuanian nation as mutually exclusive. In this context, polarisation is understood as 'a process where (. . .) differences in a society increasingly align along a single dimension and people increasingly perceive and describe politics and society in terms of "Us" versus "Them"' (McCoy et al., 2018, p. 16). Consequently, such alignment results in conflict between the 'opposite' groups. The first part of the chapter will discuss how and why same-sex sexualities became a polarising dimension in Central and Eastern Europe, including Lithuania. I will argue that anti-LGBTQ+ rhetoric has a polarising effect on societal views as it portrays LGBTQ+ people as enemies ('them') of the national collective ('us').

Polarisation that occurs along a single dimension is often incited by a discursive construction of an enemy figure 'who poses an existential threat to the community' (Gerő et al., 2017, p. 15). First, I discuss how and why same-sex sexualities became a 'successful' target for generating an image of an enemy. I argue that the 'success' can be partially attributed to the cultural and historical understanding of heterosexuality as fundamental in the process of nation building (Renkin, 2009). Therefore, rhetoric that vilifies non-heterosexual sexualities has a strong divisive impact in many CEE states (Ayoub, 2016; O'Dwyer, 2018). The rest of the chapter discusses the tactics of Lithuanian queer activists to counteract the polarising LGBTQ+ image. I will argue that the activists aim to challenge the polarising portrayal of same-sex sexualities as dangerous to the nation by fostering connection and a sense of familiarity.

I conducted seven semi-structured in-depth interviews with LGBQ+ people who organised and participated in the activist initiatives. The interviews were conducted between 2020 and 2022 in Lithuania as part of a larger project focusing on LGBQ+ (in)visibilities in Lithuania. The topics of polarisation and national belonging were not included in the interview guide but were brought up by the research participants during the interviews when they discussed their experiences of everyday life in Lithuania and explained the rationale for their activism. All names in the quotes are changed to anonymise the research participants, except for Dominykas Vaitiekūnas, who explicitly expressed his wish to use his name. I analysed the original transcripts and then translated relevant quotes into English. In the chapter, I quote the excerpts that discuss the efforts to overcome polarised renditions of national belonging in the most elaborate manner.

I conducted narrative analysis (Cortazzi, 2001) with the intent to understand how the research participants relate to the polarising imagining of same-sex sexualities in the context of belonging to the nation and how they challenge it. I address the following questions: How do the activists relate, if at all, to the anti-LGBTQ+ stance in prevalent narratives of national belonging? How, if at all, do they overcome the anti-LGBTQ+ stance? I will address these questions in the following sections of the chapter.

I employ Kulpa's (2011, 2014) concept of the nation as a hybrid space of identification to frame my analysis. The nation as a hybrid space of identification is a form of national belonging that is flexible enough to not reduce national belonging to a limited number of categories (e.g. heterosexuality), but to include multiple points of identification within the national collective. Throughout the chapter, I will argue that nationhood as a hybrid space of identification has the potential to overthrow the monopoly of polarising ideas about national belonging that come from anti-LGBTQ+ groups and politicians.

Throughout the chapter, I argue that the activist initiatives aim to overcome the polarising imagining of LGBTQ+ people. First, I will discuss the activists' negotiation of self in relation to LGBTQ+ images that were available to them. I will argue that the activists felt disconnected from the LGBTQ+ images, and this sense of disconnection informed the aims of their activism. Then, I will discuss three activist initiatives: the Living Library, *Išgirsti* (*Lith.* to hear/to be heard) and Gender Wrongs. The Living Library is an international programme that aims to challenge prejudice by facilitating a conversation between volunteers ('books') who experienced discrimination and are willing to share their experiences and the people ('readers') who ask questions about them (Orosz et al., 2016). *Išgirsti* (*Lith.* to hear/to be heard) is a platform on Facebook that promotes positive information about LGBTQ+. Gender Wrongs is a collective of LBQ+ women in Vilnius who organise parties and other LGBTQ+ inclusive events. The discussed projects are by no means the only LGBTQ+ initiatives in Lithuania, and I do not aim to provide a comprehensive overview of LGBTQ+ activism in Lithuania. Nor do I aim to discuss the extent to which the discussed strategies resonate with other activist initiatives or the broader Lithuanian LGBTQ+ population. My aim is more modest: to explore the potential and limitations of such strategies to overcome polarisation in the Lithuanian context. The similar strategies to the ones discussed above are sometimes interpreted as promoting homonationalism (Puar, 2007) and homonormativity (Brown, 2012). However, I will argue that these concepts are not suited to theorise LGBTQ+ activism in Lithuania, which is better understood as an effort to counteract the imagining of same-sex sexualities as a divisive and polarising characteristic.

Queers in CEE: Enemies of the nation

Defining LGBTQ+ rights and liberties as core European values encountered resistance in most CEE states (Ayoub & Paternotte, 2014) and incited discussions aimed at re-evaluating belonging to the European community (Graff & Korolczuk, 2021). Anti-EU nationalist discourses brand same-sex sexualities as imported from the West/EU, and thus alien to the national collectives (Guasti, 2021; Kahlina & Ristivojević, 2023). Furthemore, LGBTQ+ rights are framed as a danger from the West/EU that erode authentic national cultures based on traditional gender norms and religious values (Foxall, 2019; Kuhar & Pajnik, 2020; Kulpa, 2020). In other words, LGBTQ+ people are portrayed as an enemy figure that threatens the survival of national collectives. Such a portrayal of LGBTQ+ people resonates to varying degrees across CEE states (O'Dwyer, 2018), but it was most 'successful' in states where religion and traditional values strongly informed national identity (Ayoub, 2016). Anti-EU nationalist discourses often have a polarising effect in societies as they present same-sex sexualities as a divisive dimension between the national collectives (i.e. 'us') and the LGBTQ+ people (i.e. 'them').

The anti-EU nationalist rhetoric often reduces LGBTQ+ people to a single category of immoral sexuality that threatens the supposedly moral national collectives (Cornejo-Valle & Ramme, 2022; Hesová, 2021). The immorality of same-sex sexualities is reflected through the use of the term 'western decadence' in anti-EU nationalist discourses. The 'western decadence' refers to the set of ideas developed by Bolshevik intellectuals, who denounced sexual pleasure as a selfish act, symptomatic of the 'wrong' oppressive capitalist lifestyles and an overall lack of morals (Hoffmann & Timm, 2008; Wilkinson, 2020). Sexuality aimed at personal satisfaction was regarded as immoral, selfish, anti-social and a 'decadent predilection of the bourgeoisie' (Mole, 2019, p. 3) which needed to be uprooted to create a more just society. In other words, the anti-EU nationalist rhetoric portrays same-sex sexualities as an immoral Western import ('them'), which poses a danger to the national collectives ('us'). Due to such rhetoric, LGBTQ+ people are increasingly perceived as a group that is in opposition to national collectives.

In CEE countries where religion plays an important role in shaping national identities, religious teachings that proclaim same-sex sexualities as sin (Locke, 2004), and that sex is only permissible within marriage (Jordan, 2016), are also used to brand same-sex sexualities as immoral (Cornejo-Valle & Ramme, 2022). Such interpretations of same-sex sexualities are particularly impactful in CEE states where religion was strongly involved in the nation-building process (Mole, 2019; Sremac & Ganzevoort, 2015; Waitt, 2005). In other words, in the states where religious teachings about sexuality are perceived as building blocks of national authentic cultures (e.g. Poland, Latvia, Russia), sexualities that do not comply with those norms are easily turned into an enemy figure that threatens the survival of those nations (Máté-Tóth & Nagy, 2023). Portraying religion as a fundamental building block of the nation positions same-sex sexualities in opposition ('them') to the nation ('us').

Queers in Lithuania: A threat to the nation

Lithuanian anti-LGBTQ+ politicians and groups employ similar tactics as those in the rest of the CEE; namely, they attempt to discursively reduce LGBTQ+ people to sexuality that is immoral and dangerous to the nation (Mažylis et al., 2014). The 'danger' of same-sex sexualities is demonstrated by focusing on the sexual practices that are in opposition to the values that are considered to be the core of the nation, namely traditional family values (Wakefield et al., 2016). The portrayal of LGBTQ+ people as dangerous to the nation was well expressed in the banners of the opponents of the first Baltic Pride in Lithuania: 'gays have to sit in their homes; such processions seem acceptable in America, but not in Lithuania'; 'For the preservation of the family tradition!', 'This is not a family – it is a disease!', '[self] expression should not contradict moral values; this kind of public events is contrary to the conception of the morality of our democratic society' (Mažylis et al., 2014, p. 56). The fear of 'immoral' same-sex sexualities is often fanned by anti-LGBTQ+ media portals such as Respublika, which consistently posts anti-LGBTQ+ material (Mažylis et al., 2014), with titles such as 'Next year Vilnius will be occupied by homosexuals', accompanied by photos showing men in their underwear or wearing BDSM attire in the streets (Tereškinas, 2007). Even though such media representation of LGBTQ+ people is not the only one, and LGBTQ+ rights are also discussed (Mažylis et al., 2014; Švaraitė, 2015), the anti-LGBTQ+ press has a strong polarising effect on societal views towards LGBTQ+ people. It projects rhetoric that is a core threat to national belonging, namely unapologetically displaying sexuality in public. This way, same-sex sexualities become an increasingly divisive dimension between the national collectives (i.e. 'us') and the LGBTQ+ people (i.e. 'them').

It is not a coincidence that anti-LGBTQ+ media pairs an unapologetic display of sexuality with terms such as 'occupation' as it points to the threat of national survival and sovereignty (Beresniova, 2010). Such rhetoric invokes an image of Lithuania as 'an innocent victim of powerful neighbours' (Snyder, 1995, p. 336). Furthermore, the anti-LGBTQ+ groups position themselves as victims by comparing themselves to the historical image of the nation as a collective of 'heroic people who had suffered for centuries from efforts (. . .) to dominate and forcibly assimilate them. Yet the Lithuanians had persevered and overcome these efforts' (Clark, 2006, p. 166). Such a conflation of LGBTQ+ rights with occupation is promoted by statements from religious leaders and anti-LGBTQ+ intellectuals stating that LGBTQ+ rights are part of the communist agenda, and by displaying Soviet symbols next to rainbow and EU flags (Tereškinas, 2019). In other words, the anti-LGBTQ+ rhetoric invokes historical accounts of national suffering to highlight the 'danger' of same-sex sexualities. Indeed, before the first

Baltic Pride in Lithuania fourteen years ago, the mayor of Vilnius, Artūras Zuokas, voiced the anti-Lithuanian argument and refused to give permission for the Pride, saying that: Lithuanian LGBT organisations constitute 'a small group of people who acquire material gain from the West through escalating discrimination (. . .) initiating conflicts and (. . .) promoting propaganda' (Pumprickaitė, 2013). Such rhetorics turn same-sex sexualities into a polarising characteristic as it does not leave an option for same-sex sexualities and national belonging to coalesce in any shape or form. By portraying Lithuanian LGBTQ+ people as a small group sponsored by the West, the anti-LGBTQ+ politicians and groups negate the legitimacy and importance of the claims for recognition and protection. The anti-LGBTQ+ groups project a polarised image of the nation and the LGBTQ+ people, where the Lithuanian national collective is portrayed as heterosexual families with children who keep sexual matters away from the streets and behind closed doors (Tereškinas, 2007). Thus LGBTQ+ people, who allegedly hold oppositional values regarding sexual conduct, are portrayed as in opposition ('them') to the national collective ('us').

The depiction of LGBTQ+ people as promoting uncontrollable sexual promiscuity, and framing it as a threat to national values, was strategically used to curb any positive public information about LGBTQ+ people. Since the Constitution of the Republic of Lithuania states that family is the building block of Lithuanian society and the nation (Narkevičiūtė, 2020), it mandates legislative and executive authorities to ensure and protect its rights (Sagatys, 2010). The anti-LGBTQ+ politicians added a section to the Law of the Protection of Minors against the Detrimental Effects of Public Information, which states that public information which demeans family values and promotes family models that differ from the ones defined by the Constitution (Narkevičiūtė, 2020) is harmful to minors. In practice, the law aimed to significantly reduce any information about LGBTQ+ people on state media and in the press. The law was implemented in 2013 when announcements of the Baltic Pride were only broadcasted after 11.00 pm, with the parental guideline stating that it is 'adult content'. In 2014, the same law was applied to a book of fairy tales called 'Amber Heart', which included two stories of characters of the same-sex falling in love. It was required to limit minors' access to the book and to indicate that it is not suitable for children under 14 years old (ibid.). The book's author challenged the decision in Lithuanian courts but lost. Only in 2023, the European Court of Human Rights ruled in favour of the author.[1]

To contest the law, various Lithuanian NGOs addressed the Constitutional Court to clarify the meaning of the family. The Court ruled that the Constitution does not limit the notion of the family to a married couple with children (Narkevičiūtė, 2020) and thus the information that portrays LGBTQ+ people in a positive light does not infringe the notion of the family as defined by the Constitution. The clarification enabled broadcasters and the press to freely disseminate information about LGBTQ+ people. In my view, the fact that the NGOs addressed the Constitutional Court only to clarify the notion of the family, and not to challenge its place in the Constitution, demonstrates the importance of the family for claiming and legitimising national belonging. The NGOs' decision not to challenge the family's place in the constitution can be interpreted as succumbing to dominant and often oppressive structures at the expense of queer lifestyles. However, as I will discuss in the following sections, broadening the notion of the family as the building block of the nation, rather than challenging it, was in line with 'a domestic form' of activism (Buyantueva & Shevtsova, 2020, p. 4) which aims to challenge the polarising construction of LGBTQ+ people as the enemies of the nation by fostering connection and a sense of familiarity. I will further argue that by fostering connection and a sense of familiarity, the activists produce an alternative rendition of the nation as a hybrid space of identification (Kulpa, 2014) which disregards (same-sex) sexuality as an essential characteristic for national identification.

Longing for nuanced queerness

In this section, I explore how participants engage with the 'sexualisation' of queer people and why they attempt to downplay it. By 'sexualisation', I mean the discussed image of LGBTQ+ people promoted by anti-LGBTQ+ groups. Since 'immoral sexuality' is the main characteristic by which LGBTQ+ people are defined by anti-LGBTQ+ rhetoric, I argue that attempts to downplay sexualised aspects of LGBTQ+ people constitute a way to take ownership over one's image and introduce a more nuanced imagining of them. The activists claim that their activism was motivated by the experience of incongruence between their self-concept, that is, 'what they think they are like as people' (Troiden, 1989, p. 45) and the public images of queer people that were prevalent in the public sphere. In other words, the activists contended that the 'sexualisation' of LGBTQ+ people was a rhetorical tool used by anti-LGBTQ+ organisations to promote polarising views towards LGBTQ+ people in Lithuania, and not an accurate representation of them. The opportunity to present an image of queer people that felt more in tune with her own experiences motivated Erika, a 38-year-old lesbian woman from Vilnius, to join a Living Library project:

Erika: [The goal of the project was] to fight the stereotypes that come from not knowing much about [the minorities]. There is a stereotype that lesbians are promiscuous. But it is not true. (. . .) so we wanted to introduce people to the real situation. I really liked this about the project and that is why I agreed [to participate].

Erika claims that the image of lesbians as 'promiscuous' does not come from society's encounters with lesbians, but rather from a lack of it. By introducing people 'to the real situation', she aims to take ownership over the expression of her sexuality. In this context, Erika's rendition of 'real' is not as an authoritative or normative statement aimed at defining all lesbians, but rather an experience of what it means to be a lesbian that is real to her.

Similarly, an openly gay TV personality Dominykas Vaitiekūnas claimed that the image of LGBTQ+ people, solely focused on their sexual lives, presented a distorted image to which he found hard to relate:

Dominykas: When it comes to the image of a gay man for a long time, I had a big conflict in my head. I think that until I have come-out (. . .) the image of a homosexual man was very narrow. (. . .) It was very carnivalized (. . .) feathers, body cult, uncontrolled sexuality, open voluptuousness, polygamy, lack of subtlety, and at the same time aggressive communication. I was missing a simple, mundane, humane image of LGBT people. (. . .) I think that my generation had a bigger and a longer conflict [with their sexualities] because we were not able to identify with public gay people. They were not appealing to me.

When Dominykas defines the public image of gay men as 'carnivalized' and lacking the 'mundane', he refers to the lack of dimension in the public image of gay men. Like Erika, Dominykas does not castigate various sexual practices per se, but rather voices his inability to connect to this particular image of gay men. Dominykas notes that the lack of congruence between his self-concept and the available gay image made it more difficult for him to come to terms with his sexuality. Feeling disconnected and not being able to relate one's own queerness to the encountered queer environment led Lina (one of the organisers of Gender Wrongs parties) to feel ashamed of herself and her sexuality:

Lina: [When I first went to a lesbian bar] I was disgusted. It was simply awful. At first, I identified myself [with them] and I felt ashamed of who I am. Women used to allow themselves a lot (. . .) there were fights in the bar, and broken glasses. [From that experience] I truly used to think that homosexual people are stupid, uneducated, and horrible people.

Like Dominykas, Lina encountered a limited variety of queer culture. The absence of relatable queer images and spaces for socialisation led them to engage in activism that aimed at producing alternative images of LGBTQ+ people and spaces, which I will discuss in the next section. Shying away from sexuality rather than celebrating it is often understood as failing to subvert heteronormativity (Berlant & Warner, 1998). Indeed, such views were also expressed in the Lithuanian context (Davydova, 2012). However, in this section, I demonstrate that empowerment can also come from contesting the sexualised LGBTQ+ images that were mostly produced by anti-LGBTQ+ groups and media to 'prove' the incompatibility of same-sex sexualities and national collectives (and, in effect, turn same-sex sexualities into a polarising characteristic). Contesting the polarisation of the nation from LGBTQ+, for these activists, was about seeing sexualised public LGBTQ+ images as alien and incompatible with oneself. Activists' disengagement from 'sexualised' queer images is thus a way to take ownership of the image production of their sexualities and to introduce a more nuanced imagining of LGBTQ+ people. In the following sections, I will discuss how certain activist activities achieve this contestation of the divisions between the Lithuanian nation and LGBTQ+ people. I will argue that by introducing alternative queer images, these activities challenge the anti-LGBTQ+ rhetoric that presents same-sex sexualities as a divisive characteristic of the nation and, in this way, challenge the polarising imagining of LGBTQ+ sexualities in Lithuania.

Legitimising spaces: 'Having a good party'

When discussing the rationale behind their parties, 'Gender Wrongs' activists addressed the one-dimensional derogatory image of LGBTQ+ people produced by anti-LGBTQ+ groups. According to the activists, the 'arguments' of anti-LGBTQ+ groups (discussed above) that deemed LGBTQ+ people unfit, inappropriate or even dangerous to be seen on the streets, not only polarised Lithuanian society along the lines of sexuality but also 'traumatised' LGBTQ+ people:

Violeta: [I remember] the parties in that basement. There was a lot of violence there. And I realised that the [lesbian] community is oppressed, it is [pushed] to underground, it is traumatised.

To Violeta, 'meeting in the basement' and, supposedly, the rowdy bar atmosphere were symptoms of marginalisation and oppression. Such rationale guided the collective's concept of the parties, that is, as spaces for queer people to socialise as part of the city:

Lina: We make each party in a different well-known venue. It never happens in some unknown basement. I think it helps to promote LGBT visibility and to break some myths and stereotypes. Because people have some negative ideas about how LGBT people look and behave.

Lina sees their activity as serving two goals: providing society with an opportunity to interact with queer people and providing queer people an opportunity to become part of the broader (national) collective. I see the activities as an effort to challenge the anti-LGBTQ stance that calls for the separation and isolation of queer people, as illustrated by the slogans discussed above. Instead, they invite the public to see queer people for themselves. The organisers aim to counteract the image of LGBTQ+ people as outsiders of society by organising the parties in well-known venues at the city centre, as opposed to bars that are clandestine and primarily focused on LGBTQ+ clientele. By placing the parties in the city centre, Gender Wrongs team creates a space to counteract a polarised image of queer people as radically different from the rest of society and to form a more nuanced understanding of who queer people are, how they look and how they behave. In other words, they attempt to counteract the one-dimensional image of LGBTQ+ people as *only* sexually explicit and rowdy.

Furthermore, Lina sees the parties as serving the LGBTQ+ community by removing the stigma, which supposedly surrounds LGBTQ+ venues:

Lina: We are trying to change the attitude that queer bars are dirty holes, where you go for one-night stands. Where you only go in the middle of the night, wasted, making sure that nobody sees you. Where you go down the secret stairs. [We wanted to make] queer places that are public, where people are having fun.

Lina's rather critical opinion of one-night stands and 'getting wasted' shows her inclination towards middle-class morality and sexual norms (Mosse & Roberts, 2020). Such stance has been criticised as homonormative, that is, exclusionary of sexual lifestyles that do not conform to such norms, which lead to exclusionary politics (Kulpa, 2014). However, Lina's account can also be read not as a moralising stance on what counts as 'good' or 'not good' queer lifestyle, but rather as a lamentation of the limited queer social spaces. Lina laments that the *only* spaces for LGBTQ+ people are located at the margins, be it in a spatial or moral sense, and she voices the efforts to change that. Seeing the current LGBTQ+ bar culture as a result of exclusion and oppression, which was imposed by positioning same-sex sexualities as a divisive characteristic between LGBTQ+ people and the rest of the nation, the activists aim to rectify the situation by opening the city space to the community and helping queer people see themselves as part of it. The activists believe that organising LGBTQ+ parties in well-known venues in the city centre sends a message to the LGBTQ+ community and to wider society that LGBTQ+ people are a legitimate part of the city and society, and they should not literally and figuratively be pushed to the margins (Doderer, 2011). The parties encourage queer bodies to come together and occupy the public space in such a way that claims legitimacy to it. Such practices challenge the polarising imagining of same-sex sexualities as destructive to the fabric of the city. Instead, the parties, where people are having fun, become an integral part of the city centre.

Finally, the parties counteract the mutually exclusive rendition of queer people and the nation by downplaying the importance of sexual identity at the parties and emphasising the common goal of 'having fun'. In Lina's opinion, making the party open for all encourages the participation of people who support LGBTQ+, hence promoting integration:

Lina: The main idea of the parties is that they are open (. . .) where people can come together, not necessarily LGBT, but everyone who is LGBT-friendly. There are many people who support LGBT (. . .) the young hipster generation is not bothered by the question of sexual orientation. They want to have a good party.

I interpret Lina's emphasis on 'having a good party' as moving away from 'serious' politics that is often seen as divisive (I will discuss this point in more detail in the next section). In this context, coming together to have fun is a strategy to foster connection between people through a shared experience of fun. Thus, 'having a good party' is a form of 'queer playful politics' (Browne, 2007, p. 65) that challenges the idea of same-sex sexualities as a divisive characteristic in Lithuanian society. It aims at reconciling two subject positions (LGBTQ+ and Lithuanian) that were deemed oppositional and mutually exclusive by the anti-LGBTQ+ bodies. In effect, I argue that by creating a space for shared experiences, 'a good party' challenges polarising thinking that LGBTQ+ people pose a danger to heterosexual collective and thus need to be excluded from the national collective if not annihilated. The 'good party' shows that sexuality is not an obstacle to share a space and have positive experience as a result. Consequently, I argue that such practice contributes to the rendition of 'the nation' as a 'hybrid space of identification' (Kulpa, 2014, p. 781) which is an alternative to the polarising imagining of the nation proposed by anti-LGBTQ+ groups and politicians.

Opening up for vulnerability

In the previous section, I discussed how shared experience of fun is used to counteract the polarising rendition of LGBTQ+ people as outsiders of national collectives. In this section, I will discuss how the same goal was aimed for enacting vulnerability. Vulnerability in this context is not the opposite of strength or simply an exposure to risk and danger (Butler, 2009; Gilson, 2011). Vulnerability is understood as a condition of openness and dialogue, 'a condition of being affected and affecting in turn' (Gilson, 2011, p. 310) which, in my view, is the opposite of polarisation that calls for 'antagonistic views (. . .) where one group always benefits at the expense of the other' (Hesová, 2023, p. 22). In this sense, vulnerability, if enacted by all involved parties, enables to create a connection on a personal level and to expose unjust social and legal systems on a social and political level.

Such openness and vulnerability were enacted by Erika, a 38-year-old lesbian woman from Vilnius, and Tomas, a 29-year-old gay man from Vilnius, who participated in the Living Library[2] project (Dymond-Green, 2023; Orosz et al., 2016). The project seeks to provide a space for conversations between stigmatised minorities and the public. The participants of the project act as 'books' that the public can 'read'; that is, people can come to a designated place, usually a public library, and ask any questions. The people who act as 'books' are the members representing the stigmatised minority groups and who are ready to answer the questions. Tomas and Erika were the 'books' that represented homosexuality. The format of the project, that is, a face-to-face dialogue with a stranger, was conducive to enacting openness and vulnerability. Both participants saw their vulnerable positions as an opportunity to challenge people's convictions about LGBTQ+ people. Enacting openness and vulnerability during the conversations enabled them to present an alternative image of homosexuality to that proposed by anti-LGBTQ+ groups. Erika attempted this by reversing the questions about her sexuality:

R: Who was coming to talk to you?

Erika: All kinds of people. (. . .) the main question was: Why do you think that you are a lesbian? [And I would reply] why do you think that you are heterosexual? (. . .) I would just reverse the question and the person would start to reflect. You don't even have to say much.

The situation allowed Erika and her interlocutor to hear and reflect on each other's positions, that is, to be open to dialogue. In this situation, dialogue is a space to put polarising images of LGBTQ+ people to a test. Without clearly indicating if same-sex sexualities are 'right' or 'wrong', it invites interlocutors to make their own conclusions based on the interaction. Similarly, Tomas also employed a narration technique to induce reflection, where he was explaining his position and the interlocutors were listening:

Tomas: People might have negative convictions [regarding queer people] but when you start talking to them, they are starting to reflect. (. . .) There were people who used to come [with a conviction] that they were totally against, that [they] don't understand why they [i.e. the queer people] advertise themselves. But I would talk to them, and they listen. Most of them are not aggressive, only some.

Even faced with aggression, Tomas sees the conversations as a beneficial tool to engage with people's convictions. It is a space for interlocutors to hear a position on the topics, for example, Pride parades as an 'advertisement' that differs from their own. Such interactions can provide an opportunity to foster epistemic openness, that is, the ability to listen and to hear positions that challenge one's understanding of the self and the environment (Gilson, 2011). Listening does not necessarily lead to a complete change of heart, but at least it enables one to see an array of positions (Orosz et al., 2016). Erika was convinced that such conversations help to overcome polarising convictions as they allow to see LGBTQ+ people in all their complexity and beyond the polarised image of sexually promiscuous enemies of the nation. She expresses it in terms of shared humanity:

Erika: There were some who would come [with a goal] to 'convert' you. But then you start telling your story, answer their questions, and you see that their opinion is starting to change. They begin to understand that *I am a person just like them*. With my needs, with my strengths and my weaknesses and with my freakishness. (. . .) One conversation will not change everything. The people will have something to think about and maybe there will be some changes in the future.

For Erika, to be 'a person just like them' is to acknowledge each other's complexity as a fundamental condition of being a human. It invites looking for multiple points of connection and divergence that go beyond division based on sexuality, which challenges the polarising imagining of same-sex sexualities. Tomas and Erika believe that vulnerability, if mutually enacted, creates a connection on a personal level that can lead to better understanding and acceptance of diverse groups and consequently overcome polarising oppositional thinking about LGBTQ+ people. Such a belief was shared by Dominykas Vaitiekūnas, whose strategy I will discuss in the following section.

Eliciting empathy

Dominykas has a similar approach towards the importance of dialogue and listening in making a connection to a broader society. In Dominykas's view, eliciting empathy towards LGBTQ+ people helps to overcome societal hostility, which is a result of the polarising imagining of same-sex sexualities. In this context, empathy is understood as an affective mode of understanding (Halpern, 2003) which functions as 'a bridge between the self and other' (Cuff et al., 2016) not by becoming identical to one another, but by understanding one another's position (Decety & Sommerville, 2003). According to Dominykas, not only is an overly sexualised queer image divisive but also rights-focused LGBTQ+ activist rhetoric.

Dominykas: [For my project] I aimed at finding rhetoric that would not evoke resistance. [I aimed at] talking about LGBT topics as if it was a simple, mundane issue. Without getting into legal discussions. One of my goals (. . .) was not to talk in terms that everybody was already bored of. With strong and aggressive demands. (. . .) A critical stance (. . .) does not help to create a connection with the society.

Dominykas is critical of polarising rhetoric promoted by anti-LGBTQ+ groups, as well as LGBTQ+ rights rhetoric that, according to him, proposes 'aggressive demands'. In order to elicit empathy and foster connection Dominykas and his team started a social platform on Facebook where they, among other initiatives, shared LGBTQ+ people's stories, including ten videos about LGBTQ+ issues in Lithuania. Apart from featuring people who self-identify as gay, lesbian, bisexual and non-heterosexual, the videos included a sister of a gay man and a work colleague of a gay man from the Soviet era. Dominykas hopes that such inclusion can counteract a polarised image of LGBTQ+ people as an isolated group separate from the nation. By portraying them as members of the family, that is, as someone's siblings, he portrays them as part of kinship relations. Since family and kinship (as I have argued earlier) are considered as a building block of the Lithuanian nation, portraying LGBTQ+ people as such portrays them as an inherent part of the national kinship (Bryant, 2002), and thus challenges the dominant polarising rendition of the nation as an exclusive space for heterosexual people. In a similar manner, talking about a gay man as one's colleague from the Soviet era challenges the argument that LGBTQ+ people are imported from the West. Rather, they are part of the national history. Dominykas sees such tactics as conducive to the advancement of LGBTQ+ people's freedoms and rights.

Dominykas: The fight to freedom and rights happens in many forms. I think the most appropriate one is to win over your opponents in such a way that they would not even understand that they were won over. To change their attitudes. (. . .) We try to talk in a way that would elicit empathy in people. Not by some theoretical slogans, or theoretical discussions whether LGBT is good or bad.

Dominykas is convinced that to overcome the polarising imagining of same-sex sexualities, the thinking about sexualities needs to move beyond 'right' and 'wrong' rhetoric. He thinks that making connections through images of LGBTQ+ people that seem familiar to broader society and placing LGBTQ+ people within networks of kinship and national history is a way to achieve it.

Positioning Lithuanian domestic activism

Throughout the chapter, I discussed how Lithuanian queer activists aim at homosexualising the national canon, that is, 'writing homosexuality into the existing national master canon' (Kulpa, 2011, p. 48). Contrary to the interpretation of such practices as succumbing to heteronormativity (Davydova, 2012), or producing homonormativity (Mikulak, 2019; Plakhotnik, 2019), and/or homonationalism (Pagulich, 2017), I argue that it counteracts the polarising rendition of national belonging that is determined by sexuality. I agree with Brown (2012), Kulpa (2014) and Mizielińska (2022) (also see Glenn, 2020) that seeing such practices as homonationalist or homonormative overlooks the power dynamics in the context where the practices arise. Therefore, following Mizielińska (2022), and Kulpa (2014) I interpret the activities of Lithuanian queer activists as 'queer act[s] of replication/re-appropriation from which many opportunities to change the dominant pattern emerge' (Mizielińska, 2022, p. 195). Namely, changing the dominant polarising rendition of 'the nation' as an exclusive space for heterosexual people into a 'hybrid space of identification' (Kulpa, 2014, p. 781). By 'hybrid space of identification', I describe the imagining of nationhood that accommodates multiple points of (self)identification with the national collective.

Throughout this chapter, I argued LGBTQ+ activists were trying to achieve that by contesting the one-dimensional images of LGBTQ+ people as sexual predators and highlighting the complexity of LGBTQ+ people. As the activist quoted above summarised it: as people with their needs, strengths, weaknesses, and freakishness. If LGBTQ+ people can be seen as inherently complex and not solely defined by their sexuality alone, this allows the possibility of finding multiple points of connection and belonging which, following Kulpa (2014), I call a hybrid space of identification. Thus, I argue that, contrary to entrenching the privilege for a homogenous fraction of queer people (Sears, 2005), the activists create a vision of a nation that recognises and accommodates a diversity of subject positions (Kulpa, 2014) as an alternative to the polarising one. In my view, rendering the discussed activist strategies as homonationalist or homonormative would ignore the CEE geo-temporal modalities (Kulpa & Mizielińska, 2011) in which these strategies are embedded.

Conclusion

Some literature sees the backlash against LGBTQ+ rights in CEE as positive since it helps to mobilise societies and choose the 'right' side, which often leans towards pro-LGBTQ+ attitudes (O'Dwyer, 2018). While divisive rhetoric does indeed encourage side-picking, at the same time, it could induce irreconcilable cleavages that could lead to polarisation. It is particularly relevant to societies where national identities are strongly informed by the narratives of traditional values (Ayoub, 2016). In the chapter, I discussed how anti-LGBTQ+ groups in Lithuania portray same-sex sexualities as 'immoral' and thus exclusive of the supposedly moral Lithuanian national collective. I argued that such portrayals of same-sex sexualities have a polarising effect on societal attitudes towards LGBTQ+ people. In my view, Lithuanian queer activist initiatives can counteract polarising divisions between LGBTQ+ people and Lithuanian society. Negotiating relatable queerness, creating shared spaces to party, opening up for vulnerability and eliciting empathy as strategies to foster connection with society aimed to overcome a one-dimensional image of LGBTQ+ people as solely defined by uncontrollable sexuality.

In addition, I argued that interpreting such practices as assimilationist and using the theoretical concepts of homonormativity (Brown, 2012) and/ or homonationalism (Puar, 2013, 2007), would be unsuitable. I noted that homonormativity (Brown, 2012) and homonationalism (Puar, 2013, 2007) speak of a condition where a fraction of queer people, namely white, middle-class lesbians and gay men, have entrenched their privilege at the expense of non-white and/or economically struggling queers. Consequently, the entrenched privilege generates a national rhetoric of patriotic inclusion (Puar, 2007, p. 39) where only '[some] homosexual bodies [are]worthy of protection by nation-states' (Puar, 2013, p. 337). In other words, homonormativity and homonationalism as theoretical concepts are more suitable to explain assimilationist practices in contexts where queer people have an established legal, political, and cultural existence (albeit simultaneously exclusionary and under threat). Needless to say, that is not the case in Lithuania (or many other CEE countries), where queer people fight to prove that they are, and always have been, part of their national and cultural contexts. That they are not 'imported' from the West (Leksikov & Rachok, 2020; Vērdiņš & Ozoliņš, 2020). Thus, I argued that the discussed Lithuanian queer activist practices are better interpreted as efforts to challenge the dominant polarising rendition of 'the nation' as an exclusive space for heterosexual people into a 'hybrid space of identification' which offers multiple points of connection and belonging beyond the polarising opposition between 'us' and 'them'.

Notes

1 For the summary of the court cases please read: https://www.ilga-europe.org/news/european-court-rules-against-lithuania-labelling-lgbti-inclusive-fairy-tale-book-as-harmful-to-children/
2 For more information about the project and its goals, please see <https://www.coe.int/en/web/youth/living-library>

Chapter 6

QUEER LEGAL GEOGRAPHIES OF POLARISATION IN INTERNATIONAL LGBTQ RIGHTS LAW[1]

Kay Lalor

Introduction

Activist practice and academic literature has long recognised both the limitations and the endurance of binary patterns of 'global north'/'global south', homonationalism/homophobia and LGBT progress/LGBT suppression within international and transnational LGBTQ rights (Lalor & Browne, 2018; Rao, 2014; Weber, 2016). This chapter develops the concept of 'queer legal geography' as a novel theoretical and methodological lens for exploring the stability and tenacity of geopolitical polarisations of LGBTQ rights. It views polarisations not simply as political choices or different sides of an argument but as spatio-legal mechanisms that shape and restrict the possibility of action within international space. As such, the ways in which spatio-legal polarisations are practiced and maintained shape the forms that LGBTQ rights can take, and the different jurisdictions through which SOGI might be litigated.

Drawing upon emerging literatures of feminist legal geographies, the queer legal geography developed in this chapter uses a spatio-legal lens to trace how queer bodies are rendered 'out of place' within LGBTQ polarisations, or within polarisations that develop through and around conflicts related to sexual orientation, sexuality, sex, gender and gender identity. Such polarisations include, but are not limited to, binary patterns of north/south, homonationalist/homophobic, progress/ criminalisation, familiar/foreign. The chapter is most interested in how these binary patterns are grounded in and constitutive of structures of international law and state sovereignty, and the way that polarisations are deployed by the state as a means of affirming or signalling state power and identity against a supposed, opposite 'other'. However, it is notable that polarisations of LGBTQI+ rights and activism extend far beyond the state: binaries reverberate through many different forms of international engagement with gender, sexuality, sexual orientation and sex. Moreover, such binaries seem to persist, even when it is clear that they cannot capture the full complexity of the dynamics at play in the multiplicitous enactment of sexual and gendered lives in different spatial and temporal locations (Waites, 2017, p. 647).

In focusing on spatio-legal mechanisms of polarisation as they pertain to the operation of state power and LGBTQ rights, the chapter argues that examining how queer bodies are displaced makes clear the way in which different forms of regulation and different operations of power are simultaneously produced as 'normal' and rendered axiomatic or unquestioned within international spaces. LGBTQ polarisations are thus best understood as ontological and spatio-legal practices of 'world making' (Delaney, 2010), that are embedded and established within the foundations of international law.

Beginning with an examination of how LGBTQ polarisations are manifested in international spaces through diplomatic discussions of sexuality and gender, as well as through the operation of law in domestic courts and international bodies, the chapter draws upon recent literature on legal geography, feminist legal geography and sexual legal geography to demonstrate different spatio-legal elements of LGBTQ polarisations. It shows first how LGBTQ polarisations are deeply embedded in and supportive of axiomatic structures of international law, second how bodies 'out of place' can operate to trouble these structures, and third how the regulation of gendered and sexed bodies shapes international space. Bringing these elements together in a queer legal geography, the chapter concludes by showing how queer bodies are discursively 'stretched' across spatio-legal regulations in a way that contributes both to the continued displacement of queerness and to the ongoing stability of LGBTQ polarisations that shape queer lives.

Legal geographies of polarisations

The extent to which international legal space is shaped by polarisations of LGBTQ rights – and the extent to which these polarisations have become an organising feature of how states position and identify themselves within international arenas – is immediately evident in international diplomatic statements on LGBTQ rights. For example, following the US Presidential Memorandum of 2011 instructing 'all agencies engaged abroad to ensure that US diplomacy and foreign assistance promote and protect the human rights of LGBT persons' (White House Office of the Press Secretary, 2011), public diplomatic US support for international LGBTQ rights increased considerably, but through language that highlighted the uneven and polarised nature of LGBTQ rights protections worldwide:

> while some participating States have made tremendous progress in the fight to advance these human rights and fundamental freedoms, LGBTQ persons in many other participating States face discriminatory laws and practices that attack their dignity, undermine their safety, and abuse their human rights. (Baer, 2015)

> Despite these positive developments, we've also seen how governments use LGBTQ rights as a political wedge to bolster their own positions – in contexts such

as Nigeria and Russia, where recently passed draconian laws further undermine human rights for all people, not just LGBTQ individuals. (Berry, 2016)

We are not willing to accept an increasingly polarized world in which one set of countries moves toward greater respect for LGBT rights, while the other moves toward greater discrimination and criminalization. (Power, 2015)

These polarisations have continued: in 2023, for example, President Museveni of Uganda drew upon spatial and ideological polarisations to support the passage of the Ugandan Anti-Homosexuality Act (AHA) 2023: 'Uganda will not embrace homosexuality and the West should stop seeking to impose its views' (Reid, 2023). In response to this statement and other similar claims, activists and academics have highlighted the un-African nature of homophobia rather than homosexuality (Mafu, 2023; Tamale, 2023; Wahab, 2016). Notably however, while these statements may disagree vehemently on how and whether LGBTQ rights should be protected, they are all underpinned by a similar binary of north/south, homonationalist/homophobic, familiar/foreign, self/other. Thus, whatever the position taken on SOGI, geopolitical binaries and polarisations are maintained.

The maintenance of geopolitical, spatial and ideological binaries is not limited to diplomatic statements but extends to the courts. For example, in a 2014 Ugandan case denying the assembly rights of LGBTQ groups, the court drew explicit comparison with Europe:

Uganda and Europe have different laws and moral values and accordingly define their public interests differently... Therefore its precedents are not binding but must be read in a manner consistent with Ugandan laws and norms.[2] [Italics added]

More complex iterations of the same binary can be found in decriminalisation cases in states such as India, where some courts have protected LGBTQ rights while simultaneously preserving structures of state authority by presenting decriminalisation as a decolonial move and a restoration of indigenous practices that had been disrupted by the British Empire.[3]

Most important to this chapter is not the validity or otherwise of these various diplomatic and legal framings of LGBTQ rights, but their practical effects. LGBTQ rights polarisations are maintained through the performances and practices of state actors. Thus, legal and quasi-legal practices of polarisation shape international space and the possibility for action within it; they also shape the kinds of lexicons through which LGBTQ rights are discussed in international space and often control who has access to those lexicons. What emerges here is a co-dependence or co-constitution of human rights law and space through which international polarisations of LGBTQ rights emerge.

The co-constitutive relationship between law and space is fundamental to legal geography. Law exists not as an abstract force but as shaped by and occurring in space, while equally, space and 'social landscapes' are marked, limited and given meaning through law (Braverman et al., 2014; Brickell, Jeffrey, & McConnell, 2021; Cuomo & Brickell, 2019; Delaney, 2010, 2015; Layard & Bennett, 2015; Kessler, 2007; Robertson, 2015). This mutual dependence of law and space is multi-scalar and can be traced within the local, domestic and national, as well as in the international spaces through which the polarisations at the heart of this chapter occur.

The processes at play in the mutual co-constitution of law and space are active and responsive: when we observe the interaction of law and space, we observe not discreet or static actions, but ongoing practices of 'world-making' as law and space form around each other (Delaney, 2010).[4] An active and transformative view of the interaction of law and space is also one that attends to the tactical or knowing deployment of space in law, and to the active role and life of law, as it engages with spatial concepts to bring legal or material ends (Layard & Bennett, 2015). Equally important is the practice and performance of law within and through space (Brickell, Jeffrey, & McConnell, 2021; Jacobsen, 2021). As such we might understand the interaction of law and space as a socio-spatial-legal assemblage which is active, dynamic and subject to change.

Using a legal geographic lens, then, the world-making or 'nomospheric' (Delaney, 2010) quality of polarisations in international LGBTQ rights begins to emerge. The practice and performance of law, space and rights shape each other within such polarisations, as spatial parameters of 'global north'/'global south' are tactically deployed in discussions of rights to maintain particular boundaries, divisions or political ends. As such, the diplomatic and legal quotes above can be read as practices through which law and space are brought together to maintain particular spatio-legal geopolitical and diplomatic arrangements that coalesce around the protection or exclusion of SOGI minorities.

A further and vital aspect of LGBTQ rights polarisations is the way in which they cleave very clearly onto existing and deeply embedded norms of international law. In all the quotes above, the authority of states to regulate and legislate to govern the intimate lives of citizens goes unchallenged. These practices of regulation help to shore up state positionality as pro- or anti-LGBTQ policies become contributing factors to a state's national identity (see, e.g. Nyanzi & Karamagi, 2015; Rao, 2014; Weiss, 2013). In this way, polarisations of LGBTQ rights are predicated on axioms of sovereignty, statehood and national identity.

Tracing the relationship between LGBTQ polarisations and state sovereignty and identity allows a direct connection to be drawn between current polarisations of SOGI rights and much earlier binaries that emerged and were fundamental to the development of international law. As Anthony Anghie has argued, the 'civilising mission' of colonial states was predicated on the backwardness and 'otherness' of those that they colonised. This 'dynamic of difference' 'animated the development of many of the central doctrines of international law – most particularly, sovereignty doctrine' (Anghie, 2007, p. 3, 2006). If, as Anghie argues, the growth of key elements of international law grew from the colonial encounter, current legal and jurisdictional arrangements have long historical roots that are based in violence and conflict, and significantly, in polarisation and othering.

It is these polarised foundational structures of international law through which modern LGBTQ polarisations operate and make sense. Indeed, the spatio-legal practices of LGBTQ rights polarisations can only be fully understood through a lens that also encompasses the commingling of jurisdictional and colonial histories.

Bringing together Anghie's TWAIL (Third World Approaches to International Law) critique of international law, with legal geographic analysis, demonstrates how LGBTQ polarisation in international legal spaces rests upon and reinforces a number of assumptions, practices, norms and axioms. Most importantly, LGBTQ polarisations are expressions of state identity: a state can express 'progressive' credentials and demonstrate leadership or forward-thinking through its support of LGBTQ rights (Rao, 2014; Weber, 2016), but equally, political homophobia can be expressed with anti-colonial undertones that hints at preserving the nation from decadent external influences (Sadgrove et al., 2012; Weiss, 2013). This act of positioning recreates a long-held international legal practice of defining state identity through comparison to external 'others' and aligns with practices, common from the colonial era onwards, of condemning the sexual practices and mores of 'others' to justify colonial control (McClintock, 1995).

Thus, the spatial dimensions and mapping of homophobia and gay friendliness remain profoundly influential and tactically useful (Rao, 2014; Valverde, 2010). Polarisations are not a given; there is significant work to maintain them, but this work is not just political. It relies on a commingling and co-creation of law and space in such a way as to maintain, or at least not upset, long-established practices of state authority, state monopolies of violence, and state hierarchies of power and influence in international legal spaces. Now tied to questions of rights protections, the nexus of law-space-sexuality remains a compelling frame of organisation of international space. LGBTQ polarisations can therefore be understood as deeply embedded within long-established spatio-legal structures of international law. Beginning from this legal geographic starting point, the remainder of this chapter engages with the way in which queer bodies interact with, trouble and unsettle LGBTQ polarisations while simultaneously remaining vital to their continuation.

Feminist legal geography and feminist geolegality

The section above showed how a legal geographic approach can be used to explore the co-constitutive relations of law and space through which LGBTQ polarisations manifest and are maintained. Recent developments in feminist and sexual legal geography help to further illustrate the power relations of those polarisations through their analysis of differential movements of bodies in space, disrupting categories, scales and jurisdictions through which law and space are organised.

Introducing a recent special issue on feminist legal geographies, Dana Cuomo and Katherine Brickell note the limited sensitivity to 'the gendered character of law, and its (everyday) material sites and discourses' within many legal geographic texts (Cuomo & Brickell, 2019, p. 1043). In so doing, they highlight the lack of research on the social-spatial-legal nexus as it relates to gender or to intersections with nations, race, class or sexuality (Gorman, 2019). Concurrent with and emerging from these critiques, a number of explicitly feminist legal geographic studies have sought to fill this gap with analysis ranging from questions of intellectual property and intimate data (Farries & Sturm, 2019), land use in Cambodia (Gillespie & Perry, 2019), geolegality (Brickell & Cuomo, 2019), courtroom ethnography (Faria et al., 2020), and immigration and asylum (Gorman, 2019; Jacobsen, 2021).

An important feature of emerging feminist legal geographic literatures is their attention to the arrangement of differently categorised bodies in space 'as a site of both legal inscription and resistance' (Brickell & Cuomo, 2019, p. 108) as well as methods by and through which gendered, sexualised and racialised subjectivities occur and are constructed (Jeffrey, 2020). Thus within the legal geographic co-constitutive nature of law and space, feminist legal geography draws out the way in which bodies move and are moved in space and law. Of particular importance here are those bodies who, by virtue of gender, sexuality or other characteristics, do not easily fit within established legal, jurisdictional or spatio-legal frames or categorisations. Such bodies move unexpectedly through legal spaces, exposing the impermanence and even the vulnerability of spatial and legal categorisations, identities and jurisdictions by the very fact of their existence (see e.g. Brickell & Cuomo, 2019; Gorman, 2019). This approach allows greater attention to the gendered power dynamics of law as they are manifested in intimate and everyday spaces. It also draws focus to the multi-scalar ways in which gendered and other intimate power dynamics manifest. For example, women who seek asylum on the basis of severe domestic violence will, by their very existence, embody and challenge traditional spatial and jurisdictional binaries of global/local (in seeking refugee protection for violence that should be prohibited by the state) and public/private (by rendering domestic violence as a public concern) (Gorman, 2019). Thus, feminist legal geographic perspectives expose and interrogate established scalar and jurisdictional categories (Gorman, 2019; Valverde, 2014) and in attending to feminist legal geographic calls for sensitivity to difference in legal geographic analysis, we are compelled to attend to how law treats bodies that are differently gendered, racialised or sexualised. The nexus of the social-spatial-legal differentially resists the movement, the existence and the orientation of certain bodies over others. Concurrently, the presence of these disoriented bodies foregrounds the spatio-legal co-constitution of the traditional transnational socio-spatial-legal nexuses that are the cause of the disorientation. This process requires movement beyond the different sites, spatial issues or contexts and an exploration of the way in which acts of exclusion and welcome within law and space resonate across different legal sites and jurisdictions.

The analysis of the intersection of bodies that challenge the spatio-legal can be interestingly translated to questions of SOGI polarisations. There are numerous examples of efforts by activists and academics to manage international solidarity, create new connections and upend simplistic narratives of polarisation (Jjuuko, 2016; Kondakov, 2023; Lee, 2022; Lalor & Browne, 2018; Nyanzi, 2015; Waites, 2017). Less well explored, however, is the way in which, in the face of such efforts, the legal system will devote itself to its own continuation and protection. As the first section of this paper suggested, political polarisations of LGBTQ rights do not pose a fundamental threat to structures of state power and sovereignty that reserve to themselves the right to regulate gender and sexuality. Diplomatic polarisations represent a fundamental disagreement about *how* queerness should be regulated, and this disagreement is leveraged for political and geopolitical ends within international spaces. However, this leveraging can occur within existing international legal frameworks. There is jurisdictional investment in the construction of categorisations, and legal time and attention will be devoted to the production and consumption of 'otherness' in forms that can be recognised and regulated. Those bodies that pose a threat to established parameters are challenged and reconfigured into recognisable forms or marginalised in order to neutralise the epistemological challenge that they present. As such, by attending to marginalised bodies, we can expose and explore the international legal structures that facilitate their marginalisation and displacement. Moreover, as the final sections of this chapter explore, we can also explore how the legal and quasi-legal regulation of bodies is a spatio-legal process through which international and transnational spaces are constituted and sustained.

Sexual legal geographies of transnational space

Feminist legal geographic engagement with the movement of bodies across established categories also translates to a more specifically sexual legal geography that foregrounds questions of how spaces and places are sexualised (Browne, Lim, & Browne, 2007, p. 3). Thus space that is co-extensive with law must also be considered in terms of how spaces are heterosexualised (Binnie, 1997), 'occupied' by queer bodies (Bell & Binnie, 2004; Bell & Valentine, 1995; Binnie & Skeggs, 2004; Skeggs et al., 2004; Brown, 2014), and the way in which such bodies might claim sexual citizenship (Bell & Binnie, 2004; Binnie, 2004; Brown & Browne, 2016). Equally important are recent literatures in geographies of sexualities and beyond that have identified and questioned the way in which geopolitical hierarchies and binaries are constructed through a singular geography and politics of sexuality (Brickell & Cuomo, 2019; Browne et al., 2017; Charania, 2017; Edenborg, 2023; Kulpa & Maria Silva, 2016; Kondakov, 2023; Kulpa and Mizielińska, 2011; Rao, 2020; Shah, 2015; Lakkimsetti, 2016; Lalor & Browne, 2023). A number of texts have explored sexuality, gender and scale from the perspective of those who are caught within and move across different scales and jurisdictions as a result of their sexed, gendered and sexual subjectivities (Valverde, 2014, 2015 see also Garland, Lalor, & Travis, 2022; Lakkimsetti, 2016). The international, transnational and cross border perspective of many of these texts is notable: international legal assumptions of aspatiality or universality are here undermined by analyses of multiple spaces of international law that are sexualised in different ways, at multiple different scales.

Despite legal geographic suggestions that there was a tendency among earlier geographic texts to treat law as 'given' (Braverman et al., 2014, p. 4), geographies of sexuality research have long engaged with law and its effects on communities (Browne & Bakshi, 2013; Browne et al., 2021; Browne and Nash, 2014). Such texts move us towards what Brad Jessup and Clare McIlwraith have termed a 'legal geography of sex, and in particular the otherness of sex in place, the stigma of sex and sex being out of view' (Jessup & McIlwraith 2015, p. 1486). This sexual legal geography explores the shaping of law in sexualised spaces, and how the spaces and scales of legal regulation can impact what sexualised subjects can and cannot do (Hubbard, 2013), how changes to the regulation and governance of sexuality lead to differential engagement with or withdrawal from state structures (eg Cooper, 2019) or how boundaries such as public and private are maintained through lenses of sex and morality (Jessup & McIlwraith, 2015).

The theme of the spatio-legal regulation of sexual subjects at different scales is a particularly interesting aspect of sexual legal geography and is one that can be usefully turned to questions of LGBTQ polarisations in transnational space. Such analysis begins with consideration of transnational and international spaces, first, as places in and of themselves, rather than just abstract concepts or mid-points between the material experiences of the local and the universalised operation of international legal bodies, and second, as space that is always already gendered and sexualised. There is a significant history of the production of familiar/foreign, self/other and centre/periphery binaries within spatio-legalities of the transnational and international: from the colonial control and criminalisation of acts 'against the order of nature' (Kirby, 2013), to current discourses of LGBTQ rights and deployment of LGBTQ rights in the language of international development and leadership (Bergenfield & Miller, 2014), sexuality has long been integrated into transnational spatio-legalities.

Equally important here is the co-constitutive nature of law and space within the sexual-spatial-legal nexus. Sex is regulated, managed, 'othered' and rendered invisible or visible through its regulation at different scales. International space exists as a connected series of meeting points, physically, virtually and legally. Practices of othering, morality, disgust, inclusion and joy are all rendered visible and materialised in the interconnecting spaces of international law. In this sense, the diplomatic language from the first section of the chapter is productive of socio-spatial-legal meeting points. Thus, not only are diplomatic polarisations constitutive of *state* power to regulate sexuality, they are constitutive of the space within which states exercise their legal authority as sovereign powers: the space that is co-constitutive of international and transnational law. In short, both the practice and the discourse of rights are constitutive of the spaces that they occupy, including the polarised binaries through which those spaces are maintained.

It is possible at this point to bring together the key aspects of feminist-sexual-legal geography drawn upon in this chapter. First, legal geographic attention to the co-constitutive nature and law and space helps to demonstrate that the axioms and foundations through which international space is organised have a long colonial history that is reproduced in modern LGBTQ polarisations. These foundations are upset by the movement of bodies that do not easily fit existing categories and which bring together spaces, scales, jurisdictions and norms that are normally kept distinct. Disruptive bodies also help to reveal the gendered and sexualised nature of transnational space that has a long history of operating as a vector of polarisation and control. This perspective solidifies the perception of the constructed nature of transnational space – it is not a universal, aspatial realm or one that simply facilitates passage from the global to the local, but is spatio-legally constituted with multiple forms of regulation, often operating in conflict. Below, the final section of the paper draws upon these feminist-sexual-legal geographic points to develop a queer legal geography of LGBTQ polarisations in transnational space.

Queer legal geographies?

The distinction between a queer and a feminist legal geography is very much a matter of focus rather than a sharp categorical difference, particularly as 'queer' is necessarily a multiplicitous term operating as a form of identity, anti-normativity and a challenge to established categories (Nash & Browne, 2010). All these elements underpin a queer legal geography, in the sense that we might attend to queer identities and bodies, but in so doing, adopt an approach that is anti-normative by being curious about how 'the normal' or how norms and institutions – in this case, norms and institutions of international human rights law – are produced. From attempts to regulate the sexuality and gender of people subject to imperial rule and colonisation to the present-day polarisations of LGBTQ rights, the scalar movement of queer bodies and the materialities of queer lives often resonate beyond their embodied spaces as they unsettle or challenge accepted legal structures: love, violence, gender, sex and desire, which can thus be conceived as multi-scalar spectrums that traverse the intimate and personal but also inhere within national and transnational modes of biopolitical governance and within geopolitical manifestations of state power and public diplomacy. This means that by attending to those bodies that do not 'fit', the structures that cause their displacement come into view.

A useful representation of the way in which queerness does not conform to accepted scales is through the analysis of how the attempt to govern or regulate queer and LGBTQ bodies often leads to their metaphorical 'stretching' across borders and jurisdictions. In a physical or material sense, such bodies are located in one place and time, but legally, they can become a concern of several jurisdictions at once. Depending upon the jurisdictional or scalar lens adopted, a queer person might be legally iterated simultaneously as a criminal, a victim of a grave violation of human rights, someone seeking asylum or someone denied access to basic medical care. The same body can be differently positioned – stretched – across different spatio-legal nexuses that interact in the same assemblage.

One particularly long-running example of this could be drawn from ongoing attempts by the Ugandan Parliament to further criminalise homosexuality and the different domestic and international responses that have followed. The first attempt to introduce such legislation in Uganda was through the 2009 Anti-Homosexuality Bill. Criticised internationally and by some domestic commentators, the bill did not come to a vote until 2013 and was signed into law in 2014 amid further international criticism, which included several states and the World Bank withdrawing, redirecting or cancelling aid packages intended for Uganda (Wahab, 2016 see also Lalor, 2019). In August 2014, the Ugandan Constitutional Court overturned the AHA 2014 on the grounds that the Parliament had not been quorate when the bill passed.[5] Wider arguments about the rights of Ugandan SOGI minorities were not considered by the court.

Adrian Jjuuko, Siri Gloppen, Alan Msosa and Frans Viljoen note that following the nullification of the AHA 2014, although homosexuality remained criminalised and SOGI populations marginalised and vulnerable, there were minor improvements in terms of greater government agency engagement with LGBTQ groups and slightly less hostile press coverage (Jjuuko et al., 2022). Yet this slight improvement did not prevent the inclusion of restrictive provisions harmful to SOGI organising in the Non-Governmental Organisations Act 2016 and then the re-introduction and passage of a second Anti-Homosexuality Bill in 2023 (Shaw, 2023).

The AHA 2023 remains a grave threat to the safety of LGBTQI+ Ugandans, and without losing focus on the immediate physical violence inherent in the legislation, it is also possible to trace a pervasive epistemic violence at play. From a spatio-legal perspective, queer Ugandans are caught in domestic, transnational and international practices of world-making and of the co-constitution of law and space, which occur through the language and practice of polarisation. Thus, LGBTQ bodies are uncomfortably positioned within international sexualised spaces, as discussed in the section above, as they are stretched across multiple scalar and regulatory regimes. The argument here is that the geopolitical polarisation of here/there, self/other, familiar/foreign – a polarisation which replicates the civilisational binary upon which international law took shape – sustains and situates multiple further polarisations and oppositions that resonate through the regulation of gender and sexuality.

The multiplicity of polarisations at play can be seen in the diplomatic language of the 2023 bill:

> The . . . objective was to strengthen the nation's capacity to deal with emerging internal and external threats to the traditional heterosexual family and this Bill recognizes the fact that same sex attraction is not an innate and immutable characteristic.
>
> It was also intended to protect our cherished culture, the legal, religious and traditional family values of Ugandans and acts that are likely to promote sexual promiscuity in this country.[6]

The logic of this bill repeats, albeit in reverse form, the language of spatio-legal oppositions or polarisations used by external actors to critique the first AHA in 2014:

We have seen extraordinary advances for LGBT rights in the United States and in many countries around the world. But some governments have challenged this progress, with results that not only endanger local LGBT communities, but also pose a setback for all those around the world who share a commitment to freedom, justice, and equal rights.

The Government of Uganda's enactment of the 'Anti-Homosexuality Act' is precisely such a step in the wrong direction. (U.S. Department of State, 2016)

Thus, calls for and against increased criminal regulation of sexual orientation and gender identity are underpinned by the same spatial logics of binary opposition or self/other. The enactment of law and the critique of the enactment of law become part of a spatial practice by which states situate themselves, and through a legal, geographic lens, international and transnational legal spaces become co-constitutive of each other. In both of the quotes above, there is a polarised practice of world making or a spatio-legal dynamic of making polarised worlds. Law becomes a tool through which this world making operates, whether it be the justification of an anti-LGBTQ law as a response to an externalised threat, or the measuring of state progress towards 'freedom, justice, and equal rights' through its actions towards sexual and gender minorities.

Most importantly for this chapter, however, is the way in which the singular spatio-legal dynamic of here/there underpins multiple other oppositions that are grounded in the legal and political regulation of sexual and gendered lives. References to culture, the legal, religion and family values demonstrate how spatio-legal binaries extend far beyond diplomatic rhetoric or legal argument, as other regulatory regimes are deployed within existing polarised debates. As such, law's world-making power extends into other realms and allows for a repetition of polarised binaries that are grounded in – or at least resonate with – spatio-legal enactments.

There are multiple instances of the complex entanglement of regulatory forces that are nonetheless grounded in polarising binaries in the Ugandan context, perhaps most notably in the implication of medical, religious and financial actors in the legal debates around the AHA. For example, before signing the first Anti-Homosexuality Act into law, President Museveni sought advice from medical professionals about whether homosexuality could be 'cured' (Al-Jazeera, 2013). Equally, those opposed to the 2023 bill have highlighted the difficulty it will cause for the treatment of HIV/AIDS in marginalised communities (Nicholls, 2023) and medical professionals have responded directly to claims about the 'un-African' nature of homosexuality, with the President and CEO of the South African Medical Research Council noting, '[i]f anything, it's state-sponsored homophobia that's un-African and against the principles of Ubuntu, not homosexuality.' (Ibid)

Calls to medical authority have been mirrored by calls to religious authority as activists have condemned international religious influence on Ugandan homophobic legislation, arguing that evangelical American preachers have stoked anti-gay sentiment in Uganda and other countries worldwide (Kaoma, 2012 see also Jjuuko et al., 2022). During the first AHA in 2014, this eventually resulted in the US case of *SMUG v. Lively*, in which a Ugandan NGO brought proceedings in US courts under the US Alien Tort Statute against the US Pastor Scott Lively, claiming that his work in Uganda had contributed to harmful anti-gay sentiment in the country.[7]

Finally, one of the strongest international reactions to the AHA 2014 and 2023 was through the functioning of economics and development aid rather than through international legal action per se. In a trend that Rahul Rao (2015) has termed an example of 'global homocapitalism' after the passage of the first AHA in 2014, many states redirected financial aid to Uganda, with the World Bank withdrawing a $90 million loan in 2014 and announcing cessation of funding to Uganda in 2023 as a direct result of the anti-gay laws (Feder, 2014). There is a strong alignment here of LGBTQ rights with 'good governance': language through which the World Bank has increased its regulatory oversight and influence in aid-receiving states over many years (Bedford, 2009). In so doing the Bank has done little to undermine the north/south polarisations at the heart of other engagements with the AHA 2014 and 2023. Indeed, the imposition of punitive financial penalties upon Uganda uncomfortably resonated with histories of imperial financial control of colonised states.

The AHA is an example of the complexity that arises when different biopolitical, regulatory and epistemological regimes seek to shape the legal regulation of sexuality and gender across borders. In the varied international, transnational, activist and domestic engagements with ongoing Ugandan attempts to further criminalise homosexuality discussed here, the underlying polarisation of north/south, homonationalism/homophobia remains, but multiple different forms of regulatory power are part of the maintenance of these binaries. This is not just a legal or political process, but one of religion, economics and many other fields claiming authority and governance of queer lives within and through international legal spaces. Multiple different regulatory regimes seek to define, control and represent what queerness is, resulting in an over-determination of queerness and queer subjectivity at multiple different sites and a disorientating clamour of regulation of queer bodies. The irony that emerges is that from a starting point of polarisation, a complex and multifaceted assemblage emerges. It is possible to identify a clear socio-spatio-legal LGBTQ polarisation, but that polarisation is entangled in multiple different regulatory regimes that draw upon different iterations of how the world (and the bodies within it) should be organised, how borders should be drawn and how authority should be recognised. Within this assemblage, the queer body is both necessary and unfixed: it is the locus around which polarisations develop, but it stretches and changes shape in response to claims of different operations of law, power and regulation.

Viewing queerness in this way allows for further refinement of the argument developed in this chapter. It has been suggested thus far that LGBTQ polarisations rest upon deeply embedded structures of international law. Bodies that are 'out of place' help to reveal the spatial and jurisdictional operations of these deeply embedded structures and show that the international legal spaces through which these binaries are constituted are not aspatial, but are co-constituted with and through law and legal processes. Moreover, as this final section suggests, it is not only law but a multiplicity of quasi-legal and regulatory forces that seek to define and determine the place of sexuality and gender identity within and through international LGBTQ polarisations. Most importantly, however, within these different spatio-legal and regulatory configurations, the role of queerness or the understanding of who the LGBT or queer body is, and what purpose it serves, is constantly reiterated and redetermined. The stretching of LGBTQ bodies is a product of the requirement that they occupy multiple different subject positions within multiple different forms of regulation that shape and operate within international space.

In this way, a queer legal geography exposes the spatio-legal production of the axiomatic and the normal by attending to the movement, regulation and embodiment of those who are deemed not normal or out of place. LGBTQ polarisations and the sovereign state structures upon which they rely, as well as the scalar and jurisdictional arrangements that regulate and separate who can adjudicate questions of gender and sexuality in which arenas, rest upon the presence and performance of epistemic violence towards that which is deemed not to belong. Thus, international spatio-legal configurations of LGBTQ polarisations described here are themselves *reliant* on queerness to sustain their own logics within the cacophony of different legal and regulatory forces that are situated within international space. By attending to the over-determination of queerness by multiple regulatory regimes, the slippage of the definition of queerness or even of non-heterosexual sexualities, within these regimes becomes clear. Queerness, or LGBT rights, must be multiple things at once for LGBTQ polarisations to make sense. SOGI communities here are the excluded 'other', the vulnerable minority that must be brought within, a symbol of progress, and a scapegoat that represents colonialism and external invasion. In this way, the multiplicity of queerness, gender and sexuality is necessary to LGBTQ polarisations. LGBTQ rights operate in multiple different registers, queerness must be multiple different things, consistently open to redefinition to ensure that the polarisation is maintained.

Conclusion

The queer legal geographic approach developed in this chapter is offered as both a method and a first step towards understanding the structural elements of LGBTQ polarisations in order to better explain their tenacity. The chapter argues that approaching international legal polarisations as a spatio-legal question is a fruitful vector of analysis because by attending to the productive, co-constitutive nature of the interaction of law and space, it becomes possible to view international and transnational LGBTQ polarisations not as fixed points but as processes that reverberate through multiple regulatory regimes. With each reverberation, the underpinning legal structures of state and sovereignty – themselves built on polarised foundations – are reaffirmed. Attending to the structural elements of polarisations in this way is not to deny or discount the agency of those operating on either 'side' of them, but it does demand a recognition of the forces that shape what is possible and impossible within them and of the way that dynamic and creative political and legal action may be underpinned by long-established architectures of international law.

From this perspective, bringing feminist, sexual and queer legal geographies of scale and intimacy to bear on the experiences of queer subjects of international law exposes how queer bodies and subjects can be materially situated but discursively stretched across space and time. Queer subjects are not the only ones who experience this scalar 'stretching' – but in this case, they show how the spatial-legal production of those who cannot easily fit within international legal polarisations are essential to those polarisations' maintenance. The deployment of space in international law, and in domestic legal and diplomatic operations that follow – be it the AHA or Western attempts to seek 'leadership' on the grounds of LGBTQ rights protection – facilitates the stabilisation of state identity and state-based categorisation. It does not necessarily do the same for states' queer citizens and subjects, and as such, queer bodies are both shaped by and fundamental to the operation of LGBTQ polarisations, over which they have very little control.

Notes

1 Many thanks to Kath Browne and Emily Kazyak for their thoughtful comments on earlier drafts of this chapter. Thank you also to Beverley Clough, Jenny Kanellopoulou and participants in the Polarising Sexual and Gendered Lives symposium for the stimulating discussions of this topic and to Seán Pender for copyediting and editorial support.
2 *Nabagasera v Attorney General* Misc Cause 33 of 2012, [2014] UGHC 49.
3 In *Navtej Johar v Union of India* Writ Petition (Criminal) No.76/2016, 2, the court notes, 'A hundred and fifty eight years ago, a colonial legislature made it criminal, even for consenting adults of the same gender, to find fulfilment in love . . . Gays and lesbians were made subordinate to the authority of a coercive state . . . . Civilisation has been brutal.'
4 Delaney refers to this as the 'nomosphere': 'the cultural-material environs that are constituted by the reciprocal materialization of "the legal" and the legal signification of the "socio-spatial" and the practical, performative engagements through which such constitutive moments happen and unfold', although as Layard and Bennett observe, other terms – braiding, splicing, lawscapes – have been adopted to capture similar phenomena.
5 Oloka-Onyango and nine Others v. Attorney General [2014] UGCC 14, Constitutional Petition No. 8 of 2014 Uganda, Constitutional Court.
6 Parliament of Uganda *Official Report of the Proceedings of Parliament* Second Session, 18th Sitting, Third Meeting (21 March 2023), 7619.
7 The court, while ultimately holding it did not have jurisdiction to adjudicate the case, also found that Lively's ideas were 'crackpot' and 'pathetic' but nevertheless a harmful attempt to 'try to repress freedom of expression by LGBTI people in Uganda, deprive them of the protection of the law, and render their very existence illegal', *Sexual Minorities Uganda v Scott Lively* Civil Action 3:12-CV-30051 (MAP) (US District Court for the District of Massachusetts).

Chapter 7

UNEASY ALLIANCES

ORGANIZING ACROSS DIFFERENCE TO RESIST ANTI-TRANS LEGISLATION

Erika Slaymaker

Introduction

In 2021, in the United States, the State of Texas enacted HB (House Bill) 25, a law restricting trans students' access to athletics in K-12 public schools. This law requires that students may only participate in teams that correspond to their sex assigned at birth. HB 25 is part of a larger agenda of anti-trans policies in the state. In 2021, seventy-six anti-LGBTQ bills were filed in Texas, with a majority specifically relating to transgender people (Equality Texas, 2022). During the following legislative session, in 2023, Texas Republicans filed more than 140 anti-LGBTQ bills (Equality Texas, 2023). The legislature passed bans on gender-affirmative medical care for young people, drag performances and trans students participating in college athletics. Texas is one of the twenty-three states that has enacted similar bans on trans participation in school sports in the United States (MAP, 2023). Rather than an outlier, the case of Texas is part of a larger wave of anti-trans legislation across the United States (Connell, 2022; Jones & Travers, 2023).

The current wave of anti-trans policies reflects an increasingly polarized political context. Not only is anti-trans legislation passing in Texas, but more harsh legislation is becoming law. These laws have been met with resistance from LGBTQ advocates and their allies. This anti-trans legislative project both reflects and produces a polarized society where activists and politicians emerge on 'anti' and 'pro' sides and seek to rally the public to their side. In this chapter, I understand polarization as increasing division on political issues, as political actors' opinions on key political questions move towards further extremes across a political left-right or liberal-conservative divide (McCarty, 2019). In particular, I explore polarization around trans rights in the US and the ways that polarization is played out through anti-trans bills and their contestation. This chapter focuses on political actors, particularly the advocates who contested the anti-trans policy, to explore the relationships between polarization and coalition building.

Scholars are concerned that too much left/right political polarization can lead to breakdowns in democracy in the US (Downey, 2022; McCarty, 2019; McCoy, 2023). Still, even the foundational scholars of polarization who warn against too much polarization also argue that it is necessary to have some polarization in a functioning democracy (McCarty, 2019; McCoy & Somer, 2021). Polarization, at the very least, is important for creating options and choices for voters in elections.

Scholars and activists who push for radical social change often see polarization as necessary to accomplish their goals (Kreiss & McGregor, 2023). Indeed, social movements often encourage polarization. In this way, polarization is a tool or strategy and can be used for different ends (McCoy & Somer, 2021). Social movements, through the creation of collective identities, distinguish 'us' from 'them' (Polletta & Jasper, 2001).

It is the possibilities for social change created through and emerging because of polarization that interest me here. In particular, I am interested in how advocates construct coalitions that contest anti-trans legislation. Social movement scholars have documented that political threats contribute to collaboration and coalition building across groups and social movements (McCammon & Van Dyke, 2010; Van Dyke & Amos, 2017). For example, right-wing social movements have been very important for the consolidation and strengthening of LGBTQ social movements in the United States (Fetner, 2008). Indeed, Kreiss and McGregor (2023) argue that polarization might be 'a necessary outgrowth of efforts to achieve democracy' (2023, p. 3) and 'can fuel participation and policy-making' (2023, p. 10). I explore the complicated dynamic between polarization and coalition building in this chapter, asking whether polarization can contribute to coalition building, and in what ways can it do so.

Coalitions are necessary for broadening social movements and recruiting more people to identify with a cause and participate. Coalitions are one way to bring more people and more resources to a social movement (Jasper, 2014; Van Dyke & Amos, 2017). They can be aspirational, reaching towards larger political ideas and expanding the political vision and potential of a movement (Cohen, 1997; Chavez, 2013; Schulman, 2021). Coalitions are sometimes described as relationships between organizations and other groups that share resources, goals and strategies (Van Dyke & Amos, 2017).

However, coalitions can also be fraught. Coalitions confront what James Jasper (2014) calls the 'extension dilemma' (2014, p. 99) or the challenge of balancing organizational size and goals. As movements grow and become broader, conflict emerges and factions often form (Ghaziani, 2008; Jasper, 2014). As groups attempt to cohere a collective identity, boundaries around that identity are constructed, which, in turn, excludes some and can be limiting (Gamson, 1995). While many social movement theorists have assumed that infighting hurts movements, others argue that infighting can actually have a clarifying role (Ghaziani, 2008; Sutherland, 2023). Instead of damaging organizing, infighting 'carries meaning-rich conversations that give voice to strategy and identity' (Ghaziani, 2008, pp. 5–6). Coalitional politics are difficult as fragmentation often develops. Still, this conflict can have both weakening and strengthening effects. In the context of polarization, through sometimes fraught coalition building, social movements create new collective identities.

In this chapter, I focus on the coalition that unsuccessfully fought the 2021 anti-trans sports law in Texas. This chapter explores the coalition of advocates who fought against the bill, how it was formed and why they joined. The coalition included trans adults, mothers of trans children and cisgender lesbian, gay, bisexual and queer adults. Each group had distinct motivations to participate in the fight against anti-trans legislation targeting children. I argue that the coalition that emerged sheds light on the opportunities and challenges facing the LGBTQ movement in the midst of increasing polarization in the US. The coalition also offers lessons on how allies become politically engaged. Whereas 'LGBTQ' has become a seemingly ubiquitous coalitional term, my work illustrates the complexities and contradictions of this coalition in practice, particularly in increasingly polarized times.

LGBTQ: Constructing 'Unity through Diversity'

By bringing together lesbian, gay, bisexual, transgender and queer people, groups that organize around an LGBTQ collective identity often seek to build coalition across gender and sexuality. This has happened unevenly over time. LGBTQ collective identity has shifted from a focus simply on gay men and lesbians to include more sexual and gender identities, including bisexual, transgender, intersex, queer and non-binary identities. Scholars show how LGBTQ movements attempt to build 'unity through diversity' (Armstrong, 2002; Ghaziani, 2008; Stone, 2009). This unity is not a given; instead, this attempted cohesion is constructed and also contested by social movement actors, like all collective identities (Taylor & Whittier, 1992; Polletta & Jasper, 2001).

Scholars have argued that the coalitions that LGBTQ movement activists have built across race, gender and sexuality in the United States have been key to their success, especially in the legalization of gay marriage and increased societal acceptance of gays and lesbians (Ghaziani, Taylor, & Stone, 2016). However, these coalitions often mask power differences inside the movement. Gay men's organizations tend to control the most resources, while lesbian, bisexual and trans people wield relatively less power (Devor & Matte, 2004; Ghaziani, 2008; O'Brien, 2019). Similarly, white-led organizations have disproportionate resources and decision-making power than those led by people of color (Beam, 2018; Ward, 2008).

Identity-based movements always struggle with the question of who 'counts' as a member of the group (Ghaziani, 2008; Polletta & Jasper, 2001). Building a coalition of LGBTQ people has been especially fraught. For example, 'trans' itself is a coalitional term, often referred to as an 'umbrella term' that includes transgender, transsexual, non-binary and intersex identities (Stryker, 2017; Sutherland, 2023; Valentine, 2007). Activists, at times, police boundaries of who is 'trans enough' and at other times question if someone is 'too trans' (Sutherland, 2023, p. 71).

Transnormative logics privilege a medicalized, linear trans experience (Johnson, 2016). LGBTQ movements have a history of not only struggling over which identities should be included in the coalition but also of how broadly to define each identity. Queer and trans activists have critiqued LGBTQ movements for assimilationist politics that center normative expressions of gender and sexuality (Spade, 2015; Bey, 2021).

This points to the question: what is the role of transgender identity within the larger frame of LGBTQ politics? And how are differences overcome in political organizing? Amy Stone identifies three mechanisms through which 'ally identities' are created (Stone, 2009, p. 338). *Borrowed approximations* entail 'knowing a member of the marginalized group and being witness to their suffering' (Stone, 2009, p. 338). An example would be advocating for a cause that impacts a family member or a friend. *Overlapping approximations* occur when an ally draws an 'analogy to some oppression they have suffered' (Stone, 2009, p. 338). For instance, cisgender women sometimes draw on their experiences of sexism to understand how transgender people also face gender discrimination. Finally, *global approximations* occur when an ally makes a 'connection to their democratic or political orientations' (Stone, 2009, p. 338). Allies might draw on their beliefs about the importance of everyone being treated with dignity and respect to advocate on behalf of a certain cause. I draw upon this framework to understand how allies of trans youth came together to fight HB 25, including trans adults, mothers of trans youth, and cisgender lesbian and gay allies.

This chapter looks specifically at the advocacy against the 2021 anti-trans sports bill in Texas. In the current polarized US context, sports have increasingly become a flashpoint for conflicts over the meanings of sex and gender. Anti-trans policies are one expression of (and contributor to) the current polarization in the United States. Sports are sex-segregated and 'organized around a cisgender framework', limiting

Table 7.1: List of Participants by Race, Age and Gender

	Pseudonym	Race	Age	Gender
LGB Allies	Franny	Latinx	late 20s	cisgender woman
	Keith	white	early 40s	cisgender man
	Tony	Latinx	40s	cisgender man
	Max	white and Native American	late 20s	cisgender man
	Nicole	white	mid-20s	cisgender woman
	Taylor	white	early 30s	cisgender woman
Mothers	Christina	white	mid 40s	cisgender woman
	Mary	white	mid-40s	cisgender woman
	Sarah	white	mid-40s	cisgender woman
Trans Adults	Alex	white	early 30s	non-binary
	Cam	Asian and American	late 20s	non-binary
	Eleanor	white	early 30s	transgender woman
	Ezra	Latinx	early 30s	non-binary
	Margo	white	late 30s	transgender woman
	Skye	white	early 20s	non-binary

the access and inclusion of gender-diverse individuals (Witcomb & Peel, 2022, p. 6). US conservative advocates push to further entrench binary logics within sports by advocating for, and successfully passing, laws that explicitly exclude transgender and non-binary young people from participating in sports (Jones & Travers, 2023). In response, a range of actors advocate against this anti-trans legislation: parents, cisgender LGB activists and trans advocates. As children are more the focus of anti-trans bills, scholars note the increased political activity of parents, who are often cisgender straight mothers, in the advocacy on behalf of trans kids (Meadow, 2018; Rahilly, 2021; Travers, 2018). These parents join with the already broad, and at times unwieldy, LGBTQ coalition. In the response to anti-trans legislation in Texas, we see this coalition at work. In resisting anti-trans bills that focus on trans young people, how do advocates build a coalition across gender and sexuality? (See Table 7.1.)

Methods

This chapter draws on fifteen semi-structured interviews with advocates who organized during the 2021 legislative session.[1] This sample includes three mothers, six cisgender LGB advocates and six trans advocates. See Table 7.1. I was also a participant observer in LGBTQ activist efforts at the Texas Capitol during the 2021 legislative session, from January to October 2021. I attended rallies, lobbying trainings, office visits with legislators, committee hearings, strategy sessions, vigils and webinars over ten months.

The fifteen interviews lasted between one and three hours and were conducted between May 2021 and May 2022. I recruited interviewees who were actively involved in organizing during the 2021 legislative session, speaking at rallies, testifying at public hearings and leading organizations. I recorded and transcribed all of the interviews. I utilized a flexible coding approach (Deterding & Waters, 2021), paying particular attention to advocates' descriptions of how and why they became involved with advocacy against the anti-trans legislation.

This chapter explores the motives of the different groups to engage in the battle against the anti-trans sports bill. The following three sections walk through the three groups within the coalition, attending to advocates' motivations to participate in the fight against anti-trans legislation. As Republicans introduced anti-trans bills at the Texas Capitol, each group became mobilized to organize to keep the bills from passing. Each group had its own reasons but found ways to join the coalition. I show how these differences reveal the possibilities for and difficulties of coalition politics within a polarized context.

The allies: Lesbian, gay and bisexual cisgender adults

The first group of allies includes lesbian, gay and bisexual cisgender adults. In my interviews with these advocates, they explained that they see themselves as allies to transgender people in general and to trans kids in particular. The cisgender

LGB activists that I interviewed saw fighting anti-trans legislation as an important part of their work, either as paid staff or volunteers, supporting the larger LGBTQ movement.

The lesbian, gay and bisexual cisgender adults I interviewed drew on their own experiences with homophobia and discrimination to explain how they got involved in the fight against HB 25. Amy Stone (2009) refers to these moments as 'overlapping approximations', when cisgender gays and lesbians explain their solidarity with trans people by making links to their own experiences of oppression. One advocate, Max, explains that after coming out as gay in high school in Texas less than a decade ago, he was told by his school principal that he was a 'moral disturbance'. He explained, 'No one should hear [that] from their parents, their principal, anyone that they love or trust, their legislators.' This experience of homophobia has fueled Max's advocacy. He says, 'I was able to overcome it, but like that little nugget is what still burns inside of me to this day that keeps me going in this work.' Max was supported by his mom, who joined PFLAG and encouraged him to participate in gay pride events in Dallas. From these connections, he became active in the HRC and was called upon to help out as staff with voter mobilization efforts.

Tony, too, sees parallels with his own experience coming out as gay: 'I go back to thinking about the kids who know who they are, authentically, right. I was 6 years old, I knew that I was gay. I didn't have the words or the language for it, but I knew I was, that I was.' He draws on his own experiences and translates that experience to the way he relates to trans and non-binary kids. He explains, 'so, I believe kids when they tell me that they are non-binary or trans, or that they are kind of exploring what their identity is and they have every single right to do that.' Both Max and Tony see parallels between their cisgender gay coming out experiences and the experiences of trans and non-binary children coming out.

Like Max and Tony, the staff at LGBTQ organizations were in their twenties and thirties, mostly white and Latinx. Some have careers in LGBTQ advocacy or progressive non-profits and have moved from organization to organization. Nicole tells me about working at a non-profit organization in one of the large cities outside of Austin. She worked on the bathroom bills from the business side, trying to make the business case against the bathroom bills. When she visited Austin as part of that work, during an LGBTQ lobby day at the Capitol, she realized she was drawn to that advocacy at the Capitol, saying it was where she 'needed to be' and 'where [she] belonged'. She wanted to be directly working with community members and on the legislative strategy.

In addition to staff and volunteers at the advocacy organizations, cisgender allies included legislators at the Capitol. In 2019, after the bathroom bills session, a small group of progressive lesbian, bisexual and pansexual representatives formed the LGBTQ House Caucus. This women of color-led group hoped to not only fight against anti-LGBTQ legislation but to also create a platform for a proactive vision of more inclusive legislation in Texas. As advocates worked on messaging for testimony, organized rallies and talked with the press, the legislators worked behind the scenes and in parallel. When speaking on the issue, representatives would draw upon their own identities and experiences to connect to the sports bill. For example, at the end of the first legislative session in 2021 (and before the subsequent three special sessions where the trans sports bill continued to be on the agenda), the LGBTQ caucus members held trans flags on the House floor as the session ended without a full floor vote on the sports bill. During this celebration of an early victory, Representative Jessica González spoke movingly of her own experience participating in sports and having her gender questioned by adults. Even though González does not identify as transgender, she found the issue to be personal and connected it to her own individual experience.

This points to the earlier question: what is the role of the fight for transgender rights within the larger frame of LGBTQ politics? From the point of view of the cis leaders and from the space of LGBTQ organizations, the 'T' is a part of the larger coalition. They came to this understanding through their own experiences of homophobia and discrimination; they saw anti-trans policies as similar to the anti-gay policies they faced. In the midst of polarization around trans issues in Texas, they connected their experiences as lesbian, gay and bisexual cisgender people to the experiences of trans people, particularly trans kids. They drew on approximating experiences to make sense of their allyship with trans people. In the context of trans/anti-trans polarization, they chose their side: they saw fighting anti-trans legislation as firmly on the agenda of LGBTQ groups in Texas.

The mothers: Mothers of transgender children

Mothers of trans kids were a very visible presence at the Capitol during the fight against HB 25. They regularly participated in press conferences and testified in public hearings about their experiences as mothers of trans kids. I often saw them wearing buttons offering 'free mom hugs'. The mothers I interviewed explained that supporting their children was one of their most important duties. For them, this meant affirming their child's gender as something other than cisgender. The mothers told a similar story of first coming to the Capitol. They had an awareness that the bills being discussed in the legislature would have an effect on their kids and their family. Sarah explains, 'it's the only reason I came, because it was going to directly impact us.' She drew on *borrowed approximations* (Stone, 2009), or from knowing a trans person, her child. In the midst of polarization around anti-trans bills, the mothers were on their children's side, which, for them, meant advocating against the anti-trans bills. Through their advocacy, they joined the larger LGBTQ coalition.

The three mothers that I interviewed were involved in local politics before joining the fight against anti-trans state legislation. Christina was involved with supporting Drag Queen Story Hours, events where drag performers read books to children and their families at libraries, schools and bookstores, which have become a controversial flashpoint in her town and many others, and now state legislatures across the US. Sarah and Mary were involved in their school district's process to revise the sex education curriculum. In response to the introduction of anti-trans bills at the Texas Capitol, they got even more involved in political advocacy. In some ways, polarization around trans issues encouraged them to become more vocal and strident activists. Because of polarization, the mothers felt the need to choose a side and become part of the coalition to organize against anti-trans legislation.

The mothers became involved with these issues at the same time as they were developing new understandings of their transgender children. Throughout our interview, for example, Mary tells a parallel process of supporting her transitioning daughter and becoming involved in local political work. She makes fun of herself, saying that before her daughter transitioned, 'I always felt like [political involvement] was part of my civic responsibility, but I didn't do shit about it, you know. It was like yeah, we all, we have to stand up! And I'll do it with this sign for Wendy Davis in my yard! And by donating ten dollars to ActBlue, but not really doing anything.' She felt a lot of 'discomfort' with getting more involved with politics at the time and looks back on this time with some self-deprecation.

The mothers I interviewed shared a feeling of responsibility not just to their own children, but also to others who shared their situation but could not be at the Capitol. They knew that they were unusual in their privileged access to resources and flexible schedules that made it possible for them to be active in the protests. They mentioned the moms of trans kids that lived too far away to be able to show up at hearings and rallies on a regular basis. Sarah explains that she 'felt really obligated because I am two miles from that building [the state Capitol] and I know so many people across the state who couldn't be there who are going to be impacted'. She felt a deep sense of responsibility to people who could not be there, including mothers whom she had met through Facebook groups and support spaces for mothers of trans children. She was very aware of her own proximity and access to resources, which added a sense of wanting to show up at the Capitol.

Mary began to get connected with organizations, including Equality Texas, to support her daughter and build relationships with LGBTQ adults and other mothers of trans children. Doing so taught her new information and organizing skills. She became an advocate through her daughter's transition: 'we talked to her school, we talked to her teachers, she came too, I was modeling how to advocate for herself'. From there, she became involved in organizing at the school district level. She explains that 'while all that was happening, AISD, Austin Independent School District, and the Texas Board of Education were both reviewing their curriculum. And so, I got involved with Informed Parents of Austin.' Through supporting her daughter, she became more active in local politics.

This sense of responsibility expanded over time for Sarah. She expresses solidarity with the trans adults at the Capitol, too: 'These trans adults would continue to show up and they're not even directly impacted and they're showing up for my kid, who they don't even know. So, I'm going to keep showing up for them, you know? I felt like I would be abandoning my team or my post if I moved.' She has a feeling of responsibility to an expanded 'team', one that includes trans adults. Through this, her sense of allyship is growing and her connection to the wider LGBTQ coalition is developing.

Emotion was a motivator and a resource for the mothers. Social movement scholars argue that feelings are 'fundamental to political life' (Gould, 2009, p. 3); they not only motivate political action, but they are also shaped by that action (Jasper, 2014). Angst was especially important, particularly for Sarah. She explains, 'I turned all my angst into action and that always feels really good, and even though we didn't get the outcome we wanted for every single bill, it felt like I was working towards something.' Christina showed up and had a positive emotional experience that it was a 'cup-filling experience to be in there and get to meet so many people, so many diverse backgrounds, and experiences'. Emotions were a motivation to get involved at the beginning, and they were also a motivation for staying. Social movement scholars recognize that emotions '[do] not disappear', but instead 'motivate continued mobilization' (Jasper, 2014, p. 30).

Throughout this, relationships were also important. Relationships got them to the Capitol through invitations and through seeing that people were attending via social media, especially Facebook. They were all either invited by a person or saw a person they respected post about a rally. Relationships kept them at the Capitol, feeling responsible to the broader community and to more immediate friendships.

The mothers also describe a shift from being intimidated by the Capitol, the legislators and the political process to a feeling of 'I can do this'. They shared an 'aha' moment of realizing that advocacy is a learnable skill. They experienced some demystification of the political process. After seeing someone she knew from PFLAG post on Facebook about an event at the Capitol, Christina decided to attend. Once she joined the event, it became less scary. Sarah, too, explains a learning curve at the beginning, 'now that I have gone through that process and see that yes it's a lot but it's like not insurmountable' and that it is a learnable skill, 'you can just show up and learn it.'

Through the mothers, we see a development of a wider sense of community. This is the potential of coalition, a developing sense of solidarity. From their specific relationship with their child, they became connected to a larger movement. In the context of polarization around the anti-trans bills, the mothers felt the need to pick a side. They chose to fight the anti-trans bills. By entering this advocacy effort, they connected with the broader LGBTQ coalition. In this way, polarization around anti-trans bills was constitutive, driving the mothers' activism and the coalitions they found and joined.

Trans advocates

A third group, made up of trans adults, fought against anti-trans legislation. Trans people I interviewed explained that they advocated at the Capitol because they want trans kids to be supported. Cam explains that they are generally involved in LGBTQ activism 'for the sake of my own survival, for the sake of my own education, and for the sake of all the people I fell in love with'. They connect their own experiences with their political work. In moments of polarization where their lives are being scrutinized, people can, and do, draw on their own experiences to situate themselves in relation to the debate. Ezra, too, explains that 'that's also part of why I do this work, why I think it's important, because I lost one of the most important people in my life to anti-LGBTQ hate.' Later, they explain, 'this is not just like a political arena, it determines our lives and the future possibilities for ourselves and the people we love.' Both Cam and Ezra reference their own experiences and their relationships with other queer and trans people. Even when they had very different life experiences to the trans children, by coming out later in life, the adults still identified with the trans youth. They drew on *approximating experiences* as trans adults to connect with the experiences of trans young people.[2] Their lived experience shaped the way they became allies to trans kids and, in turn, it shaped the way they chose to engage with the polarized political context.

The six trans adults that I interviewed had mixed feelings about the strategies and messaging that were used to resist the anti-trans legislation. Whereas LGBTQ organizations were invested in including transgender issues as a part of their larger work, some trans organizers were worried that this would decrease the visibility of trans people themselves. Eleanor, for example, questions the framing of the bills as 'anti-LGBT'. Eleanor explains, 'Certain organizations will send out emails saying our org defeated this many anti-LGBT bills last year. And you are like uh, no, you fought anti-trans bills.' She wants to bring more attention to how trans people were at the center of the legislative fights. This is a shift in focus. She is skeptical of the ways that trans people get incorporated within LGBTQ politics and is worried about an 'erasure of actual trans people'.

In my interview with Cam, they referenced 'the community' multiple times. When I asked them who they were imagining as part of that community, they explained, 'I'm talking about the people who are going to be affected on a very deep and personal level by the legislation that we are either advocating for or advocating against down to the simple of question is this going to be able to increase the wellness of our community or not.' They went on to say, explicitly, that allies are included in their vision of the community. Ezra, too, explicitly included allies in their understanding of the community at the heart of the activism. Ezra tells the story of one particularly intense hearing on anti-trans bills during the 2021 legislative session. After being asked by a mom of trans kids to confront a legislator outside the hearing, they felt like their 'only option was to run up to her and beg her to listen to this child's story'. They explain that this is not normally how they interact with legislators, but they did it because 'a mom asked me to and I would fucking do anything for those parents'. They have a fierce sense of loyalty to and solidarity with the parents of trans kids. At the same time, as they are trying to understand where they found the courage to confront the legislator, they explain the mix of emotions that they experienced that evening. They 'felt some guilt because I had talked and other people had ceded their time to the kids'. They had testified at the hearing, when other adults had ceded their time to trans young people in the hearings. They explained that others 'made me feel like I should have given up my time, but I was just like I am one of the only trans adults here in this room. It's important that they hear from that, too'. Even as they felt pressure to more specifically center trans kids and to share their time with trans kids, they also were clear that they had a specific experience that they felt could influence those in the hearing room. They did this despite their fears, and the bravery they showed was for others who they would 'do fucking anything for'.

Adult trans women occupy a fraught position at the Capitol because of the polarization of trans lives. They have fought to be spokespeople and leaders; they often argue that it is important for trans people to be at the front of the rallies, to be talking to the media and so on. Transfemininity is at the center of the polarized discourse about the anti-trans legislation; this is driven by proponents of the anti-trans sports bill who often invoke images of scary or dangerous trans women in their arguments for the bills.

Two of the trans women I interviewed had particularly strong critiques of the leading LGBTQ organizations, for the lack of representation of trans women. Margo, an ordained minister, was a very visible presence in rallies and testimonies against the 2021 anti-trans legislation. She was in the process of coming out during the 2017 'bathroom bills' legislative session and was navigating presenting as a woman at work and with family. She wanted to participate in the rallies against the bathroom bills but was not ready.

After she left her job and went back to school, the Capitol was more accessible to Margo. She was no longer worried about backlash from her boss or the HR department for her activism. She also had a flexible schedule that allowed her to be there. And she was more confident and grounded in herself as a trans woman. In her telling of it, things changed from year to year and from legislative session to legislative session. It was hard to show up during the bathroom bill session. Then, in 2019, she was present, but nervous. And then 2021 hits and something else happens. She's present in a big way. She explains that when she went to the Capitol in 2021, 'for my first testimony, I wanted to be visible in a way that made the people that showed up there feel good.' She wore what she called 'the ridiculous clergy dress', a skintight black maxi dress with a high slit on one side and a clerical collar sewn on. She explains why she chose this outfit: 'When I'm scared, I like to turn it up to 11. It's part of kind of putting on armor in a way. And it is such a ridiculous, sexy, clergy outfit, that I find it just delightful.' Her visibility was a coping mechanism and also a way to connect with the other advocates. She explains that she also saw this visibility as a part of her strategy: 'I also thought some of the game here is to get media attention and maybe they'll pay more attention to me if this is a spectacle. And I wanted to be seen, I wanted to be that sort of lightning rod, because I was like I can handle that.' She was aware that she was a visible trans woman at the Capitol, and she was intentional in how she leveraged that visibility.

Over time, Margo's audience changed from trying to convince legislators to speaking more directly to the trans community. During the 2019 session, she focused on 'tight', 'clever' arguments in her public speaking. She referenced her philosophy training in college and her divinity schoolwork in how she prepared testimony for the legislators. Over time, though, she cared less and less about the argument. She explained, 'so what I noticed was it didn't matter how clever I was, how funny I was, how tight the argument was, how much they paid attention, it didn't seem to do anything.' Margo began to question the utility of the testimonies: 'I wonder sometimes has this process radicalized me and I look at the rhetoric and how I have entered into this and I think in some ways it has, because I have experienced the trauma of it, and you're like, no one here, no one in the GOP is showing up in good faith and that changes the conversation.' By good faith, Margo emphasized a belief in the process, that the public hearings are supposedly a place for legislators to listen to the public comment on bills. Her belief in this process faded over time. Instead of talking directly to the legislators, she started to focus her testimony and public speaking on the trans community. She began to 'shift from talking only to the people who are in the room to talking to the people who will see it on social media later. There is a distinct shift in saying I'm here, I'm not here for you, I am here for them [trans people and allies]'. As advocates became increasingly frustrated with the legislators, they focused their testimony and messaging on the trans community to try to counterbalance the negative messaging that trans people were hearing. Margo's engagement with and understanding of the political process changed over time, becoming more antagonistic with the successive introduction of anti-trans bills in the Texas legislature.

Margo is unsure if the LGBTQ organizers want her there. She says that she 'weaseled myself into a rally'. She explains that she would respond to invitations to rallies affirmatively,

> I kept being, oh, like I would be happy to do it, what do I do to prepare, so I kept replying to the automated message, and it was like the day before, and I was like hey, I really want to come to this, did you want me to speak or did you just want me to be there? and at the very last minute they would be like, oh we want you to speak and I spoke like next to last.

Repeatedly throughout our interview, Margo describes being unsure if the cis-led organizations want her at the Capitol. 'They were not asking me to interview for things, they weren't even inviting me out, they didn't even want me, I'm fairly certain, they didn't want me to testify.' For example, I observed a press conference against the anti-trans sports bill where Margo was the only trans woman to speak out of seventeen speakers in total. She was one of four trans people to speak, and she spoke in the last fifteen minutes of the hour-long press conference.

Margo is not the only one who noticed these dynamics of trans women being left out or pushed to the end. Eleanor, a white trans woman in her late twenties, also felt like she had to fight to take up space within the advocacy. Eleanor started her own organization in reaction to the difficulties of working with the larger non-profit organizations. Eleanor explains:

> I was really connected with a lot of trans people in Austin, especially trans women on the more radical politically active side of things, but we had issues where we were going to these events and not being heard or even in some cases feeling

like we were scooted into the back and put out of sight, as part of respectability politics coming up again.

She tells about going to a rally where most of the speakers were cisgender people, along with one trans child and one trans man. She was 'frustrated', explaining that 'it was so conspicuous how much they were removing trans women from this fight.' Eleanor echoes Margo's concerns about the place of trans women in the advocacy. She is also concerned specifically about Margo's presence. She says,

> instead of elevating trans women, especially people like Margo, who is like a fucking goddess, first of all, but then also a Reverend, like, I can't think of anyone who is a better example of who we should be putting in front of humans and then treating her like she is a pariah and letting her do stuff in the background, not giving her a platform.

Eleanor and Margo are both concerned about the sidelining of trans women in the advocacy.

This was not experienced by all trans people, though. Skye, a non-binary young person, was a teenager during the legislative session and testified at committee hearings along with their supportive parents. They were invited back repeatedly and explicitly by organizational leadership. They explain, 'I did everything through Equality Texas, I do not think I could have done it without them.' Trans men also participated in the advocacy but were more often staff of non-profit organizations than trans women.

In addition to feeling like trans women should have been more at the center of the protests, Eleanor wishes that the reach of who showed up at the Capitol was wider. She is frustrated that 'there is just not enough people.' She explains, 'it would be experts and really dedicated community members for hours' arguing against the anti-trans bills, but then 'everyone on the right's side would be some like yahoo that's like, "yeah I had nothing better to do then come here." And why don't we have more people that had nothing better to do but come here?' She argues that the advocates need a bigger coalition – a coalition that includes people who are not as directly impacted by the issues. She is arguing here for both more trans women to be centered in the organizing and also for a broader group of people to be mobilized. She is not only critiquing the need to be directly impacted in order to show up but also critiquing a too narrow frame of who sees themselves as directly impacted. In other words, more people need to see it as worth their time to advocate against the legislation. Also, her take on the conservative testimony is different from many of the other advocates. Many advocates would make fun of the random 'yahoo' who was there and see it as a sign of weakness about the quality of testimony from those who supported the anti-trans legislation. Eleanor, however, saw it as a sign of strength that so many people were testifying despite not having a deep connection to the issue. In this context, the polarization of trans issues was having uneven impacts on who was becoming involved at the Capitol. Not only is Eleanor critiquing that trans women are not centered in leadership and visible at public events, but she is also pushing for a wider coalition of actors than the narrow group of LGBTQ organizations. Many of the LGBTQ advocates I spoke to framed the issue as protecting a small vulnerable population (trans young people). This, in turn, shaped, and perhaps limited, who and how people were mobilized to participate in advocacy against the anti-trans bills.

Trans adults occupied a precarious position at the Capitol within the larger, also precarious, coalition. Some, particularly the trans women, were volunteers who were often unsure of their role within the advocacy. Margo and Eleanor were critical of LGBTQ organizations for not making a more explicit place and role for trans women. Trans advocates who were also staff at organizations were conflicted, as they navigated insider and outsider roles. In response to polarization, trans adults advocated against anti-trans bills and joined the larger LGBTQ coalition, but they occupied a more fraught position in the coalition. Like the other groups, their personal experiences and relationships with trans people informed their advocacy against anti-trans bills and shaped how they chose sides within the polarized political context.

Conclusion

While these groups of cisgender lesbian, gay and bisexual advocates, parents of trans kids, and trans people were unsuccessful in defeating the 2021 Texas anti-trans sports bill, they did achieve something else: a coalition across gender and sexuality. They each came to the issue out of their own interests and motivations. Sometimes they struggled to work together. Mothers saw their experience of the LGBTQ community expanded by showing up at the Capitol; they gained a new 'team'. Trans advocates found that space to be stifling. Instead of an expanded coalition, they found a space that was limited. Two trans advocates, in particular, wanted a more explicit focus on transness and, at the same time, a wider base of support to be showing up. The cisgender lesbian, gay and bisexual organizers, especially those who were staff at LGBTQ organizations, were comfortable with the status quo and saw fighting anti-trans policies as a core part of the larger LGBTQ coalition.

This study contributes to our understanding of the LGBTQ movement and the complicated coalitions that challenge anti-trans legislation in polarized contexts. Polarization creates a context within which coalitions can emerge. As advocates become mobilized to join political fights and pick sides, they join with others, and in this process, new coalitions can form. These coalitions are responding to, being pulled into, and even contributing to, polarization. Building on scholars like Kreiss and McGregor (2023) in seeing the ways that polarization can be necessary for organizing against social injustice, I have shown how coalitions are both created through polarization and how they, in turn, can contribute to that polarization.

This chapter also contributes to the scholarship that examines the fraught process of transgender inclusion within the LGBTQ movement (Stone, 2009). Whereas Stone's analysis examines how cisgender gay men and lesbians develop ally identities with transgender people, my work broadens the scope by including parents of transgender children and trans people themselves. Even within the identity of 'trans', advocates rely on *approximating experiences*. These experiences shaped how advocates became allies to trans youth and, consequently, how these advocates found their 'side' within polarization, and worked to create better conditions for trans young people. The coalition of parents, cisgender LGB activists and trans advocates found each other within a polarized political context. More broadly, this study contributes to our understanding of coalitional dynamics and collective identity as something that is constructed.

As the current wave of anti-trans legislation continues to take hold in the United States and political debates are increasingly polarized about trans issues, this coalition of actors has continued and will continue to come together. In 2023, similar coalitional configurations advocated against the most recent wave of anti-trans legislation in Texas. The coalition was not large enough to defeat the anti-trans sports bill in Texas in 2021, but perhaps, as the advocates' narratives in this chapter suggest, it is possible, the coalition will continue to expand in the future.

Notes

1 This chapter is part of a larger study of anti-trans legislation in Texas. As part of that project, I have interviewed thirty-nine advocates who organized against anti-trans legislation, including the 2017 bathroom bills and the 2021 anti-trans sports bill.
2 Trans youth themselves also testified and rallied at the Capitol. Elementary school students sometimes testified in public hearings in an attempt to directly appeal to legislators.

Chapter 8

IDENTITY WORK IN THE HUBRISTIC PRESENT

HOW GENERATIONS AS GROUPISM CREATE POLARIZATION[1]

S. L. Crawley

Judgments that are based in the protection of a singular vision of a Western feminist past, present, and future are bound to reproduce rather than challenge the amenability of Western feminist political grammar.

Hemmings (2011, p. 226)

Introduction

Copious public media in recent years points to political polarization in the United States and globally. Such debates as Brexit, the MAGA Republican/Democrat divide, putatively growing global populism, Russia's war on Ukraine and the Israeli/Palestinian conflict have controlled media headlines. Similarly, polarized debates have taken place among LGBTQ+ communities, including the so-called TERF wars (Gill-Peterson, 2022; Hines, 2020; Mackay, 2014, 2015a, Pearce, Erikainen, & Vincent, 2020) and debates over whether lesbian community and identity are diminishing in response to the proliferation of trans and queer identities (Forstie, 2018,2020; Herzog, 2020; Morris, 2016; Sullivan, 2022; Thurlow, 2024). Polarization seems pervasive.

While political polarization is typically assumed to be related to allegiance to religious or political ideologies or logic-based political agendas, more recent theories focus on 'affective polarization' – emotive-based political polarization based on dislike and opposition to social group identity (Iyengar, Sood, & Lelkes, 2012; Iyengar, Lelkes, Levendusky, Malhotra, & Westwood, 2019). In short, they argue, recent political polarization stems not from espousing opposing political agendas but simply from mistrusting perceived social out groups.

In this chapter, I theorize how the narrative production of generations as putative real groups leads to polarization among LGBTQ+ communities. I examine how the tendency toward generational 'groupism' – the analytical and activist construction of social groups (Brubaker, 2004) – coupled with affective polarization may play out within LGBTQ+ communities over time. Utilizing a constructionist/

interpretivist ontology – which I have elsewhere termed interpretive-materialism (Crawley, 2022) – can help explain how working across time will likely cause discord. Drawing on the work of GH Mead, I offer two concepts regarding time – the Present Past and the Hubristic Present. My goal is to theorize and question the production of identities themselves – noting particularly how groupism is implicit in the ever-emergent production of our pasts – and how remembering the past for everyone involves revision through what is presently known. Aligning very closely with the original queer illumination that conceiving people as identity types (members of putative real groups) necessitates trouble, I theorize how our narrations of the past will tend toward creating polarization.

Groupism, categories and polarization in everyday identity work

Quite a lot of research and politics have focused on generational polarization. Much of this putatively demographic work has relied ontologically on realism, using positivist epistemologies via collecting large datasets of attitudinal data to measure some sense of truth or concreteness of polarity. The work tends to see group membership in realist terms – actual, concrete, binary (either one or the other) – as though membership were an independent variable. (See, for example, Risman, 2018.) Despite decades of social constructionist theory, group-based, collective identity continues to be conceived as though it were constant, countable and largely unchanging. This suggests that persons must be unitary and whole – such that any one person is either in or out of the group – rather than seeing identity as multiple, fragmented, situational or emergent over time or life course. Rather than conceiving identity as an independent variable, constructionism would understand identity as negotiated outcomes of our lived experiences at particular moments as practical actors in a world of constrained possibilities (Crawley, 2022).

Much excellent constructionist work recognizes the production of sexual generations as narrative productions of reality (Ben Hagai, Annechino, & Antin, 2022; Plummer, 2010; Ryan-Flood, 2024). Even so, these works still tend to compare putative generations, as though some hint of reality persists. I wish to push constructionism yet further such that the very concept of stable generations can be called into question – even as we understand the referencing and remembering of lived experience. Schutz (1970) offers the concept of direct and indirect social experience, which helps us understand differential narrations of historical moments – how we remember moments we lived through and those we did not. Pairing Schutz with Mead, I demonstrate that our 'looking back' involves remembering the past for everyone through the present – that is, through what we know now. In this chapter, I question how everyday identity work involves remembering – that is, revisioning – the past through the present for everyone and how various direct and indirect social experiences with past moments may lead to narrating generational and – potentially polarizing – groupism.

In everyday and activist settings (and, indeed, among positivist social scientists), sexual, racial and gender identities are often referred to as representative of and as belonging to an individual – as a (realist) thing or a type. Setting up identities as types (i.e. Lesbian, Gay, Bisexual, Trans, straight, non-binary) necessarily draws boundaries (Zerubavel, 1991). Am I one of these or one of those? 'Social identity is always exclusionary, since any inclusion necessarily entails some element of exclusion as well' (Zerubavel, 1991, p. 41). Such boundary-making leads to groupism (Brubaker, 2004) – a belief in and everyday (and often scientific) deployment of the relevance of group membership as a real and largely fixed experience. Brubaker (2004) opines 'groupism' as: 'the tendency to take discrete, bounded groups as basic constituents of social life, chief protagonists of social conflicts, and fundamental units of social analysis', 'as if they were internally homogeneous, externally bounded groups, even unitary collective actors with common purposes (8)'. As Zerubavel and Brubaker note, drawing such bounded groups necessitates exclusions.

Groupism plays out in terms of the production of so-called generations, including among LGBTQ+ communities (Ben Hagai, Annechino, & Antin, 2022; Plummer, 2010; Ryan-Flood, 2024). There has been much public and academic discussion of generations – Baby Boomers, Gen X, Millennials and Gen Z – as though each of us fits neatly into one and only one. There seems to be a received wisdom that people experiencing a similar political moment do so similarly and in fixed ways – hence, by definition, at odds with other age groups. The 'culture wars' between self-identified radical feminists (pejoratively named TERFs – Trans-exclusionary radical feminists), a seemingly older generation of self-identified feminists who wish to found notions of gender and feminist activism on possession of a female body at birth (Mackay, 2015a, 2015b; Webster, 2022) and trans people who purportedly are often aligned politically with a more recent queer culture that values gender fluidity, inclusion and malleability of bodies and identities (Bettcher, 2014; Gill-Peterson, 2022; Perkins, 2022). This divide addresses those who came of political and sexual age before or after Judith Butler (1990) [following de Beauvoir (1952)] asked whether the category woman can even be said to exist. Similarly, some generational literature explores whether lesbian as an identity is disappearing (Escudero-Alías, 2022; Forstie, 2020; Morris, 2016), including a recent issue of the *Journal of Lesbian Studies* (vol 26, issue 3), asking: 'Is Lesbian Identity Obsolete?' Within LGBTQ+-identified communities, politics and identity lexicons have proliferated, often in discord. Yet, not all authors argue for the polarization of trans, feminist and lesbian identities (Escudero-Alías, 2022; Garber, 2001; Rudy, 2020). Rudy (2020, p. 354) asks readers to see a historical alignment of the 1970s notion of 'lesbian' and the present-day identity of 'queer woman', recognizing that history provides the context through which each person has a language to 'speak this recognition' of aligning with a gender identity. What should be imminently clear from this discussion is that what history is and the composition of identities within moments are imminently in motion and under debate.

To counter groupism, Brubaker (2004) encourages us to question categories and categorization, 'We can ask how people – and organizations – do things with categories' (12–13). Focusing then on practices of categorization 'allows us to treat groupness as an event, as something that "happens"' (12). Gender and sexual identities are not a feature of 'types' of individuals but, rather, comprise ongoing categorical *identity work* – negotiated relations between and among us over time – which can be normalizing or resistant (Crawley & Green, 2021). Following an interpretive materialist approach, identity is constituted by pervasive, thoroughgoing, *situational organizing practices* of meaning-making experienced through our worlds, which are always *relational and emergent* among people in institutional contexts at historical moments (Crawley, 2022). Yet, how does this help us understand polarization?

The debate over identities involves who and what counts. Martin and Lynch (2009, p. 244) demonstrate how 'counting emphasizes the relations between enumeration and classification' and point to Foucauldian and Goffmanian concerns for 'how the administration of classifications, codes, and rankings produces, orders, and controls human multiplicities and individual fates'. Prophetically, they write:

> People are often counted as objects without being aware of being counted (and, in some cases, while being deceived, or despite attempting to evade being counted), but many instances of counting involve a variable degree of collaboration between counters (persons doing the counting) and countees (persons being counted). For example, in roll calls and shows of hands, countees themselves perform or facilitate the work of counting. *Membership*, rather than personhood, is the key issue (255).

Implicit in a discussion of history and polarization, then, is: what might it mean when we make ourselves countable as specific identities – as generations? How might our own collusion with classification set in motion the political discord of identity politics?

Plummer's (1995) *Telling Sexual Stories* comprised part of the 'narrative turn' that shifted our attention from life stories as individual representations of self to communal, public narratives. That is, in constituting self, we narrate ourselves using the timelines, stocks of knowledge and common-sensical narratives that make a life story coherent (see also Linde, 1993). Life stories, then, are acts of claims-making, which involve giving accounts that have to make sense by following, to some degree, a kind of script – classically, for example, the coming out story. In my dissertation research (Crawley, 2002), at the start of each interview, *every* participant fell into the dance of telling me their coming out story and frequently requesting mine – though my research was not on coming out and I did not ask for a coming out story. I learnt that telling a coming out story was a requisite step in beginning any conversation on LGBTQ+ identity. Talk about time and experience is similarly scripted *as about generation.*

In later work, Plummer (2010) focuses on the narrative production of generational categories, recognizing how 'sexual generations' can become oppositional. [See also Spišák (2023).] Plummer (2010) points out that when lived from various moments in history, we experience different references to material culture/objects, embodiments, languages and memories – including silences. These putative generations for Plummer are based around turning-point events in history around which public narration of generations is generated. Thus, for Plummer, we should expect generational nostalgic re-creations of histories as collective generational projects – that is, as groupism. Yet, while Plummer bases this notion of the narration of sexual generations as a project of construction (including citing GH Mead), he then turns to discussions of generational comparison, capitulating to the existence of lived generations. My goal in this chapter is to invert that notion in a much more queer direction. Not only is the notion of generations a narrated production of reality (as opposed to a 'real' thing), but GH Mead (1932) helps us understand that the past itself is an emergent production – always being generated in the present. Similar to more queer orientations to time (Halberstam, 2005; Muñoz, 2009), Mead helps us question ever-present references to a linear, bounded past.

Mead, present pasts and the hubristic present

Though the narrative turn is premised on interactionism, much of which is based on the work of George Herbert Mead, Mead's theory of the present in reconstructing a past has been underutilized (Järvinen, 2004; Maines, Sugrue, & Katovich, 1983). For Mead, the past is not a thing, but rather, an emergent constitutive process or (my term) a *Present Past* – an articulation of historical moments that is necessarily viewable only through the present. For Mead (1932, p. 3), 'Cognition is reconstructive.' Hence, the past is not a singular thing to be 'accurately' remembered. Instead, Mead (1932, p. 2) introduces the notion that the past is always emergent:

> It is idle, at least for the purposes of experience, to have recourse to a 'real' past within which we are making constant discoveries; for that past must be set over against a present within which the emergent appears, and the past, which must then be looked at from the standpoint of the emergent, becomes a different past.
> . . . There is a new past, for from every new rise the landscape that stretches behind us becomes a different landscape. (9–10)

Mead's point is that nothing escapes the lens of the present – 'the present in which the emergent appears accepts that which is novel as an essential part of the universe, and from that standpoint rewrites its past' (11). Summarizing Mead, Järvinen (2001, p. 265) writes, 'The materials out of which individuals create the past lie in the present.' Maines et al. (1983, p. 163) add:

> The symbolic reconstruction of the past thus involves redefining the meaning of past events in such a way that they have meaning in and utility for the present.

... Each present, therefore, must reconstruct its past, and there are as many reconstructed and functional pasts as there are novel events.

Mead's insight about the present reordering of all pasts has implications for our production of selves as well. Järvinen (2001, pp. 266–267) notes that people tell life history narratives that weave a unified plot line. 'Life histories, then, do not speak directly of things bygone; they speak of things in progress, something that is and has been becoming.' And finally, as Maines et al. (1983, p. 164) point out, our present pasts are also mythical: 'These pasts are creations, rather than re-creations, because they are not empirically grounded. They are fictitious.'

Present Pasts also have affective components. Järvinen (2001, p. 281) notes, 'all life histories can be read, not as representations of the interviewees' actions, but as presentations of the interviewees' preferred interpretations of the actions.' That is, they are willed-for pasts. Love (2001, p. 515) articulates a tendency among stigmatized communities to see only what is perceived as positive as we recreate our pasts:

We tend to read history according to the successes of the past and to see in its failures only ideology at work. Proceeding in the mode of affirmation, we construct a genealogy that steps from stone to stone, looking for high points of pride, gender flexibility, and resistance.

Several authors have empirically recorded how people remember their pasts in ways that put them at a better advantage in the present, either aligning with present narratives or aligning with a wished-for present (Brown-Saracino, 2020; Henriksen & Järvinen, 2023; Mason-Schrock, 1996). In short, as Keeling (2019) points out, people in their everyday lives 'are motivated by a desire to look to the past for *recognizable signs that might authorize the existence of particular collective sociopolitical formations in the present*' (91, emphasis added).

The collective insights of these authors – that the past is necessarily a reproduction that can only be viewed through the lens of the present, negotiated through communal narration and negotiation, typically as an affectively, willed-for past – points to the common tendency that I refer to as the *Hubristic Present*: everyday actors and activists often motivate a modernist notion of progress, assuming that the present is the smartest, sexiest, happiest, most revolutionary, most politically astute moment. Hence, when producing our Present Pasts, not only does the present stock of knowledge necessarily change *what we can know and articulate* about a past, but the past is often seen wanting for the beauty, valor and keenness of our present knowledge. In short, there is a hubris to our present – an arrogance that we are correct *now*, that we now know better what conflicts or experiences people had at moments in the past, exercising retroactive judgement of what was or wasn't revolutionary, agentic or proper. It assumes a direct connection between the present and the past with a clear (and improved!) analytical lens lacking messiness. Those are very big assumptions. For as Love (2001) argues, prior narratives of historical events or people may not sit comfortably with present-day political narratives or wished-for utopias.

The colloquial concept of misremembering, then, is the wrong notion. *There is no accurate account of the past*. There is only the present past – indeed, there are many, many present pasts. Remembering always involves redoing the membering. Our Present Pasts are always being rearticulated through the lens of the recent – and often left wanting or made too simplistically shiny, or both simultaneously.

The paradigmatic case of reclaiming history may be Garfinkel's (1967) archetypal case of Agnes, a person with a penis who lived as a woman and who participated with a research team at UCLA during the 1960s in order to receive a sex-change operation (e.g. O'Brien, 2016; Stokoe, 2006; West & Zimmerman, 1987). More recent analyses of what took place between Garfinkel, the research team and Agnes (among other research participants) have become a site of contestation and reclamation (e.g. Rubin, 2017; Stryker & Whittle, 2006). Subsequent self-titled transgender studies scholars (e.g., Stryker & Whittle, 2006) harshly critique the research team for the mistreatment of Agnes – debating who Agnes really was, as though to claim a present-day comrade. Another recent attempt to re-frame Agnes occurred through the celebrated short and 2022 feature films titled, *Framing Agnes* (by Chase Joynt). Posing questions about identity, history, representation and power, the filmmakers performatively recreate Agnes, Garfinkel and several other people who were the objects of research for the UCLA lab at the time. They ask compelling questions about how Garfinkel's singular use of Agnes, whose subjectivity as a white, typical suburban would-be housewife was used by Garfinkel as an archetypal case, lends itself to racist and classist imaginings of gender and heteronormativity. Yet, the film itself seems to reach back and forth through history, inter-splicing between the theatrical performances of historical moments and the interview-like chats among the film's writers, producers and actors speaking about the putative truths of trans lives – as though there is a more concrete truth – constituting groupism of trans experience.

Importantly though, the lexicons of 'transgender', 'queer theory', 'intersectionality' and the concept of 'LGBT' did not exist in the 1960s when Garfinkel was interviewing Agnes. In the introductory issue of *Transgender Studies Quarterly* claiming the position as 'the journal of record' for transgender studies, Stryker and Currah (2014, p. 1) point to Sandy Stone's 1991 essay, 'The Posttranssexual Manifesto', as the foundational moment for trans studies. Queer theory did not emerge until the early 1990s (Jagose, 1996) and the term intersectionality is commonly attributed to Kimberle Crenshaw's (1991) essay 'Mapping the Margins'. Though clearly developing over a long period of time, these theoretical concepts as they are named and understood now were not available to Agnes or Garfinkel at the time that they spoke. Similarly, people who articulate a life different than their sex assigned at birth have been recorded at many points in history (Feinberg, 1996), yet the lexicons for gender have changed markedly – and lexicons matter. The Agnes we often articulate today through our current lexicons is not the Agnes that Garfinkel spoke with. Agnes today is a creation of our own making – our own present past. As such, these works are *re-claiming Agnes* – remaking Agnes in the present-day through the lens of current theories and activist tools. Similar to Halperin's (1993) queer historicity of sexuality asking:

were the ancient Greeks 'gay'? the answer must be no. 'Gay' is a twentieth-century subjectivity. Agnes could not have been 'transgender'. In the 1960s, the concept of transgender and the entire queer theoretical oeuvre and pursuant lexicons did not exist, yet today these concepts have been so pervasive and important that *there is no un-queering*. Present-day scholars and activists imputing how Agnes must have felt – that her experience must have been like theirs in defense of trans experience and scholarship – renders intelligible only what can be accountable now. The reclaiming of Agnes is a hubristic, present-day reality production – not a truth of the past.

Thus, discursive, affective and experiential emergence is probable in reclaiming a past. These kinds of categorical rememberings (such as in Joynt's film) are set up at odds with pasts – implicitly claiming themselves to be more omniscient and perhaps more caring than members of the past. Differing lived experiences as well as ongoing narrations of a willed-for past will implicitly put some at odds with various perceived pasts – potentially causing polarization. Our life stories, even our sexual life stories, are narrated as generational, often in wilfully concrete terms. Yet, what is more likely is that we each have different timeframes of experiential reference which will necessarily cause conflicting views of the present and the past.

Temporality and changing lexicons

The lexicons used to describe gender and same-sex sexuality have changed over time. Lexicons matter in articulations of history. Scholarly paradigms shift how we know ourselves and how we know our pasts. Our Present Pasts reorganize how we understand what we think transpired in the past.

In Figure 8.1, I illustrate how looking backwards presently over historically changing gender and sexuality lexicons necessitates articulating a present past – but one which is relative to anyone's direct experience of history or what I call the timeframe of reference. In the lower part of Figure 8.1, the original 'Timeline of Recent (US) Feminist/"Queer" Lexicon' (a similar figure originally published in Crawley & Green, 2021) demonstrates how the lexicon available to describe gender and/or sexuality has changed markedly over time, especially with reference to changing academic schools of thought. Terms emerge as self-references, epithets and/or markers of collective identity. 'Thought bubbles' place academic ideas chronologically in relation to (US) identities taken up in everyday usage over about 70 years. The timeline demonstrates the inextricable links between genders, sexualities and bodies (wherein the terms above the timeline are related to gender, the terms below it are related to sexuality or bodies, and the italicized terms emerge from racial minority communities). This timeline shows waves, recessions and sometimes recursions of identities in moments. Each academic school of thought (displayed above in the cloud icons) offered an important paradigm shift, alongside a changing public lexicon of identities to show: (1) that the everyday lexicon of gender and sexual identities has shifted and expanded greatly over time, (2) that various lexicons are implicitly racialized, historicized and spacialized and

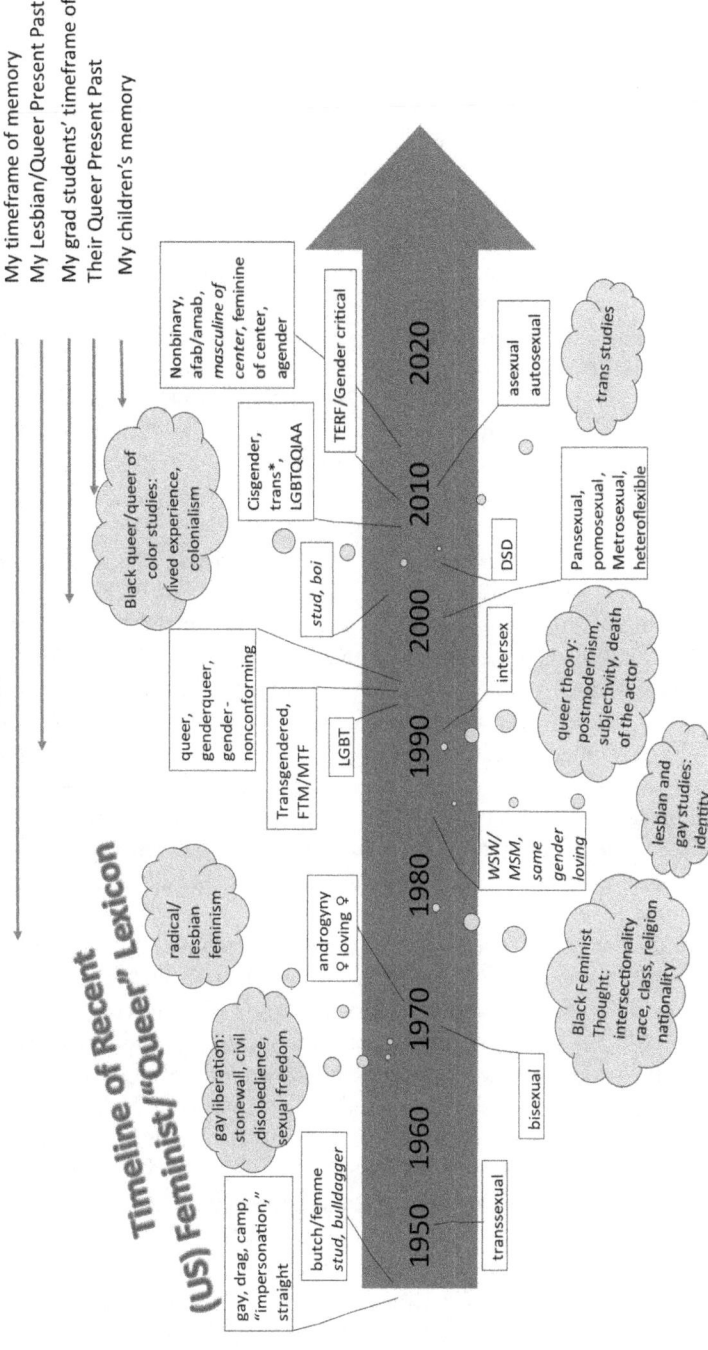

Figure 8.1: Timeframe of reference on the timeline of (US) feminist/queer lexicon. *Source:* (Adapted from Crawley & Green, 2021.)

(3) that in many ways public lexicons respond to academic schools of thought. Gay liberation, radical feminisms, Black feminist thought, gay and lesbian studies, queer theory, Black queer studies and trans studies each emerged with an intent for a paradigm shift, which seems to have played out to some extent with consequences to the public lexicon of available identities. Importantly, paradigm shifts across schools of thought invoke discord.

The history of activist lexicons and academic theorizing can be told chronologically, as is the case in the lower part of Figure 8.1. Early feminist responses to queer theory argued that it had a tendency to be too playfully glib about performance and power while ignoring material inequalities, lived experience and the body (Connell, 2012; Fonow & Cook, 2005; Gannon & Davies, 2012; Hawkesworth, 1997; Martin, 1994; Smith, 1999; Walters, 1996). Grounded in women of color feminisms such as Hill Collins's (1990) or Moraga and Anzaldua's (1981), Black queer studies critique queer studies for having ignored materiality, including intersectionality and embodied racial experience (Cohen, 2005; Ferguson, 2004; Johnson, 2005; Muñoz, 1999).Subsequent authors have taken up race explicitly in response to such critiques (Ahmed, 2012; Patil, 2022). Importantly, this lexicon and the timeline I have drawn are US-based. It is vital to recognize that the experience of time and history is also necessarily related to place and space, such that US articulations of gender, sexualities and race are implicitly Westernized (Patil, 2022; Spivak, 1988). For example, Mizielińska (2011) points out that the political context in Poland – the fall of Stalinist communism and transition to a more Westernized liberal democracy from 1989 to 1991 – coincided with the advent of queer theory, skipping the lesbian and gay identity politics era that happened in the 1980s in the United States. Hence, present-day sexual and gender subjectivities in Poland – quite unlike in the United States, according to Mizielińska – were conceived as queer, not through LGBT identity politics, from the initial reengagement with international communities post-communism. See also Kao's (2021, p. 1) critique of how falsely assumed universalism of queer theory in Taiwan 'produces "radical queer temporality" and Orientalist double standards that collude with imperialist epistemology'.

Yet, we do not experience history chronologically but recursively as we look back from the present – our present past. Further, given the historical moments in which we 'came of age', came out, experienced various identities and so on, each of us has a different *timeframe of reference* for the first-person, lived experience of our present pasts – as represented by the backward-facing arrows in the upper right part of the figure. Our own direct and indirect experience of historical moments will affect how we know a present past. For example, my older child recently told me that Ellen DeGeneres is an 'asshole'. Somewhat surprised and a bit defensive, I replied, 'Ellen DeGeneres was one of the first people to come out on national TV. It was pretty brave and she took a lot of shit for that. Do you even know who Ellen is?' To which they replied, 'Yeah, of course. I know who Ellen is. She used to have a good game show but now she's an "asshole".' Leaving open the question of Ellen's ethics and morality, it is clear that my kid's timeframe of reference is much shorter than mine. A graduate student recently reminded me of the experience of those who know Ellen primarily as the animated, forgetful fish. Theorizing intersubjectivity (how we know an Other), Schutz (1970, p. 219) lays out how we can know something which we have not directly experienced, typically through the experience of others. Naming one's own understanding of experiences of others as 'they-orientations', Schutz writes:

> The object of my They-orientation is my own experience of social reality in general, of human beings and their conscious processes as such, in abstraction from any individual setting in which they may occur. My knowledge of my contemporaries is, therefore, inferential and discursive. . . . They are treated as typical conscious experiences of 'someone' and, as such, as basically homogeneous and repeatable. (1970, p. 225)

In short, I can 'know' the experiences of others only through typified discursive narrations – which, as we will see, are not accurate so much as constantly mobile and under revision. In the top right section of Figure 8.1, I demonstrate how the timeframe of reference will necessarily cause uneven articulations of histories. My very first memory of time is of a moment in 1971 – the first year that I understood what a year was. My lesbian/queer present past begins around 1990. My graduate students were either quite young or yet to be born at that time. Hence, their (collective)[2] timeframe of reference is much shorter and necessarily indirectly reconstructive (if at all) of the moments through which I lived and they did not. I regularly hear younger people citing events while completely swapping entire decades as though the 1980s were ancient history. (One undergraduate in the mid-2000s argued that AFI – the punk rock band with the hit song 'Miss Murder' in 2006 – was the first gender non-conforming pop band. Are you kidding me??? David Bowie? A Flock of Seagulls? Boy George?)

My point is not to re-articulate a notion of bounded generations but rather that first-person experiential knowledge of historical moments, as opposed to indirect re-articulations of a past in some other moment which one did not experience, will necessarily affect how we each know a present and, hence, our present pasts. Tactile, lived experience must necessarily be different in character than narrations of pasts we did not experience. My timeframe of reference for my present past is necessarily longer than my grad students' and much longer than my children's. Still, one cannot say that my Present Past (of direct experience) is more 'accurate'. My present past too is reconstructive – of lived experience (Plummer, 2010), as well as through reading and hearing subsequent re-accounts of past moments. All of us are reconstructing a present past through what we now know. My notion of early 1990s lesbian bars will necessarily be contextually different from my students' notion of lesbian bars, yet neither of us can now avoid reconstructing these present pasts through 'queer' and 'non-binary' concepts that are available today.

Further, we must also recognize that *the world and how we communicate have changed* over time (Adams-Santos, 2024; Crawley & Green, 2024). With the advent of the internet, smartphones, social media and virtual communication apps, digital access to the lived world has changed. Among the changes are digital divides from the timeframe of reference (Spišák, 2023) as well as debates about identities playing out in virtual spaces (Chanady, 2022; Crawley & Green, 2024; Webster, 2022). It is not simply that the way people communicate has changed, but how we can know our present pasts is now virtually mediated. We often remember online.

Ongoing narrations of political generations seem to actively be reconstructed as differing political alliances. (See, for example, Mackay, 2014, 2019.) Ben Hagai et al. (2022, p. 216) found: 'participants across generations articulated their sexual identities strategically to express not only a sexual orientation but more importantly political and community alliances.' Their interview work, which divided respondents into classic generations of baby boomers and millennials – effectively separating the pre-queer theory coming of age from the post-queer theory coming of age generations – found: 'For Baby Boomer lesbians, lesbian identity connoted an alliance with feminism, and for Millennials their sexual identity indicated a political alliance with queer and trans* movements (216).' Hence, scholarly paradigm shifts matter with regard to the present-day creation of putative political generations. As Maines et al. (1983, p. 165) note: 'If a past is created which believably "fits" with other pasts, presents and futures, and is acted upon as such, it is real.' Hence, everyday actors often accomplish groupism – the belief in specific political generations – and do so at odds with other putative generations.

Conclusion: Hubristic accounts, life history-telling and polarization

What does this turn to time help us know and what are the implications for polarization? First, *we reconstruct our pasts hubristically to put ourselves in the best light*. Affective polarization in our digital social media-soaked hubristic present would seem only increasingly likely to encourage the taking up of identities through uneven referencing of experience and mythical nostalgic rememberings such that people across age and experience will come into conflict (Iyengar et al., 2012, 2019). Järvinen (2001, p. 267) presciently writes, 'Accounts are born out of the distinctly human capacity to be blamed, charged, and held responsible. . . . Accounts presuppose that individuals socially negotiate the meaning of events and can change them by reconfiguring their underlying meaning.' There are implications for articulating pasts but also implications for producing our willed-for selves.

> Accounts involve not only a presentation of an action but also a presentation of the accounter's self. When we justify and excuse our actions, we simultaneously try to recast ourselves as sensible and proper human beings. The accounter's primary search seems to be for situational definitions that will blunt the effects of anticipated censure from others (and/or self), thereby reintegrating the self into the moral order of the community. (Järvinen, 2001, p. 267–268)

Given the soapbox moment of indignant Twitter wars, DIY TikTok reels, self-righteous influencers, self-curated news via podcasts and social media echo chambers, the stakes and tactics of expressing oneself in a hubristic present past seems ripe for conflict.

Second, *social movement organizing seemingly longs for collectivity as groupism* – the making of each of us into identity types. Groupism is pervasive in the high-stakes common practice of virtual world-making, all the while through historically morphing lexicons for storying identity. Importantly, implicit in making our identities intelligible, we are also making ourselves countable. Assessing the Western proclivity for counting in and through science itself, Martin and Lynch (2009, p. 261) recognize what it means to be answerable to the exigencies of the imperative to count: 'Substantive qualities of the things did not simply precede and constrain the work of counting them; instead, those qualities were themselves assembled by and assimilated within the work of counting.' Naming identities makes us countable – accountable, intelligible. As Foucault and Goffman pointed out, becoming recognizable as an identity and being counted as such involves classification (Martin & Lynch, 2009, p. 245). To be a member is to be classified and categorized – to be made into a type. Aligning with group membership – being countable/intelligible – is a seemingly requisite step in social movement organizing. There are quite a number of good political reasons to be countable. Conceptually, measurement of inequalities requires counting in order to demonstrate scales of disparity. Yet, is there always utility and unity of bounded identity in our everyday lives? Need we imagine that being born about the same time necessitates a similar experience?

Third, *though gender categories have proliferated, we still use them categorically*. Gender specificity of womanhood seemed implicit in feminist organizing until Butler asked their famous and troubling question, which, in part, led to new queer possibilities. Queer theory originally intended to counter the notion of fixed identities, favoring anti-essentialism and anti-normativity that refuse rules, science and counting itself. Still, 'queer' has subsequently emerged as a political subjectivity, albeit one that hopes to be unintelligible and uncountable. Yet, queer as the un-category has famously grappled with the question of how to organize around no social identity (Gamson, 1995). Some scholars have argued for the move toward multiplicity and indeterminacy in mixing gender non-specific identities with sexually or body-specific identities such as 'non-binary lesbian' (Hord, 2022) or 'trans dyke' (Helton, 2022). Maybe the virtual, less geographically and temporally fixed moment will result in somewhat less bounded identity categories. Nonetheless, empirical social scientists continue coming up with more particularized ways to count the proliferation of identity categories (Westbrook & Saperstein, 2015).

In any case, lifestory-telling is ubiquitous and necessary for political movements and self-making alike. Hemmings (2011) argues for the importance of telling stories of our histories differently:

there are particular costs to a presumption of shared agreement about the proper subject of the Western feminist present because it produces a common history that she is presumed to inherit.... that history is marked by oppositions between materiality and culture, politics and theory, and good and bad feminist subjects, and relies particularly on a separation between poststructuralism and feminism, whether positively or negatively inflected. Such oppositions produce a history of feminist theory caught into decades and pit racial and sexual meanings and identities against one another. (193)

Hemmings' point is that there is a surprising tendency to tell the story of feminisms as a story of a unified feminism centered on one idea, one subjectivity that is putatively Western (and presumably White?). Not only is this ahistorical, it also lends itself to misappropriation. As Hemmings suggests, we might do well to pay more attention to multiplicities within and around historical moments, their conflicts and disruptures, rather than seek a correct or putatively accurate history.

Finally, *in our rememberings, we each might take greater care to reflect affectively on how we remember if we wish to work toward reducing polarization.* Love (2001, p. 515) warns us against focusing on the positive while disavowing loss and pain, suggesting that political change can also arise from its recognition: 'it is through such shaming acts of identification that we come to terms with the difficulty of queer history and its legacy in the present.... Celebration gets us only so far, for pride itself can be toxic when it is sealed off from the shame that has nurtured it.' Remembering the pain, joy and legacy of each moment will be uneven, inaccurate and mired in the referential difference of time and experience. If we wish to reduce polarizations across our diverse temporal experiences and begin to attend to our own affective impulses to willed-for pasts, perhaps we can share our present pasts with greater empathy, respect and generosity, and less hubris if indeed the goal is to produce the most mythic grouping of all – community.

Notes

1 I would like to thank Kath Browne and Emily Kazyak for the opportunity to enjoy a very generative trip to Dublin through their grant, which made this paper possible. I also thank the wonderful collective in Dublin whose work inspires me, especially Jody Moore-Ponce for helping to name the hubristic present, a concept that I have been mulling over for a while.
2 In order to avoid singling out any one person, I speak in terms of my 'collective' graduate students as an amalgam, not as a representation of one person's experience, but as a recognition that they are comparatively younger than me.

Chapter 9

'GENDER DEBATE' DISCOURSE

POLARISING, BIGOTED AND VALIDATING[1]

Elizabeth Peel

Introduction

Feminist psychotherapist Susie Orbach (2023) recently claimed that 'Twitter is a marketplace of hate.' This polemic comment certainly contains a seed of truth. In the so-called culture wars around the underpinning ideological edifices of sex/gender in contemporary British culture, media in general and social media in particular, are implicated in multifarious ways. In this chapter, I draw on two aspects of the *Future of Legal Gender* (FLAG) project which ran from May 2018 to May 2022 (see further Cooper et al., 2020; Cooper et al., 2022, 2023; Cooper & Renz, 2023). Firstly, and substantively, I focus on how FLAG project participants constructed the influence of the media on their perceptions of gender. Second, I explore how the project was received on social media and, as such, situate the research within the wider landscape of 'gender wars'. Taken together, these two lenses contribute to our understanding of the salience of discourse and the place of media in constructing divisions in sexual and gendered lives and landscapes. I conclude by offering some thoughts on how we might heal some divisions and envision a more conducive environment for articulating divergent perspectives.

As Nash and Browne (2020, p. 115) note, '[t]ransgressions of normative gender identity and expression have long been a concern of heteroactivists.' These concerns have also been vociferously articulated by 'gender-critical feminists' – some of whom hold minoritised sexual identities – in recent years (Peel & Newman, 2020; Browne, 2020). These fault-lines and (potentially) new alliances create unsettling terrain for feminist researchers exploring progressive questions, such as what would happen to conceptual understandings of gender if legal sex weren't a concern of the State. We found in our FLAG 'Attitudes to Gender' survey that was conducted in the autumn of 2018, that biological essentialist arguments for retaining a binary sex classification of female and male in law were dominant (Peel & Newman, 2020). The impassioned investment in the status quo from (predominantly) women who identify as feminist speak to new polarisations and, as Browne (2020, p. 3) rightly acknowledged, the experience we discussed in Peel and Newman (2020) highlights 'what had become somewhat accepted in gender and feminist academic circles regarding the performativity of sex/gender binaries and the constitution of sex and gender since the 1990s, is increasingly and overtly contested.' Some of this contestation, as I discuss in the second part of this chapter, is conducted through the medium of social media.

In the first empirical part of this chapter,[2] I focus on how the media is constructed in UK participants' (n = 2550) responses to the FLAG project survey question, 'Have your views on gender changed as a result of recent media coverage on gender and transgender issues?' Although participants were equally split on whether the media had influenced their views ('yes' 50.04 per cent, n = 1276; 'no' 49.96 per cent, n = 1274), most (56.67 per cent, n = 1445) provided qualitative information to explain their response. It is this qualitative material that forms the basis of my analysis using a discursive thematic approach (e.g. Peel & Newman, 2023). These additional qualitative comments amounted to 100 pages, or 60,000 words of data. In these qualitative comments, there were over 300 instances of various permutations of being aware or awareness (e.g. 'just more aware'), and these were judged to be too generic to be included analytically. My thematic analysis (Braun & Clarke, 2022) focuses on three main constructions of the media's role in UK 'gender debates'. These constructions are that the media is (a) polarising, (b) bigoted against trans people and (c) validating of trans, non-binary and/or gender-diverse experiences.[3]

Both/and discourse

Polarised thinking, argumentation and discourse could be claimed to be ubiquitous. Certainly, philosophical ideas of thesis versus antithesis leading to synthesis are encountered in numerous disciplines. It does seem, though, that in the UK and many other cultural contexts, we're living in a time where progressivity cannot be in any sense guaranteed through dialectical movement or anything else. Feminists such as Davina Cooper (2019, 2022) have both acknowledged the binary nature of the current sex/gender 'drama' and also carefully attempted to move beyond particular practices becoming seen as 'shorthand' for a particular stance on pro/anti-trans issues. For instance, Cooper's (2022) blog post on the significance of presenting or not presenting gender pronouns is a well-rounded exploration of the topic. Other feminists too have explicitly articulated seeing the 'gender debate' from 'both' sides. For example, Finn Mackay (2021, p. 114) remarked that

> like many GC[4] activists and queer activists, I believe gender is indeed a social construction [. . .] CG activists argue only sex matters, as in the sex we were recorded at birth. I agree that sex matters; it affects our life trajectory and places us into one of two hierarchical sex classes [. . .] However, I disagree that gender identity is irrelevant. Gender too shapes how we understand and experience our bodies.

In their different ways, Cooper and Mackay, and many other academics, activists and feminists wish to engage in 'both/and' thinking, holding two potentially opposing positions in mutuality.

If binary discourse is considered rigid and certain, though perhaps simplistic, then a 'both/and' stance allows – at least theoretically – for more fluidity, and arguably could become an antidote to polarisation or extremism. In Pauline Boss' (2022) recent exploration of ambiguous loss in the pandemic times, she usefully draws our attention to the importance of *both/and thinking* encapsulated in the fact that 'it was both a terrible time and a time of growth; it was both a time of loss and a time of gaining new insight' (p. 67). And in the accessible *Life Isn't Binary*, Meg-John Barker and Alex Iantaffi (2019, p. 15) 'take bisexual and non-binary gender experiences as starting points for an exploration of the whole idea of being between or beyond binaries in several key aspects of our lives'. As well as posing questions which encourage non-binary thinking, such as 'are both "sides" of this debate equally valid, for example according to the research evidence in this area?' (p. 189) or whether both poles have equal power, they embed reflection tasks and stress actively slowing down as a reader to pause, feel and think into the text. This reflexive approach sits in stark contrast to the apparatus of social media platforms such as Twitter – fast, short, (often) unnuanced posts scrolled through at speed. Reflexive engagement on the one hand; impulsive engagement on the other.

Barker and Iantaffi's (2019, pp. 189–190) gloss[5] on the British 'trans debate' is a trans-exclusionary feminist versus trans feminist binary which, I agree, does 'fit into a much older media pattern of pitching different feminists against each other in "cat fights" which delegitimizes feminism as a whole [. . .] and away from the broader – essential – fight to dismantle patriarchy'. Nevertheless, it is important to scrutinise the detail and the contours of media 'debates' (see also Knott-Fayle et al., 2021, 2022). Or, in the case of the current chapter, consider themes in how the media is positioned and tease out both/and discourse from – and alongside – binarising representations of *LGBTQI+* lives and intersections with feminisms.

Polarising media

In the theme of polarising media, typically those who either implicitly or explicitly held 'gender-critical' positions about gender would be in agreement that the media had changed their views. Indeed, claiming, as we will see below in some instances, that they had been radicalised by media consumption. Conversely, those who were trans inclusive tended not to ascribe power to the media in influencing their perspective. Some, while not being influenced personally, ascribed polarising power to the media in general. For instance,

> [a] lot of the media coverage has been so polarizing as to be unhelpful and has pushed a lot of people who probably wouldn't be all that bothered, to taking one side or the other. (no – F, 36, bisexual/pansexual)[6]

Media, in this example, has 'pushed' those who otherwise would not be 'bothered' into taking sides. And although in this instance the respondent is neutral about which 'side' people might take, there were many instances of respondents in this theme explicitly arguing that they had been radicalised to become 'gender-critical feminists' by their exposure to media, for instance: 'I have been radicalized in my gender critical views by transgender activists abusing and silencing women' (yes – F, 45, lesbian) in the media. The emotionality of the changing connotations of social media identities, on Twitter specifically, is highlighted in the respondent quote below:

> I'm just more scared and sad than I was. I share the goal of abolition of gender with radical feminists, and I remember them being my allies in this – I used to have 'radfem' in my twitter handle! – but now if I see someone describe themself as a 'radfem' I'm immediately on guard, scared that they will be spreading lies that hurt all trans people and especially trans women, under the guise of 'women just have Concerns'. (no – No gender, 32, bisexual/pansexual/queer)

Sadness and fear are ascribed as being generated by radical feminist ('radfem') being appropriated on Twitter by anti-trans feminists 'spreading lies'. The minimising 'just' at the start of this example belies what has not only been a profound shift in politics attached to the person's 'handle' but also a sense of pervasive interpersonal threat from the identity politics on this particular platform – conveyed through the phrase 'immediately on guard'. By contrast, for both lesbian and heterosexual feminists, media was deemed as 'increasing alarm' about the 'rights of the female sex class', or to be 'thanked' for enabling (implied) anti-trans views, as encapsulated in the example below:

> An increasing alarm and determination that personal gender choices must not be allowed to negatively impact on the rights of the female sex class to define themselves or have the right to privacy, dignity and safety in situations of personal vulnerability (yes – F, 45, lesbian).

> Thanks to coverage over the past couple of years, I have given this subject *much* more consideration and this has therefore solidified my belief that *gender identity* is a load of old cobblers (yes – F, 44, heterosexual).

As well as polarisation within feminist communities, 'them and us' groupings across majority/minority lines were attributed to media representation. For instance:

> I feel that the focus in recent years is starting to be a bit gimmicky. The important issues for the LGBTQ+ communities are being trivialized and I think the population is getting fatigued by the gender debate in general. The issues are not being handled properly in the media to include those that identify as male and female, but only focus on the LGBTQ+ groups. The focus is only on the

differences and not on what makes us the same. Therefore there is becoming a 'them and us' culture (yes – F, 32, straight).

For this respondent, the focus on 'differences' is becoming divisive. They contrast the ploys of the media in 'the gender debate' with trivialising issues for *both* LGBTQ+ and 'male and female' communities, though in so doing, they make a heteronormative claim that the binary gender norm is being marginalised.[7]

As mentioned above, polarisation is associated with extremism, and there were many examples in these data of claims of radicalisation from those at the 'gender-critical feminist' pole. Commonly, as in the two examples below, there was a contrast made to 'before' media exposure to 'trans activists' or TRA,[8] which entailed either a laissez-faire attitude or little thought about 'sex/gender issues'.[9]

> As someone who had not given biological sex/gender issues much thought before and could hardly spell the word misogyny, I have been shocked at the frightening degree of misogyny as well as racism and homophobia (specifically lesbophobia) and ableism by trans activists. It has completely radicalized me and so many other women I know. (yes – F, 47, heterosexual)

> Before recent media coverage I generally thought 'live and let live' and didn't care much that other people continued to believe in gender as a real thing. Recently I have realized how much this matters, because the TRA campaign seeks to prevent women from being able to name themselves as a class, and without a word that can describe us, it is impossible to monitor any improvements or deteriorations in sexual discrimination in society. Lesbians are also being erased as a class, with some TRAs claiming that it is transphobic to have a sexuality that excludes the male body. This makes 'live and let live' impossible. (yes – F, 43, lesbian)

We can see that in the rhetorical construction of both these examples, extremism is built into the contrast, as well as the attitudinal outcome, namely '*completely radicalized*' and 'live and let live' *impossible*. There were many more examples of extremist claims against 'trans activists', which, likely in part due to the anonymity of the survey method of data collection, made noxious references to trans and gender-diverse people and allies being 'sex offenders' and trans young people being 'transed'.[10] The example below is especially offensive given the Nazi SS physician who conducted inhumane and often lethal experiments on Auschwitz prisoners of war is invoked.

> I now think anyone who uses the word gender when they mean sex is a sex offender as ONLY sex offenders benefit from self ID so I now assume all those pushing it ARE sex offenders. I also now realize transing children is flat out eugenics and supporters of the trans cult are modern day Dr Josef Mengeles [*sic*]. (yes – F, 25, heterosexual)

Another aspect of the polarising theme was responses to the question of whether the media had changed views on gender and transgender issues, invoking the facticity of claims. As the two examples below demonstrate, 'pseudo science' and 'misinformation' and 'learn[ing]' versus public ignorance are contrasted with the destruction of 'classic gender roles' and explicit reference to sexed bodies (mutilation and penises):

I'm concerned that people claiming to be progressive and working in the public interest are using pseudoscience to destroy classic gender roles and causing confusion among our youth to such an extent that they will be more inclined to mutilate their bodies irreversibly as a result of misinformation. (yes – M, 32, heterosexual)

> As I have learned more I have become more gender critical. In particular I have learned that transgender and transsexual are not synonyms. The public do not seem to realize that a large percentage (86% IIRC[11]) of transmen [sic] retain their penis. (yes – F, 60, heterosexual)

Interestingly, these two examples deploy factual and scientific evidence in different ways, which is common in polarised discourse (e.g., Clarke, 2000). The first respondent labels the current evidence base around gender diversity as 'pseudoscience'. The second deploys a 'fact' that is specific enough to suggest plausibility but inaccurately attributes this to the wrong category of trans person, which endogenously undermines its accuracy. Although less common in the FLAG survey data, there were instances where respondents discussed the media influencing them towards the trans-positive pole, as the two examples below illustrate:

> This year's GRA consultation and the 'feminist' campaigning against it has made me more actively involved in supporting trans people – the increase in transphobia from left/feminists is very concerning, and coincides with the increase in overtly anti-trans right wing politics. (yes – F, 62, queer)

> I'm more determined than ever to speak up, transgender issues in the media are constantly misrepresented & lied about in an attempt to push back trans rights either by a rising right wing or as a distraction to brexit, this is a coordinated well funded attack. (yes – F, 38, lesbian)

Interestingly, both these responses link their more 'active' and 'determined' support for trans people to wider party politics. The first observes a 'very concerning' and growing alignment of some left-wing feminists and explicitly anti-trans right-wing politics. The second directly implicates the media in being driven by 'rising right-wing' agendas. Implicit in this response is trans people being used as a scapegoat by the media, which ties into the second theme of the media being bigoted against trans people. Before discussing this second theme, another form of rupture or new polarisation was evident in some responses, namely division in previously understood 'natural' ideological alignment between marginalised groups:

I've thought about it a lot more, and become more committed to challenging the transphobia that has been shown in recent coverage. My assumptions that cis women would 'naturally' show solidarity with trans people as another group affected by gender stereotypes and prejudice have been challenged. It hasn't affected my understanding of my own gender, but has made me reflect on experiences I had as a child in wanting to express my gender in ways which were not traditionally feminine. (yes – F, 40, lesbian)

Discussion of this new polarisation feels very different from the earlier comment, also from a lesbian in their 40s, that lesbians are being 'erased'. Rather, this respondent has been prompted to 'reflect' on their experience. And others had been prompted to become '[f]ar more aware of the importance of using my cis privilege to challenge transphobia' (yes – F, 44, bisexual). Transphobia in and through the media was the second most common theme in these data.

Media is bigoted against trans people

There were many responses which, although typically not agreeing that the media had changed their views, placed the media in a powerful position in terms of scaremongering, generating hate and attacking trans people. For instance, '[m]edia coverage has been mainly vile and one-sided. Living in the UK right now is not a good place to be as we're targeted and vilified. Hate is at its peak right now' (no – Transwoman, 50, lesbian). The emotional impact of being 'targeted' and denigrated is clear from this response which, interestingly, perhaps alludes to the #peaktrans through naming the divergent perspective of peak hate. The sense of media bigotry and attack is evident in responses such as '[a]ll I've learned is a lot of people don't like us. It feels like the media is out to get trans people' (no – Agender 30, asexual), '[a]s a trans person it isn't news to me (though the backlash and misinformation has been unpleasant to watch)' (no – trans male, 37, asexual), and '[g]reater awareness of the challenges and prejudice faced by trans people as they have been attacked repeatedly in the media' (yes – M, 41, bisexual).

Some responses explicitly labelled the media as transphobic, for example, '[r]ecent coverage is basic or worse, transphobic TERF nonsense' (no – Genderqueer, 22, queer) or '[m]edia coverage has been in general transphobic and sensationalized' (no – F, 63, bisexual) or '[t]he coverage is so uniformly mendacious and unenlightening that it's only contributed to my views on the standards of media organizations. It's clear that nobody's worried about libel when the victim is trans' (no – F, 39, lesbian). Moreover, trauma, anxiety and 'terror' were also evident in more detailed responses to the question, such as the three examples below:

The recent media coverage of the GRA consultation was traumatic. It didn't make me change my views but it did make me considerably more anxious about the inexplicable and vitriolic transphobia directed primarily at trans women but all trans people generally. (no – NB, 38, queer)

The recent media has made me feel incredibly concerned that I will again be on the receiving end of transphobia. I worry that some I work with may share the views I see online (I have no evidence to suggest any of them feel this way). I am frustrated, hurt and angry and the passion with which these people shout their misinformation and bigotry means I would only waste my time trying to reassure them that we're not monsters. People like dirtywhiteboi, Clare Dimyon, websites like http://transcrimeuk.com are just the tip of a very ugly iceberg which calls for genital checks, using scaremongering and misinformation as justification. Frankly, it's terrifying. (no – Male, 33, straight)

I'm appalled and gutted by the media coverage. Although I am cis, I feel devastated by the level of transphobic vitriol and the dedication of anti-trans groups. I can only imagine what it's like living in this world as a trans person when people are calling for you to stop existing. My partner is trans as are many of my friends and I am really aware of the toll this has had on their wellbeing and mental health. Last night I had to collect my partner who was having a panic attack after reading the website of Fair Play for Women. All that has changed is my deepening commitment to push trans rights further, and realizing how hateful and misinformed most of the public is. (no – F, 27, bisexual/queer)

There are a number of interesting aspects of these responses to highlight regarding both the impact of transphobia and the potential interpersonal impact of polarising discourse. First, phrases such as 'misinformation and bigotry', 'scaremongering and misinformation', and 'hateful and misinformed' are used in two of these examples. There is some similarity here with language used in the polarising theme from the anti-trans side also claiming use of 'misinformation' and pseudoscience. Second, the 'inexplicable' transphobia of the first extract is in stark contrast with the 'justified' attack on gender-diverse and trans people implied in the polarising theme. Third, the implications of media representation on people's mental health and well-being are foregrounded. In the first example, the impact is 'considerably more anxious', and in the third example, this is conveyed perhaps more persuasively through the third-party account of a cisgender person with a transgender partner. The proximity of the negative impact (i.e. a panic attack last night prompted by a named sex-based rights organisation's website) also works to convey the depth and real human impact of the media. Similarly, the online transphobia translated to offline and workplace transphobia concerns articulated in the second example illustrate the profundity of the impact of 'recent media'.

Finally, there are aspects of these examples that signal perceptions of intergroup relations being irretrievably damaged. In the third example, 'most' of the public is positioned as transphobic rather than a minority.[12] In the second example, extremist and fundamentalist beliefs are implied through the perceived inability of education or positive intergroup contact to have any impact – 'I would only waste my time trying to reassure them that we're not monsters.' There is a futility in interacting across differences here, which is very different from efforts from LGBTQI+ members to educate and reduce prejudice from majority group members (e.g. Peel, 2005). Other responses in this theme focus on the wider or individual impact of 'bigoted coverage', for example, the two responses below:

> A bunch of transphobic people spouting lies in every news outlet every day while screaming they are being no platformed and silenced is a pretty obvious attempt at removing equal rights. It's sad. (no – F, 49, lesbian)

> All the recent bigoted coverage has done is make me feel more protective of my trans friends and acquaintances and more able to empathize with their pain. (no – F, 33, straight)

In the first example, the erosion of 'equal rights' is deemed the aim of 'transphobic people'. This respondent conveys this in a rhetorically compelling way, using extreme contrasts between the volume and scope of coverage ('every news outlet every day') and the extremity of the supposed exclusion ('screaming they are being no platformed and silenced'). In this second, and final, example in this theme, individual feelings of protectiveness and empathy are foregrounded. The final, and contrastive, theme in these survey responses was that, rather than bigoted, media coverage conversely functions to validate non-binary and gender-diverse identities and experiences.

Media validates trans, non-binary and/or gender-diverse experiences

Though the smallest of the themes in these data, the positive impact recent media has had on enhancing the public visibility of LGBTIQ+ communities in general, and trans, non-binary and gender-diverse people in particular, was salient for both majority and minority group respondents. For instance, in the two examples below, 'interest' and 'delight' are expressed by straight respondents due to heightened 'awareness' and increased visibility of LGBTQIA+ communities.

> Before social media, people from the LGBTQIA+ community were invisible to me, I didn't know anything about them or their struggles within our society. I am very interested by this topic actually and I think that our obsession with genders is just a way of limiting our freedom. Society wants us to behave a certain way, and I believe that imposing genders is a way of creating predictable behaviors and controlling us better. It controls the way we feel in society and what we are supposed to want. (yes – F, 25, straight)

> becoming more aware of how other people identify, becoming aware of some people not having a gender or being gender fluid – delighted this is becoming more in the public eye and people are more able to be themselves. (yes – F, 52, straight)

In this first example, the placement of 'actually' implies that as a cisgender, and perhaps previously cisnormative and heteronormative woman, she was unaware of the negative implications of gender norms and conventions. There is an 'eyes-opened' flavour to this response and perhaps a resistance to 'control', which has been seeded by media exposure to sexual and gender-diverse people and our lives. The second example also speaks to a sense of liberation, but more from the perspective of others 'more able to be themselves'. This liberal humanist interpretation of the media sits in stark contrast to the tone and tenor of the previous theme. The antithesis of bigoted media, in this theme is constructed as enlightening.

Finally, there was a small number of instances of the media having a validating and 'hugely positive impact' on non-binary people themselves. As conveyed through the following examples, '[a]round 3 years ago I realized I was non-binary and saw this as a valid gender for the first time due to media reporting' (yes – NB, 27, Bisexual), and '[m]edia coverage, which has depicted trans and non-binary people as even *existing*, has had a hugely positive impact on my life and self-acceptance' (yes – NB, 48, queer). In the first example, in contrast to the claims of media 'transing' (i.e. unduly influencing) young people to *become* trans or gender diverse in the first theme, the understanding conveyed by the person themselves is very different. Rather than 'transing', the media is attributed as valorising an identity 'realized' some years previously. In the second example, the respondent emphasises 'existing' foregrounds the profoundly positive impact the media can have. (See also Newman & Peel, 2022 for wider discussion of non-binary people's perspectives in this project.)

In the second substantive section of this chapter, I further explore toxicity and division in the 'gender debate' discourse itself and also how the mainstream media and the social media platform Twitter engaged with the findings of the FLAG project in May/June 2022. This is for two reasons. First, to illustrate how media discourse is inextricably linked to human lives and experiences; and second, to provide an evocative 'hook' for some thoughts, by way of conclusion, which may support communicating across difference and division.

Toxicity and division

The discussion of the polarising, bigoted and validating themes has demonstrated some division and hostility between different groups, though perhaps it doesn't fully communicate the depth of feeling evident in some of the data collected in the autumn of 2018.[13] For instance, this respondent's use of the term 'yeet', which stresses the forcefulness of throwing something and a lack of concern for what is being thrown, captures some of the strength of feeling: 'I want to "yeet" all of the "gender critical" "feminists" into the sea. Also the media. I want to "yeet" lots of things into the sea but I'm worried I might pollute the sea too much' (yes – F, 24, bisexual/pansexual). Similarly, on the other side, comments such as 'I wish the new generations would do their homework about sexism and feminism pre 1990 and shut up about bullshit unicorn rainbow gender binary bullcrap; as soon as they have babies and are left holding them (the women) they will soon change their tune' (yes – F, 50, bisexual).

Before exploring how the FLAG final report was engaged with by the media and how that national media coverage was reacted to on Twitter in May/June 2022, it is worth discussing two responses which together highlight additional dimensions of the debate. First, the role 'dynamics of platforms' have to play in the production and maintenance of polarisation, and second, the place of personal attack in research practices which aim to interrogate and deepen understanding of issues pertaining to the 'gender debate'. These dimensions are represented in the responses below from heterosexual/straight participants:

> My awareness of a spectrum has increased, as well as some of the controversies in gender politics (e.g. arguments between trans activists and 'TERFs'). My skepticism about the latter has increased in tandem with my compassion for the former; I think there is a lot of tribal politicking going on that is obfuscating the realities of individuals' lived experiences that is ultimately unhelpful to everyone. This is a reflection of the social media-isation of political discourse – understanding has not been helped at all by the dynamics of platforms that encourage people to retreat to their ideological bunkers. (yes – M, 33, heterosexual)
>
> Gaslighting people to accept identity politics for the sanitisation of fetish is a bit grim, please stop, or at least figure out what you are doing and why you are being used this way. (yes – F, 56, straight)

With regard to implicating social media platform dynamics in 'encouraging' polarisation in the first example above, this speaks to a substantial literature that suggests that the cause of polarisation is both political 'and tied to broader shifts in media, including the rise of social media and platforms' (Kriess & McGregor, 2023, p. 2). Platforms themselves are positioned as 'a reliable go-to for both blame and intervention' (Kriess & McGregor, 2023, p. 2). There is much debate about the role of 'filter bubbles' and 'echo chambers' in political polarisation, though the acronym SMIP – Social Media Induced Polarisation – is used in the information systems literature (e.g., Wakefield & Wakefield, 2022). Empirical research shows that social media engagement can also increase, rather than constrain, exposure to a diversity of information (e.g. Moller et al., 2018). Though a systematic review found that media and social media use tends to increase polarisation, there are flaws in how research in this field is conducted, including Twitter being overused as a study site (Kubin & Von Sikorski, 2021). Certainly, though, the relative or complete anonymity of Twitter and other online media, and the operation of algorithms that may encourage a 'bunker' mentality are elements at play in the 'gender debate'.

The second response above, accusing us of 'gaslighting people to accept identity politics for the sanitisation of fetish', was not uncommon at times during the four years of the FLAG project (2018–22). Personal attacks on the motives and 'side/s' the research team had in the 'gender debate' occurred regularly and largely via social media or anonymously through responses to the 'Attitudes to Gender' survey.[14] As we have discussed elsewhere, we were positioned as both 'anti trans' and as having 'NO respect for the 99% of the population who do NOT follow trans ideology' (Peel & Newman, 2020, pp. 11–12; Peel & Newman, 2019). In this particular example, the suggestion is that we're 'dopes' being 'used' by unarticulated others with no understanding of how to conduct research. This leads to the final aspect of my exploration of toxicity and divisiveness in this chapter, the public reception of the FLAG final report.

Two national outlets ran a story on the project final report (Wakefield, 2022; Rustin, 2022).[15] One was in the online-only *PinkNews* (Box 9.1), which, according to its website, reaches a global audience of more than 100 million users a month via its website and social media channels and 'stand[s] for the fundamental rights of the entire LGBTQ+ community and its allies'.[16] The other story was in the *Guardian* (Box 9.4), a mainstream British national newspaper which also doesn't have a paywall for its online content, is on the left of the political spectrum and is 'known for its non-conformist opinions and support of innovative, non-traditional approaches'.[17]

In Box 9.1 leading LGBTQ+ human rights activist and Director of the Peter Tatchell Foundation, Peter Tatchell, engages with the radicalism of the final report on its terms and puts a positive valence on the *PinkNews* article in his retweet in personal terms ('sounds liberating & progressive to me'). In another positive response to Wakefield's (2022) *PinkNews* article, a structural feminist analysis of the 'foundations' of legal sex for supporting heteropatriarchal practices labels current social practice as 'bizarre'.

Box 9.1: Engaged and/or positive responses to *PinkNews* coverage of the FLAG final report (Cooper et al., 2022)[18]

Abolishing legal sex & gender identity comes with many pros, radical new report finds. Getting ride of gender roles & breaking down divisions based on sex & identity sounds liberating & progressive to me. These are challenging ideas worth considering!

*(Includes a link to the article in *PinkNews*.)

– @PeterTatchell, 17 May, 2022

Honestly it's bizarre that anyone would argue for legal sex given its very foundations are in making sure women are a tradable good between fathers and husbands, and keeping women and girls from inheriting property.

*(Includes a link to the article in *PinkNews*.)

– Anonymous Twitter user

Given that it's been found that 'those with high group identification tend to use Twitter for negative interactions' (Wakefield & Wakefield, 2022, p. 658) it is perhaps unsurprising that the FLAG researchers were accused of encouraging the trafficking of women, inciting rape and committing child abuse from gender-critical accounts and individuals on Twitter. I'm not reproducing that material here as I deem it too offensive[19] although Box 9.2 provides a flavour of the negative reaction the reporting of the final project garnered.

Box 9.2: Examples of negative reactions to media coverage of the FLAG final report

Welp, I've abused my eyeballs enough for one evening. Can someone just defund this garbage, so I never ever have to think of it again?

*(Accompanied by a *GIF of Homer Simpson, the cartoon character from* The Simpsons, *screaming as he pours a large bottle of bleach into his open eyes.*)

– Anonymous Twitter user

Are you on glue?

– Anonymous Twitter user

This has all got to be a big joke. I can't make myself believe there are people out their spending time and energy writing this utter shit.

– Anonymous Twitter user

As the three tweets in Box 9.2 demonstrate, the criticism here is not with the substantive content of the *PinkNews* article, but rather a generic trashing of the research – referred to as 'garbage', 'a big joke' and 'utter shit'. The extreme image of Homer Simpson from the US Simpsons cartoon pouring bleach into his own eyes enhances the visceral nature of this negative response. Although the use of 'welp' rather than 'well' is, according to Kilkenny (2012) 'a linguistic shrug'. Nevertheless, this combination of the self-harming gif and extremely negative, if resigned, text does result in the question from another Twitter user, 'are you on glue?' Though it is not made clear whether this rhetorical question is a challenge to the tweeter or an additional attack on the *PinkNews* article – and by extension the FLAG research team – twitter bubbles and echo chambers would suggest it's the latter. Box 9.3, below, is an example of how the other 'side' of the 'gender debate' reacted to the article.

> **Box 9.3: Tweet about the *PinkNews* coverage of the FLAG final report engaging with the 'gender debate' rather than the substantive article**
>
> I can see the GC cult now
>
> *(Accompanied by a GIF of a White individual with shoulder-length brown hair and wearing glasses, seated in a car and secured with a seatbelt. The person is screaming in visible rage, and the word 'TRIGGERED' appears in bold dark red text at the top right corner.)
>
> (Includes a link to the article in *PinkNews*.)
>
> - Anonymous Twitter user

As can be seen in Box 9.3, which also combines a gif and text, the substance of the article isn't engaged with; rather, the gif depicts a person in or driving a car screaming with the word 'TRIGGERED' in the background. The text speaks to the content of the gif, commenting with immediacy, 'I can see the GC cult now.' 'Cult' is generally not viewed as a neutral or benign term to describe a social group, and the article is positioned as 'fodder' for a strong and uncomfortable emotional reaction. Given 'triggers' and trigger warnings are given in contexts with reference to serious issues which may negatively impact mental health, this tweet ironises both the gender-critical position (implied but not labelled in Box 9.2) and the *PinkNews* article content.

Lastly, I reflect on the 'new' divisiveness evident in the *Guardian* article (Box 9.4) and the letters in response (Box 9.5). As can be seen in Box 9.4 below, the Rustin (2022) headline labels the substance of the FLAG final report as 'dangerous', and the sub-heading to the opinion piece frames the article as the 'feminist case' against gender self-identification. If we compare this 'gender-critical feminist' framing of the debate to the feminist analysis in Box 9.2, the crux of the issue around the place of 'sex' in feminisms becomes evident: in the former, inequality against women is largely a vestige of the past, and therefore the idea of removing legal sex is progressive; in the latter, women's oppression is currently so prevalent and insidious that, without legal sex, protections for women would be eroded or erased.

> **Box 9.4: Coverage and reaction in the mainstream media to the FLAG final report**
>
> Article heading in the 'Opinion' section of the *Guardian*:
>
> Trying to erase the biological definition of sex isn't just misguided – it's dangerous.
>
> Susanna Rustin
>
> *(Accompanied by a headshot of Susanna Rustin)
> Proposals to rewrite the law take gender self-identification too far. Here's the feminist case against.

> Tues 28 June 2022 16:16 BST
>
> I wrote about the idea of 'abolishing legal sex' (yes this is a real thing! gender critical feminists aren't making it up).
>
> *(Includes a link to the article in the *Guardian*.)
>
> – @SusannaRustin, 28 June, 2022, Pinned Tweet
>
> Twitter responses:
>
> I am reading it and it is a painful read. Probably the most poorly researched piece of work I have ever read. It is appalling that after 4 years and more than 500.000 pounds, these 48 pages pamphlet is the best they could produce.
>
> – Anonymous Twitter user
>
> And read how nuts it is.
> Wow! Cannot believe you got this published in the *Guardian*. Well done.
>
> – Anonymous Twitter user
>
> This is excellent, Susanna. I can't quite believe I'm reading it in the *Guardian* though! On a Tuesday!
>
> – Anonymous Twitter user

The examples from the 'gender-critical' Twitter responses that followed Rustin's pinned tweet about her article capture the notable features of the comments, namely generic criticism of the research and both glee and amazed pleasure (e.g. 'wow!') at encountering an explicitly 'gender-critical' article featured in a left-wing national newspaper such as the *Guardian*.

Box 9.5: Letters in response to Susanna Rustin's *Guardian* article

Heading from the 'Letters' section of the *Guardian*:

Opening up the debate about abolition of legal sex and gender status

Anne Phillips says The Future of Legal Gender report raises important questions, while Peter Tatchell says biological sex and gender identity are equally valid and important

*(Accompanied by a photograph of five infants of diverse racial backgrounds seated on a white floor. Two of the infants are dressed in light pink outfits, two in white, and the baby in the centre is wearing a light blue outfit. The image's caption reads '"Most of us would recoil in horror at the idea of people being stamped at birth with a specific racial or religious identity". Photograph: Alamy'.)

Interestingly, though the *Guardian* published the Rustin (2022) piece as the opening interpretation of the FLAG project final report, the letters in response and the headline above them (Box 9.5) stressed 'openness'. Phillips challenged Rustin's 'misreading' of the project's research question of whether 'decertifying' sex and gender as legal categories makes it easier or harder to challenge the many gender-based forms of inequality in our society'. And she ended her letter in perhaps a veiled counter to the many comments roundly dismissing the whole project – 'and I for one find the report genuinely thought-provoking'. Tatchell took a different stance in his letter, emphasising that 'many of us say that biological sex and gender identity are both equally valid and important.'

Taken together, participant perspectives on whether and how the media has influenced their views on gender and transgender issues, in combination with a (necessarily selective) social media and media representation of the FLAG project key findings, illuminate various aspects of sexual and gender positionalities. While these positionalities are not exhaustive and, for some, may feel well-trodden, sedimented and resistant to reformulation or change, they do reflect a particular cultural moment. In concluding this chapter, I suggest a 'bunker mentality' is antithetical to any hope of a peaceful outcome from a 'gender war'.

Concluding thoughts: Leaning into difference?

At the time of the release of the FLAG project final report, I had an exchange with another project team member about the media coverage and the 'feedback' we'd received on Twitter. They said, 'I'm trying hard to see the funny side... but it's just depressing and takes the enjoyment out of doing research when it then just gets endlessly rubbished.' On one reading of the FLAG project, it failed to intervene productively in the 'binary drama' (Cooper, 2019) of this debate, and the lack of embodied human connection during the pandemic and (for some) overreliance on social media perhaps exacerbated this. But Cooper (2023, p. 34) usefully reminds us that when polarisation occurs, '[p]ublic divisions can *feel* deeply embedded, but they are not fixed, stable phenomena' (my emphasis). Divisions are not static and enduring, and taking a stance of principled hopefulness, there *is* potential for growth and change if divergent perspectives are heard.

Kreiss and McGregor (2023, p. 3) suggest that 'polarization is often the outcome of struggles for justice.' This analysis of new media is not solely the preserve of media and communication scholars such as Kreiss and McGregor. As one of the FLAG respondents commented, '[t]he recent press coverage is, in the main, exactly the same sort of hate speech that was used against gay people under Clause 28, and against black people in the US fight against desegregation' (no – F, 60, lesbian). Feminist politics, too, has a long history of division as well as solidarity, as does the LGBTIQ+ community (e.g. Ellis & Peel, 2011; Clarke & Peel, 2007). A key difference in our contemporary mediatised times is that representations of these divisions are visible to the mainstream and are no longer intra-community disagreements. As such, exploring differences and 'leaning in' across those – even seemingly entrenched

– differences remains vital for human relating (Emilion et al., 2022) and potentially community (re)building (e.g., Nodin et al., 2023). The FLAG project may have been the 'right' project at the 'wrong' time, the 'wrong' project at the 'right' time, or some blend of these evaluative poles. Either way, listening to divergent perspectives will likely ultimately strengthen, rather than diminish, LGBTQI+ equalities.

Notes

1   This chapter is based on research conducted as part of the ESRC-funded project, *The Future of Legal Gender* (FLAG), award number ES/P008968/1. Warm thanks to Davina Cooper (PI), fellow Co-Is Flora Renz and Emily Grabham, and research associates Han/Hannah Newman, Robyn Emerton, and Jess Smith. Thanks also to Lauren Hall, Jessica Robles and all the participants at the Polarising Sexual and Gendered Lives symposium at University College Dublin (June, 2023).
2   For details about the overall FLAG project including methodology and key overall findings, please see https://futureoflegalgender.kcl.ac.uk/final-report/ for the full report and https://www.kcl.ac.uk/law/research/future-of-legal-gender-abolishing-legal-sex-status-report-overview.pdf for a briefer project overview (Cooper et al., 2022).
3   I purposely do not quantify the prevalence of these three themes in order to give parity of 'weight' to the differing constructions of the media. This is in keeping with my stance on the FLAG project data more broadly to either/or (a) analyse cisgenderism and endosexism when it is present rather than elide prejudicial discourse (e.g., see Peel & Newman, 2020) and (b) foreground minoritised perspectives or identities (e.g. see Newman & Peel, 2022).
4   GC means 'gender critical' in this context.
5   This was seen too in the survey data I discuss in this chapter, that is, '[t]he intensely negative coverage of – trans issues – (focusing only on trans women to the exclusion of everyone else; depicting "trans people" and "feminists" as mutually exclusive and adversarial groups, rather than overlapping and contiguous) has been awful, awful, awful' (yes – NB, 48, queer).
6   Data quotes are tagged with whether the person responded yes or no to the question, 'Have your views on gender changed as a result of recent media coverage on gender and transgender issues?' and their gender, age and sexuality. Data are represented as they were written, and any changes to aid readability are indicated in square brackets.
7   This is reminiscent of claims of 'prejudice against heterosexuals' when non-heterosexuals are more visible or gain an incidental benefit, which is connected to the apparatus of heteronormativity (Peel, 2001), as well as cisnormativity.
8   TRA stands for Trans Rights Activist.
9   Less frequently, there was the contrast of shifting from pro to anti-trans. For example, '[b]efore the cruise India stories about transgender and the things I see on social media from transgender activists, I would've counted myself as a very pro transgender person' (yes – F, 53, bisexual).
10 There were instances where it was claimed 'transing children is child abuse' (yes – F, 44, straight) and 'transing' was alluded to but not named explicitly, for example, 'Media coverage fuel the ridiculousness of the so called myriad "genders" and "non genders" causing vulnerable people including children to become confused and unable to understand what is real and what is not' (no – F, 43, heterosexual).

11　IIRC means 'if I recall correctly'.
12　Conversely, in the polarising theme, the public was invoked in a different way ('The public do not seem to realize') to emphasise the foundational 'truth' of trans women's bodies.
13　In partial overlap with the UK Government consultation on the Gender Recognition Act 2004 (Fairburn et al., 2022).
14　This also occurred during the book launch event for Witcomb and Peel (2022) which largely showcased the work of doctoral and early career researchers.
15　A critical opinion piece was also published in The *Scotsman* (Dalgety, 2022).
16　See https://careers.thepinknews.com/?_gl=1*1uzjywk*_ga*NzIwMTQ4NzI3LjE2O DQ3NjU5NTU.*_ga_BX9CRJ4BBP*MTY4NDc2NTk1NC4xLjEuMTY4NDc2 NTk2NC41My4wLjA.
17　Quote from https://www.newworldencyclopedia.org/entry/The_Guardian.
18　In keeping with standard ethical guidance around the use of materials in the public domain, I did not seek formal ethical approval for their use. I have, however, anonymised text from those I assume to be members of the public. Journalists and/or public figures such as Peter Tatchell have not anonymised because they contributed to engaging with the project's final report in a professional capacity. These comments were captured at the time the articles were published and responded to and, as such, represent a moment in time rather than (necessarily) the full reach and extent of social media engagement with the final report.
19　While not engaging directly with criticism of the FLAG project on social media or on Mumsnet, we did engage with questions and critique via the project website at https://futureoflegalgender.kcl.ac.uk/qas/ and offered our perspective on some of this material in talks about the project (e.g., Peel, 2022), journal articles (Peel & Newman, 2020) and similar to other LGBTIQA+ researchers (e.g., Riggs & Ciccarello, 2023) blog posts (e.g., Peel & Newman, 2019).

Chapter 10

MISINFORMATION IN THE 'GENDER WARS' IN BRITAIN

AFFECTIVE ATTACHMENTS IN THE USE AND MISUSE OF EVIDENCE[1]

Sarah Lamble

Introduction

Amid Britain's recent 'culture wars', debates about transgender rights have gained prominence, becoming a significant arena for social, political and legal conflicts. Discussions are highly polarised, often portrayed in the mainstream media as a clash between trans rights and women's rights, and a dispute over the meaning and significance of sex versus gender (the *Guardian*, 2018; Cooper, 2019; Hines, 2020). While initially focused on proposed reforms to the UK's 2004 Gender Recognition Act to enable greater gender self-determination (self-ID),[2] the debates have expanded to encompass broader issues around trans people's access to gender-segregated spaces (e.g. toilets, refuges, hospitals, prisons and sports). The 'gender wars' now feature regularly in British news, parliamentary discussions and celebrity culture, leading to high-profile legal cases and significant implications for equality law, policy and practice.

Polarisation in these disputes can be characterised by the division of opinions into two starkly opposed and firmly entrenched camps, where there appears little scope for common understanding, dialogue or shifting perspective. In Britain, divisions over trans rights have been actively stoked by political leaders, corporate news outlets and social media, who capitalise on such disputes as part of a wider culture war and actively encourage a 'zero-sum conception of rights' where the protection of one group is contingent on the exclusion of another (GATE, 2022, p. 12). This culture war frame strips nuance from debate and channels different perspectives into competing factions who wrestle over which social norms and values will be applied to public policy decisions on health, education, welfare and governance.[3] While initially seen as a sub-theme within the wider culture wars, disputes over trans rights and sex/gender policies in Britain have escalated to such a heightened state of polarisation that they are now regularly referred to on their own terms as 'gender wars'.

However, unlike in North America, Latin America and Europe, where anti-trans politics often align with right-wing populism and opposition to feminist and LGBTQ+ issues more broadly (Graff & Korolczuk, 2022; Kuhar & Paternotte, 2017; Corrêa, 2021), in Britain these debates do not map easily into conventional left-right divisions (Lamble, 2024). Prominent 'gender-critical'[4] feminists in Britain, for example, who are sceptical of trans rights, identify as left-wing (Stock, 2021; Bindel, 2021; Ingala Smith, 2023). Conversely, key proponents of trans rights hail from conservative circles, including the original government commitment to reform the Gender Recognition Act in England and Wales.

As such, the opposing factions in the British gender wars defy the existing literature on culture war polarisation, which has tended to focus on divisions along partisan lines (e.g. Tory versus Labour, Republican versus Democrat); ideological perspectives (e.g. left versus right, conservative versus liberal); and demographics (e.g. age, gender, ethnicity, sexuality and class) (Muste, 2014). Gender-critical perspectives in Britain do not fall neatly within these standard divisions, with advocates crossing many demographics as well as political and partisan lines (GATE, 2022). Gender-critical groups not only include expected players from right-wing religious and conservative organisations but also liberal, left and radical positions. This includes groups that advocate for women but explicitly disavow feminism (e.g. Standing for Women);[5] left-wing feminists (e.g. Women's Place UK);[6] 'non-partisan' women's and children's advocacy groups (e.g. Fair Play for Women, For Women Scotland, Transgender Trend, Sex Matters);[7] and lesbians, gays and bisexuals who seek separate organising from trans communities (e.g. LGB Alliance)[8] including those who eschew both left and right politics (e.g. Get the L Out).[9] There are also gender-critical sub-groups within all major political parties across Britain, with the exception of the Welsh nationalist party Plaid Cymru.[10]

What broadly unites British factions in opposing trans rights are concerns for safety. Gender-critical groups commonly share claims that trans rights and 'gender ideology' pose a danger to (non-trans) women and children (Pearce et al., 2020; Turnbull-Dugarte & McMillan, 2023). Likewise, counter-claims by trans rights advocates also rely on assertions of danger and harm from gender-critical views and trans-hostile politics (Baska, 2023). As such the gender wars in Britain are dominated by claims about risk, safety and danger in relation to contested claims about sex and gender identity.

Polarisation between supporters and opponents of trans rights has escalated due to fears of harm on both sides, leading to a perception that gains for one side are losses for the other – with high-stakes consequences. As such, emotions often run high, and the demeanour of the debates, particularly on social media, has become increasingly toxic in tone (Tryl et al., 2022). Interestingly, although some groups are highly invested in these debates, the gender wars do not rank as a key political priority for the broader British public (Smith, 2022; Tryl et al., 2022). Nevertheless, the disputes have been amplified by a dramatic increase in (frequently negative) news stories about trans issues (Julian, 2020; Baker, 2019; Gwenffrewi, 2022) and exacerbated by click-bait-driven media. Particularly when framed as matters of safety and harm, these narratives are designed to invoke moral outrage, thereby intensifying the emotional and political stakes of the debates and giving the impression of two highly polarised positions.[11] Ceding any ground is then often perceived by opposing sides as tantamount to capitulating to violence. Hence, some feminist and LGBT+ groups that otherwise share common concerns (e.g. gender and sexuality-based oppression and violence) have become positioned as diametric opponents.

This chapter examines how misinformation, combined with safety fears, has deepened polarisation around trans rights in Britain. Tracing why and how false narratives have taken hold in news, social media and parliamentary debates, the chapter argues that fears of 'dangerous others' have dovetailed with misinformation about trans people to create a climate where safety concerns have become a key feature of the disputes. The chapter suggests that underpinning the widespread circulation of misinformation is a set of misdirected fears combined with affective investments in punitive safety politics and outrage economies (Lamble, 2013; Phipps, 2020, p. 107). Polarisation in the British gender wars has manifested in an 'us/them' mentality, which is not characterised by the conventional left/right divide, but instead sutured to a safety politics where the political stakes revolve around divergent accounts of dangerous and threatening 'others'.

The new gender wars in Britain: Mobilising safety claims

In 2017, UK Prime Minister Theresa May pledged to reform the Gender Recognition Act 2004 (GRA) in response to concerns that the existing act, though groundbreaking when initially passed, was no longer fit for purpose (Mason, 2017). The medical and bureaucratic requirements for those seeking legal recognition of gender were widely seen as outdated, pathologising and unnecessary. Proposed changes intended to bring the UK in line with best practices internationally and allow greater self-determination of gender identity (Whittle & Simkiss, 2020).[12] Given that it was already possible in the UK to change gender on key documents such as driver's licences, passports and bank accounts (irrespective of whether one held a Gender Recognition Certificate), the proposed GRA reforms were seen as a relatively minor bureaucratic issue that would reduce barriers for changing birth and death certificates. The proposed changes, however, proved highly contentious, as groups opposing trans rights quickly mobilised against reform, including newly formed 'gender-critical' groups organising under the banner of women's 'sex-based rights'.[13]

While internal disputes about trans inclusion within feminist and lesbian communities have a long-standing history, particularly during the 1970s and 80s, by the early 2000s they had largely dissipated in Britain, with overtly trans-hostile sentiments mostly limited to fringe groups (Thurlow, 2022). As such, many UK feminist and LGBTQ+ communities were shocked when, during the July 2018 Pride March in London, half a dozen lesbians from the group 'Get the L out: Lesbian Not Queer' took over the front of the parade, carrying banners claiming that 'trans ideology' was harmful to lesbians (BBC News, 2018b). This action marked a key moment in the growing backlash against trans rights and the emergence of what would become known as the new 'gender wars' in Britain.

In the same month, the UK government launched a public consultation on potential reforms to the Gender Recognition Act (Fairbairn et al., 2022). Various groups orchestrated responses, garnered media attention and lobbied MPs. Among various tactics, the claim that trans rights endangered women's safety proved most effective in generating media attention. Two key arguments surfaced: first, gender self-identification would allow predatory men to access women-only spaces under false pretences (the 'trans faker' argument) (e.g. Kirkup, 2018; Massie, 2021); and second, that trans women pose an inherent threat due to their 'previous status' as men or because of their 'biological sex' (the sex essentialist argument) (e.g. Turner, 2018; Keep Prisons Single Sex, 2023c). These arguments, bolstering a wider narrative that associated transness (whether 'fraudulent' or 'authentic') with sexual predation, gained prominence (Lamble, 2023b), despite evidence from countries with gender self-ID indicating otherwise (e.g. Anarte, 2022; Sharpe, 2020a).

Despite the lack of factual support, portraying gender self-ID as a risk to women's safety gained momentum in the UK debates, including within the liberal press (e.g. the *Guardian*, 2018).[14] The 'trans danger' frame was a deliberate strategy among gender-critical groups. For instance, Fair Play for Women (FPFW), initially formed in 2017 to address concerns about the 'fairness' of trans inclusion in sports, soon shifted focus to issues of crime, justice and safety. Other groups adopted a similar narrative, such as the campaigning group Keep Prisons Single Sex (KPSS, 2023b). This emphasis on safety, coupled with claims around trans people, risk and sexual danger, not only deepened polarisation but arguably played a key role in the shelving of GRA reforms in England & Wales,[15] and the unprecedented constitutional blocking of the Gender Recognition Reform Bill in Scotland.[16] Concerns about safety for women and girls, and the potential for fraudulent applications by 'malicious actors' were cited as reasons for blocking the Scottish Bill (UK Government Equalities Office, 2023). Similar safety concerns were behind proposals to roll back trans rights by redefining sex in the Equality Act on 'biological' terms (Elgot, 2023).

Public opinion in Britain has shifted since these safety claims gained media traction. While support for trans rights had been rising over decades, recent surveys indicate a significant drop. The 40th annual British Social Attitudes Survey showed a 28-point decline (from 58 per cent in 2016 to 30 per cent in 2022) in support for changing sex on birth certificates. It also found an 18-point decline (from 82 per cent to 64 per cent) in those who describe themselves as not at all prejudiced towards trans people (Clery, 2023).[17] These shifts were likely due to hostile media and campaigning by gender-critical groups (Turnbull-Dugarte & McMillan, 2023). This was the assertion made by groups like Fair Play for Women, who claimed in their 2022 'year in review' report that their most significant achievement was shifting public perception (Fair Play for Women, 2023). While other social attitudes around family form, sexual relationships and abortion continue to follow trends of liberalisation (Clery, 2023), the rapid shift in views on trans rights indicates a lurch towards greater polarisation, spurred on by narratives of safety concerns and threats to women's rights.

Misinformation: From misleading claims to accepted 'facts'

Misinformation has played a pivotal role in framing trans rights as a threat to women's safety, in turn deepening polarisation in the gender debates. Scholars differentiate *disinformation* (intentionally sharing false information) from *misinformation* (inadvertently sharing of unchecked information), with both being exacerbated by rapid circulation on social media (Tandoc, 2019). While there are many examples of disinformation in the gender wars, particularly on social media (Billard, 2023), misinformation seems to be the primary problem within mainstream media, parliamentary and policy debates in Britain. Much of the misleading, false or incorrect information in news media and parliamentary debates appears to be circulated in good faith, though it is difficult to evidence intent. However, a widespread lack of public awareness around trans issues (Faye, 2021), combined with popular misconceptions around prisons, crime data and criminal justice policies, and amplified by trans-hostile media and poor press regulation, (Akrivos, 2022; Baker, 2019) have converged to create the conditions for inaccurate and misleading claims to regularly circulate unchecked. Genuine concerns about gender-based violence have also been used to mobilise against trans-inclusive policies – despite evidence that trans people, especially trans women, are at heightened risk of such violence and that trans-inclusive policies do not pose safety risks for non-trans women (Rymer & Cartei, 2015; Serano, 2021; Stonewall, 2018; Stokes, 2021; Hasenbush et al., 2019).

Dominant narratives portraying trans individuals as a danger can be traced to several inaccurate claims repeatedly voiced by gender-critical groups and amplified by British media. Key examples include assertions that: (1) trans people are disproportionately likely to be sexual offenders; (2) trans women exhibit 'male-pattern' criminality; and (3) crime statistics are being distorted by trans people. These narratives have circulated in the press, on social media and in political lobbying, fostering public apprehension regarding trans rights and deepening polarised views.

False claim 1: Half of trans prisoners are sex offenders

In October 2017, Fair Play for Women (FPFW) released a report claiming that 'Half of all trans prisoners are sex offenders or dangerous category A inmates.' The report suggested that trans people in prison were more frequently convicted of sexual offences than non-trans people. Released amid discussions about gender recognition law reform in England, Wales and Scotland, FPFW's report warned that, 'If self-declaration of gender becomes law, these trans-identifying males [sic] will become eligible for transfer to women's prisons' (Fair Play for Women, 2017a). While this claim misrepresented existing prison policy at the time (since location decisions in England, Wales and Scotland were done on a case-by-case risk-assessed basis rather than solely by legal gender),[18] it was part of a deliberate effort to associate gender recognition reform with sexual danger for women.

The self-published[19] report was admittedly speculative[20] – it did not rely on official prison population statistics or offender records but instead pieced together partial and inconsistent information gleaned from Prison Inspectorate and Independent Monitoring Board reports spanning several years. The FPFW report used dehumanising language throughout, referring to trans women as 'TIMs' ('trans-identifying males'), making inflammatory remarks about cross-dressing and referencing out-of-date studies from the 1980s and 1990s to pathologise gender and sexually non-conforming people. A summary of its findings also claimed, with no corresponding evidence, that 'Crimes committed by trans-identifying males (including violent and sexual crimes) are being recorded as female offences, distorting female crime figures' (Fair Play for Women, 2017a).

Despite its serious methodological weaknesses, the FPFW report was pushed to several newspapers, which used the story to warn against the potential perils of gender self-identification reforms. The *Sunday Times*, for example, ran a headline declaring, 'Up to half of trans inmates may be sex offenders: Plans to allow people to self-define their gender could put female prisoners at risk, campaigners warn'(Gilligan, 2017b). The *Daily Mail* ran a similar headline, warning that 'predatory inmates' were '"falsely" defining their gender to target vulnerable women' (Matthews, 2017). As the *Times* described, 'With the government soon to consult about allowing people to change gender on demand, prisons will be on the front line. No other single-sex place – no changing room, lavatory or shower area – forces you to live in it for up to 24 hours a day, confined with others who are there because their behaviour is extreme'(Gilligan, 2017b).

While the *Times* acknowledged 'the imprecision of the figures' in the report, it nonetheless legitimised FPFW's claims (Gilligan, 2017b). That same week, the *Mirror* ran a story with the headline 'Prisoners at Europe's biggest sex offender jail celebrate transgender day to support 12 male inmates living as women' – reinforcing the association between transness and sex offending (Dorman, 2017). Similar stories followed, with another *Times* article published two weeks later under the headline 'Number of trans prisoners rises by 80%' (Gilligan, 2017a). This article reported on prisoner equalities data released by the Ministry of Justice but offered little context or explanation for why the *recorded* numbers (versus actual numbers) might be increasing – other than suggesting nefarious motives by male prisoners and reasserting the association between trans prisoners and sex offending. While there were some challenges to these claims (Fisher, 2017 (amended 2018))[21] – including an unsuccessful complaint to the press regulator (IPSO, 2018) – the general assertion that most trans prisoners were sex offenders would continue to circulate widely in the press, largely treated as a de facto truth. On social media, some misread these claims as a statistic about trans people in general rather than prisoners specifically.

BBC News subsequently ran a 'Reality Check' report, which explained why FPFW's claims were misleading. The BBC noted that the Ministry of Justice had itself stated that its data was 'not yet a reliable reflection of the true numbers' of trans people in prison (BBC News, 2018a). The Ministry's figures only counted individuals who had undergone a transgender case board and were more likely to include those with longer sentences and serious convictions – which partly explained the higher-than-expected numbers with sexual offences. At the time, those figures also didn't count individuals with Gender Recognition Certificates. Since the overall official number of trans prisoners was highly unreliable, any claims about offence percentages were also unreliable (Bent Bars Project, 2020).

Unmentioned in the BBC Reality Check report was that Ministry of Justice official figures were based on *staff* reports of trans prisoners (captured on a 'snapshot' basis once a year) and differ vastly from figures based on prisoner *self-reporting*. For example, Official Ministry of Justice figures in 2022 indicate that 0.3 per cent (i.e. less than 1 percent) of the prison population identify as transgender (230 out of 78,058 total prisoners in March 2022). In contrast, the Prison Inspectorate's Annual Reports, which allow prisoners to self-report their identities through direct surveys, have repeatedly found 1–2 per cent of prisoners identify as transgender – a significant difference.[22] One percent of the 2022 prison population would be 780 prisoners; 2 percent would be 1,561; this is compared to the official figures of 230. If self-reported figures are used, the proportion of trans people in prison for sexual offences is considerably smaller than claimed and could be as low as 6 per cent.[23]

Even if a disproportionate number of trans people were imprisoned for sexual offences, this does not mean that trans people are more likely to commit sex offences. Rates of offending (how often people commit a crime) differ significantly from rates of criminalisation (how often people are charged/convicted of a crime), with the latter shaped by factors of inequality, discrimination and selective enforcement, which directly impact trans people (Bent Bars Project, 2020). Yet Fair Play for Women continued to present their 2017 report as 'fact' and claimed their data was 'confirmed by the MOJ' (Fair Play for Women, 2019) despite the Ministry repeatedly saying the data is unreliable (BBC, 2018a, Ministry of Justice, 2022).

The same media pattern of suggesting rapidly growing numbers of trans prisoners, high numbers of trans sex offenders and allegations of fraudulent identities continued for several years (e.g. Beckford, 2019; McCann, 2022; Beckford, 2022). A disproportionate media focus on a small number of high-profile cases routinely gave the impression of increasing numbers of trans people with sexual offences filling prisons. Other news stories contributed to this narrative, some of which turned out to be entirely false. For example, in 2017, the tabloid press ran a widely shared story claiming, 'Child murderer Ian Huntley wants SEX CHANGE to get cushier life in women's jail' (Dickinson, 2017). The story ran across numerous papers including the *Daily Mail*, the *Mirror*, the *Sun*, *Telegraph* and the *Times*, as well as ITV and Good Morning Britain – and was included in an opinion piece in the *Guardian*, though subsequently corrected (Freeman, 2017). Follow-up reports also appeared in 2018, with headlines designed to incite outrage (Dickinson, 2018). The story about Huntley was entirely false and a retraction was printed two years later. However, the original reports included full-page stories with large attention-grabbing headlines and photos, while the retraction was limited to a small text box (*Daily Star*, 2019). Similar stories were used to reinforce narratives that, on the one hand, dangerous prisoners were claiming to be trans to supposedly get special treatment, and on the other, that trans people were disproportionately likely to be, or associate with, murderers and sex offenders. Both narratives played on long-standing cultural tropes where trans identities are deemed suspect, fraudulent and sexually deviant (Sharpe, 2018; Feder, 2020).

False claim 2: Trans women have male-pattern criminality

The boldest and most unevidenced claim by FPFW was their assertion that 'trans-identifying males exhibit a male pattern of criminality' (Fair Play for Women, 2017a). This claim was partly based on FPFW's own faulty assertions about trans prisoners' convictions and partly on the misinterpretation of a 2011 Swedish study examining the long-term outcomes of trans individuals after sex reassignment surgery (Dhejne et al., 2011). While the study's main finding highlighted the need for comprehensive social and mental health support for trans individuals to address the social impact of discrimination, it was misinterpreted to suggest that medical transition leads to suicide, ill health and criminality, and misconstrued to suggest that trans women follow 'male-pattern' crime trends (Tannehill, 2014; Williams, 2015). However, the study's lead author, Cecilia Dhejne, has clarified that the male-pattern criminality claim is inaccurate and the study is widely misunderstood (Williams, 2015).

Nonetheless, the unsubstantiated 'male-pattern criminality' claim was widely repeated across news, social media, and political campaigning. It featured prominently in oral and written evidence submitted to the UK Parliament during the Women & Equalities Committee Inquiry on GRA reform (Freedman et al., 2020; Women and Equalities Committee, 2020; for counter evidence, see Sharpe, 2020b; Pearce, 2021). The Scottish National Party 'Women's Pledge Group' opposing gender recognition reform echoed this claim in its submission to the Scottish government and in its online template for individual submissions (SNP Women's Pledge, 2020). A report by the right-wing think tank Policy Exchange, on 'Transgenderism and policy capture in criminal justice', reinforced the claim (O'Hara, 2022, p. 10).

The assertion also gained traction in the news media. The *Scotsman* newspaper, for example, quoted the Women's Pledge Group's assertion that trans women follow male crime patterns (Gourtsoyannis, 2020). The *Mail on Sunday* featured an opinion piece claiming that 'either transwomen [*sic*] are more likely than other males [*sic*] to be sexual predators, or – more probably – gender self-ID provides sexual predators with a marvellous loophole. Whichever is true, allowing males [*sic*] to self-identify into women's spaces makes women less safe' (Joyce, 2021). Similar claims appeared in other pieces in the *Mail* (Harrington, 2022) and the *New Statesman*, which claimed that 'Trans-identified males retain male patterns of offending and criminality. A gender recognition certificate is not a magic piece of paper that removes this risk' (Hatchet, 2022).

The male-pattern criminality claim spread widely on social media, particularly on high-profile Twitter accounts. For example, author JK Rowling, who has 14 million followers, tweeted that 'Trans women retain the same pattern of sex offending/violence as males' (Rowling, 2022b). She further claimed that 'Trans women retain male strength advantage and male patterns of violence and sexual offending. We know TW aren't all predators. However, the evidence shows that some are' (Rowling, 2022a). She referenced the gender-critical parliamentary submission as evidence for her claims (Freedman et al., 2020). Despite the lack of evidence, stating these claims repeatedly and assuredly was sufficient to turn them into perceived 'facts' among those opposing trans rights.

False claim 3: Recording gender rather than sex is skewing crime statistics

Following claims that crime data was being distorted because police were recording gender identity rather than sex (Fair Play for Women, 2017a), calls began to mount for 'sex-based' record-keeping (McLaughlin, 2021). These calls culminated in petitions to the UK and Scottish Parliaments calling for rape charges to be recorded by sex rather than gender (Petition 1, 2021; Petition 2, 2021; Petition 3, 2022).

To support the Scottish petition, sociology professor Alice Sullivan submitted evidence to Parliament alleging that record-keeping was distorting crime statistics (Sullivan, 2021). Using unofficial[24] rape charge statistics in England and Wales (Office for National Statistics, 2018), Sullivan cited the number of defendants recorded as men versus women. Sullivan noted that in UK law, the offence of rape must involve a penis but acknowledged women could be charged as accessories to this offence. However, her submission suggested that any number – and perhaps all – of the defendants recorded as women could be trans women (Sullivan, 2021).

While Sullivan later clarified on her personal website that not all 436 cases were trans women,[25] her tweets and responses from followers suggested otherwise. For example, criminal defence barrister Allison Bailey (co-founder of the LGB Alliance, which opposes trans rights) retweeted Sullivan's rape statistics claims with the following:

> Under English law rape can only be committed with a penis. That means 436 males, accused of rape, identified as women. 436 victims of male sexual violence, overwhelmingly women, were required to call their male rapist 'she' and 'her'.
> (Bailey, 2021b)

When challenged, Bailey replied that charges against women for rape are rare and suggested that the last time the press reported on such a case was 2001 – further implying that most of the 436 cases were likely trans women (Bailey, 2021a). Bailey eventually issued a correction (three months later) but asserted that it was impossible to know how many were actually 'natal females' (Bailey, 2022).

Criminology Professor Jo Phoenix also retweeted Sullivan's statistics and suggested the defendants were not women:

> Let me drive the point home. In law, people can only be charged with rape if what has happened is non-consensual penetration by a penis. In a six-year period 436 prosecutions for rape were recorded as prosecutions against women. Take. The. Time. To. Let. That. Sink. In. (Phoenix, 2021a)

Phoenix further elaborated (incorrectly) that 'rape charges can only be levelled against someone with a penis' and argued for record-keeping on the basis of biological sex (Phoenix, 2021b). While these tweets did not directly state that the rape statistics referred to trans women, it was implied. Comments in response to Sullivan, Bailey and Phoenix also assumed this, no doubt spurred on by the fact that these claims were made by a sociology professor, a criminal barrister and a criminology professor, all of whom might reasonably be assumed to be credible on such matters.

These misleading claims extended beyond social media to newspapers. The *Daily Mail* repeated Sullivan's 'findings' without explaining that women can be charged as accessories, leaving the impression that all 436 cases involved trans women perpetrators (Owen, 2021). The *Times* published an article by Alex Massie echoing the claim:

> In Scotland, as in other parts of the UK, reality gives way to fantasy. We pretend that women can – and do – commit rape. This absurdity is not restricted to Scotland. In England and Wales 436 male-bodied sex offenders were classified as women from 2012 to 2018 and at the weekend Police Scotland confirmed that if a man who rapes a woman wishes to be considered a woman, the authorities will honour that request. (Massie, 2021)

The *Times* subsequently issued a correction and replaced the reference to 'male-bodied sex offenders' with 'defendants' (Massie, 2021), but the wording still implied these were likely trans women.[26]

These misleading rape statistics also circulated in Parliament. Speaking at an International Women's Day debate in the House of Commons in 2022, Conservative MP Bernard Jenkin said, 'there is a new and growing category of violence against women committed by people who call themselves women but are biologically male.' He went on to claim that there were 436 cases of rape 'committed by men presenting themselves as women' (HC Deb, 2022; Dawson, 2022). Jenkin's comments were repeated without correction in a Press Association article (Bet, 2022) and in the *Daily Mail*, under the headline: 'Why do police and the NHS insist that some male-bodied rapists are women?' (Lawson, 2022). Another *Daily Mail* article repeated the claim that all 436 cases involved trans women (York, 2022) and it was reiterated in a piece published by the Centre for Crime and Justice Studies, which acknowledged that 'a tiny number' women are convicted of rape but nonetheless referred to '436 male crimes recorded as female crimes' (Asteriti, 2023).

These assertions were deeply flawed. Sullivan's claims were entirely speculative, based on unreliable data,[27] and offered no proof that the cases involved trans women. The Crown Prosecution Service stated it was incorrect to assume the data referred to trans women (Dawson, 2022). While Sullivan was correct that inconsistent recording practices across police forces mean that charging records were unreliable, more reliable data from the Ministry of Justice showed that rape convictions involving women have remained fairly stable since 2010 and have not changed significantly following shifts in recording practices on the basis of gender (Moore, 2022).

In Scotland, where detailed data is available, as of 2021, among '17,000 reports over 8 years documenting rape and attempted rape, none have been suspected by Police Scotland to have been committed by a trans woman' (Collier & Cowan, 2022, p. 761). Further, 'since trans women have been able to secure a GRC without surgery since the GRA in 2004, 17 years ago . . . not one trans woman has been a suspect in a rape/attempted rape in Scotland' (Collier & Cowan, 2022, p. 761; see also Police Scotland, 2021). While a subsequent public furore emerged in 2023 over the Isla Bryson case (a top news story when the Gender Recognition Reform Bill was being debated in Scotland), even in that case, Bryson's convictions for rape were not recorded as committed by a woman because Bryson identified as a man at the time of the offences (Grant, 2023).

While the media took considerable interest in calls for crime statistics to record biological sex rather than legal sex or gender identity, the impracticality of this proposal was rarely acknowledged. Yet, as the Home Office explained in response to one of the petitions, recording biological sex poses serious practical and ethical issues. Since 'biological sex' refers to a combination of factors (including chromosomes, gonads, hormones and primary and secondary sex characteristics), undertaking checks of these factors would be logistically and ethically unworkable (Petition 3, 2022). In April 2022, the Home Office announced new official guidance advising police to consistently use legal sex (based on birth certificate or GRC) for crime statistics (Dodds, 2022).[28] However, the concerns that gender identity was distorting crime statistics persisted, despite a lack of credible evidence.

The repetition of different misinformation claims – each reinforcing the broader assertion that trans rights pose a safety threat to women – worked to embolden those with gender-critical views and antagonise those who recognised the claims as misleading, further escalating polarisation between the two positions. The deployment of misinformation through the lens of safety claims also worked to draw in new sympathisers to the gender-critical cause, including those who might otherwise hold more moderate views or previously see themselves as supporters of trans rights. This has been a common refrain among those explaining how they became 'gender critical'; many describe being initially supportive of trans rights but then changing their minds when they became aware of safety concerns (Phillimore & Peters, 2022).

How misinformation circulates and escalates polarisation

With each of these examples, a similar pattern can be seen. Gender-critical groups self-publish claims based on unsound or speculative evidence. These claims gain traction on social media via endorsements from academics, community groups, social media influencers and so-called 'experts'. Claims are subsequently pushed to mainstream news outlets and lobbied to parliament. The mainstream press amplifies and legitimises these claims, contributing to a trans-hostile media environment. By repeatedly asserting misleading claims connected to safety concerns, framing them as fact and seeking endorsements from those with social standing, the claims eventually begin to be treated as credible evidence, impacting public opinion and influencing political and policy decisions. In turn, trans rights groups who recognise the inaccuracy of these claims but have far less influence in media and politics become increasingly determined to counter gender-critical views, and polarisation becomes more entrenched.

The pattern of legitimising misleading narratives through strategic circulation and endorsement appears to be a deliberate tactic by gender-critical groups. For example, during a Keep Prisons Single Sex event in Parliament in March 2023, Lord Blencathra revealed the strategy behind two amendments he proposed to the Police, Crime, Sentencing and Courts Bill, which aimed to exclude trans women from women's prisons. Blencathra admitted that these amendments had little chance of passing but emphasised their importance in recording the debate in Hansard and obtaining media coverage as a crucial political move: 'Although these [amendments] did not proceed to a vote . . . their significance in contributing to the groundwork that saw the recent change to policy by the Ministry of Justice is clear' (Keep Prisons Single Sex, 2023a). The change in policy he was referring to was the decision in February 2023 to roll back the existing trans prison policy in England & Wales and introduce new restrictions on housing trans women within the women's prison estate – decisions driven by political pressures rather than evidence and likely to have highly discriminatory effects (Bent Bars Project, 2023; Lamble, 2023a).

Lord Blencathra's proposed amendments occurred alongside a highly orchestrated social media strategy. In the lead-up to the proposed amendment in January 2022, a social media campaign launched on Twitter under the hashtag #KeepPrisonsSingleSex. Baroness Fox, speaking in favour of the amendment, referred to the 'huge amount of interest' outside parliament, noting that #KeepPrisonsSingleSex had been 'trending for the last 36 hours' on Twitter (HL Deb, 2022). At that point, the hashtag had 37,000 mentions. However, a subsequent investigation by Logically, a fact-checking company that specialises in fighting disinformation on the internet, revealed that the vast majority of those tweets were likely generated by bots rather than actual people (Muller-Heyndyk & Ondrak, 2022). While there was no evidence suggesting that Keep Prisons Single Sex instigated the bots, the Twitter trend created the impression of more support for the campaign than actually existed.

These examples reveal several overlapping tactics:

1) *Decontextualised claims*: Campaigners present ostensibly accurate statistics or data, but without adequate contextual information such that the claims portray a highly distorted picture of the phenomenon they are describing.
2) *Unevidenced claims, endorsed by 'experts'*: Unsupported claims are presented as facts and repeated by academics, NGOs and other 'experts', giving them legitimacy. This often amounts to what Jules Gill-Peterson describes as 'the laundering of conspiracy', whereby outlandish theories from fringe groups are repackaged by seemingly respectable commentators into more palatable, 'reasonable' and 'common sense' forms (Gill-Peterson, 2021).
3) *Playing on fears of sexual danger/otherness*: Concerns about gender-based violence are linked to trans individuals, conflating male violence with trans women. Tactics of deliberately asserting misleading associations, or what Ahmed (2011) calls 'problematic proximities', reinforce supposed links between trans identity and risk, which demonise trans people. These tactics also work to invoke punitive responses towards trans and gender non-conforming people more broadly – including increased scrutiny, surveillance and exclusion – and position trans people as undeserving of rights.
4) *Distortion of risk/prevalence*: Campaigners highlight anecdotal cases of alleged violence by trans individuals (and/or people asserted to be trans) and then overstate the prevalence of such cases. This reflects what Gillian Harkins (2020: 37) describes as the problem of 'amplification and misdirection', where fears of violence are amplified and misdirected in ways that misconstrue danger and undermine efforts necessary to address key sources of violence.
5) *Appeals to moral outrage*: Policy decisions are presented in an inflammatory way to spark what Alison Phipps (2020: 107) describes as 'outrage economies', which are designed to mobilise people on the basis of emotive claims, often attached to sexual violence and racialised safety politics. Such outrage also generates punitive and reactionary responses towards those deemed blameworthy for the problem in question.

These combined tactics gain legitimacy by leveraging concerns about safety and by reframing attacks on trans rights as protective measures for women. Since misinformation spreads rapidly on social media, alarmist claims can have a significant impact before being corrected, if corrected at all (Figueira & Oliveira, 2017). While sweeping, outrage-inducing claims are easily asserted on social media, explaining why these claims are incorrect and generating interest in those corrections requires greater time and effort. Particularly with criminal justice statistics and policy, complicated technical explanations rarely appeal to the soundbite demands of social media audiences. Even when specific claims are disproven, the accumulative effect of repeatedly asserting misleading narratives over time solidifies the association of transness with risk, ultimately turning them into 'common sense' concerns. This, in turn, escalates polarisation between those who recognise these claims as being based in false information and those who see objections to those claims as dismissing their feelings and concerns, especially when related to safety fears.

Why misinformation sticks: Emotional investments

While gender-critical groups repeatedly present their positions as based on 'fact' and 'common sense', what seems to solidify these claims is their incitement of emotions and invocation of safety fears (Thurlow, 2024; Turnbull-Dugarte & McMillan, 2023). Appealing directly to concerns about gender-based violence and establishing affinities with potential supporters through a narrative of women's shared vulnerability to violence, gender-critical groups actively channel fears of gender-based violence towards anti-trans positions. This emotional appeal, combined with long-standing cultural tropes of trans and gender-diverse people as deviant and dangerous, strategically plays on fear to generate and amplify concerns about trans rights – even when there is little empirical evidence to support such claims (Thurlow, 2024).

Many gender-critical groups exemplify this strategy of coupling 'facts and fear' tactics. Fair Play for Women, for example, claims a reputation for 'calm, rational, fact-checked, accurate information, statistics, and good-faith debate' (2022), but relies heavily on emotive language and imagery in their campaigns. During the public consultation on proposed GRA reforms in 2018, FPFW released a series of emotionally charged campaign videos, exploiting concerns about violence against women to oppose gender reform. Drawing on alarmist language and imagery and using dramatic accounts of survivors of sexual and domestic abuse, the videos suggested that proposed legal reforms would allow men, including convicted rapists, to enter women-only spaces and violate traumatised women (Fair Play for Women, 2018b; Fair Play for Women, 2018d). They also suggested that supporting GRA reform equated to disregard for survivors of sexual violence. As stated in one article,

> If this legislation happens . . . We are saying, that as a society we don't *care* if you were sexually abused as a child. We don't *care* if you went through the care system, winding up as a sex worker. We don't *care* if your husband beat you up a couple of times a week. We don't care about any of that or about what you need. (Fair Play for Women, 2017b)

FPFW also placed a full-page ad in the Metro (the free national paper distributed on public transport networks throughout the UK) to oppose reforms to the Gender Recognition Act (Duffy, 2018). The ad featured a large red square with simple white text in the centre that read: 'Think about it. #Choose Reality.' Underneath, the main campaign message stated: 'Say No to Sex Self-ID. Say YES to common sense.' The headline was deliberately paired with misleading content designed to spark outrage:

Do you think adult males should be able to enter female-only sleeping and changing areas or domestic violence refuges? Do you think fully intact, male-bodied prisoners should be allowed to live with women in prison? Do you think males should be allowed to compete against women in sport, if they feel like women? Do you think someone with a penis is a woman? . . . If you think Sex Self-ID is wrong, tell the Government not to make it law. There's no time to lose . . . Do it now, for your mum, your sister, your daughter or yourself. (Duffy, 2018).

A similar strategy was used in March 2020 by the LGB Alliance and For Women Scotland, who jointly ran a full-page ad in the *Scotsman* newspaper with the bold headline: 'Self-ID gives predators the green light.' The ad claimed that the Scottish Gender Recognition Bill would allow violent men to access women-only spaces and harm women and girls. The language in the ad was highly emotive and designed to invoke fear: 'We know that every predator typically abuses hundreds of times. So this change to the law will harm thousands of women' (Turnbull-Dugarte & McMillan, 2023, p. 635).[29]

Another widely circulated opinion piece titled 'Pronouns are Rohypnol' equated respecting trans people's pronouns with succumbing to the 'date rape drug' rohypnol (Kerr, 2019). A further article described non-binary identities as 'The new wolf in sheep's clothing' (Fair Play for Women, 2021). These tactics repeatedly associate trans rights and identities with sexual threats and danger, capitalising on widespread fears of gender-based violence to fuel opposition to trans rights.

This pairing of 'facts, reason and science' with tactics that play on fear and outrage also serves to deflect allegations of transphobia. For instance, an FPFW infographic presenting statistics about trans prisoners and sexual convictions featured the statement: 'Data isn't transphobic. Evidence isn't hateful. Facts aren't bigoted' (Fair Play for Women, 2018a). The coupling of misleading information framed as fact alongside alarmist narratives worked to garner public concern, legitimise misinformation and solidify emotional attachments to gender-critical narratives. When strong emotions are reinforced by misleading but widely believed 'facts' (and vice versa), this dynamic can also contribute to more absolutist positions, removing space for nuance, complexity and alternative viewpoints, thereby contributing to further polarisation.

Conclusion

As the 'gender wars' in Britain show little sign of abating and public debates become increasingly divisive, it is worth considering what lessons can be learnt from the role of misinformation in the escalation of polarisation. Such lessons are not limited to the UK; they hold relevance for other contexts where similar strategies are gaining momentum – particularly in North and South America, Europe, Asia and the Pacific, where tactics from British gender-critical advocates are circulating and where international anti-trans alliances are being forged. For those seeking to challenge polarisation and misinformation trends at local, national or international levels, it may be necessary to rethink existing strategies and tactics.

First, because of the distinct character of the gender wars in Britain and the leading role that women's groups and feminist voices play in the debates, conventional strategies employed for responding to left-right and conservative-progressive divisions are unlikely to be effective in reducing anti-trans misinformation or addressing polarisation. Although gender-critical feminists and women's groups are relatively small in number in Britain, they nonetheless cut across a range of political perspectives and 'enjoy a disproportionate amount of media coverage and influence over public discourse and policy' (Michaeli & Fischler, 2021, p. 110). This means counter tactics which simply dismiss all gender-critical concerns as right-wing or as solely hate-motivated are likely to fuel further backlash (Lamble, 2024).

Second, combating misinformation will require more than factual corrections (Kuo & Marwick, 2021; Reinsborough & Canning, 2017). Because anti-trans sentiments are mobilised around fear and attached to concerns around safety – which are then channelled into a shared sense of belonging and community – fact correction alone is unlikely to shift current discourse. While many of the fears underlying the gender wars are misdirected, they often stem from genuine concerns about gender-based violence that do warrant attention. Without addressing those fears, polarisation will continue to escalate, particularly if gender-critical advocates perceive objections to such fears as equivalent to dismissing concerns about sexual violence.

Third, the ease with which misinformation spreads raises key questions about the role of corporate media, the lack of media regulation in propagating misinformation and the impact of academics, NGOs and social media players in legitimising misinformation. This means that strategies targeting individual figures are unlikely to be effective in reducing misinformation or addressing polarisation. A greater focus on the role of institutions is needed.

Finally, because polarisation in the British gender wars is not characterised by the conventional left-right divide but is sutured to a wider-ranging safety politics which are invested in narratives of dangerous 'others', these deeper attachments to regressive safety politics and logics of 'us/them' need to be questioned and challenged (Lamble, 2023b). Confronting these divisions – and the wider social and political conditions which underpin and escalate them – will require new visions of safety which are grounded in principles of solidarity and collectivity rather than demonisation and othering.

Notes

1 This chapter was generously supported by a Research Fellowship from the Leverhulme Trust (RF-2023-640\8) for the project, *Beyond sex versus gender: Rethinking the 'gender wars' in Britain*. Many thanks to Kath Brown, Emily Kazyak and all the workshop participants at the Polarising Sexual and Gendered Lives

symposium at University College Dublin, in June 2023. Thanks also to Mallory Moore, Gina Gwenffrewi, Lindsey Shively, Nim Ralph, Mo Mansfield and Wayne Burnette for helpful feedback on earlier drafts.

2   The proposed reforms, considered in England, Wales and Scotland, aimed to update the legislation and remove financial, medical and bureaucratic barriers that trans people face in acquiring a Gender Recognition Certificate. Despite a lengthy public consultation process which demonstrated support for reform, the Conservative government decided in 2020 not to pursue reforms in England and Wales beyond reducing the fees to acquire a Gender Recognition Certificate and allowing online applications. In contrast, following its separate consultation processes in 2017–18, 2019–20 and 2022, Scotland passed a Gender Recognition Reform bill in 2022, but it was blocked by the UK government. Although the Scottish government launched a legal challenge against the block, it lost its case and in December 2023, decided not to appeal.

3   Many commentators have challenged the 'culture wars' frame as deliberately stoked by politicians, media and selected campaigning groups to obscure underlying class politics. E.g. See Singh Dhillon A (2023) *The Culture War Doesn't Exist: Call it what it is: class war*. Available at: https://novaramedia.com/2023/04/19/the-culture-war-doesnt-exist/ (accessed 26 August 2023).

4   Advocates of gender-critical beliefs assert that gender is a harmful concept and sex is binary and immutable, and therefore oppose trans-inclusive feminism. For a genealogy of the term in Britain, see Thurlow C (2022) From TERF to gender critical: A telling genealogy? *Sexualities*, 27(4): 962–978.

5   The founder and leading figure of Standing for Women, Kellie-Jay Keen-Minshull (also known as Posie Parker), well known for the slogan 'Women = Adult Human Female', has repeatedly stated that she is not a feminist and has been repeatedly associated with the far-right. See, for example, Posie Parker: 'To Protect Women's Rights, We Must Abandon Feminism' Maiden Mother Matriarch, YouTube, 9 May 2023, Available from: https://www.youtube.com/watch?v=NxBXNQZOR80; see also Elliards X (2023) Who is Posie Parker? The anti-trans founder of Standing for Women. *The National (online)*. Available at: https://www.thenational.scot/news/23299549.posie-parker-anti-trans-founder-standing-women/ (accessed 27 October 2023).

6   Women's Place UK describes its movement as including people 'from across the political spectrum' but explicitly defines its values as 'left and progressive' and has distanced itself from right-wing groups and figures such as Posie Parker. See: https://archive.ph/che7B & https://womansplaceuk.org/2024/07/08/the-resurgence-of-the-far-right/

7   Fair Play for Women (https://archive.ph/xTqbu); For Women Scotland (https://archive.ph/wip/Hvou3), Transgender Trend (https://archive.ph/wip/F90p0)and Sex Matters (https://sex-matters.org/about-us/) all explicitly describe themselves as non-partisan and/or having no political, ideological or religious affiliation.

8   See Lesbian, Gay, Bisexual Alliance: https://archive.ph/iqXvT

9   Get the L Out UK, a group of 'lesbian radical feminists' formed to oppose trans activism, states on its website that it is opposed to 'any kind of misogynistic politics and systems that prioritise men's interests', including 'right-wing politics and left-wing politics'. See: https://archive.ph/jjWHn

10 See, for example, the Labour Party Women's Declaration Group (https://archive.ph/wip/TbIZ4); Liberal Voice for Women (Liberal Democrats) (https://archive.ph/WhWy3); Green Women's Declaration (https://archive.ph/WKUT8); Scottish

National Party Women's Pledge (https://archive.ph/Ox6Cd); and Conservatives for Women (https://archive.ph/mPsbt). In Wales, there are gender-critical groups but, at the time of writing, no public subgroup of Plaid Cymru.

11   Some research suggests that the British culture wars are characterised by four distinct groups (traditionalists, moderates, progressives and disengaged) rather than two. See: Duffy B, Hewlett K, Murkin G, et al. (2021) Culture wars in the UK. June 2021. London: The Policy Institute, King's College London. Available at: https://www.kcl.ac.uk/policy-institute/assets/culture-wars-in-the-uk.pdf (accessed 27 October 2023).

12   Countries that have adopted self-ID to date include Argentina (2012), Belgium (2018), Brazil (2018), Colombia (2015), Costa Rica (2018), Denmark (2014), Greece (2017), Iceland (2019), Ireland (2015), Luxembourg (2018), Malta (2015), New Zealand (2023), Norway (2016), Portugal (2018), Spain (2023), Switzerland (2022), Uruguay (2018).

13   Legally, 'sex-based rights' do not exist; this is a political term. Legal protections prohibit discrimination on grounds of sex (as well as gender identity, sexual orientation and other categories), but there are no special rights granted because of a person's sex.

14   Notably, the Guardian's stance in the UK was contested by its US and Australian counterparts. See Levin S, Chalabi M and Siddiqui S (2018) Why we take issue with the Guardian's stance on trans rights in the UK. The *Guardian*, 2 November. Available at: https://www.theguardian.com/commentisfree/2018/nov/02/guardian-editorial-response-transgender-rights-uk (accessed 16 August 2023).

15   In September 2020, the government confirmed that it would not be reforming the GRA. BBC News (2020) Changes to gender recognition laws ruled out. *BBC News*, 22 September. Available at: https://www.bbc.com/news/uk-politics-54246686 (accessed 24 August 2023).

16   See footnote 2.

17   Other polls indicate increased negativity towards trans people in Britain, though results vary depending on the demographics of survey participants and the questions asked. A YouGov poll, for example, found that, in contrast to the general public, cis gay, lesbian and bisexual Britons feel overwhelmingly positive towards trans people. Smith M (2023) What do lesbian, gay, bisexual and transgender Britons think the British public thinks of them? *YouGov*. Available at: https://yougov.co.uk/topics/society/articles-reports/2023/08/11/what-do-lesbian-gay-bisexual-and-transgender-brito (accessed 24 August 2023).

18   At that time, placement decisions for trans prisoners in Scotland, England and Wales were not contingent on having a Gender Recognition Certificate. All placement decisions were made on a case-by-case, risk-assessed basis, rather than simply legal gender.

19   Though not peer-reviewed, the report was nonetheless repeatedly portrayed by Fair Play for Women as if it were an academic study. Its author, Dr Nicola Williams, was also presented as an expert, despite the fact that her academic credentials (biochemistry) are unrelated to criminology, sociology or gender studies. The report offers an example of a common pattern where gender-critical advocates use their academic credentials in one area to claim expertise in an unrelated area. While this is unacceptable in most disciplines (e.g. a literary scholar would not be credibly asked their view on astrophysics), it is a common problem in relation to gender issues.

20 The report acknowledges that 'No official statistics are systematically recorded by prisons stating the number of trans-identifying inmates and the types of offences for which they are convicted. It is impossible to precisely calculate the percentage of TIMs [sic] who are sex offenders. However, using the incomplete data set available, we have provided the best estimate available . . . we have inferred their convictions depending on the prison in which they are housed' (Fair Play for Women, 2017a).

21 Notably, when the Independent ran a comment piece by Owl Fisher challenging the claims, Fair Play for Women responded with a legal claim of defamation. According to FPFW, the case was settled out of court, with the headline changed, and some facts corrected. Fair Play for Women (2018c) *Victory for Women Tonight . . . [tweet]*. Available at: https://twitter.com/fairplaywomen/status/1053033005021847553 (accessed 23 August 2023).

22 The 2018–19 HMIP annual report found that 2 per cent of prisoners surveyed in the adult male estate and 1 per cent in the female estate identified as trans. It also found higher percentages among foreign nationals (3 per cent), Travellers (10 per cent) and disabled prisoners (3 per cent). The 2019–20 report had similar findings: 2 per cent of male and 1 per cent of female, with higher figures for foreign nationals (3 per cent), Travellers (7 per cent) and disabled prisoners (3 per cent). The 2020–1 report did not include information on trans prisoners. The 2021–2 HMIP annual report data indicated that 1 per cent of prisoners surveyed in the male estate and 2 per cent of prisoners in the female estate identified as trans. It also found a higher rate of 3 per cent in the open estate. Because HMIP reports do not necessarily cover a representative sample of prisons, there are limits to generalising the findings, but they provide an important indication of the differences between self-reporting and staff reporting of prisoners' gender identities. Self-reporting is also standard in other identity-collecting for race, ethnicity, disability and sexuality.

23 Some of those additional people could also be in prison for sexual offences. However, the key issue is that the percentage of trans people with convictions for sexual offences is entirely dependent on the overall number of trans people in prison, and that figure varies significantly depending on the data collection method.

24 The Office for National Statistics distinguishes between 'official' and 'unofficial' statistics, with the former being those whose reliability is considered robust. The latter applies to secondary sources of information which are seen as less reliable due to discrepancies in reporting. The statistics that Sullivan relied on were explicitly described by the ONS as 'not designated as official statistics'. In 2014, the UK Statistic Authority downgraded the status of police-recorded crime figures due to unreliability and concerns that some figures had been subject to 'a degree of fiddling' – Travis A (2014) Police crime figures lose official status over claims of fiddling. *The Guardian*. Available at: https://www.theguardian.com/uk-news/2014/jan/15/police-crime-figures-status-claims-fiddling (accessed 24 August 2023).

25 Sullivan noted: 'Some commentators may have assumed that all 436 defendants were male. This assumption is not justified.'

26 Notably, the claim itself was visible to the public, but the correction, placed at the bottom of the article, was only visible to subscribers of the *Times* (Moore 2022).

27 See footnote 24.

28 While the new guidance was considered voluntary for police forces from 2022 onwards, it is expected to become compulsory.
29 The ad also included a number of inaccuracies about the bill. See testimony of MP John Nicolson: https://mermaidsuk.org.uk/wp-content/uploads/2022/09/2022.01.31-Witness-Statement-of-John-Nicolson-MP-1.pdf

Chapter 11

NAVIGATING THE TENSIONS OF CREATIVITY AND DIVISION

PLANNING AN ARTIST-LED WORKSHOP TO ADDRESS POLARISATIONS AROUND SEXUALITIES/GENDERS/ABORTION[1]

Carol Ballantine, Leah Hilliard and Kath Browne

Introduction

Significant socio-legal changes have taken place related to gender, sexuality and abortion in Ireland, Great Britain and Canada, towards the liberalisation of legal regimes and greater reproductive and sexual rights. Nonetheless, there are significant divisions, differences and polarisations around these issues. We understand social polarisation in this chapter as processes that construct deep, oppositional and/or fundamental divisions around sexuality, gender and/or abortion, with our specific focus on divisions regarding socio-legal changes. We see these emerging through popular votes, media and social media but under-investigated in terms of how they manifest and how they might be addressed.

In Ireland, popular votes on the implementation of same-sex marriage and abortion passed in two separate referendums by a majority vote, demonstrating mainstream public support for the changes. At the same time, in both cases, significant minorities opposed the changes: the 'No' vote in each referendum was higher than 34 per cent (Elkink et al., 2020). The question of living with/ across polarisations is a timely one that needs multiple explorations. This chapter, coming from the project Beyond Opposition, explores one approach to researching the question – how might we live together if we cannot change everyone's 'hearts and minds'? In doing so, we examine 'tackling' polarisation through presumptions of division/difference that will not disappear. We take as given that other work needs to be done alongside education, activism and other political and academic work to tackle marginalisation. With this in mind, we came to work together as an artist and researchers to create a one-day artist-led workshop in Dublin that brought together members of the public who held fundamentally different positions on the topics of gender, sexuality and/or abortion. We set out to enable up to fifteen workshop participants to directly encounter the 'other' in relation to their positions, in a space that would be simultaneously open and imaginative, yet also carefully managed and controlled. The workshop was designed to facilitate creative and imaginative inquiry, while also deliberately bringing people directly in contact with difference and opposition. The purpose was not to attempt to resolve differences between participants; nor to debate the issues and come to an agreement; nor to find commonalities across them. Rather, we aimed to creatively consider how we live alongside/with difference and division in this arena. We chose artistic research methods in order to move outside of established modes of discussion and debate, to provide the opportunity to think in new, experimental and utopic ways about sharing space.

In this chapter, we outline the approach we took to meeting this challenge, offering insights into the 'how to' when considering addressing polarisations creatively across complex and fraught differences. We introduce the idea of using an experimental artist-led workshop[2] to facilitate a space for creatively imagining new ways of living together with difference, recognising the potential and importance of creative methods in this vein as social science research praxis.[3]

In exploring the collaborations and eventual plan for the day, this chapter speaks to the possibilities of research intervening in divisions and polarisations in new ways that do not negate the importance of activism, conflict resolution and other modes of engaging others. It addresses a key tension that drove our considerations of how to address polarisation through research, namely how to facilitate creative and imaginative research with a group of strangers on a topic that they fundamentally disagree about.

The chapter begins with a discussion of the rationale for the Beyond Opposition project; the 'New Ireland' as a place to address the polarisations explored in Beyond Opposition; and the creative methods we used in the Irish artist-led workshops. It then outlines the process of building a research partnership between a research team and a visual artist researcher. Next, we present an annotated version of the timetable that we devised for the Irish day-long workshop. The timetable is followed by a discussion of the considerations of key aspects of facilitating this space, recognising the tension between creativity and polarisation, when we are not seeking common ground or resolutions to differences between participants. We end with reflections on the aspects that made it possible to set up this workshop and note that the replication of these workshops, as is often a presumption of social scientific research, is not a given and should be undertaken with caution.

Beyond Opposition: Working creatively across difference

Beyond Opposition is an ERC five-year research project that is interested in addressing social divisions in places where there have been changes to policies and laws related to gender, sexualities and abortion; namely Ireland, Canada and Great Britain (see www.beyondopposition.org). It arises out of work that Kath did with Catherine Nash on heteroactivism (Nash & Browne, 2020), that conceptualised and explored twenty-first-century resistances to LGBT equalities in Canada, Ireland and Great Britain. Beyond Opposition arose because, while documenting the shifting changes in contestations of LGBT inclusions as they were manifested in countries that had adopted socio-legal changes, including same-sex marriage, gender recognition and abortion provision, it became apparent that these resistances were not simply 'dying out'. Instead, they were and are morphing and adapting in geographically specific ways (Nash & Browne, 2020). It became clear that the playing out of these contestations around sexualities, genders and abortions have increasingly retrenched certain positionings in this arena. This is driving forms of social divisions in these areas that have yet to be understood and addressed, particularly outside of the United States.

This project does not negate work that seeks to educate, protest or engage in developing social justice in ways that oppose, contest and challenge. Instead, this research asks for a different engagement alongside these approaches, one that considers the effects of opposition itself on lives and how it might be addressed. Refusing a singular answer, we take the perspective that there is no one 'right' tactic that is appropriate for everyone, every situation and that can offer a universal blueprint. Therefore, *only* vilifying opponents risks playing into narratives of opposition and exclusion that further their political appeal (which we will explore further in papers in draft, see www.beyondopposition.org for updates on publications).

Beyond Opposition initially conducted 161 interviews with those who are opposed to or concerned about socio-legal changes in gender, sexuality and abortion, exploring their experiences of everyday life, including in 'New Ireland' (Browne & Nash, 2020, 2023a, 2023b). One of the most striking recent shifts in Irish politics is the extensive changes to 'middle Ireland' social and political positions related to gender, sexualities and abortion (McCartan, 2022; Browne et al., 2018, Reidy, 2020). With the passing of referenda on marriage equality (2015) and abortion (2018), and the enactment of the Gender Recognition Act (Government of Ireland, 2015), Ireland moved from having among the most regressive social legislation in Europe to being widely seen as a progressive front-runner (McAuliffe, 2018). This has fed into the nation's imaginings of itself as progressive, cosmopolitan and 'equal' (Browne et al., 2018; McCartan, 2022; Neary, 2016). However, in both referenda, more than 34 per cent of voters rejected the proposed changes, and divisions and contestations on these subjects persist (Nash & Browne, 2020), illustrating that division and difference remain. Such divisions can fuel polarisation.

This chapter focuses on addressing these social polarisations through the Irish artist-led workshop to consider how we might live together where we fundamentally disagree. Arts-based research methods are well-established within the social sciences for generating and disseminating new knowledge (Chilton & Leavy, 2014, Kara, 2015). They can go beyond the more established methods of interviewing, focus groups and questionnaires, in thinking about exploring lives and possibilities that offer new approaches to research (Barone & Eisner, 2011). Creative and arts-based inquiry resists rigid and narrow approaches to knowledge-production, instead privileging 'play, intuition, serendipity, imagination and the unexpected as resources for making sense' (Kara et al., 2015, p. 22). An objective of Beyond Opposition is to collectively imagine utopic alternative ways of sharing space: we chose arts-based methods in order to access imaginative and creative conceptualisations rather than purely discursive or linguistic ones. We did this in the hope that through creative exploration, new insights into how to address social polarisation might be generated. However, in choosing arts-based methods, we confronted a challenge: how to introduce a discussion around living with differences in relation to positions on gender, sexuality and/or abortion with their attendant tensions, while also facilitating a space that could be creative and imaginative.

The Beyond Opposition artist-led workshops not only draw on creative methods but they extend their possibilities for research on polarisation related to gender and sexuality. We created workshops that bring together people who hold different views, but in doing this, our intention was explicitly not to debate the issues in ways that wish to change 'hearts and minds' for the benefit of specific marginalised groups, as can be key in social justice research, policy interventions and other forms of engaging with those who disagree (Denzin, 2018; Enright, McNeely & de Londras, 2020, Guyan, 2022). We also did not seek common ground or attempt to build trust or shared objectives across differences, as can be key to facilitating research workshops for conflict management and peacebuilding (e.g. Linabary et al., 2017, Julian et al., 2019, Fernandez Martínez et al., 2018). Instead, these spaces ask for people to consider and play with the possibilities of (new) worlds, where we don't assume everyone will eventually hold the same positions in relation to gender, sexuality and abortion or that finding commonality is necessary. Before outlining our plan for the day and its rationale, we first use our separate voices to explore how we came to work together to create an arts-based workshop, and then together discuss the process that brought us to designing a space for creating visual art inspired by circles, cups of tea and encountering those who disagree with us.

The dance of creating the Irish artist-led workshop

Researchers: Working as social science researchers, Carol and Kath recruited Leah. We were drawn to her diverse and interconnected practice, which brings together facilitation, performance and making with fabric and other materials, all connected by themes of conversation, relationships and everyday life. Leah's practice aligned with our research interest in daily life and day-to-day spaces. Her expertise in facilitation, coupled with her joyful artistic approach, made her well-placed to lead a workshop that was experimental, novel, potentially uncomfortable and required creative, confident and flexible leadership.

Leah: When I first heard about Beyond Opposition, I was daunted by the scope of the project but knew it was opening a door to an amazing opportunity to work with an incredible team. I didn't run through the door; I was guided in through a well-crafted brief[4] which allowed me to reflect and consider the task. My primary concern was that it was to be a solo run, facilitating the workshop as a service provider, but I agreed to take part when it was clear that I would be working in concert with a team.

Together: The brief that the Beyond Opposition research team created structured our initial meeting. The three of us met at the very beginning of the collaboration (in December, in advance of an early-March workshop) to establish what Beyond Opposition was seeking to understand and how we hoped to use an artist-led space to explore this. We took baby steps together at first, working out the dance of who would lead certain sections of the day and who would guide others, and like good dance partners, we played to our strengths and where we had expertise. Some of Leah's previous work (Hilliard, 2018a, 2018b) had drawn on the motif of a kettle and cups of tea to explore everyday relationships and the power of conversation. In other work, Leah had used the figure of concentric circles, which she used from teaching boundaries (Raising Children Network, ND). Carol read these as reflecting on socio-ecological models of the person in relation to others in society (Brofenbrenner, 1977), while Kath associated them with Burgess's (1925) land use model, still taught to Geography students! We agreed to build the workshop structure around the two motifs of cups of tea and concentric circles of social relationships – to bring participants to think about fundamental differences related to gender, sexuality and/ or abortion in day-to-day life. By overlaying the motif of cups of tea (representing relationalities and ordinariness) with the concentric circles (a simple visual depiction of everyday spatialities) (see Figure 11.1), we sought to give participants an entry point to imagine different ways of relating to the 'other' in place (as we explore in detail in the next sections).

We planned the workshop over a series of meetings – initially monthly, then weekly coming closer to the workshop. We often met at one of our kitchen tables, and inspired by Sara Ahmed (2006), our thinking about the outputs of the workshop frequently drew on the idea of domestic tables as relational and social spaces infused with power. In this way, the outline of the day-long workshop was devised through a collaborative process: Leah offering up ways of working and approaches, and all of us as a team exploring/playing with/ critiquing them.

Our process involved first agreeing on a structure that emphasised the participant experience. This was led by Leah in the preparation, and she took the lead in facilitating this aspect. Once this was agreed upon, we explored ways to deliberately and sensitively introduce the themes of gender, sexuality, abortion and difference without discussing, debating or attempting to resolve them. This thematic/conceptual part was handled through the planning and workshop facilitation by the researchers Kath and Carol (as discussed below). We aimed for participants to build their skills and confidence with the artistic activities over the course of the day. We wanted participants and the research team to feel reassured by providing clarity as to the roles each person (Leah/ Carol/Kath) played in the space. The activities and prompts were developed iteratively, moving between the artistic and conceptual prompts to ensure that each supported the other.

We turn now to explore the final annotated timetable of the day, offering new insights into a plan for an artist-led workshop that seeks to address polarisation by exploring how we engage with those whom we disagree with, without seeking common ground or resolutions to these differences.

Artist-led workshop: The run of the day

This workshop was planned for a Sunday in March 2023, in Dublin city centre. It was led by Leah, Kath and Carol, supported by the rest of the Beyond Opposition research team: two postdoctoral researchers (Katherine Young and Andrew McCartan) and the project manager, who is also a trained counsellor responsible for project oversight, logistics and psycho-social care (Aoife Grant).

The workshop was structured to move from the specific, concrete and individual to the non-specific, abstract and collective, across two pillars: the artistic *making* process and the conceptual *thinking and talking* process (see Table 11.1). Reading through the timetable, we explore the activities and plan for the day. These worked across and between our interests and expertise to offer new ways of doing, understanding and engaging with creative methods across polarisation and difference. We initially show our own technical notes in *italics* and then expand on the rationale for these in each section.[5] This offers new insights into ways in which we might work across differences and bring people together to imagine creatively alongside their disagreements around gender, sexuality and/ or abortion.

Table 11.1 Timetable for Artist-Led Workshop

	Timetable for Artist-Led Workshop
10.00	Start
10.05	Introduction: Kath
	Housekeeping/Ethics/Outline of session
	Participants seated in circle at/near screen.
	Kath begins the day with a detailed outline of the project's ethical standards and the guidelines that participants have agreed to abide by to make the research possible.
10:30	**Introduction to Leah**
	Participants seated in circle at/near screen – Kath reads short bio.
10:35–11:00	**Mugs introduction** (Leah)
	Choose a mug;
	Grab a cuppa and a pastry;
	Sitting in the circle, share why you chose that mug.
	We use mugs in an introductory exercise to get participants speaking: this gives everyone something to associate each person with as a shorthand. On arrival, participants are asked to select a mug they like before getting tea or coffee. The mugs are carefully chosen to avoid any association with any 'side' and are differentiated in terms of colour, shape, size and texture. Upon returning to the plenary circle, participants are asked to talk about why they selected each particular mug. This icebreaker gives everyone some small insights into people's daily lives without requiring them to reveal anything personal about themselves or their positionalities. The icebreaker leads to the mug representing the individual within the concentric circles model that is introduced next.
11:00	**Leah: Introducing the tea/coffee/circles device**
	Participants seated in circle around the white tablecloth with concentric circles: see Figure 11.1.
	Leah delivers this script about teas and coffees and the concentric circles as she places objects and labels onto each circle (see Figure 11.1).
	Leah:
	This Mirrorball kettle was a piece of work that I made to discuss the electric kettle as the centre of the Irish home. As a nation of tea and coffee drinkers, we spend about eleven minutes a day on average waiting for the kettle to boil. Each of us knows the sound of our own kettle when it is clicked on and when it's about to come to the boil.
	I'd like to invite you to consider the different ways we encounter people and cups of tea and coffee in our everyday lives. The centre circle is the individual represented by **a mug**. *The cup of tea or coffee that we make ourselves exactly the way we like it.* **A personal or private space.**
	Next ring is those people who, when making them a cuppa, the milk is taken directly from the fridge, and **the carton** *plonked on the table. There is no standing on ceremony. You may know them well enough to put the milk in for them. For example, pouring until it appears to come back up, or the tiniest drop to alter the colour.* **So this ring is home.**
	Then there's the people, where it calls for **a jug.** *Putting some effort in. These are people who might visit you at home or whom you might go out with. People who wouldn't necessarily know where you keep your teabags.* **Here we are talking about spaces where we socialise.**

(Continued)

Table 11.1 (Continued)

*The **teapot** represents a wider community – on a wider ring, this is a broader group of people, people who might be part of a club, a church, a book group. People you have something in common with, maybe a shared passion – and also a lot of differences: the tea in the pot may be too weak or too strong; you have to make compromises when you're working with groups.* **So this ring is community spaces.**

*This **stackable cup** is the type you find to the side of a tea or coffee urn, a cup that never holds quite enough. This cup represents workmates, colleagues, people who you work with, volunteer with and are part of your professional life.* **This level refers to the world of work.**

*Finally, the outer edge is **the takeaway cup** that you might see out on the street. This represents public space, and it might include things like people you see on posters or on TV, or strangers you pass in the street.* **Public space.**

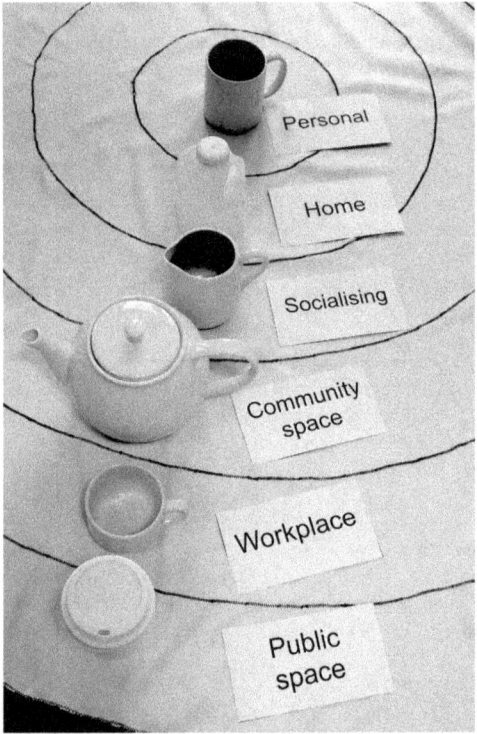

Figure 11.1: The concentric circles with objects.

We return to this visual device throughout the day to anchor participants' reflections on the spatialities of their everyday lives and 'the other', as related to issues concerning gender, sexuality and abortion. The metaphor of cups of tea is used to ground conversations in the day-to-day and the relational.

(*Continued*)

Table 11.1 (Continued)

11:10–12:00	**Sharpie pen exercise** **Leah:** *Explain how to make the sharpie stick* **Kath/Carol**. *Prompt: Consider people who hold different views from you on gender, sexuality and/ or abortion and where you meet or encounter them, how you engage with them. They might be real individuals in your life, strangers that you know of, or specific organisations, or anything/anybody else. Which of these items/objects/locations best represents where and how you relate to those people in your day-to-day life?* **Leah:** *Using your stick, draw the object(s) that you have chosen.*

Following the visual of the concentric circle, we invite participants to reflect individually and privately on the idea of 'the other', as related to issues concerning gender, sexuality and abortion in their own lives. As per the prompt above, we ask participants to draw one of the objects in the circle that represents where and how they relate to people who disagree on issues related to gender, sexuality and/ or abortion in their everyday lives. They use an 'extended sharpie pen' to make the drawing (Figure 11.2).

Participants make the extended pen by using masking tape to attach a Sharpie marker to the end of a piece of doweling approximately four feet long. These could have been pre-made, but by having participants make the tools themselves, we aim to give them ownership. With this task, the participants start handling the materials and sharing resources, through the passing of masking tape and pens.

For the first art activity, participants are asked to either stand or sit and draw using the extended pen onto cardboard with a circle already drawn; they are guided by the prompt and by the concentric circles and crockery model. The white cardboard is robust, so easy to handle and doesn't need to be taped to the floor; at A2 there is plenty of space for someone to work while standing up. The aim of the extended pen activity is to have the participants generate a wobbly drawing so that individual skills are not showcased: it is inherently hard to achieve a perfect line using the extended pen (see Figure 11.2).

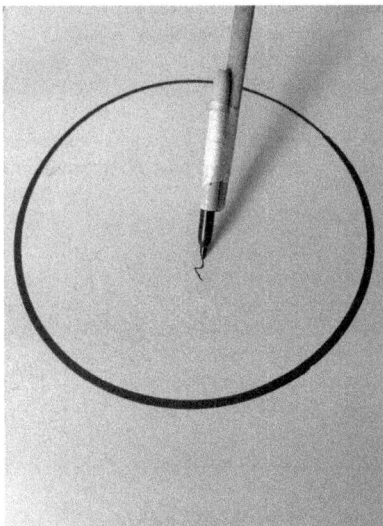

Figure 11.2: Drawing using the extended sharpie pen.

(*Continued*)

Table 11.1 (Continued)

    Work work work

    Group reflection
    Leah: *How did you find that activity? Invite responses in plenary.*
- *Probe (if necessary): Leah techniques, art*
- *Probe (if necessary): Kath + Carol – ideas, representations – tell us about your object,* **please share your position/ or the people you disagree with, if you want to.**
- *If you want to, write down your thoughts about that object on a* **post-it note***. You can share with the research team anonymously or with your participant sticker/number.*

Participants come back together in the circle with their completed drawings for a group discussion. In plenary, we invite anybody who wants to share thoughts about either the artistic process or the decisions they made about what to represent and why. This is the first time in this workshop that participants are invited to share their own positions on the subject of gender, sexuality and/or abortion – or more specifically, to identify the positions that they considered to be *against* their own. Participants are free to share/reveal as much or as little information about their own positions and those they disagree with as they choose. Alternatively, they can write their thoughts on a post-it note and share them confidentially with the research team only.

12:00–1:00   *Placemat exercise*
    Leah *Prompt: how to make the placemat – wobbly and fragile may move.*
In the next activity, participants recreate their drawings in collage form, using coloured paper inserted into a clear A3 lamination pouch to make a placemat. They are not given any scissors, glue or pens, instead they have to rip the paper into the shapes they require and then place it within the fold of the laminate pouch. The paper is held in place by static electricity and gravity, so it is quite precarious. The emphasis here is on not being perfect or literal but aiming to make the images further abstracted and to get the participants working with colour and shape, removing any reliance on line. This activity is physically immersive and very free-form, playing with colour and texture. Scissors at this stage could lead to precision, which is the opposite of the approach we want to promote. There are inherent constraints in the paper choices: none of the paper is larger than A4, so the participants can't fill the background of their image easily. While we don't curtail a solid image, the materials steer participants so that some of the transparency of the lamination sheet is likely to remain (Figure 11.3).

Kath/Carol: *On hand to answer questions or prompt further*
– are there colours or shapes that speak to how you relate to the people you disagree with?

Work work work

Lamination stations

Once complete: bring placemat to one of three laminators: three researchers on hand to laminate and record brief individual discussions.
Open question: *Do you want to tell me about your placemat? Object/position*
(Prompts if wanted: What object did you choose? Would you like to tell me why that object?)

At three laminator stations set up at the side of the room, participants are invited to reflect individually with a postdoctoral researcher about the object they selected, and the reasons behind their artistic choices. This allows for a relatively private audio-recorded conversation between the participant and the researcher, and it gives participants the opportunity to share their thought process directly with the research team, without having to tell any other members of the group. As the art becomes increasingly abstract, we invite them to provide interpretations, if they want to, of the choices they are making: colours, symbols, shapes and so on (Figure 11.3).

(Continued)

Table 11.1 (Continued)

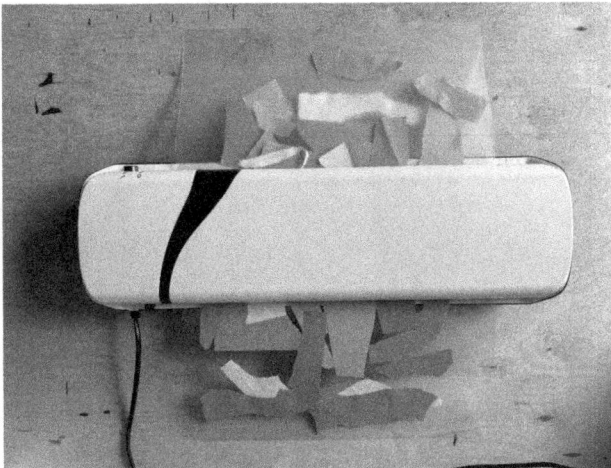

Figure 11.3: A placemat moving through the laminator: loose and flimsy as it enters above; fixed and shiny after lamination below.

1:00–1:30	**Lunch**
	During a deliberately short lunch break to avoid too much informal interaction, Carol and Kath determine the allocation of participants into three groups of four for the afternoon activities. Each group is organised to ensure some degree of diversity in positions related to gender, sexuality and abortion and in relation to their interactions during the morning; as researchers we have information about positions from questions asked confidentially during the recruitment process, although participants do not, necessarily. The group composition is not explained to the participants in any detail. The hope is that in working directly with those who disagree, participants might encounter the 'other', and this might lead to creative possibilities. In each of the three groups, we choose to have at least one person with concerns about or opposition to legal and social changes related to gender, sexuality and abortion, and at least one person who told us during recruitment that they were fully in favour of these changes.
1:30	***Placemat group discussion***
	Concentric circles (white table cloth) *Participants standing/sitting around the circle in plenary.* **Leah** – *invite participants to remember where the different objects go.* **Kath/Carol Prompt:** *Take your placemat, and position it on the circles in the place that makes the most sense to where you see people who disagree with you and how you relate to them. This doesn't have to be the same as when you started, and the object and the place might be different.* Once the collages are fixed by the laminator they are transformed – now robust and shiny they can be handled easily (Figure 11.3). Gathering in the plenary space after lunch, once all the placemats are laminated, participants are asked to place their placemats back onto the concentric circles model (Figure 11.1), considering their response to it and therefore increasing their familiarity with it. The transparency of the laminate allows the lines of the circle bands to be seen through the placemats. Additionally, participants can layer their collages on top of each other if they wish.

(Continued)

Table 11.1 (Continued)

1:45　　　*Decorating wedges of the tablecloth (group exercise)*

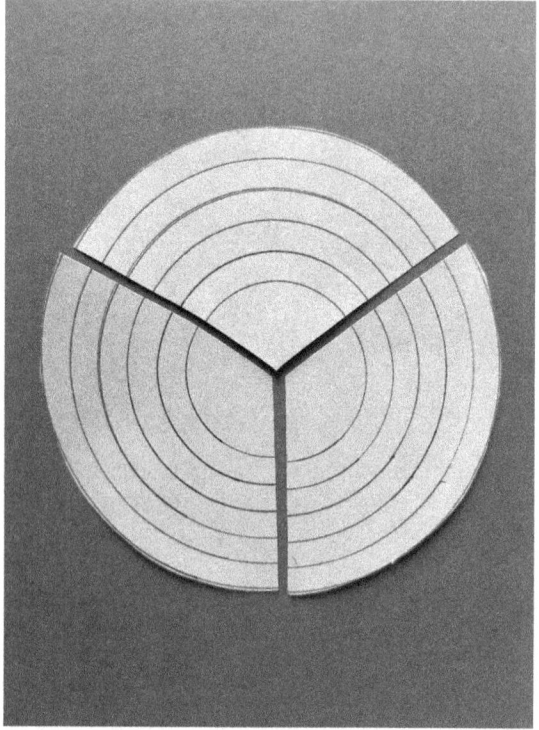

Figure 11.4: Diagram of a tablecloth with concentric circles, divided into three wedges.

Leah: instruction:
You're going to break into three groups (we'll assign you).
Outline how to move from placemats to wedges.
Note that the wedges are arranged in concentric circular layers (Figure 11.4).
Carol/Kath: prompt (on slide):
Consider how and where we relate to each other when we don't agree. What might we do differently? How can we live with each other? What would a 'perfect world' look like?
Carol/ Kath assign people to groups (as decided at lunch)
Carol/Katie/Andrew at three tables, four participants at each table, with audio recorders in mugs.

Each of the tables is given a third of the circle to work on, a wedge (see Figure 11.4, above). The wedges are white felt with black stitched lines to indicate the bands of the concentric circle (Figure 11.4). Each participant receives scissors and craft glue, and instructions on how to use the glue best. Coloured fabric is available at the top of the room and requires the group to select and gather what fabric they want. The colours of the fabrics match those of the paper they used earlier in the day in the placemat activity. Working at separate tables not only breaks up the group for documentation and conversation purposes, it also allows for access to the materials so that there aren't too many people crowding around the one set of resources.

(Continued)

Table 11.1 (Continued)

The instruction to the groups is to create a collective artwork on a wedge of fabric, bringing together the placemats that participants made earlier in the day. The placemats represent individual experiences of difference related to gender, sexuality and abortion; with this wedge exercise, participants are challenged to integrate their respective 'others' collectively on a piece of fabric that maintains the different levels of the concentric circles. We invite them to think about the different social spaces where we encounter difference related to gender, sexuality and abortion; and to try to bring together the colours, shapes and ideas that fed into their individual placemats, accepting and acknowledging that difference persists and is not going away. The key challenge in this activity is to answer the question, 'what would a "perfect world" look like?'

An important dimension here is that we do not know how participants will respond to the invitation: as artists and researchers we deliberately relinquish control of the afternoon activities and invite participants to be exploratory and creative. We provide materials and techniques to allow participants to collectively imagine shared space that accommodates difference, deliberately offering a minimum of instruction, removing our own framings of difference, opposition and polarisation. We invite participants to imagine visually and texturally a different way of experiencing opposition.

Leah on hand to give technical guidance, feedback, ideas.
Katie/Andrew/Carol oversee ground rules (adhere to guidelines Use people's own language etc.)
Offer prompts + probe as necessary.
Prompts for researchers:
How are we connecting across different places?
Are there differences in different places that make it easier/harder?
What might it mean to live together and not agree?

Work work work

Each table is overseen by a researcher who is responsible for observing adherence to the guidelines (respect, confidentiality, using preferred terms, not debating issues) and offering help where it is required. If help needed is technical or artistic, Leah is on hand to provide it; researchers are on hand to facilitate the conversation, particularly the conceptual aspect of the activity, and to ask prompt questions.

3:15	**Final plenary**
	Leah: *gather group together in plenary at screen* *Lay out the three sections together* *[if time] Organize to fit together well.*
	In the final session of the day, participants gather back together in a circle to reflect on the overall experience, process and the art produced. We steer the discussion deliberately to ask participants to acknowledge and accept differences related to gender, sexuality and abortion; and to imagine a 'perfect world' that does not seek to overcome or silence that difference. Participants are invited to share the art that they have created, the discussions they had and to reflect on what this tells us about others and othering. There is no image to represent this session, as it is impossible for us as researchers to anticipate what the participants will create.
3:30	*Reflection on day as a whole, feedback* *Prompts: How was that for you?*
4:00	*Wrap up – Kath thank you*

Discussion

Social polarisation around sexuality, gender and abortion requires attention, including, but not limited to, engaging across differences. How this is undertaken has yet to be explored, particularly in places like Ireland, where recent changes have resulted in the liberalisation of legal regimes and the provision of new reproductive, gender and sexual rights. While scholars, activists and practitioners will continue to seek ways of deepening these changes, the continued presence of fundamental differences demands that we consider the question: how do we live together if we accept that we cannot change everybody's 'hearts and minds'? The workshop we designed set out to facilitate creative and imaginative responses to this question, requiring us to maintain a focus on contestations around gender, sexuality and abortion without attempting to debate, resolve or indeed ignore these issues. By deliberately bringing together people with fundamentally different positions related to these topics, we were inviting a degree of discomfort, and potentially conflict, into the room, and the workshop design needed to respond to this discomfort while facilitating creativity. In this section, we present four aspects of the approach we developed to address the tension between inviting creativity while sustaining a focus on polarisation. These are: employing artistic activities that don't require expertise; developing a clear artistic and conceptual narrative arc for the day; carefully managing the invitation to share individual positions related to the topics of gender, sexuality and/or abortion; and collecting data in multiple, varied ways. Overall, we develop understandings of how workshops across fundamental differences that seek to address polarisation might be constituted, and some limits of these approaches.

First, **the visual art activities were devised in such a way that no particular level of expertise was needed**. This meant that pre-existing artistic skill sets were not a criteria for inclusion, and there was a 'levelling' that allowed all participants equal space to create, regardless of their skill level. Specific techniques, such as drawing with a modified Sharpie pen (see Sharpie pen exercise, Figure 11.10 and Figure 11.2 in the timetable above) and collaging without scissors or the colours black and white (see the placemat exercise, 12.00/Figure 11.3), deliberately sought to make the activities equally new and difficult for all participants. This also allowed for the activities themselves to be part of the process, rather than the learning of skills/techniques forming the centrepiece of the day.

Second, the individual activities were created within a **deliberate and co-constitutive artistic+conceptual arc to the day**. The artwork was an outcome in itself and was further used to scaffold the discussions and explorations of what it means to live with/across difference related to gender, sexuality and/or abortion. In developing how the day would progress, we carefully orchestrated art+conceptual prompts to facilitate mutual explorations.

This art+prompts for discussion creation also developed through how participants were asked to work. We prompted them to move from working individually before the lunch break (albeit socially, alongside one another, with room for spontaneous conversation) to working in pre-defined groups made up of diverse positions related to gender, sexuality and abortion in the final artistic exercise decorating the wedges of a tablecloth (1.45/Figure 11.4). At the same time, they moved from working figuratively, directly representing ideas connected to place and the social other, to working more abstractly both in terms of artistic techniques and conceptualisations of 'utopia'. The final group exercise, decorating one of three wedges in small groups, was the longest activity (one hour: 1.45/Figure 11.4), and the one where the key tension outlined in this paper – between creativity and polarisation – was designed to be most present. Here, participants were given autonomy to create without extensive instructions, either technical or conceptual. In doing this, our intention, having equipped the groups with tools and ideas to work with earlier in the day, was to leave enough space for participants to encounter the fundamental differences within their groups and to experiment creatively within this encounter to imagine utopian ways of sharing space.

While our intention in using creative methods was to open a space for free-flowing imaginative work, because of the topics involved, we provided a level of clarity and specificity in our instructions prior to moving to abstraction. The spaces that we sought to create between people offered time for participants to work individually and find their place in the workshop, before working collectively with others with whom they disagreed.

The third important aspect of our approach to the tensions in this workshop relates to the sharing of essential but sensitive information. There are unique challenges to working with a group where we deliberately **introduce and seek to address topics that we know result in/from polarisations and choose not to discuss/resolve/ignore these**. Our planning did not include formats or aims that would be typical of most arts-based research workshops, such as establishing commonalities or developing interpersonal relationships (Fernandez Martínez et al., 2018, Linabary et al., 2017), because we wanted to hold open the likelihood that participants would view one another as opponents, and ask them to work *with* that fact rather than moving past it. To facilitate this, we planned the Irish workshop to provide enough space for individuals to encounter, engage and explore the idea of fundamental differences throughout. Each activity asked people to think about those with whom they disagreed, and through invitations to share their work in pairs, small groups and in plenary, there was an opportunity for participants to identify their own positionalities should they so choose. We coupled this with explicitly inviting people to withhold their views and positionings, should they prefer. The data we wanted to collect related to topics that are often avoided in conversations with strangers, and so we needed to provide prompts that were direct enough to bring participants straight to the topic at hand while also allowing people to maintain confidentiality as much as they needed. We made sure to both offer opportunities for disclosure of positionalities, and simultaneously ensure nobody was required or pressured into disclosing their position against their will. This was to enable participants to move forward cautiously in a group space with strangers where they might be fearful of the repercussions of people knowing their positions; while also encouraging as much disclosure as participants were comfortable with, for the sake of rich and insightful research data.

Finally, we created a **diverse and multiplicitous approach to creating data** from the Irish workshop. Specifically, we offered a variety of ways for participants to communicate with the research project: speaking in small and large groups that were audio recorded (in group discussions after each activity) and in smaller groups at the final activity decorating the wedges (1.45/Figure 11.4); speaking individually and confidentially to individual researchers with audio recorders (at the lamination stations: 12.00/Figure 11.3); and providing everybody with pen and paper to write notes for the research team that could be identified or kept anonymous. We also invited all participants to follow up by email if they wished; and we video recorded the entire day – participants actively consented to all of these methods of data capture.[6] This approach to data gathering had two purposes:

- we sought for it to be light and unintrusive, but still obvious so that people were not covertly recorded, keeping participants oriented towards free and creative experimentation;
- we created various modes of engagement, allowing those who were less comfortable speaking in groups to find other ways of making their voices heard – or their creations and actions recorded – at the workshop.

We planned this light and varied approach in order to capture as much information from the workshop as possible, knowing that participants may be reticent to speak in front of certain others.

These four aspects of our workshop design demonstrate the way in which we planned the workshop to manage the core tension between inviting exchanges in a potentially charged context (that of social differences related to gender, sexuality and abortion) and facilitating creative research in a workshop setting. We offer this workshop plan and commentary to start considerations of exploring how to navigate this tension. We will return to these methods in later papers to consider their effectiveness and the lessons we learnt from putting them into practice.

Conclusion

Polarisation in relation to sexualities and genders can take many forms. In this chapter, we have focused on divisions around socio-legal changes such as same-sex marriage, abortion and gender recognition. We have shown that researching polarisation can make use of creative methods. Beyond Opposition started from the recognition that while campaigning, advocacy and education efforts would continue, previous research and contemporary events have shown that different positions related to gender, sexuality and abortion continue to exist, sometimes to the extent of extreme polarisation. In order to explore the possibilities of new ways of addressing social polarisation, we chose a creative, arts-based space to facilitate open, exploratory and imaginative thinking, and invited people with a range of positions into the space. We worked to create a space that was productive in the tension between the invitation to create and the dynamics of oppositionality.

The process of designing this approach to an Irish artist-led workshop deliberately centred on the tensions between creative collective work and fundamental differences offers insights into how this might be achieved. Creativity can be daunting in a workshop space at the best of times; more so in a space that has already been flagged as being organised across fundamental differences related to gender, sexuality and/ or abortion. In laying out this workshop plan, our intention is not to provide a set of instructions for replication, but rather to introduce key areas that might then lead to further developments and discussions, including about the potentials *and* limitations of bringing people together to work creatively across fundamental differences with relation to gender, sexuality and/ or abortion.

A key aspect of this discussion should be replicability. Typically, methodology papers presume replicability. In the case of this Irish artist-led workshop, we do not take it for granted that any of our methods can or should be replicated. We would caution against attempting anything similar without careful consideration and the full resources in place. We would also be slow to recommend simply replicating the plan above; instead, this needs careful contextual considerations, development of appropriate ethical plans, researcher skills (including facilitation, interpersonal skills and self-care) and security (see Maguire et al., 2018) and an artist collaborator with a thorough understanding and acceptance of the research aims.

Future papers will explore what happened when we put the methods into practice and the outcomes of this workshop, including the implications of the careful recruitment of participants and the ways in which participants responded to the artistic and conceptual prompts. In this chapter, we offer this process and approach as one possible new way of working collectively across fundamental differences without seeking to address/resolve/avoid them.

Notes

1 This chapter is funded by the European Union under the Horizon 2020 programme, Grant no. 817897. The authors would like to thank all those who took part in the research and all who made the workshops possible: Dr Andrew McCartan, Dr Katherine Young, Aoife Grant, Tracy Bryce-Smith and Sarah Foudy.
2 The design and plan for the artist-led workshop will be the focus of this chapter. Here, we give a brief summary of aspects that are beyond the scope of this chapter but will be developed elsewhere. We recruited via direct contacts, groups and Facebook advertising. This was followed by a detailed process involving an email exchange and two screening phone calls in advance of inviting participants to the workshop. Strict guidelines were agreed to in advance, including that people engage respectfully with each other, in particular, that participants use other participants' preferred terms (e.g. pro-life/pro-choice; gender critical; preferred pronouns), even when they disagreed with them. Participants agreed not to debate the issues or seek to change other

people's minds. In advance of the workshop, we put in place protocols for dealing with discomfort, conflict and protest should these arise.
3   Future papers will explore the implementation of this and subsequent arts-based workshops carried out in Canada and Great Britain, as well as discussion group activities carried out in the same two countries.
4   The two-page brief developed to recruit an artist outlined the unusual nature of the workshop. It explained that participants would hold a wide range of views related to gender, sexuality and/or abortion, which are not easily divided into two categories. It noted that discomfort was inevitable and that measures were in place to manage outright conflict. It mapped out lines of responsibility between the artist, who would be responsible for activities and output, and the researchers, who were responsible for ethical oversight and data collection. This brief served as an opening to a process of exploration and negotiation.
5   In this chapter, we focus on the plan that we devised to bring people together creatively across differences. Future papers will explore the outcomes when we put this plan into action.
6   The consent process involved a detailed information sheet and opt-in consent form; these are posted on the project website at https://beyondopposition.org/wp-content/uploads/2023/01/InformationSheet_-DiscussionGroups_and_Workshops.pdf

The project ethics, including data collection, were outlined to participants in advance of the workshop in a phone call with a member of the research team, and again at the beginning of the day (see introduction: Kath, 10:05 in the timetable above). Once Kath had outlined the ethical protocols, participants completed the consent form, opting in to each method of data collection. At the end of the day, before they left, participants returned their consent forms to the project manager, confirming their retrospective consent for the use of their data. They were informed that any subsequent withdrawal from the project could only be partial, as it would not be possible to remove individual contributions from the art produced.

Chapter 12

CRUMBLED WORLDS OR IMPERFECT UTOPIAS

DISCUSSING OUR POLARISED SEXUAL AND GENDERED LIVES

Andrew McCartan, Jody Moore-Ponce, Ann Burke,
Sarah Foudy and Eliza Thor

Introduction

The Polarising Sexual and Gendered Lives symposium held in Dublin, June 2023, captured the intensity and multiplicity of contemporary ideological debates over sexuality and gender, and the challenge of how to address them in queer and feminist scholarship.[1] The symposium papers make clear that this is an especially charged time when polarisation around sexual and gendered lives is intensifying in complex and nuanced ways, with serious implications not least for those whose lives are considered 'up for debate'. These debates polarise societies through contested social relations, and the papers interrogate how this plays out in the home, within communities, online and in the media, through national and transnational activist campaigns, and government interventions. Key to these interrogations is the changed sociopolitical landscape in terms of LGBTQ rights and equalities globally. Together, the papers reveal the complexity of how polarisations form and the urgent need to better understand the processes and discourses through which polarisation impacts our lives.

There is, perhaps unsurprisingly for those in these contexts, a dominant focus on the 'gender wars' that position transgender rights and recognition in opposition to sex-based rights for cisgender women. Groups are shown to become polarised over trans lives through multiple sociopolitical debates relating to everyday lives and practices, including trans inclusion in sports (Slaymaker, 2023; Rahilly & Tecklenburg, 2023), trans inclusion in women's-only spaces, including prisons (Lamble, 2023), and the collection of sex-based statistics (Lamble, 2023). Polarisation intensifies when debates manifest around specific legislations such as HB 25 in Texas (Slaymaker, 2023), Title IX in the US (Rahilly & Tecklenburg, 2023) and the Gender Recognition Act in the UK (Lamble, 2023). Crucial for addressing polarisation is a recognition of how debates that are framed around seemingly singular issues or legislation mask deeper social anxieties around gender, sexuality and the nature of reality, which persist and take multiple forms across generations and borders. Although trans issues emerge most prominently across the symposium, the papers teased out broader gender and sexual issues, such as LGBTQ Pride events (Kamarauskaitė, 2023), same-sex marriage and abortion (Ballantine, Hilliard, & Browne, 2023), bisexual identities and kink communities (Strobel, 2023), and language surrounding butch/femme dyke and queer identities (Crawley, 2023), as issues which remain polarising and challenge imaginaries of equality, tolerance and progress in places with same-sex marriage, abortion and other big legislative wins for progressive social movements.[2] While the papers name gender-critical feminists (Peel. 2023; Lamble, 2023), heteroactivists (Strobel, 2023) and LGBTQ, trans and queer activists (Slaymaker, 2023; Rahilly & Tecklenburg, 2023), as key groups engaged in actions that polarise sexual and gendered lives, the papers make clear that we are all implicated in reproducing the web of polarising power relations, and groups on all 'sides' of any given debate can often be made up of people with nuanced and sometimes contradictory positions, solidarities and disagreements.

Grappling with this complexity, the papers together make a convincing case of how polarisation operates: that polarisation around sexuality and gender is produced through systemic power relations, which sustain the sociopolitical hierarchies and norms that privilege certain sexual and gendered lives over others by aggravating social divisions along us/them and good/bad binaries. This chapter presents an edited conversation between postdoctoral and postgraduate discussants at the symposium, which reflects on the key insights from the papers at this event. Here, we elaborate on the major themes that emerged in our discussion, around progress, relationality and utopian thinking, to highlight the complex and negotiated process of (un)polarising our sexual and gendered lives.

Polarisation and progress

Andrew: The papers develop the relationship between social polarisation and the realities and imaginings of 'progress' for sexual and gender rights, where polarisation is constant but fluctuates in intensity as concerns are alleviated for some groups while simultaneously heightened for others over timelines of 'progressive' social change. Narratives of progress are never egalitarian but 'inherently hierarchical' to render 'some forms of violence particularly visible while marginalising others' (Lalor & Browne, 2018, p. 211). Groups rely on spatial and temporal boundaries to make divergent claims, and disallowances, over who is on 'the right side of history' and what violences against sex, gender or sexuality get recognised as such.

Ballantine, Hilliard and Browne (2023) discuss spatial imaginaries of Ireland as 'new' and 'equal' in unambivalent terms following two successful referenda on same-sex marriage and abortion, through which previously unimaginable LGBTQ and women's rights became resolutely in place, altering previous dominant imaginings of a 'backwards' Catholic nation oppressive in terms of sexual and gender relations. However, while the polarised debates of the referendum are in the past, 'New Ireland' is not a 'post-polarised' social landscape. Rather, opposition, and thus polarisation, 'morphed and adapted' past the homophobic divisions witnessed in the referendum to re-emerge in new ways within the uncharted sociopolitical and legal context of progress. When progress is configured differently, such as in Kamarauskaitė's (2023) paper where Lithuanian LGBTQ activists view progress as sustaining a positive relationship between Catholic, traditional nationalities and behaviours with LGBTQ identities and lifestyles, polarisation still operates to much of the same oppositional ends. The power relations governing and operating through the opposition in the Irish and Lithuanian contexts of progress are different, wherein the reasons through which 'subordinated populations are deemed inconvenient to the privileged who made them so' are place-specific, but in each case, the polarisation has the same goal: to maintain this domination of the subordinated by the privileged (Berlant, 2022, p. 4).

Reading those two papers together demands a recognition that polarisation, much like progress, does not occur in a coherent movement following a linear 'further apart' direction. National gender and sexual social movements are on different timelines, not necessarily heading in similar directions nor from similar beginnings. Although progress is not uniform, it might be a useful framework for unpacking how different national polarisations compare and converge in transnational spaces, and if understanding the relationship between progress and polarisation might offer a tool for addressing ongoing divisions.

Eliza: Developing transnational conceptualisations of polarisation risks inaccurately and problematically extending Anglo-American critiques around progress if norms associated with heteronormativity, as it is understood within Anglo-American contexts, are applied to national contexts with different ideas surrounding sexual and gendered lives that would not be considered heteronormative within their culture. Kamarauskaitė (2023) discussed how LGBTQ activists in Lithuania were combating a Western narrative of what it meant to be gay or queer, and what progress for a 'new' Lithuania could be. When up against perceptions held by those in opposition that being gay was against Lithuanian values, the LGBTQ activists sought to win support through arguments of sameness so opponents would 'begin to understand that I am a person just like them. With my needs, with my strengths and my weaknesses and with my freakishness . . .'. These arguments might recall in their similarity homonormative critiques, yet Kamarauskaitė avoids the imposition of Western-centric concepts into the analysis, as it would be wrong – perhaps as it would not allow for the necessary 'freakishness' in the 'free and cosy' sameness of Lithuania.

Ann: In Ireland, LGBTQ activists during the marriage equality referendum were also appealing to Irish 'values', so in both cases polarisation around sexual and gender identities was also about the ability to claim inclusion in national identity and what it means to be Irish or Lithuanian more broadly. What's normative has changed considerably in Ireland, and the marriage referendum has been instrumental in that change. Ireland as a society is arguably so politically left-leaning now that there are perceptions of 'traditional' ways of life being, or having been, ambivalently destroyed. When people see their ways of life being disrupted, the earth crumbles underneath them, and we need to deal with the fear, anxiety and resentment involved in that. There is also a perception held by some that nothing outside of the 'new' progressive orthodoxy is up for debate, and a growing feeling and dissatisfaction that there is no dialogue at all by those feeling left behind in the reconfiguration of sexuality, gender and the nation. Hegemonic positions in the public sphere are being debated and claims regarding marginal voices are made from surprising quarters and indeed not from those we have come to acknowledge and expect. Lamble (2023) states in their paper that similar debates in the UK 'do not map easily into traditional left and right political divides' and my own research interviewing pro-life feminists in Ireland is testament to that.

In comparison to the election of Donald Trump and the overturning of Roe versus Wade in the US, and the Brexit vote in the UK, for example, Ireland appears to be an outlier in terms of political shifts to the right. Irish politics is influenced by different dynamics compared to these processes happening elsewhere, as activists in Ireland have long been fighting for the smallest of victories in a narrow, repressive and punitive Catholic-driven society that privileged stereotypical gender roles and the nuclear family. It remains very contextually specific, but those structures of religion, law and nationalism are deeply implicated in how the polarisation of sexual and gendered lives takes hold.

Sarah: Several complex structures such as the church, the law and the state overlap to constitute, shape and maintain the polarisation of sexual and gendered lives in ways that problematise what progress means, and how progress is experienced, within different geographical contexts. The United States may be considered 'progressive' nationally following the introduction of marriage equality; however, Loder's (2023) paper draws attention to the regionally specific sociopolitical climates for LGBTQ communities in the United States, particularly for Black transgender women in the regressive South due to the prevalence of anti-LGBTQ legislation introduced in 2023, and the influence of church gatekeepers and the nuclear familial structure. The contrast in the sociopolitical climate for LGBTQ communities across different regions within nation states reminds us that polarisation in relation to sexual and gendered lives does not only play out evenly in relation to progress for LGBTQ communities, in terms of legislative protections and/or social and cultural inclusions. Crawley's (2023) paper draws from ethnomethodological sensibilities to show how polarisation is also experienced differently across generations. Noting the limitations of binary thinking, they argue that polarisation around sexual and gendered lives across generations is not as straightforward as being pro/anti-LGBTQ rights or inclusions or identities. This disrupts the temporality of the LGBTQ progress narrative, the idea that things used to be bad and now they are good for sexual and gender minorities.

Upholding polarisation through complex, overlapping structures is not inevitable, and Lalor's (2023) paper grapples with the intricacies of the labour involved in keeping sexuality and gender polarised. In foregrounding the productive force of polarisations and looking specifically at geopolitical polarisations around LGBTQ rights in international law, Lalor notes the limitations of binary thinking in terms of LGBTQ progress/LGBTQ suppression. She draws on feminist, sexual and queer legal geography to think 'unconventionally about the construction, deployment and maintenance of political polarisations in international law' around LGBTQ rights.

In order to think 'unconventionally' about political polarisations, she develops a concept of queer legal geographies, which makes visible the magnitude of work involved in upholding and maintaining polarisations and draws attention to the conditions under which polarisation can thrive. Considering polarisation through this queer legal geography lens, in the context of international law surrounding LGBTQ rights, offers key insights into the role of institutions like the church and the nation in the sexual and gendered organisation of contemporary societies.

Jody: The omnipresence of the normative structures upholding polarisations in society means polarising tendencies come to infiltrate different communities through heated contestations which become difficult to escape or be immune to. Foucault said that history is 'Fragile' (1986:187), not solid, and more like a spiderweb than anything unyielding, so it can and should be picked at. Contemporary non-binary gendered identities and LGBTQ sexualities problematise normativity and are oppositional to the traditional structures that uphold it, as they pick at the spider web of epistemological and historical certainties. Gendered, sexual, patriarchal and colonial histories are being re-examined, 'identity lexicons' and categories are re-defined (Crawley, 2023), and for some, the world they know must already feel like it's splintering. This unearths a pushback from those who reject frameworks for understanding society outside the traditional and hegemonic views that are, to them, familiar, comprehensible and comforting.

Crawley (2023) discussed the need to give time to both present knowledges of sexuality and gender, and those of the past, to form a discursive space that can offer an 'agonistic' (Mouffe, 2007), but also hopeful, place of discourse. Progress emerges from the past; the present does not spring unbidden into contemporary progressive enlightenment. Crawley's past/present space of discourse offers 'narrations of past that can only be viewed through our present' but which incorporates 'differing generational lived experience'. It is difficult to have nuance and hold ambivalent feelings in the spaces where one feels embattled, but in a space where the 'lived experience' of past and present can be discussed, perhaps a space opens for individuals on all sides to be more receptive of differing epistemological certainties, and indeed uncertainties. In the polarised posture of defensiveness, it is not possible to engage in listening spaces of past/present lived experience. Polarisation keeps people in embattled trenches.

This section has focused on the spatiotemporalities of polarisation, to consider the sociopolitical contexts which foster and are shaped by polarisation. Ideas of progress towards LGBTQ-inclusive societies are prominent in discussions of contemporary sexualities, but progress is a nebulous idea that is contextual and contested. Cultural and place specificity is integral to how progress will be negotiated in terms of sexual and gendered lives. Subjectification as queer, trans or other forms of sexual and gendered subjects means navigating the 'norms' and power relations that are woven into every fibre and fabric of our lives, and intertwined into narratives of progress and change. Opposition is present in social relations in the places where 'progress' is being fought for and present still in the places where progress has been 'won'. The idea of progress can be a catalyst, fought for or against, that turns up the heat on oppositional politics to seemingly split societies into polarised factions. These polarised spatiotemporalities of progress are unevenly felt between groups in support and opposition to what is considered progress. Polarisation can be a goal of those in opposition, and/or an outcome ignited by reactive fears and anxieties over how to protect 'traditional' sexual and gendered selves, norms and hegemonic worldviews from new threatening ideologies. On all sides, polarisation in progress may be informed by a fear that hard-won rights will be lost; freedoms can never be overestimated or taken for granted. In these terms, progress becomes a fragile dynamic that requires endless negotiation. The next section moves to explore what the symposium papers tell us about the relations through which these negotiations take place, between various groups implicated in the polarisation of sexuality and gender.

Polarisation beyond 'Us-versus-Them'

Andrew: Across the papers, we see how the increasing polarisation of sexual and gendered lives does not play out with two distinct groups/'poles' getting further apart while those at the poles are drawn ever closer into each other. Power dynamics within specific temporal moments, such as public votes, may hold in place an image of there being only 'two camps', but even in those cases, the papers show how there are multiple standpoints. There is no simple 'us' versus 'them' when there are multiple, shifting boundaries between and within both the us and them, and those that fall outside of either; yet people on all sides of the debates can be guilty of putting others into reductive categories, disavowing complexity in their imagining of the 'other'. This creates a complex web of social relations shaping the 'crisis of meaning' Strobel (2023) discusses, where within the 'us' and 'them' there are questions of how to honour diversity and not homogenise groups in unity.

Ann: Polarisation is about how we relate to each other, particularly those with whom we disagree, and this relationality is intrinsically linked to ontological security. Butler (2023) talks about embodied anxiety, embodied resentment and embodied fear at a somatic level in terms of anti-gender movements. Polarisation is deeply implicated with the pathological need for certainty of self and certainty in believing oneself to be on the 'right' side of right/wrong understandings of societal issues. For those who feel the structured order of their worlds splintering, certainty in traditional understandings disavows ambivalence and refuses the shifting boundaries of present reconfigurations of gender and sexuality to ensure the maintenance of 'normal' ways of life. In this way, adhering to certainties works to maintain hierarchies of credibility around gender and sexuality (Becker, 1967; Howard, 1967).

Certainties fuel misinformation when the need to confirm biases, whether conscious or otherwise, becomes more important than truth. Lamble (2023) discusses how misinformation 'sticks' in those terms, for instance, in 'framing trans rights as a key threat undermining women's safety, gender critical campaigners tap into widely felt concerns about male violence but direct them to a new target'. Gender-critical groups will employ the certainties of 'science' 'facts', 'reality' and 'reason' to make an emotional case that plays on fears and anxieties. These tactics are highly successful, with messages such as 'facts aren't bigoted' (FPFW cited in Lamble, 2023) resonating with people and justifying positions. While Lamble has demonstrated that simply correcting facts does not work, finding ways to innovatively take control of narratives that misinform and create fear and anxiety within and outside queer communities requires a patience and willingness to dwell in those discursive and 'agonistic' spaces (Mouffe, 2007). Such work is uncomfortable, but doing so also offers the opportunity to dismantle dehumanising narratives and challenge those hierarchies of credibility, allowing for uncertainties and ambivalences in our understandings of the self and others.

Sarah: The way in which polarisation plays out in relation to sexual and gendered lives in practice, as evidenced by many of the papers in this collection, is nuanced and complex. Yet polarisation is necessarily uncomfortable with this nuance. It does not allow for having mixed feelings and holding multiple views or contradictions. There's so much nuance that people do not want, or are unable, to negotiate or interrogate their own beliefs. Examining the operation of polarisation in this context is often uncomfortable, and I wonder if this discomfort is an effect of the large-scale polarisation about these sexual and gendered issues, to keep things as they are?

Jody: The unknown of the other and unyielding certainty in the self are often coupled with fear, and in places of fear and uncertainty, defensive postures can be engaged wherein it feels necessary to protect every inch of the views we hold, or else the whole ground might fall apart beneath us. These defensive postures are instrumental in the growing chasms of contemporary polarisation as fear often incites attack and fuels division, and individuals are terrified that their epistemological certainties and foundations are crumbling. This is particularly seen online on social media platforms, where there is ubiquitous denunciation of seemingly everything.

To maintain certainty in self is often to cling to fixed beliefs and a sense of rightness. The rightness or virtue that is attached to an individual's certainty often comes with a deep suspicion of engaging with 'the other side' as often that 'other side's' views are seen as harmful and dangerous for societal cohesion and progress, both socially and economically. Hearing what the other has to say opens the gateway to examining how and why one thinks the way they do about gender and sexuality. Ballantine, Hilliard and Browne's (2023) paper unearths how recent referendums have led to 'retrenched positions' on these topics. It becomes evident that it requires real bravery to want to sincerely seek out opportunities to be open with each other across, and despite, our differences – to embrace, what Keating (2013) calls, 'interconnectivity', such as in the Beyond Opposition artist-led workshop, which brought together people who held opposing views, but who worked together in an interesting expression of interconnectivity across difference (Ballantine, Hilliard, & Browne, 2023).

In the tribal environment of contemporary polarisation it becomes necessary in these spaces to prove allegiance to the tribe and secure one's place of belonging.

Slaymaker (2023) writes, 'identity based movements always struggle with the question of who "counts" as a member of the group'. In this setting, how individuals relate to others is governed by the social relations of the tribe. It becomes important to eliminate the chance of wandering towards the edge and realising that 'this other tribe over there seems quite nice, actually'; thinking in this open-handed way, with the capacity to empathise with the 'other', is often interpreted as a threat to the tribe. Labelling 'the other side' as dangerous is a way of staying in the safe centre of a group or tribe. Ballantine, Hilliard and Browne (2023) however, argue 'What we think is "dangerous" is only deploying vilification, a politics of condemnation'. Deploying vilification and condemnation ensures distance, and prevents conversations that have the possibility of softening 'retrenched' resistance. In this polarised political and social atmosphere of vilification and condemnation of 'the other side', no one is permitted to wander to the edge of nuance.

There are so many lived experiences that other individuals simply won't or can't acknowledge or recognise or accept, choosing to attack rather than affirm other lives that do not fit their own understandings of gender and sexuality. Groups can become so threatened by the other that they fundamentally believe the other should be eradicated, should not deserve to exist, saying, 'your reality isn't a reality'. This kaleidoscope of existences becomes splintered, broken shards of realities with sharp edges that cut deeply. While Ballantine, Hilliard and Browne resist appeals to commonality in this kaleidoscope, they instead offer insights into ways in which we might 'work across difference' to reduce the chasm of polarisations.

Andrew: Within these 'chasms', groups become protective of the boundaries around their tribes, as extended boundaries of their 'self'. Crawley (2023) discusses people's desire to be able to claim their own identity and their own histories in their own lexicon. In other words, they want to protect the cohesion of a narrative over their sovereignty as gendered/sexed subjects that they do not want to give up. Berlant (2022: 3) argues the defence of a sovereign self is a 'fantasy . . . a defence of entitlement', where 'sovereignty is the name for a confused, reactive, often not-quite-thought view that there ought to be a solution to the pressure of adapting to "other people"'. Crawley's discussions of disagreements over terminologies and identity categories may illustrate 'the pressures of coexistence' and the 'problematic of receptivity to the stimulus and situations of the world' (Berlant, 2023, p. 7) when the 'world' is plural in terms of how it is conceived for sexual and gendered lives. People who get angry at terms like 'cisgender' may do so because, to them, it represents someone else's idea over their reality being imposed on them and rewriting who they are without their permission, as indeed some of Peel's (2023) participants suggest how cisgender identities become associated with ignorance and bigotry against transness. Rather than a willingness for new ideas around sex and gender, there is a fear in some camps that 'others' will rewrite the common sense rules around identities to either say something new about them that they do not want to accept or eradicate them completely. I see in certain online spaces, particular activist groups of gay men and lesbians mourning themselves in alternative timelines in which they fear they would have been 'transed' as a child growing up in trans-inclusive school environments. To me, Crawley's paper suggests that to address polarisation will be to offer a process through which people can develop confidence in their own relational identity actualisation. Although the papers do not touch on this, such a process will require unpacking cisnormative fears of transness and being trans and challenging claims such as the eradication of gay and lesbian lives, which are nonsense to some and world-shattering to others.

Eliza: Polarisation is also at times really focused on who's allowed to represent identity groups, such as trans women speaking at the legislature described in Slaymaker's (2023) paper. Questions over representation and who has the authority to be speaking on behalf of a community are also very polarised. People on the same side may have the same basic goals, but not the same specifics. There's then this polarisation over who's actually allowed to speak and actually allowed to represent this camp that has formed. When they're not all in agreement on what should be happening, strategic decisions are made through tense negotiations of equality and difference. As Slaymaker shows us, forming coalitions and working together to create an 'us' can mask power differences to create new sets of marginalisations between those who agree with each other.

Ann: Slaymaker's (2023) insightful characterisation of 'uneasy alliances' arguably needs to extend beyond organisations under the anti-trans umbrella to inform a much-needed shift in thinking by those willing to explore finding solutions to polarisation. Peel's (2023) article explored the idea of considering both/and thinking, that people can hold two conflicting views at the same time. It allows us to recognize the complexity of positions people have in polarised debates beyond either/or, so someone can absolutely agree that trans rights are really important, and people should have trans rights but might still have questions to be explored, nuances that make them uncomfortable. Taking a both/and approach acknowledges this complexity so that we don't demonise people straight away for living in the space in between the poles. Peel suggests that thinking in terms of 'both/and' 'allows – at least theoretically – for more fluidity and arguably can become an antidote to polarisation and extremism'. This type of thinking played out in the living library discussed by Kamarauskaitė (2023), where queer people sat with people from 'a general public' to discuss the lived experience of being queer while also asking questions about the lived experience of heterosexuality, in essence demystifying 'the other'. Imagining more spaces like this that allow us to identify our common humanity, also, to identify ways that we can see each other as just humans instead of separate identities.

Andrew: Yet, in planning their Beyond Opposition workshops, Ballantine, Hilliard and Browne (2023) did not aim for participants to find commonalities or seek common ground. Claims to 'humanity' have allowed marginalised sexual and gender minorities to be recognised through legal and human rights discourses, but there are limits to how far claims of common humanity can take us in addressing social polarisation. The most toxic forms of polarisation dehumanise trans and gender non-conforming lives as 'aliens to humanity' (O'Shea, 2020), so it is not the case that humanity is missing from these debates but that it is disavowed and actively, violently argued against. Even if some of us want to hold on to the hopeful rhetoric that 'we are all human', it remains that we have fundamentally different ideas over the realities of human life and how human identities are understood. A focus on commonalities risks forgoing the differences which lead to sexual and gender lives being polarised, differences which are very important to our lives, on all sides. Rahilly and Tecklenburg (2023) discuss how 'sides are often "talking past each other", focusing on entirely different issues and logics', as what and how issues are understood as important to one group does not easily map onto the perspectives of other groups. No one desires to compromise those differences or lose really core parts of themselves to appease others, so how would we live together once we've made a recognition of common humanity? Where do we go from that point if 'to live and let live' is impossible (Peel, 2023) and we still have fundamentally different ideas of what the world is, what the future should look like and at some point, you are going to have to address that?

Eliza: We know from current affairs that so much of the anti-trans discourse has been grounded in beliefs that 'they're grooming children' or 'they're paedophiles', also seen in Lamble's (2023) example of false claims perpetuated in the media that 'half of trans inmates' are 'predatory sex offenders'. If these are beliefs that you really hold, that's not something you can really push to the side to find other common ground. There's a level where we have to overcome certain things before that common ground can even be accessed. I don't know that just sitting two people down in a room would solve that automatically.

Ann: Recognising that someone is a person, a human being just like you, does not have to entail ignoring differences. In fact, producing a recognisable subject as Kamarauskaitė (2023) demonstrated is often the starting point to 'creating a connection' and maybe a key to creating alliances, however uneasy. In many ways, the Lithuanian queer communities within Kamarauskaitė's paper were appealing to commonalities, seizing opportunities to express shared values and a desire for communitarian and national pride and belonging, but they were also changing the negative narratives of deviance associated with being queer, despite differing opinions regarding the appropriateness of strategies.

Moreover, recognising that there are 'people' behind the stats and the media reports can be a powerful recognition for many. An appeal to personhood involves creating for the audience – as Kamarauskaitė, citing Judith Butler, referred, 'a subject who is living, whose life is worth sheltering and whose life when lost would be worth mourning' (Butler, 2009, p. xi). We need more visibility for those affected by anti-trans and anti-queer bigotry that goes beyond simply seeing them as 'other'. The Irish Repeal Campaign demonstrated that the pragmatic decision to utilise the stories of those affected by the eighth amendment meant that the people behind the numbers were suddenly visible, also demonstrating that walking in someone else's shoes does work, as many opposed to abortion on a fundamental ideological level voted to Repeal the eighth amendment despite ongoing misgivings.

Indeed, 'working across difference', as Ballantine, Hilliard, and Browne (2023) suggest involves 'leaning in' as Peel (2023) puts it, and that leaning in can take many forms. The fact that social and personal capital is experienced asymmetrically requires that we remain open to all the possibilities. However, what is feasible will depend on the context and people involved, as the effects of misinformation and disinformation continue to take hold. Lamble (2023) has discussed how simple fact correction does not seem to work, which suggests that abstract initiatives will only go so far, creating liminal spaces that create room for reflexive thinking may ensure that we don't inadvertently reinforce polarisation as Loder (2023) suggests.

Sarah: Even when you are trying to find common ground across polarised issues, you still have to acknowledge the complex web of power relations that are at play, and how some positions on that web are closer to social norms than others, which places certain people higher on social hierarchies than others. Those dynamics and power relations do not go away because you're finding some commonality. Lalor (2023) highlighted how sometimes, by acknowledging polarisation we can end up reiterating polarisation, but I don't really know how to get away from that, or if we want to?

Beyond Opposition's artist-led workshop created a space that allowed for artistic collaboration to carve out a pathway for being able to live better with people with fundamentally different worldviews (Ballantine, Hillard, & Browne, 2023). Artist workshops like this offer different ways to relate with people who you disagree strongly with. In everyday life, situations like those, where you are coming together across fundamental differences can feel impossible and unsafe and already so politically charged, because the possible loss to you is too great that it might not be worth engaging with. Do spaces of collaboration through art offer a different, safer means of engaging with polarisation? Or what do they offer, and how could we bring some of that to everyday situations?

This section has examined how polarisation forms through the relationality of sexuality and gender identity formation, and through the conceiving of the 'self' in relation to the other. What becomes evident is that expressions of selfhood and difference exist in a tangled web of worldviews and identities that collide in oppositional and tribal ways to produce and maintain the polarisation of sexual and gendered lives. These complexities don't simply exist in a binary 'us' and 'them', but in a web of polarities created through the ways oppositional communities view themselves in relation to each other, and which also exist inside those communities. Gaining ground in terms of polarisation can therefore feel like a Sisyphean task in an increasingly complicated scene where polarisation is happening both between and within demographics. This is illustrated in Strobel's (2023) description of the 'double discrimination' experienced by many who are stigmatised by heteronormative classifications and fall prey to the vagaries associated with classifying and ordering within queer communities.

Identifying a discreet 'us' versus 'them' seems futile as generally the conflictual heterogeneity within polarised societies defies easy categorisation or indeed characterisation. Yet, in a world of 'multiplicities and plurals', people often look for 'the singular' to feel safe (Plummer, 2019, p. 39). Ballantine, Hilliard, and Browne (2023) highlight the need for 'skilful navigation' of these multiple polarities to honour fundamental differences and, perhaps, recognise commonalities without diminishing identities. The artist-led workshop run by the Beyond Opposition project provides a model for navigating the tangled web of polarisation by producing a research space 'for open, playful, creative thinking' but with 'enough structure and guidance for self-care, self-regulation'. However, in this chapter, we do not reach a conclusion about how groups might interact and work 'across difference' in everyday spaces across the 'us' versus 'them' paradigm. There is no agreement between ourselves, or simple answer to find, over how to engage with those who fundamentally oppose our worldviews. Is living with this difference, to engage with those on 'the other side' without questioning their viewpoints, more or less brave than being willing to question one's own outlook and certainties through creative discourse? We leave this unanswered but, in the next section, bring together our thoughts around progress and relationality to speculate through the papers how we might create spaces that address polarisation moving forward.

After polarisation

Andrew: When Strobel (2023) reviews the emergence and persistence of heteroactivist actions in places 'won' for LGBTQ rights, we are cautioned not to fall into the trap of imagining progress as leading to an 'end point' in which sexual and gender rights are no longer polarised. Progress is always going to be resisted and be seen as regressive for those with fundamental oppositions to what is considered progressive. If, for example, in Ireland after the introduction of marriage equality and the repeal of the 8th amendment, people on the 'losing' sides now feel oppressed and marginalised, will there ever be a time after polarisation? When do people on all sides get to be happy in their everyday life? When Ballantine, Hilliard, and Browne (2023) invite participants to imagine utopian spaces, they imagine utopias where the people they disagree with are still there. These speculative futures do not overcome the polarisation of our sexual and gendered lives but carve out pathways for being able to live better with the fundamentally divergent worldviews that underpin polarisation. I wonder what the best is that we can hope for?

As it is hard to imagine futures after polarisation, the pressing question becomes over how we can make life more liveable so that we can thrive better within this landscape. Ballantine, Hilliard and Browne recognise that as 'not all minds can be changed', the act of believing you can change other people's minds works to maintain polarisation. Loder's (2023) paper similarly suggests that polarisation is maintained by holding a belief you can change people's 'lifestyles'. Spaces of polarisation are not just the oppositional, activist, protest spaces of societies split into factions but also the everyday, intimate, private spaces of communities and families divided. Loder revealed all the negative, upsetting things that can happen when people fail to accept and accommodate the coexistence of fundamentally different worldviews, to believe that their energies should focus on a lifestyle or mind that can be changed. The concept of liminality was used by Loder to explore how the women she interviewed carved out temporary spaces in resistance to the ways in which 'polarisation has created ruptures between Black transgender women and their ties to native communities that hold critical resources'. The backdrop of Loder's paper was the very negative, polarised climate around trans people in the US South and how this relates to the marginalisation of trans people, but a lot of the narrative coming through from the women was around the communities of care and support they formed for themselves. In exploring the ways in which bisexual people excluded from hetero- and homo-spaces found other non-normative communities, Strobel explored realities and relationality within BDSM and furry communities that may not have otherwise occurred outside of the current polarised climate. There's a lot of optimism and positive things to be taken from the networks that we forge with each other as our lives are debated, so that to imagine better futures is to look at how some of the least privileged of us are already surviving and thriving in the face of marginalisation and polarisation.

Jody: Increasingly, in contemporary sociopolitical landscapes of 'progress', people in less progressive, more traditional groups are beginning to make claims of their own marginalisation and victimisation for continuing to hold their normative, once hegemonic, positions. Strobel (2023) articulates how sexuality and gender differences that are not easily defined or categorised often create a 'crisis of meaning', wherein individuals feel that they are living through a crisis in which they are a victim. Polarisation is fuelled by the victim mentality of those who feel their view is not supported by majority public opinion or political trajectory, as evidenced, for example, by testimony quoted in Rahilly and Tecklenburg's (2023) paper that sought an 'acknowledgment that women and girls are the victims here' regarding trans inclusion in competitive sports. The belief from those who unambivalently feel like victims of a society that they no longer understand is that everyone's out to get them, and that they are being persecuted for their views. Those who feel cornered tend to 'retrench' (Ballantine, Hilliard, & Browne, 2023), as a defensive and aggressive positionality.

It is difficult to lean in and engage in utopian thinking and fruitful communication 'across difference' when doing so within a societal milieu of crisis, victimhood, retrenchment and attack; these positionalities are powerful narratives that engage impassioned tribal support but do not encourage discourse across difference. If the shared goal of reducing polarisation is present, then perhaps coalition building across difference might also be possible in this societal space. Slaymaker (2023) reveals that within the Trans community, tensions of difference exist, but shows how coalition building amid difference is possible. Utopia in this sense works better as an imperfect Utopia. In visualising this imperfect utopia, sameness or the dominance of a particular view is not the overriding image it generates. In the imperfect utopia, a commitment to 'working across difference' emerges as a creative way forward. To give up the utopian dream of everybody agreeing on every single thing opens new pathways of embracing nuance and difference and yet being able to function together in an imperfect embrace of difference.

Ann: Sexuality and gender have been so absorbed in the culture wars now that it can seem impossible to have a conversation, so how do we get around that to reach those new pathways? A 'democratic ideal' (Anderson, 2022, p. 68) would see us listening to voices we may not agree with. That said, within that, the presence of undemocratic voices remains an ever-challenging spectre. However, while there will always be those who are unreachable, for those of us who possess a 'democratic ethos' (Anderson, 2022, p. 86), then the meaning and outworkings of democracy are something that we have to consider and interrogate in attempting to address and perhaps overcome polarisation. We are arguably experiencing a current 'crisis' of democracy created by the toxic discourses, fear and distrust created by the spread of misinformation and disinformation by mainstream and social media, and others with vested interests to do so, as Lamble (2023) and Peele (2023) describe. However, how we respond to the undermining of democratic principles (Anderson, 2022) created by these discourses as academics and potential influencers in society requires a commitment to higher ideals that may not always be easy to follow through on. In papers by both Ballantine, Hilliard, and Browne (2023) and Slaymaker (2023) we see examples of these higher ideals at work despite differences.

I believe we need to embrace channels where people feel that they can be heard without us shouting each other down or talking past each other, as Rahilly and Tecklenburg (2023) described in their paper. Indeed, Rahilly and Tecklenburg found that because of the partisan nature of legislative debates, these may not be the best places to try to 'sway rivals', suggesting a variety of other locations where 'productive dialogue may be achieved'. In order to conceive of a future where every person is valued, we must find ways to do so by remaining open to new possibilities. It may not be a future of reconciliation of positions, but hopefully we can imagine and form more points of connection where we can, at the very least, enact a respectful recognition of difference.

Butler (2023) speaks about the need to create and develop a counter-imaginary that responds to the phantasm circulating around gender. Butler argues that fascist incitement works through fantasy and 'fears around the body . . . contamination or expropriation'. Butler resists trying to explain how gender should be defined, especially to those who are clearly 'suspicious of argument', while knowing the work that needs to be done, which Lamble alludes to in their paper also. There is, Butler says, a 'certain kind of work' being executed by the 'phantasmic circulation' of information around gender, and many of the papers in this volume illustrate those processes; hence, a 'counter-imaginary' is needed that requires 'appealing to fundamental passions in a different way', which in turn means going beyond responses which are purely academic to make public arguments or appeals. Moreover, negativity towards academics who are seen to be indoctrinating students behoves us to be innovative in our approaches, in our attempts to develop a shared imaginary beyond polarisation.

There can be a real resistance to Utopian thinking, where it can be viewed as being naive. As 'narrative power is dialogic, contentious and fragile' (Plummer, 2019: 38), labouring in the negative can become nihilistic and defeatist. By instead focusing on 'positive power', as demonstrated in Kamarauskaitė's (2023) paper, we might consider Solnit's (2016, p. xvii) proposal that 'what we dream of is already present in the world' and build from there. Rather than seeing utopia as some grand, elusive phantasm of our imaginations, Solnit and others elucidate more 'grounded utopias', which are already all around us. Furthermore, if, as Levitas (2013) proposes, we think of utopia as a method through which subordinated standpoints are championed and normative visions for the future pursued, rather than as a goal, then perhaps the realities explored in the symposium papers are evidence that we are all already engaged in utopian action 'to make it better if we can for those that come after' (Levitas, 2013, p. x).

This final section has engaged with the idea of utopian thinking to consider the futurity of polarisation and how we might imagine social life after polarisation for those implicated in the heated contemporary divisions over sexuality and gender. Our readings of the symposium papers suggest that 'leaning in' across differences, both between and within demographics, has never been more urgent if we are to conceive of future imaginaries where all sexual and gendered lives are equally liveable. How that is to be achieved is contested, as differences in opinions in this chapter demonstrate. The symposium papers pose challenging questions about how to be good allies to one another, how to affirm new possibilities for sexualities and genders and work across difference and how best to address polarisation as academics – questions which are not answered but reflected on to explore if we can move beyond polarisation without reconciliation. As many of the symposium papers demonstrate, our narratives surrounding sexuality and gender recursively shape the power relations which sustain and/or ameliorate polarisation to form the potentials of utopian thinking. Developing a receptivity to hear other narratives without trying to reframe them to fit our own may be crucial for creating the imperfect utopias that can counter oppressive hegemonies surrounding gender and sexuality without requiring the minds and lifestyles of others to be changed. How we might develop and engage in that receptivity is the challenge for those who desire such futures.

Conclusion

The symposium papers call for a nuanced approach to understanding and addressing polarisation that takes seriously the relationality of gender and sexuality to challenge the binary certainties of self/other, us/them and good/bad that underpin the polarising of sexual and gendered lives. Dichotomous conceptualisations of polarisation as splitting societies across clear boundaries are shown to be restrictive and reductive, not fully grasping the heated spatiotemporalities of contemporary polarisation nor allowing clear pathways to alternative futures after polarisation. Not giving attention to, nor allowing more space for, ambivalence and disagreement may reinforce polarisation and push people into harder positions, as well as bolster the positions of those embracing the certainties fostered by misinformation. Embracing ambivalence and nuance surrounding progress around sexuality and gender might alternatively offer a point of entry into ameliorating polarisations by allowing for a more reflexive relationality which resists the urge and danger to vilify others. Finding ways to foster ontological security while holding uncertainties and ambivalences across difference appears key for attempts at mitigating polarising positions.

Avoiding aspatial and ahistorical understandings and critiques of polarisation and taking control of contextual polarising narratives on the ground also becomes a key imperative for those seeking to address polarisation and support those whose lives and rights are up for debate. However, the impasse over how to work across difference without reconciliation, and make space for fundamental disagreement without being oppositional, remains in the challenge of seeing the both/and in binaries of right/wrong for issues regarding sexuality and gender. Allowing for conversation of issues, negotiation of positions and ambivalent recognition of conflicting worldviews creates a present threat and places a burden on those already marginalised. If this burden can be shared and the threat mitigated by allies and those with the capital to make a difference both within and outside of the academy, the struggle to address polarisation through democratic processes may be sustainable. Despite the challenges shown across the symposium papers over the societal milieu of progress, crisis and victimhood, we interpret the collection to be overall optimistic and hopeful. While there will be many who remain sceptical and find such sentiments naive and idealistic, it is optimism and hope that may make utopian thinking and activism work to create futures beyond polarisation.

Notes

1 Note that this commentary includes all the papers in the symposium, some of which are not in this special special collection.
2 Kazyak's chapter in this volume also shows sexuality and gender in public school curriculum to remain polarising. Kazyak's chapter was not presented at the symposium, so was not discussed by the authors of this chapter.

REFERENCES

Abramowitz, A. I., & Saunders, K. L. (2008). Is polarization a myth? *The Journal of Politics, 70*(2), 542–555.

ACLU. (2023). Mapping attacks on LGBTQ rights in U.S. state legislatures. https://www.aclu.org/legislative-attacks-on-lgbtq-rights?state= (accessed 24 May 2023).

Adams-Santos, D. Desiring technologies: Digital pathways towards black queer sociality. In R. Ryan-Flood & A. Tooth Murphy (Eds.), *Queering desire* (1st ed., pp. 255–271). Routledge.

Ahmed, S. (2006). *Queer phenomenology: Orientations, objects, others*. Duke University Press.

Ahmed, S. (2011). Problematic proximities: Or why critiques of gay imperialism matter. *Feminist Legal Studies, 19*(2), 119–132.

Ahmed, S. (2012). *On being included: Racism and diversity in institutional life*. Duke University Press.

Akrivos, D. (2022). Transgender reporting in the British press: Editorial standards and discursive harms in the post-Leveson era. *Journal of Media Law, 14*(2), 406–441.

Al-Jazeera. (2013). Uganda leader says he will sign anti-gay bill. Al-Jazeera, 15 February. https://www.aljazeera.com/news/2014/2/15/uganda-leader-says-he-will-sign-anti-gay-bill

Anarte, E. (2022). Do trans self-ID laws harm women? Argentina could have answers. *Openly News*, 1 June. https://www.openlynews.com/i/?id=21757767-4909-4844-922f-41903ff042f8 (accessed 26 August 2023).

Anderson, E. S. (2022). Can we talk?: Communicating moral concern in an era of polarised politics. *Journal of Practical Ethics, 10*(1).

Anghie, A. (2006). The evolution of international law: Colonial and postcolonial realities. *Third World Quarterly, 27*, 739–753.

Anghie, A. (2007). *Imperialism, sovereignty and the making of international law*. Cambridge University Press.

Armstrong, E. A. (2002). *Forging gay identities: Organizing sexuality in San Francisco, 1950–1994*. University of Chicago Press.

Asteriti, A. (2023). Canaries in the coalmine. *Centre for Crime and Justice Studies*, 30 January. https://archive.is/6u32I (accessed 24 August 2023).

Auchmuty R. (2004). Same sex marriage revived: Feminist critique and legal strategy. *Feminism and Psychology, 4*(1), 101–126.

Ayoub, P. M. (Ed.). (2016). Internalizing new norms: Attitudes toward sexual minorities. In *When States come out: Europe's sexual minorities and the politics of visibility* (pp. 127–157). Cambridge University Press; Cambridge Core.

Ayoub, P. (2018). Perils of success: Backlash and resistance to LGBT rights in domestic and international politics. In A. Brysk & M. Stohl (Eds.), *Contracting Human Rights: Crisis, Accountability, and Opportunity* (pp. 89–104). Edward Elgar Publishing.

Ayoub, P. M., & Paternotte, D. (2014). Introduction. In P. M. Ayoub & D. Paternotte (Eds.), *LGBT activism and the making of Europe: A rainbow Europe?* (pp. 1–25). Palgrave Macmillan UK.

Bächtiger, A. (2014). Debate and deliberation in legislatures. In S. Martin, T. Saalfeld & K. Strøm (Eds.), *The Oxford handbook of legislative studies* (pp. 145–166). Oxford University Press.

Baer, D. B. (2015). On the International Day against Homophobia, Transphobia, and Biphobia (IDAHOT): Statement to the OSCE permanent council, 21 May. https://www.osce.org/files/f/documents/8/1/161751.pdf

Bail, C. A., Argyle, L. P., Brown, T. W., Bumpus, J. P., Chen, H., Hunzaker, M. F., Lee, J., Mann, M., Merhout, F., & Volfovsky, A. (2018). Exposure to opposing views on social media can increase political polarization. *Proceedings of the National Academy of Sciences*, *115*(37), 9216–9221.

Bailey, A. (2021a). It's rare that a female…[tweet], 27 September. https://twitter.com/BluskyeAllison/status/1442449150818324484 (accessed 23 August 2023).

Bailey, A. (2021b). Under English law…[tweet], 27 September. https://twitter.com/BluskyeAllison/status/1442427273076948994 (accessed 23 August 2023).

Bailey, A. (2022). *Correction: of the 436 'women' recorded…[tweet], 7 January. https://twitter.com/BluskyeAllison/status/1479465707113009157 (accessed 23 August 2023).

Baker, J. O., & Edmonds, A. E. (2021). Immigration, presidential politics, and partisan polarization among the American public, 1992–2018. *Sociological Spectrum*, *41*(4), 287–303.

Baker, P. (2019). Representing trans people in the UK press - A follow-up study. ESRC Centre for Corpus Approaches to Social Science (CASS). https://cass.lancs.ac.uk/representing-trans-people-in-the-uk-press-a-follow-up-study-professor-paul-baker/ (accessed 27 October 2023).

Baker, R. S. (2022). The historical racial regime and racial inequality in poverty in the American South. *American Journal of Sociology*, *127*(6), 1721–1781.

Ballantine, C., Hilliard, L., & Browne, K. (2023). Researching and addressing polarisation around gender, sexuality and abortion. Beyond Opposition: An artistic collaboration [Symposium paper] *Polarising Sexual and Gendered Lives: Divisions, Differences and LGBTQI+ Equalities*, University College Dublin, 23 June.

Banerjea, N., & Browne, K. (2018). Liveable lives: A transnational queer-feminist reflection on sexuality, development and governance. In C. L. Mason (Ed.), *Routledge handbook of queer development studies* (pp. 169–179). Routledge.

Banerjea, N., & Browne, K. (2023). *Liveable lives: Living and surviving LGBTQ equalities in India and the UK* (p. 208). Bloomsbury Academic.

Banerjea, N., Browne, K., Ferreira, E., Olasik, M., & Podmore, J. (Eds.). (2019). *Lesbian feminism: Essays opposing global heteropatriarchies*. Bloomsbury Publishing.

Barker, M-J., & Iantaffi, A. (2019). *Life isn't Binary*. Jessica Kingsley.

Barone, T., & Eisner, E. (2011). *Arts based research*. SAGE Publications, Inc.

Baska, M. (2023). UK Politicians may have contributed to rise in anti-trans hate crime, government confirms. *Pink News*, 6 October. https://www.thepinknews.com/2023/10/06/uk-government-hate-crimes-lgbtq-trans-rishi-sunak/

Baumer, D. C., & Gold, H. J. (2010). *Parties, polarization and democracy in the United States* (1st ed.). Routledge.

BBC News. (2018a). How many transgender inmates are there? *BBC News Reality Check*, 13 August. https://www.bbc.com/news/uk-42221629 (accessed 24 August 2023).

BBC News. (2018b). Pride in London sorry after anti-trans protest. *BBC News*, 8 July. https://www.bbc.com/news/uk-england-london-44757403 (accessed 24 August 2023).

BBC News. (2020). Changes to gender recognition laws ruled out. *BBC News*, 22 September. https://www.bbc.com/news/uk-politics-54246686 (accessed 24 August 2023).

Beam, M. (2018). *Gay, Inc.: The nonprofitization of queer politics*. University of Minnesota Press.

Becker, H.S. (1967). Whose side are we on?. *Social Problems*, 14(3), 239–247.

Beckford, M. (2019). One prisoner in 50 'identifies as the opposite sex': Survey suggests 1,400 inmates are transgender - but are they conning staff for easier conditions? *Mail on Sunday*, 17 February, 4. https://login.ezproxy.lib.bbk.ac.uk/login?url=https://www.proquest.com/newspapers/one-prisoner-50-identif-ies-as-opposite-sex/docview/2182082825/se-2?accountid=8629 (accessed 24 August 2023).

Beckford, M. (2022). 4 in 10 trans inmates guilty of sex crimes. *Daily Mail*, 2 December, 2. https://login.ezproxy.lib.bbk.ac.uk/login?url=https://www.proquest.com/newspapers/4-10-trans-inmates-guilty-sex-crimes/docview/2744437930/se-2?accountid=8629

Bedford, K. (2009). *Developing partnerships: Gender, sexuality and the world bank*. University of Minnesota Press.

Beech, N. (2011). Liminality and the practices of identity reconstruction. *Human Relations*, 64(2), 285–302.

Bell, D., & Valentine, B. (1995). *Mapping desire: Geographies of sexualities*. Routledge.

Bell, D., & Binnie, J. (2000). *The sexual citizen: Queer theory and beyond*. Polity Press.

Bell, D., & Binnie, J. (2004). Authenticating queer space: Citizenship, urbanism and governance. *Urban Studies*, 41, 1807–1820.

Bennett, L., & Layard, A. (2015). Legal geography: Becoming spatial detectives. *Geography Compass*, 9(7), 406–422.

Ben Hagai, E., Annechino, R., & Antin, T. (2022). Comparing conceptions of gender, sexuality and lesbian identity between baby boomers and millennials. *Journal of Lesbian Studies*, 26(3), 216–234.

Bent Bars Project. (2020). *Trans prisoners info sheet #2: Frequently asked questions*. https://www.bentbarsproject.org/resources/trans-prisoner-info-sheet-2 (accessed 24 August 2023).

Bent Bars Project. (2023). *Revised trans prison policy in England & Wales*. https://www.bentbarsproject.org/news/revised-trans-prison-policy-in-england-wales-2023 (accessed 17 August 2023).

Beresniova, C. (2010). When intolerance means more than prejudice: Challenges to Lithuanian education reforms for social tolerance . In I. Silova (Ed.), *Post-Socialism is not dead: (Re)Reading the global in comparative education* (Vol. 14, pp. 247–269) Emerald.

Bergenfield, R., & Miller, A. (2014). Queering international development? An examination of new 'LGBT Rights' Rhetoric, policy, and programming among international development agencies. *LGBTQ Policy Journal*, March 2014.

Berlant, L., & Warner, M. (1998). Sex in Public. *Critical Inquiry*, 24(2), 547–566.

Berlant, L. (2022). *On the inconvenience of other people*. Duke University Press.

Bermon, S., & Garnier, P. (2017). Serum androgen levels and their relation to performance in track and field. *British Journal of Sports Medicine*, 51, 1309–1314.

Bernstein, M., & Taylor, V. (Eds.). (2013). *The marrying kind?: Debating same-sex marriage within the lesbian and gay movement*. University of Minnesota Press.

Berry, R. (2016). Briefing by Special Envoy for the Human Rights of LGBTI Persons Randy Berry, 13 April. U.S. Department of State. https://2009-2017.state.gov/r/pa/prs/ps/2016/04/256425.htm

Bet, M. (2022). Commons trans row after Tory MP says 'a woman is an adult female human'. *The Independent*, 20 March. https://www.independent.co.uk/news/uk/bernard-jenkin-anneliese-dodds-commons-joanna-cherry-mps-b2033109.html (accessed 24 August 2023).

Bettcher, T. M. (2014). Trapped in the wrong theory: Rethinking trans oppression and resistance. *Signs: Journal of Women in Culture and Society*, 39(2), 383–406.

Bey, M. (2021). Trouble genders: 'LGBT' collapse and trans fundamentality. *Hypatia*, 36(1), 191–206.

Beyerlein, K., & Eberle, C. J. (2014). Who violates the principles of political liberalism?: Religion, restraint, and the decision to reject same-sex marriage. *Politics and Religion*, 7(2), 240–264.

Biegel, S. (2018). *The right to be out: Sexual orientation and gender identity in America's public schools*. University of Minnesota Press.

Billard, T. J. (2023). 'Gender-critical' discourse as disinformation: Unpacking TERF strategies of political communication. *Women's Studies in Communication*, 46(2), 235–243.

Bindel, J. (2021). *Feminism for women: The real route to liberation*. Constable Press.

Binnie, J. (1997). Coming out of geography: Towards a queer epistemology? *Environment and Planning D: Society and Space*, 15, 223–237.

Binnie, J. (2004). *The globalization of sexuality*. SAGE Publications, Inc.

Binnie, J., & Skeggs, B. (2004). Cosmopolitan knowledge and the production and consumption of sexualized space: Manchester's gay village. *The Sociological Review*, 52(1), 39–61.

Binnie, J., Holloway, J., Millington, S., & Young, C. (2006). *Cosmopolitan urbanism* (1st ed. 1). Routledge.

Bliuc, AM., McGarty, C., Thomas, E., Girish, L., Berndsen, M. & Misaj, R. (2015). Public division about climate change rooted in conflicting socio-political identities. *Nature Climate Change* 5, 226–229.

Borbáth, E., Hutter, S., & Leininger, A. (2023). Cleavage politics, polarisation and participation in Western Europe. *West European Politics*, 46(4), 631–651.

Bosia, M. J., & Weiss, M. L. (2013). Political homophobia in comparative perspective. In M. L. Weiss & M. J. Bosia (Eds.), *Global homophobia: States, movements, and the politics of oppression* (pp. 1–29). University of Illinois Press.

Boss, P. (2022). *The myth of closure: Ambiguous loss in a time of pandemic and change*. W W Norton.

Boulila, S. C. (2019). *Race in post-racial Europe: An intersectional analysis*. Rowman & Littlefield.

Boxell, L., Gentzkow, M., & Shapiro, J. M. (2017). Greater Internet use is not associated with faster growth in political polarization among US demographic groups. *Proceedings of the National Academy of Sciences*, 114(40), 10612–10617.

Boxell, L., Gentzkow, M., & Shapiro, J. (2024). Cross-country trends in affective polarization. *The Review of Economics and Statistics*, 106(2), 557–565.

Braun, V., & Clarke, V. (2006). Using thematic analysis in psychology. *Qualitative Research in Psychology*, 3(2), 77–101.

Braun, V., & Clarke, V. (2022). *Thematic analysis: A practical guide*. SAGE Publications, Inc.

Braverman, I., Blomley, N., Delaney, D., & Kedar, A. (Eds.). (2014). *The expanding spaces of law: A timely legal geography*. Stanford University Press.

Brewer, P. R. (2003). Values, political knowledge, and public opinion about gay rights: A framing based account. *Public Opinion Quarterly, 67*(2), 173–201.

Brickell, K., & Cuomo, D. (2019). Feminist geolegality. *Progress in Human Geography, 43*(1), 104–122.

Brickell, K., Jeffrey, A., & McConnell, F. (2021). Practising legal geography. *Area, 53*(4), 557–561.

Bronfenbrenner, U. (1977). Toward an experimental ecology of human development. *American Psychologist, 32*(7), 513.

Brooks, S. (2016). Staying in the hood: Black lesbian and transgender women and identity management in North Philadelphia. *Journal of Homosexuality, 63*(12), 1573–1593.

Brown, G. (2012). Homonormativity: A metropolitan concept that denigrates 'ordinary' gay lives. *Journal of Homosexuality, 59*(7), 1065–1072.

Brown, G., & Browne, K. (Eds.). (2016). *The Routledge research companion to geographies of sex and sexualities* (pp. 13–20). Routledge.

Brown-Saracino, J. (2020). From situated space to social space: Dyke bar commemoration as reparative action. *Journal of Lesbian Studies, 24*(3), 311–325.

Brown, M. (2014). Gender and sexuality II: There goes the gayborhood?. *Progress in Human Geography, 38*(3), 457–465.

Browne, K. (2007). A party with politics? (Re)making LGBTQ Pride spaces in Dublin and Brighton. *Social & Cultural Geography, 8*(1), 63–87.

Browne, K. (2020). Doing feminist research in contested moments: Commentary on 'Gender's Wider Stakes: Lay Attitudes to Legal Gender Reform'. *feminists@law, 10*(2).

Browne, K. & Banerjea, N. (2023). *Liveable Lives: Living and Surviving LGBTQ Equalities in India and the UK*. Bloomsbury Publishing.

Browne, K., & Bakshi, L. (2013). *Ordinary in Brighton?: LGBT, activisms and the city*. Routledge.

Browne, K., & Nash, C. J. (2010). *Queer methods and methodologies: Intersecting queer theories and social science research*. Taylor & Francis.

Browne, K., & Nash, C. J. (2014). Resisting LGBT rights where 'we have won': Canada and Great Britain. *Journal of Human Rights, 13*(3), 322–336.

Browne, K., & Nash, C. J. (2018). Resisting marriage equalities: The complexities of religious opposition to same sex marriage. In N. Bartolini, S. MacKian & Pile (Eds.), *Spaces of spirituality* (pp. 37–53). Routledge.

Browne, K., & Nash, C. J. (2020). In Ireland we 'love both'? Heteroactivism in Ireland's anti-Repeal ephemera. *Feminist Review, 124*(1), 51–67.

Browne, K., & Nash, C. J. (2023a). From hegemonic to where? The public spatialities of shifting positionings for those who are opposed to/concerned about socio-legal changes in sexual and genders. *Tijdschrift voor Economische en Sociale Geografie, 114*(4), 271–288.

Browne, K., & Nash, C. J. (2023b). What do 'we' do with 'them'?: A response. *Tijdschrift voor Economische en Sociale Geografie, 114*(4), 298–299.

Browne, K., Nash, C. J., & Gorman-Murray, A. (2018). Geographies of heteroactivism: Resisting sexual rights in the reconstitution of Irish nationhood. *Transactions of the Institute of British Geographers, 43*(4), 526–539.

Browne, K., Banerjea, N., McGlynn, N., Bakshi, L., Banerjee, R., & Biswas, R. (2017). Towards transnational feminist queer methodologies. *Gender, Place & Culture, 24*(10), 1376–1397.

Browne, K., Banerjea, N., McGlynn, N., Bakshi, L., Beethi, S., & Biswas, R. (2021). The limits of legislative change: Moving beyond inclusion/exclusion to create 'a life worth living'. *Environment and Planning C: Politics and Space, 39*(1), 30–52.

Browne, K., Munt, S. R., & Yip, A. K. T. (2010). *Queer spiritual spaces: Sexuality and sacred places*. Routledge.

Brubaker, R. (2004). *Ethnicity without groups*. Harvard University Press.

Bryant, R. (2002). The purity of spirit and the power of blood: A comparative perspective on nation, gender and kinship in Cyprus. *Journal of the Royal Anthropological Institute*, 8(3), 509–530.

Burack, C. (2008). *Sin, sex, and democracy: Antigay rhetoric and the Christian right*. State University of New York Press.

Burgess, E. W. (1925). The growth of the city: An introduction to a research project. In R. E. Park, E. W. Burgess, & R. D. McKenzie (Eds.), *The city: Suggestion for investigation of human behaviour in the urban environment* (pp. 47–62). University of Chicago Press.

Burke, K. (2016). *Christians under covers: Evangelicals and sexual pleasure on the internet*. University of California Press.

Burke, K. (2023). *The pornography wars: The past, present, and future of America's obscene obsession*. Bloomsbury Publishing USA.

Burke, K., & Kazyak, E. (2021). Religion, sexuality, and freedom: The social and legal landscape of religious liberty and LGBTQ rights. Paper presentation. Vanderbilt University.

Burke, K., Kazyak, E., & MillerMacPhee, A. (2022). LGBT employment nondiscrimination: Debating sexuality and citizenship. *Sexuality Research and Social Policy*, 19(2), 470–482.

Burke, K., Kazyak, E., & Behrendt, M. (2023). 'In a religious celebration': The religious defense of LGBT rights in U.S. federal courts. *Journal of Homosexuality*. Online advanced access.

Burke, K., Kazyak, E., Oliver, M., & Valkr, P. (2023). LG but not T: Opposition to transgender rights amidst gay and lesbian acceptance. *The Sociological Quarterly*, 64(3), 471–492.

Butler, J. (1990). *Gender trouble: Feminism and the subversion of identity*. Routledge.

Butler, J. S. (2006). *Born again: The Christian right globalized*. Pluto Press.

Butler, J. (2009). Performativity, precarity and sexual politics. *Revista de Antropología Iberoamericana*, 4(3), I–XIII.

Butler, J. (2023). Who's afraid of gender? Judith Butler's public lecture at University of Cambridge 2023 [Lecture], Centre for Gender Studies, University of Cambridge, 26 April.

Buyantueva, R., & Shevtsova, M. (2020). Introduction: LGBTQ+ activism and the power of locals. In R. Buyantueva & M. Shevtsova (Eds.), *LGBTQ+ activism in central and Eastern Europe: Resistance, representation and identity* (pp. 1–19). Springer International Publishing.

Castle, J. (2019). New fronts in the culture wars? Religion, partisanship, and polarization on religious liberty and transgender rights in the United States. *American Politics Research*, 47(3), 650–679.

Carothers, T., & O'Donohue, A. (Eds.). (2019). *Democracies divided: The global challenge of political polarization*. Brookings Institution Press.

Chanady, T. (2022). Shifting inclusions: Identities and spaces of political lesbianism in Montreal from 1970 to 2020. *Journal of Lesbian Studies*, 26(2), 121–132.

Chapkis, W. (1997). *Live Sex Acts: Women Performing Erotic Labor*. Routledge.

Charania, M. (2017). Outing the Pakistani queer: Pride, paranoia and politics in US visual culture. *Sexualities*, 20(1–2), 41–64.

Chávez, K. R. (2013). *Queer migration politics: Activist rhetoric and coalitional possibilities.* University of Illinois Press.

Chilton, G., & Leavy, P. (2014). Arts-based research practice: Merging social research and the creative arts. In P. Leavy (Ed.)., *The Oxford handbook of qualitative research methods* (pp. 403–422*).* Oxford University Press.

Clark, T. D. (2006). Nationalism in post-Soviet Lithuania: New approaches for the nation of 'innocent sufferers'. In L. W. Barrington (Ed.), *After Independence: Making and Protecting the Nation in Postcolonial and Postcommunist States* (pp. 162–186). University of Michigan Press.

Clarke, C. (1983). The failure to transform: Homophobia in the Black community. In B. Smith (Ed.), *Home girls: A Black feminist anthology* (pp. 197–208). Rutgers University Press.

Clarke, V. (2000). 'Stereotype, attack and stigmatize those who disagree': Employing scientific rhetoric in debates about lesbian and gay parenting. *Feminism & Psychology, 10*(1), 152–159.

Clarke, V., & Finlay, S.-J. (2004). 'For better or worse?' Lesbian and gay marriage. *Feminism & Psychology, 14*(1), 17–23.

Clarke, V., & Peel, E. (2007). From lesbian and gay psychology to LGBTQ psychologies: A journey into the unknown (or unknowable)? In V. Clarke & E. Peel (Eds.), *Out in psychology* (pp. 11–35). Wiley.

Clery, E. (2023). A liberalisation in attitudes?, September 2023. National Centre for Social Research. https://natcen.ac.uk/sites/default/files/2023-09/BSA%2040%20Moral %20issues.pdf (accessed 27 October 2023).

Cloke, P., May, J., & Williams, A. (2017). The geographies of food banks in the meantime. *Progress in Human Geography, 41*(6), 703–726.

Cohen, C. J. (1997). Punks, bulldaggers, and welfare queens: The radical potential of queer politics? *GLQ, 3*(4), 437–465.

Cohen, C. J. (2005). Punks, bulldaggers and welfare queens: The radical potential of queer politics? In E. P. Johnson & M. G. Henderson (Eds.), *Black queer studies* (pp. 22–51). Duke University Press.

Collier, B., & Cowan, S. (2022). Queer conflicts, concept capture and category co-option: The importance of context in the state collection and recording of sex/gender data. *Social & Legal Studies, 31*(5), 746–772.

Comte, J. (2014). Decriminalization of sex work: Feminist discourses in light of research. *Sexuality & Culture, 18,* 196–217.

Connell, C. (2022). *A few good gays: The gendered compromises behind military inclusion.* University of California Press.

Connell, R. (2012). Transsexual women and feminist thought: Toward new understanding and new politics. *Signs, 37*(4), 857–881.

Conover, M. D., Ratkiewicz, J., Francisco, M. R., Gonçalves, B., Menczer, F., & Flammini, A. (2011). Political polarization on twitter. *Proceedings of the International AAAI Conference on Web and Social Media,* 5(1), 89–96.

Conrad, R. (Ed.). (2014). *Against equality: Queer revolution, not mere inclusion.* AK Press.

Cooper, D. (2019). A very binary drama: The conceptual struggle for gender's future. *feminists@law, 9*(1).

Cooper, D. (2019). *Feeling like a state: Desire, denial, and the recasting of authority.* Duke University Press.

Cooper, D. (2019). A very binary drama: the conceptual struggle for gender's future. *feminists@law*, 9(1).
Cooper, D. (2022). Presenting our pronouns: When feminist politics pull in different directions. *LSE Engenderings*. https://blogs.lse.ac.uk/gender/2023/01/30/4784/
Cooper, D. (2023). Crafting prefigurative law in turbulent times: Decertification, DIY law reform, and the dilemmas of feminist prototyping. *Feminist Legal Studies*, 31, 17–42.
Cooper, D., & Renz, F. (2023). Introduction to special issue: Decertifying legal sex – prefigurative law reform and the future of legal gender. *Feminist Legal Studies*, 31(1), 1–16.
Cooper, D., Grabham, E., & Renz, F. (2020). Introduction to the special issue on the future of legal gender: Exploring the feminist politics of decertification. *feminists@law*, 10(2).
Cooper, D., Emerton, R., Grabham, E., Newman, H. J. H., Peel, E., Renz, F., & Smith, J. (2022). *Abolishing legal sex status: The challenge and consequences of gender-related law reform. Future of Legal Gender Project. Final Report*. King's College London, UK.
Cornejo-Valle, M., & Ramme, J. (2022). 'We don't want rainbow terror': Religious and far-right sexual politics in Poland and Spain. In C. Möser, J. Ramme, & J. Takács (Eds.), *Paradoxical right-wing sexual politics in Europe* (pp. 25–60). Springer International Publishing.
Corrêa, S. (2017). Gender ideology: Tracking its origins and meanings in current gender politics. *LSE Engenderings*. Available at: https://blogs.lse.ac.uk/gender/2017/12/11/gender-ideology-tracking-its-origins-and-meanings-in-current-gender-politics/
Corrêa, S., (Ed.). (2021). *Anti-Gender politics in Latin America: Summaries of country case studies. Rio de Janeiro*, Sexuality Policy Watch. https://sxpolitics.org/summaries-of-country-case-studies/22094 (accessed 19 July 2024).
Cortazzi, M. (2001). Narrative analysis in ethnography. In P. Atkinson (Ed.), *Handbook of ethnography* (pp. 384–394). SAGE Publications, Inc.
Cramer, R., Hexem, S., LaPollo, A., Cuffe, K. M., Chesson, H. W., & Leichliter, J. S. (2017). State and local policies related to sexual orientation in the United States. *Journal of Public Health Policy*, 38(1), 58.
Crawley, S. L. (2002). Narrating and negotiating butch and femme: Storying lesbian selves in a Heteronormative world. Doctoral Dissertation. Department of Sociology, University of Florida. https://ufl-flvc.primo.exlibrisgroup.com/discovery/fulldisplay?docid= alma990325751240306597&context=L&vid=01FALSC_UFL:UFL&lang=en&search_scope= MyInst_and_CI&adaptor=Local%20Search%20Engine&tab=Everything&query=any,con tains,crawley,%20sara&offset=0
Crawley, S. L. (2022). Queering doing gender: The curious absence of ethnomethodology in gender studies. *Sociological Theory*, 40(4), 366–392.
Crawley, S. L. (2023). From Butch/Femme dykes to trans and queer folx: Why time and space create discord from talking in identity types [Symposium paper] *Polarising Sexual and Gendered Lives:Divisions, Differences and LGBTQI+ Equalities*, University College Dublin, 23 June.
Crawley, S. L., & Green, A. (2021). Gender and embodiment as negotiated relations. In W. H. Brekhus, T. DeGloma, & W. R. Force (Eds.), *The Oxford handbook of symbolic interaction*. Oxford University Press.
Crawley, S. L., & Green, A. (2024). From Butch and Femme lesbians to non-binary and queer women: Intergenerational shifts from in-person places to digital spaces. In R. Ryan-Flood & A. Tooth-Murphy (Eds.), *Queering desire: Lesbians, gender and subjectivity*. Routledge.

Crenshaw, K. (1991). Mapping the margins: Intersectionality, identity politics, and violence against women of color. *Stanford Law Review*, *43*(6), 1241–1299.

Cuff, B. M. P., Brown, S. J., Taylor, L., & Howat, D. J. (2016). Empathy: A review of the concept. *Emotion Review*, *8*(2), 144–153.

Cuomo, D., & Brickell, K. (2019). Feminist legal geographies. *Environment and Planning A: Economy and Space*, *51*(5), 1043–1049.

Daily Star. (2019). Ian Huntley: Clarification. *Daily Star Sunday*, 10 February, 2. https://login.ezproxy.lib.bbk.ac.uk/login?url=https://www.proquest.com/newspapers/ian-huntley-clarification/docview/2177872326/se-2?accountid=8629

Dalgety, S. (2022). Abolishing legal status of sex would rob women of sex-based rights and protections. The *Scotsman*, 20 May. https://www.scotsman.com/news/opinion/columnists/abolishing-legal-status-of-sex-would-rob-women-of-sex-based-rights-and-protections-susan-dalgety-3702218

Davis, A. Y. (1981). *Women, race & class* (1st ed.). New York: Random House.

Davydova, D. (2012). Baltic pride 2010: Articulating sexual difference and heteronormative nationalism in contemporary Lithuania. *Sextures*, *2*(2), 32–46.

Dawson, B. (2022). MP wrongly suggested 436 transgender women committed rape between 2012 and 2018, says Crown Prosecution Service. *Business Insider*, 6 April. https://www.businessinsider.com/cps-mp-wrongly-claimed-436-trans-women-committed-rape-in-6-year-period-2022-4?r=US&IR=T (accessed 24 August 2023).

De Beauvoir, S. (1952). *The second sex*. H. M. Parshley (trans.). Knopf [1st American ed.]

De La Cretaz, F. (2022). IOC and Trans inclusion. 23 March, *Sports Illustrated*. https://www.si.com/olympics/2022/03/23/transgender-athletes-testosterone-policies-ioc-framework

Decety, J., & Sommerville, J. A. (2003). Shared representations between self and other: A social cognitive neuroscience view. *Trends in Cognitive Sciences*, *7*(12), 527–533.

Delaney, D. (2010). *The spatial, the legal and the pragmatics of world-making: Nomospheric investigations*. Routledge-Cavendish.

Delaney, D. (2015). Legal geography I: Constitutivities, complexities, and contingencies. *Progress in Human Geography*, *39*(1), 96–102.

Democratic National Convention. (2020). Platform of the Democratic Party, 2020, Cleveland, OH. Issued by the Democratic National Committee, Washington, DC.

Dentice, D., & Dietert, M. (2015). Liminal spaces and the transgender experience. *Theory in Action*, *8*(2), 69.

Denzin, N. K. (2018). *The qualitative manifesto: A call to arms* (2nd ed.). Routledge.

DeSilver, D. (2022). The polarization in today's congress has roots that goes back decades. Pew Research Center, 10 March. https://www.pewresearch.org/short-reads/2022/03/10/the-polarization-in-todays-congress-has-roots-that-go-back-decades/

Deterding, N. M., & Waters, M. C. (2021). Flexible coding of in-depth interviews: A twenty-first-century approach. *Sociological Methods & Research*, *50*(2), 708–739.

Devor, A. H., & Matte, N. (2004). ONE Inc. and Reed Erickson: The uneasy collaboration of gay and trans activism, 1964–2003. *GLQ: A Journal of Lesbian and Gay Studies*, *10*(2), 179–209.

Dhejne, C., Lichtenstein, P., Boman, M., et al. (2011). Long-term follow-up of transsexual persons undergoing sex reassignment surgery: Cohort study in Sweden. *PloS One*, *6*(2), e16885.

Diaz, A., & Figueredo, V. (2022). Transgender in pediatrics. *Pediatric Medicine*, 6.

Dickinson, I. (2017). Child murderer Ian Huntley wants SEX CHANGE to get cushier life in women's jail. *Daily Star* (Online), 15 January. https://archive.is/Ag5vS (accessed 24 August 2023).

Dickinson, I. (2018). 'Call me Nicola' Evil double murderer Ian Huntley in wig and make-up prison stunt. *Daily Star* (Online), 8 April.

Di Feliciantonio, C. (2016). In Italy It's Different: Pride as a Space of Political Contention. In G. Brown & K. Browne (Eds.) *The Routledge research companion to geographies of sex and sexualities*, (1st ed., pp. 97–104). Routledge.

Dodds, I. (2022). Police told to use birth sex for trans crime victim stats. *The Independent*, 12 April. https://www.independent.co.uk/news/uk/home-news/home-office-trans-crime-statistics-grc-birth-sex-b2056345.html (accessed 24 August 2023).

Doderer, Y. P. (2011). LGBTQs in the city, Queering Urban Space. *International Journal of Urban and Regional Research*, 35(2), 431–436.

Dorman, N. (2017). Prisoners at Europe's biggest sex offender jail celebrate transgender day to support 12 male inmates living as women. *The Mirror*. 18 November. https://www.mirror.co.uk/news/uk-news/prisoners-europes-biggest-sex-offender-11545803 (accessed 13 August 2024).

Downey, D. J. (2022). Polarization and persuasion: Engaging sociology in the moral universe of a divided democracy. *Sociological Perspectives*, 65(6), 1029–1051.

Druckman, J. N., Peterson, E., & Slothuus, R. (2013). How elite partisan polarization affects public opinion formation. *American Political Science Review*, 107(1), 57–79.

Du Bois, W. E. B., & Marable, M. (1903). *The souls of black folk: Essays and sketches*. A.C. McClurg.

Duffy, B., Hewlett, K., Murkin, G., et al. (2021). Culture wars in the UK. The Policy Institute, *King's College London*, June. https://www.kcl.ac.uk/policy-institute/assets/culture-wars-in-the-uk.pdf (accessed 27 October 2023).

Duffy, N. (2018). Metro newspaper runs full-page ad attacking transgender right reforms. *Pink News*, 21 April. https://www.pinknews.co.uk/2018/10/10/metro-newspaper-full-page-ad-attacking-transgender-reforms/ (accessed 24 August 2023).

Duggan, L. (2002). The new homonormativity: The sexual politics of neoliberalism. *Materializing Democracy: Toward a Revitalized Cultural Politics*, 10, 175–194.

Duggan, L. (2003). *The twilight of equality: Neoliberalism, cultural politics, and the attack on democracy*. Beacon Press.

Duggan, L., & Hunter, N. D. (2006). Sex wars: Sexual dissent and political culture (10th Anniversary ed.). Routledge.

Duggan, L., & Hunter, N. D. (2014). *Sex wars: Sexual dissent and political culture*. Routledge.

Dymond-Green, B. V., & Neil D-G. (2023). The living library – A participatory approach to societal research impact. In A. Urbaniak & A. Wanka (Eds.), *Routledge international handbook of participatory approaches in ageing research* (pp. 273–286). Routledge.

ECPS or European Center for Populism Studies. (n. d.). Political polarization. https://www.populismstudies.org/Vocabulary/political-polarization/

Edenborg, E. (2022). Time, queerness and global politics. *Lambda Nordica*, 26(4–1), 183–187.

Edenborg, E. (2023). 'Traditional values' and the narrative of gay rights as modernity: Sexual politics beyond polarization. *Sexualities*, 26(1–2), 37–53.

Elgot, J. (2023). Kemi Badenoch could rewrite law to allow trans exclusion from single-sex spaces. The *Guardian*, 4 April. https://www.theguardian.com/society/2023/apr/04/kemi-badenoch-could-rewrite-law-to-allow-trans-exclusion-from-single-sex-spaces (accessed 24 August 2023).

Elkink, J. A., Farrell, D. M., Marien, S., Reidy, T., & Suiter, J. (2020). The death of conservative Ireland? The 2018 abortion referendum. *Electoral Studies*, 65, 102–142.

Elliards, X. (2023). Who is Posie Parker? The anti-trans founder of standing for women. *The National* (online), 4 May. https://www.thenational.scot/news/23299549.posie-parker-anti-trans-founder-standing-women/ (accessed 27 October 2023).

Ellis, S. J., & Peel, E. (2011). Lesbian feminisms: Historical and present possibilities. *Feminism & Psychology, 21*(2), 198–204.

Emilion, J., Halacre, M., & Lee, C. (2022). Difference by its nature is a relational concept. *Therapy Today, 33*(10), 22–26.

Enright, M., McNeilly, K., & De Londras, F. (2020). Abortion activism, legal change, and taking feminist law work seriously. *Northern Ireland Legal Quarterly, 71*, 359.

Equality Texas. (2022). Anti-transgender sports ban, HB 25 goes into effect today. https://www.equalitytexas.org/anti-transgender-sports-ban-hb-25-goes-into-effect-today/ (accessed 24 May 2023).

Escudero-Alías, M. (2022). The institutionalization of queer theory: Where has lesbian criticism gone? *Journal of Lesbian Studies, 26*(3), 253–268.

Fairburn, C., Pyper, D., & Balogun, B. (2022). Gender recognition act reform: Consultation and outcome. House of Commons Library, UK Parliament. https://researchbriefings.files.parliament.uk/documents/CBP-9079/CBP-9079.pdft.uk

Fair Play For Women. (2017a). Half of all transgender prisoners are sex offenders or dangerous category A inmates, 9 November. https://web.archive.org/web/20171119115401/https://fairplayforwomen.com/transgender-prisoners/ (accessed 24 August 2023).

Fair Play for Women. (2017b). Women in prison are highly vulnerable, 1 August. https://archive.is/QZyjN (accessed 24 August 2023).

Fair Play For Women. (2018a). Government figures back Fair Play's report on transgender offenders, 3 June. https://archive.is/vBh3e (accessed 24 August 2023).

Fair Play for Women. (2018b). Rebirth [video]. YouTube. https://youtu.be/mzDEAz8Qztk (accessed 24 August 2023).

Fair Play For Women. (2018c). Victory for women tonight…[tweet], 18 October. https://twitter.com/fairplaywomen/status/1053033005021847553 (accessed 23 August 2023).

Fair Play for Women. (2018d). What will Sex Self-ID mean for women? [video]. YouTube. https://youtu.be/rxmq6e026s0 (accessed 24 August 2023).

Fair Play for Women. (2019). Our research: Transgender prisoner study, 4 February. https://archive.is/MREch (accessed 24 August 2023).

Fair Play For Women. (2021). Non-Binary: The new wolf in sheep's clothing, 11 July. https://archive.is/KdZmy (accessed 24 August 2023).

Fair Play For Women. (2022). Our aims. https://archive.is/0PQu8 (accessed 24 August 2023).

Fairbairn, C., Pyper, D., & Balogun, B. (2022). Gender recognition act reform: Consultation and outcome – Research Briefing No 09079. House of Commons Library, UK Parliament. https://researchbriefings.files.parliament.uk/documents/CBP-9079/CBP-9079.pdf (accessed 24 August 2023).

Farries, E., & Sturm, T. (2019). Feminist legal geographies of intimate-image sexual abuse: Using copyright logic to combat the unauthorized distribution of celebrity intimate images in cyberspaces. *Environment and Planning A: Economy and Space, 51*(5), 1145–1165.

Farris, S. R. (2017). *In the name of women's rights: The rise of femonationalism*. Duke University Press.

Faria, C., Klosterkamp, S., Torres, R. M., & Walenta, J. (2020). Embodied exhibits: Toward a feminist geographic courtroom ethnography. *Annals of the American Association of Geographers, 110*(4), 1095–1113.

Fausto-Sterling, A. (2000). *Sexing the body*. Basic Books.

Faye, S. (2021). *The transgender issue: An argument for justice.* Penguin UK.
Feder, J. L. (2014). World bank delays $90 million loan To Uganda as bank President Blasts Anti-Gay Laws. *BuzzFeed News*, 27 February. https://www.buzzfeednews.com/article/lesterfeder/world-bank-delays-90-million-loan-to-uganda-as-bank-presiden
Feder, S. (2020). *Disclosure: Trans lives on screen* [film]. Netflix.
Feinberg, L. (1996). *Transgender warriors: Making history from joan of arc to Dennis Rodman.* Beacon Press.
Feinberg, M., & Willer, R. (2015). From gulf to bridge: When do moral arguments facilitate political influence?. *Personality and Social Psychology Bulletin, 41*(12), 1665–1681.
Ferguson, R. A. (2004). *Aberrations in black: Toward a queer of color critique.* University of Minnesota Press.
Fernández Martínez, A., Meschede, S., & Zolchow, G. (2018). *Impossible Glossary.* Hablarenarte: Madrid. Available at: https://www.hablarenarte.com/catalogos/doc_glosario_ed2/PDF/glosario2018_es.pdf
Fetner, T. (2008). *How the religious right shaped lesbian and gay activism* (Vol. 31). University of Minnesota Press.
Fields, J. (2008). *Risky lessons: Sex education and social inequality.* Rutgers University Press.
Figueira, Á., & Oliveira, L. (2017). The current state of fake news: challenges and opportunities. *Procedia Computer Science, 121,* 817–825.
Fiorina, M. P., & Abrams, S. J. (2008). Political polarization in the American public. *Annual Review of Political Science, 11*(1), 563–588.
Fiorina, M. P., Abrams, S. J., & Pope, J. C. (2008). Polarization in the American public: Misconceptions and misreadings. *The Journal of Politics, 70*(2), 556–560.
Fiorina, M. P., Abrams, S. J. & Pope, J. C. (2010). *Culture war? The myth of a polarized America.* Longman.
Fisher, O. (2017). A recent study claimed that 41 per cent of transgender prisoners are sex offenders – this is why I'm not convinced. *The Independent*, 23 November (amended 18 October 2018). https://www.independent.co.uk/voices/41-per-cent-trans-transgender-trans-women-prisoners-sex-offenders-false-study-statistic-this-is-why-a8072431.html (accessed 24 August 2023).
FitzGerald, F. (2017). *The evangelicals: The struggle to shape America.* Simon & Schuster.
Flores, A. R. (2014). *National trends in public opinion on LGBT rights in the United States.* Williams Institute (UCLA). https://escholarship.org/uc/item/72t8q7pg (accessed November 2023).
Ford, R., & Jennings, W. (2020). The changing cleavage politics of Western Europe. *Annual Review of Political Science, 23,* 295–314.
Forstie, C. (2018). Ambivalently post-lesbian: LBQ friendships in the rural midwest. *Journal of Lesbian Studies, 22*(1), 54–66.
Forstie, C. (2020). Disappearing dykes? Post-lesbian discourse and shifting identities and communities. *Journal of Homosexuality, 67*(12), 1760–1778.
Foxall, A. (2019). From Evropa to Gayropa: A critical geopolitics of the European Union as seen from Russia. *Geopolitics, 24*(1), 174–193.
Foucault, M. (1986). An interview with Michel Foucault by Charles Ruas. (pp. 171–188). In M. Foucault (Ed.), *Death and the Labyrinth: The world of Raymond Roussel,* trans. Charles Ruas, Continuum.
Freedman, R., Stock, K., & Sullivan, A. (2020). *Evidence and data on trans women's offending.* Women and Equalities Select Committee, UK Parliament, 9 December. https://committees.parliament.uk/writtenevidence/18973/pdf/ (accessed 24 August 2023).
Freeman, H. (2017). Identity is the issue of our age: so why can't we talk more honestly about trans women? The *Guardian*, 18 March, 6. https://archive.is/xlOZj (accessed 24 August 2023).

Frey, J. J., Hall, W. J., Goldbach, J. T., & Lanier, P. (2021). 'Here in the bible belt, it's predominantly negative': Sexual identity stigma in the American South, 50 years after Stonewall. *Frontiers in Psychology, 12*, 804064.

Futterman, M. (2022). FINA restricts transgender women from competing at elite level. New York Times, 22 June. https://www.nytimes.com/2022/06/19/sports/fina-transgender-women-elite-swimming.html#:~:text=The%20vote%20by%20FINA%2C%20which,age%2012%2C%20whichever%20occurred%20late

Gallup. (2023). LGBTQ+ Rights. https://news.gallup.com/poll/1651/gay-lesbian-rights.aspx (accessed November 2023).

Gamson, J. (1995). Must identity movements self-destruct? A queer dilemma. *Social Problems, 42*(3), 390–407.

Gannon, S., & Davies, B. (2012). Postmodern, post-structural, and critical theories. In S. N. Hesse-Biber (Ed.), *Handbook of feminist research* (pp. 65–91). SAGE Publications, Inc.

Garber, L. (2001). *Identity poetics: Race, class, and the lesbian-feminist roots of queer theory.* Columbia University Press.

Garfinkel, H. (1967). *Studies in ethnomethodology.* Prentice Hall.

Garland, F., Lalor, K., & Travis, M. (2022). Intersex activism, medical power/knowledge and the scalar limitations of the United Nations. *Human Rights Law Review, 22*(3), ngac020.

GATE. (2022). Mapping anti-gender movements in the UK. *Global Action for Trans Equality (GATE)*, 12 July. https://gate.ngo/mapping-anti-gender-movements-in-the-uk/ (accessed 26 October 2023).

Gerő, M., Płuciennicak, P. P., Kluknavska, A., Navrátil, J., & Kanellopoulos, K. (2017). Understanding enemy images in central and Eastern European politics: Towards an interdisciplinary approach. *Intersections, 3*(3).

Ghaziani, A. (2008). *The dividends of dissent: How conflict and culture work in lesbian and gay marches on Washington.* University of Chicago Press.

Ghaziani, A., Taylor, V., & Stone, A. (2016). Cycles of sameness and difference in LGBT social movements. *Annual Review of Sociology, 42*(1), 165–183.

Gidron, N., Adams, J., & Horne, W. (2020). *American affective polarization in comparative perspective.* Cambridge University Press.

Gill-Peterson, J. (2021). From gender critical to QAnon: Anti-Trans politics and the laundering of conspiracy. *The New Inquiry*, 13 September. https://thenewinquiry.com/from-gender-critical-to-qanon-anti-trans-politics-and-the-laundering-of-conspiracy/1/15 (accessed 26 August 2023).

Gill-Peterson, J. (2022). Toward a historiography of the lesbian transsexual, or the TERF's nightmare. *Journal of Lesbian Studies, 26*(2), 133–147.

Gillespie, J., & Perry, N. (2019). Feminist political ecology and legal geography: A case study of the Tonle Sap protected wetlands of Cambodia. *Environment and Planning A: Economy and Space, 51*(5), 1089–1105.

Gilligan, A. (2017a). Number of transgender prisoners rises by 80%. *Sunday Times*, 3 December, 12. https://www.thetimes.co.uk/article/number-of-transgender-prisoners-rises-by-80-7stz2bfvl (accessed 26 August 2023).

Gilligan, A. (2017b). Up to half of trans inmates may be sex offenders: Plans to allow people to self-define their gender could put female prisoners at risk, campaigners warn. *Sunday Times*, 19 November, 7. https://www.thetimes.co.uk/article/up-to-half-of-trans-inmates-may-be-sex-offenders-26rz2crhs (accessed 30 August 2023).

Gilson, E. (2011). Vulnerability, ignorance, and oppression. *Hypatia, 26*(2), 308–332.

Glenn, C. (2020). We are the new Lithuania. *Lambda Nordica, 25*(3–4), Article 3–4.

Gorman, C. S. (2019). Feminist legal archeology, domestic violence and the raced-gendered juridical boundaries of US asylum law. *Environment and Planning A: Economy and Space, 51*(5), 1050–1067.

Gould, D. B. (2009). *Moving politics: Emotion and ACT UP's fight against AIDS.* University of Chicago Press.

Gourtsoyannis, P. (2020). SNP has 'no mandate' for sex self declaration, campaigners warn. The *Scotsman,* 24 February, 11. https://login.ezproxy.lib.bbk.ac.uk/login?url=https://www.proquest.com/newspapers/snp-has-no-mandate-sex-self-declaration/docview/2718820299/se-2?accountid=8629 (accessed 24 August 2023).

Government of Ireland. (2015). *Gender recognition act.* Dublin: Stationery Office.

Graff, A., & Korolczuk, E. (2021). *Anti-gender politics in the populist moment* (1st ed.). Routledge.

Graff, A., & Korolczuk, E. (2022). *Anti-gender politics in the populist moment.* Taylor & Francis.

Graham, L. F., Crissman, H. P., Tocco, J., Hughes, L. A., Snow, R. C., & Padilla, M. B. (2014). Interpersonal relationships and social support in transitioning narratives of Black transgender women in Detroit. *International Journal of Transgenderism, 15*(2), 100–113.

Grant, A. (2023). Police Scotland must record all rapists as men, say Tories. The *Scotsman,* 28 January. https://www.scotsman.com/news/politics/police-scotland-must-record-all-rapists-as-men-say-tories-4004903 (accessed 24 August 2023).

Greene, J. (2021). Labor of love: The formalization of care in transgender kinship organizations. *Organization, 28*(6), 930–948.

Grimsley, J. (2001). *Myth and reality: The story of gay people in the South.* In J. Howard & K. E. Pratt (Eds.), *Out in the South,* (pp. 229–235) Temple University Press.

Grosz, E. (2001). *Architecture from the outside: Essays on virtual and real space.* MIT press.

Guasti, P. (2021). Same same, but different: Domestic conditions of illiberal backlash against universal rights in the Czech Republic and Slovakia. In A. Lorenz & L. H. Anders (Eds.), *Illiberal trends and anti-EU politics in East Central Europe* (pp. 179–206). Springer International Publishing.

Guyan, K. (2022). *Queer data: Using gender, sex and sexuality data for action. Bloomsbury studies in digital cultures.* Bloomsbury Publishing.

Gwenffrewi, G. (2022). *The stoning of Stonewall during the new trans panic.* University and Colleges Union. https://www.ucu.org.uk/media/13245/The-stoning-of-Stonewall-during-the-new-trans-panic/pdf/The_stoning_of_Stonewall_Nov22.pdf (accessed 19 July 2024).

Hagai, E. B., Annechino, R., & Antin, T. (2023). Comparing conceptions of gender, sexuality and lesbian identity between baby boomers and millennials. In E. B. Hagai (Ed.), *Is lesbian identity obsolete? In conversation with queer and trans perspectives* (pp. 92–110). Routledge.

Hahm, H., Hilpert, D., & König, T. (2022). Divided by Europe: Affective polarisation in the context of European elections. *West European Politics, 46*(4), 705–731.

Halberstam, J. (2005). *In a queer time and place: Transgender bodies, subcultural lives.* New York University Press.

Halperin, D. M. (1993). Is there a history of sexuality? In H. Abelove, M. A. Barale, & D. M. Halperin (Eds.), *The lesbian and gay studies reader* (pp. 416–431). Routledge.

Halpern, J. (2003). What is clinical empathy? *Journal of General Internal Medicine, 18*(8), 670–674.

Halley, J. (1997). 'Like race' arguments. In J. Butler, J. Guillory, & K. Thomas (Eds.), *What's left of theory?* (pp. 50–70). Routledge.

Hamilton, M. (2009). *God vs. the Gavel: Religion and the rule of law*. Cambridge University Press.

Haritaworn, J. (2015). *Queer lovers and hateful others: Regenerating violent times and places*. Pluto Press. https://doi.org/10.2307/j.ctt183p5vv

Harkins, G. (2020). *Virtual pedophilia: Sex offender profiling and U.S. security culture*. Duke University Press.

Harper, J., O'Donnell, E., Khorashad, B. S., McDermott, H., & Witcomb, G. L. (2021). *British Journal of Sports Medicine, 0*, 1–9.

Harper, J. (2015). Race times for transgender athletes. *Journal of Sporting Cultures and Identities, 6*(1), 1–9.

Harrington, M. (2022). How could the Lords vote to let trans women into female prisons after this fiasco? [Scot Region]. *Mail on Sunday*, 16 January, 25. https://login.ezproxy.lib.bbk.ac.uk/login?url=https://www.proquest.com/newspapers/how-could-lords-vote-let-trans-women-into-female/docview/2619815458/se-2?accountid=8629

Harteveld, E., Mendoza, P., & Rooduun, M. (2022). Affective polarization and the populist radical right: Creating the hating? *Government and Opposition, 57*, 703–727.

Hasenbush, A., Flores, A. R., & Herman, J. L. (2019). Gender identity nondiscrimination laws in public accommodations: A review of evidence regarding safety and privacy in public restrooms, locker rooms, and changing rooms. *Sexuality Research and Social Policy, 16*(1), 70–83.

Hatchet, J. (2022). Female prisoners shouldn't be used as a shield for trans women from male violence: The House of Lords must vote to keep prisons single-sex. *New Statesman*, 10 January. https://www.newstatesman.com/comment/2022/01/female-prisoners-shouldnt-be-used-as-a-shield-for-trans-women-from-male-violence (accessed 26 August 2023).

Hawkesworth, M. (1997). Confounding gender. *Signs: Journal of Women in Culture and Society, 22*(3), 649–685.

HC Deb. (2022). 10 March 2022, vol. 710, col. 537. *Hansard*. https://hansard.parliament.uk/Commons/2022-03-10/debates/1C377E5F-9903-48CD-A036-1F1728D726B2/InternationalWomen'SDay (accessed 24 August 2023).

Helton, L. (2022). Learning butch: Tracing lesbian and trans becoming in the classroom. *Journal of Lesbian Studies, 26*(2), 148–158.

Hemmings, C. (2005). Telling feminist stories. *Feminist Theory, 6*(2), 115–139.

Hemmings, C. (2011). *Why stories matter: The political grammar of feminist theory*. Duke University Press.

Hemphill, L., & Shapiro, M. (2019). Appealing to the base or to the moveable middle? *Journal of Information Technology & Politics, 16*(4), 325–341.

Henriksen, T. D., & Järvinen, M. (2023). 'Looking back, I don't quite recognise myself': Narratives of the past in prostitution. *Sexualities, 0*(0), 13634607231174536.

Herek, G. M. (2007). Confronting sexual stigma and prejudice: Theory and practice. *Journal of Social Issues, 63*(4), 905–925.

Herman, D. (1997). *The antigay agenda: Orthodox vision and the Christian Right*. University of Chicago Press.

Herman, D. (2000). The gay agenda is the devil's agenda: The Christian Right's vision and the role of the state. In C. Rimmerman, C. Wilcox, & K. Wald (Eds.), *The politics of gay rights* (pp. 139–160). University of Chicago Press.

Herman, J. L., Flores, A. R., & O'Neill, K. K. (2022). *How many adults and youth identify as transgender in the United States?* Williams Institute (UCLA). https://williamsinstitute.law.ucla.edu/publications/trans-adults-united-states/

Herzog, K. (2020). Where have all the lesbians gone? *The Weekly Dish*, 27 November. https://andrewsullivan.substack.com/p/where-have-all-the-lesbians-gone-0a7 (accessed 6 March 2024).

Hesová, Z. (2021). New politics of morality in central and Eastern Europe. Intersections. *East European Journal of Society and Politics*, 7(1), 59–77.

Hesová, Z. (2023). Culture wars in Central Europe: A different playbook with evolving actors. In S. A. Samoilenko & S. Simmons (Eds.), *Culture wars in Europe* (pp. 21–28). IERES.

Hetherington, M. J. (2009). Putting polarization in perspective. *British Journal of Political Science*, 39(2), 413–448.

Hill Collins, P. (1990). *Black feminist thought: Knowledge, consciousness, and the politics of empowerment*. Routledge.

Hilliard, L. (2018a). *Digital Transformations Conference*, Ballina Arts Centre, Mayo, May 2018.

Hilliard, L. (2018b). *Taking Back the Web Conference*, Centre for Critical Media Literacy (CCML) Dublin Institute of Technology, October 2018.

Hilton, E. N., & Lundberg, T. R. (2021). Transgender women in the female category of sport. *Sports Medicine*, 51, 199–214.

Hines, S. (2020). Sex wars and (Trans) gender panics: Identity and body politics in contemporary UK feminism. *The Sociological Review*, 68(4), 699–717.

HL Deb. (2022). 10 January 2022, vol. 817, col .883. Hansard. https://hansard.parliament.uk/lords/2022-01-10/debates/DE31B0AB-B2E4-4687-B021-6D127741D254/PoliceCrimeSentencingAndCourtsBill#contribution-50DA8DF8-8B32-4D53-93BE-C4F2B9DB04FD (accessed 24 August 2023).

Hobolt, S. B., Leeper, T. J., & Tilley, J. (2021). Divided by the vote: Affective polarization in the wake of the Brexit referendum. *British Journal of Political Science*, 51, 1476–1493.

Hoffmann, D. L., & Timm, A. F. (2008). *Utopian biopolitics: Reproductive policies, gender roles, and sexuality in Nazi Germany and the Soviet Union* (pp. 87–130). Cambridge University Press.

Hogan, R. (2001). Class, race and gender inequality. *Race, Gender & Class*, 8(2), 61–93.

Hord, L. C. (2022). Specificity without identity: Articulating post-gender sexuality through the 'non-binary lesbian'. *Sexualities*, 25(5–6), 615–637.

HRC (2023). MAP: Attacks on gender affirming care by state. https://www.hrc.org/resources/attacks-on-gender-affirming-care-by-state-map

Hubbard, P. (2006). Out of touch and out of time? The policing of prostitution. In M. O'Neill & R. Campbell (Eds.), *Sex work now*, (pp. 1–32). Willan.

Hubbard, P. (2013). Kissing is not a universal right: Sexuality, law and the scales of citizenship. *Geoforum*, 49, 224–232.

Hunt, S. (Ed.). (2009). *Contemporary Christianity and LGBT sexualities*. Ashgate.

Ingala Smith, K. (2023). *Defending women's spaces*. Polity Press.

IPSO. (2018). *20177-17 O'Connell v The Sunday Times*. Report no. 20177-17, 23 March 2018. Independent Press Standards Organisation. https://www.ipso.co.uk/rulings-and-resolution-statements/ruling/?id=20177-17 (accessed 26 August 2023).

Iyengar, S., Sood, G., & Lelkes, Y. (2012). Affect, not ideology: A social identity perspective on polarization. *Public Opinion Quarterly*, 76(3), 405–431.

Iyengar, S., & Westwood, S. J. (2015). Fear and loathing across party lines: New evidence on group polarization. *American Journal of Political Science, 59*(3), 690–707.

Iyengar, S., Lelkes, Y., Levendusky, M., Malhotra, N., & Westwood, S. J. (2019). The origins and consequences of affective polarization in the United States. *Annual Review of Political Science, 22*(1), 129–146.

Jacobsen, M. H. (2021). Practical engagements in legal geography: Collaborative feminist approaches to immigration advocacy in Denmark. *Area, 53*(4), 595–602.

Jagose, A. (1996). *Queer theory.* New York University Press.

James, S. E., Herman, J. L., Durso, L. E., & Heng-Lehtinen, R. (2024). *Early insights: A report of the 2022 US transgender survey.* National Center for Transgender Equality, Washington, DC. https://transequality.org/sites/default/files/2024-02/2022%20USTS%20Early%20Insights%20Report_FINAL.pdf

Järvinen, M. (2001). Accounting for trouble: Identity negotiations in qualitative interviews with alcoholics. *Symbolic Interaction, 24*(3), 263–284.

Järvinen, M. (2004). Life histories and the perspective of the present. *Narrative Inquiry, 14*(1), 45–68.

Jasper, J. M. (2014). *Protest: A cultural introduction to social movements.* Wiley.

Jeffrey, A. (2020). Legal geography II: Bodies and law. *Progress in Human Geography, 44*(5), 1004–1016.

Jessup, B., & McIlwraith, C. (2015). The sexual legal geography in 'Comcare v PVYW'. *University of New South Wales Law Journal, 38*(4), 1484–1506.

Jjuuko, A. (2016). International solidarity and its role in the fight against Uganda's anti-homosexuality bill. In K. Lalor, E. Mills, A. S. García & P. Haste (Eds.), *Gender, sexuality and social justice: What's law got to do with it?*, (p. 126) Institute of Development Studies.

Jjuuko, A., Gloppen, S., Msosa, A., & Viljoen, F. (Eds.). (2022). *Queer lawfare in Africa: Legal strategies in contexts of LGBTIQ+ criminalisation and politicisation.* Pretoria University Law Press.

Johnson, A. H. (2016). Transnormativity: A new concept and its validation through documentary film about transgender men. *Sociological Inquiry, 86*(4), 465–491.

Johnson, E. P. (2005). 'Quare' studies, or (Almost) everything i know about queer studies i learned from my grandmother. In E. P. Johnson and M. G. Henderson (Eds.), *Black queer studies* (pp. 124–157). Duke University Press.

Jones, A. (2020). *Camming: Money, power, and pleasure in the sex work industry.* New York University Press.

Jones, C. J. (2021). Unfair advantage discourse in USA powerlifting. *Transgender Studies Quarterly, 8*(1), 58–74.

Jones, C. J., & Travers. (2023). The sports issue: An introduction. *Transgender Studies Quarterly, 10*(2), 93–99.

Jones, K. L., Noorbaloochi, S., Jost, J. T., Bonneau, R., Nagler, J., & Tucker, J. A. (2018). Liberal and conservative values. *Political Psychology, 39*(2), 423–443.

Jordan, M. D. (2016). Love in the vocation of Christian sexual ethics. In F. V. Simmons & B. C. Sorrells (Eds.), *Love and Christian ethics* (pp. 290–302). Georgetown University Press

Jost, J. T. (2006). The end of the end of ideology. *American Psychologist, 61*(7), 651–670.

Joyce, H. (2021). Why it's wrong – and profoundly damaging - to make us all agree that someone is whatever gender they say they are. *Mail on Sunday*, 4 July, 32. https://login.ezproxy.lib.bbk.ac.uk/login?url=https://www.proquest.com/newspapers/why-wrong-profoundly-damaging-make-us-all-agree/docview/2548076749/se-2?accountid=8629 (accessed 24 August 2023).

Julian, V. (2020). New research on reporting of trans issues shows 400% increase in coverage and varying perceptions on broader editorial standards. *Independent Press Standards Organisation*, 2 December. https://www.ipso.co.uk/news-analysis/new-research-on-reporting-of-trans-issues

Julian, R., Bliesemann de Guevara, B., & Redhead, R. (2019). From expert to experiential knowledge: Exploring the inclusion of local experiences in understanding violence in conflict. *Peacebuilding*, 7(2), 210–225.

Kahlina, K., & Ristivojević, D. (2023). Desire to resist: EU border-making and anti-LGBT mobilisation in Serbia. In E. Helms & T. Pulkkinen (Eds.), *Borders of desire* (pp. 162–177). Manchester University Press.

Kamarauskaitė, R. (2023). We are just like everybody else: Strategies of inclusion of homosexuality within Lithuanian national(ist) discourses [Symposium paper] *Polarising Sexual and Gendered Lives: Divisions, Differences and LGBTQI+ Equalities*, University College Dublin, 23 June.

Kane, M. (1995). Resistance/transformation of the oppositional binary: Exposing sport as a continuum. *Journal of Sport and Social Issues*, 19(2), 191–218.

Kara, H. (2015). *Creative research methods in the social sciences* (Vol. 10). Policy Press.

Kao, Y. C. (2021). The coloniality of queer theory: The effects of 'homonormativity' on transnational Taiwan's path to equality. *Sexualities*, 27(1-2), 136–153.

Kaoma, K. (2012). *Colonizing African values: How the US Christian right is transforming sexual politics in Africa*. Political Research Associates. https://www.sxpolitics.org/wp-content/uploads/2012/08/colonizingafricanvaluespra.pdf

Kazyak, E., Burke, K., Kichler, R., & McGraw, L. (2021). 'Pee in peace' or 'make everyone uncomfortable': Public perceptions of transgender rights. *Socius: Sociological Research for a Dynamic World*, 7, 1–16.

Kazyak, E., & Stange, M. (2018). Backlash or a positive response?: Public opinion of lgb issues after obergefell v. hodges. *Journal of Homosexuality*, 65(14), 2028–2052.

Kazyak, E, Burke, K., Behrendt, M., & Oliver, M. (2023a). Religious exemption, LGBT rights, and the social construction of harm and freedom. *Law & Social Inquiry*. Online advanced access.

Kazyak, E., Burke, K., Oliver, M., & Behrendt, M. (2023b). Making the case: Examining outcomes of religious claims in federal litigation involving LGBT rights. *Sexuality Research and Social Policy*. Online advanced access.

Keating, A. (2013). *Transformation now! Toward a post-oppositional politics of change*. University of Illinois Press.

Keeling, K. (2019). *Queer times, black futures.– 'Yet still: Queer temporality, black political possibilities, and poetry from the future (of speculative pasts)'*. New York University Press.

Keep Prisons Single Sex. (2023a). 200 Years since the Gaols act: What next? [Event held 28 March, London]. https://archive.is/nxmVw

Keep Prisons Single Sex. (2023b). About us. https://archive.is/BV5Qb (accessed 26 August 2023).

Keep Prisons Single Sex. (2023c). I am deeply concerned.... [tweet], 24 January. https://twitter.com/NoXYinXXprisons/status/1617919454800932864 (accessed 24 August 2023).

Kelley, R. D. (1996). *Race rebels: Culture, politics, and the black working class*. Simon and Schuster.

Kerr, B. (2019). Pronouns are rohypnol. *Fairy Play for Women*, 4 June. https://archive.is/ZJuTV (accessed 26 August 2023).

Kessler, M. (2007). Free speech doctrine in American political culture: A critical legal geography of cultural politics. *Connecticut Public Interest Law Journal*, 6, 205.

Kilkenny, K. (2012). Where did the expression 'welp' come from? *Slate*, 30 November. https://slate.com/culture/2012/11/welp-slang-term-has-longer-history-than-you-might-think.html

Kirby, M. (2013). 'The sodomy offence': England's least lovely criminal law export? In C. Lennows & M. Waites. (Eds.), *Human rights, sexual orientation and gender identity in the commonwealth: Struggles for decriminalisation and change* (pp. 61–82) Institute of Commonwealth Studies.

Kirkup, J. (2018). The cautionary tale of Karen White, the transgender rapist. *The Spectator*, 11 October. https://www.spectator.co.uk/article/the-cautionary-tale-of-karen-white-the-transgender-rapist# (accessed 26 August 2023).

Kline, N. S., Webb, N. J., Johnson, K. C., Yording, H. D., Griner, S. B., & Brunell, D. J. (2023). Mapping transgender policies in the US 2017–2021: The role of geography and implications for health equity. *Health & Place*, *80*, 102985.

Knobloch-Westerwick, S., Jingbo Meng. (2011). Reinforcement of the political self through selective exposure to political messages. *Journal of Communication*, *61*(2), 349–368.

Knott-Fayle, G., Peel, E., & Witcomb, G. L. (2021). (Anti-)feminism and cisgenderism in sports media. *Feminist Media Studies*, *23*(3), 1274–1291.

Knott-Fayle, G., Peel, E., & Witcomb, G. L. (2022). Representing diverse genders in sports media: The discursive production of cisgenderism in the UK press. In G. L. Witcomb & E. Peel (Eds.), *Gender diversity and sport: Interdisciplinary perspectives on increasing inclusivity* (pp. 134–155). Routledge.

Knox, T., Anderson, L. C., & Heather, A. (2019). Transwomen in elite sport. *Journal of Medical Ethics*, *45*(6), 395–403.

Kondakov, A. S. (2022). *Violent Affections: Queer sexuality, techniques of power, and law in Russia*. UCL Press.

Kondakov, A. S. (2023). Challenging the logic of progressive timeline, queering LGBT successes and failures in Ireland and Russia. *Sexualities*, *26*(1–2), 105–124.

Korolczuk, E. (2023). Anti-gender campaigns as a threat to liberal democracy. In E. Orofino & W. Allchorn (Eds.), *Routledge handbook of non-violent extremism* (pp. 347–359). Routledge.

Kreiss, D., & McGregor, S. C. (2023). A review and provocation: On polarization and platforms. *New Media & Society 26*(1), 556–579. .

Kubin, E., & Von Sikorski, C. (2021). The role of (social) media in political polarization: A systematic review. *Annals of the International Communication Association*, *45*, 188–206.

Kuhar, R., & Paternotte, D. (2017). *Anti-gender campaigns in Europe: Mobilizing against equality*. Rowman & Littlefield.

Kuhar, R., & Pajnik, M. (2020). Populist mobilizations in re-traditionalized society: Anti-gender campaigning in Slovenia. In G. Dietze & J. Roth (Eds.), *Populist mobilizations in re-traditionalized society: Anti-gender campaigning in Slovenia* (pp. 167–184). Transcript Verlag.

Kulpa, R. (2011). Nations and sexualities – 'West' and 'East'. In *De-Centring Western sexualities*. Routledge.

Kulpa, R. (2014). On attachment and belonging: Or why queers mourn homophobic president? *Sexualities*, *17*(7), 781–801.

Kulpa, R. (2016). Nations and sexualities–'West'and 'East'. In *De-Centring Western sexualities* (pp. 43–62). Routledge.

Kulpa, R. (2020). National menace: Mediating homo/sexuality and sovereignty in the Polish national/ist discourses. *Critical Discourse Studies*, *17*(3), 327–343.

Kulpa, R., & Mizielińska, J. (2011). 'Contemporary peripheries': Queer studies, circulation of knowledge and East/West divide. In R. Kulpa & J. Mizielinska (Eds.), *De-Centring western sexualities* (pp. 11–26). Routledge.

Kulpa, R., & Silva, J. M. (2016). Decolonizing queer epistemologies: Section introduction. In G. Brown & K. Browne (Eds.), *The Routledge research companion to geographies of sex and sexualities* (pp. 139–142). Routledge.

Kuo, R., & Marwick, A. (2021). Critical disinformation studies: History, power, and politics. *Harvard Kennedy School Misinformation Review*, 2(4), 1–11.

Ladson-Billings, G., & Donnor, J. (2005). Waiting for the call: The moral activist role of critical race theory. In N. K. Denzin & Y. S. Lincoln (Eds.), *The Handbook of Qualitative Research* (pp. 279–301), SAGE Publications, Inc.

Lagerman, J. (2023). Neo-Nazi heteroactivism and the Swedish nationalist contradiction. *ACME*, 22(3), 1093–1114.

Lakkimsetti, C. (2016). 'Empowered criminals and global subjects': Transnational norms and sexual minorities in India. *Qualitative Sociology*, 39, 375–396.

Lalor, K. (2019). Encountering the past: Grand narratives, fragmented histories and LGBTI rights 'progress'. *Law and Critique*, 30(1), 21–40.

Lalor, K. (2023). Queer legal geographies of polarisation and silencing in international LGBTQ rights law [Symposium paper] *Polarising Sexual and Gendered Lives: Divisions, Differences and LGBTQI+ Equalities*, University College Dublin, 23 June.

Lalor, K., & Browne, K. (2018). Here versus there: Creating British sexual politics elsewhere. *Feminist Legal Studies*, 26(2), 205–213.

Lalor, K., & Browne, K. (2023). Introduction – Here versus There: Beyond comparison in queer and sexuality politics. *Sexualities*, 26(1–2), 3–11.

Lamble, S. (2013). Queer necropolitics and the expanding carceral state: Interrogating sexual investments in punishment. *Law & Critique* 24(3), 229–253.

Lamble, S. (2023). Misinformation in the 'gender wars' in Britain: Affective attachments in the use and misuse of evidence [Symposium paper] *Polarising Sexual and Gendered Lives: Divisions, Differences and LGBTQI+ Equalities*, University College Dublin, 23 June.

Lamble, S. (2023a). Prisons have never been safe for women – removing trans people won't change that. *i-news*, 17 August. https://archive.is/3Wd2p (accessed 24 August 2023).

Lamble, S. (2023b). Sexual peril and dangerous others: The moral economies of the trans prisoner policy debates in England and Wales. *Sexualities*, 28(1-2), 492–513.

Lamble, S. (2024). Confronting complex alliances: Situating Britain's gender critical politics within the wider transnational anti-gender movement. *Journal of Lesbian Studies*, 8(3), 504–517.

Laver, M. (2021). Analyzing the politics of legislative debate. In H. Back, M. Debus, & J. M. Fernandes (Eds.), *The politics of legislative debates*. Oxford Academic.

Lawson, D. (2022). Why do police and the NHS insist that some male-bodied rapists are 'women'? *Daily Mail*, 21 March, 16. https://www.dailymail.co.uk/debate/article-10634127/DOMINIC-LAWSON-police-NHS-insist-male-bodied-rapists-women.html (accessed 26 August 2023).

Levin, S., Chalabi, M., & Siddiqui, S. (2018). Why we take issue with the *Guardian's* stance on trans rights in the UK. The *Guardian*, 2 November. https://www.theguardian.com/commentisfree/2018/nov/02/guardian-editorial-response-transgender-rights-uk

Levitas, R. (2013). *Utopia as method: The imaginary reconstitution of society*. Springer.

Leksikov, R., & Rachok, D. (2020). Beyond Western theories: On the use and abuse of 'homonationalism' in Eastern Europe. In R. Buyantueva & M. Shevtsova (Eds.),

LGBTQ+ activism in central and Eastern Europe: Resistance, representation and identity (pp. 25–49). Springer International Publishing.

Lee, P. H. (2022). Struggle for recognition: Theorising sexual/gender minorities as rights-holders in international law. *Feminist Legal Studies, 30*(1), 73–95.

Levendusky, M. (2010). Clearer cues, more consistent voters: A benefit of elite polarization. *Political Behavior, 32*, 111–131.

Liinason, M. (2023). 'The loved home' and other exclusionary care discourses: A multiscalar and transnational analysis of heteroactivist resistances to gender and sexual rights in Sweden. *ACME, 22*(3), 1047–1068.

Linabary, J., Krishna, A., & Connaughton, S. (2017). The conflict family: Storytelling as an activity and a method for locally led. *Community-Based Peacebuilding Conflict Resolution Quarterly, 34*, 431–453.

Linde, C. (1993). *Life stories: The creation of coherence*. Oxford University Press.

Locke, K. A. (2004). The bible on homosexuality: Exploring its meaning and authority. *Journal of Homosexuality, 48*(2), 125–156.

Loder, K. (2023). Liminal spaces as refuge for black transgender women navigating the U.S. South [Symposium paper] *Polarising Sexual and Gendered Lives: Divisions, Differences and LGBTQI+ Equalities*, University College Dublin, 23 June.

Love, H. (2001). 'Spoiled identity': Stephen Gordon's loneliness and the difficulties of queer history. *GLQ: A Journal of Lesbian and Gay Studies, 7*(4), 487–519.

Mackay, F. (2014). Open space: Reclaiming revolutionary feminism. *Feminist Review, 106*, 95–103.

Mackay, F. (2015a). Political not generational: Getting real about contemporary UK radical feminism. *Social Movement Studies, 14*(4), 427–442.

Mackay, F. (2015b). Radical feminism. *Theory, Culture & Society, 32*(7–8), 332–336.

Mackay, F. (2019). Always endangered, never extinct: Exploring contemporary butch lesbian identity in the UK. *Women's Studies International Forum, 75*, 1–9.

Mackay, F. (2021). *Female masculinities and the gender wars*. IB Taurus.

MacKinnon, C. A. (1989). Sexuality, pornography, and method: 'Pleasure under Patriarchy'. *Ethics, 99*(2), 314–346.

MacKinnon, C. A. (1982). Feminism, Marxism, Method, and the State: An Agenda for Theory. *Signs, 7*(3), 515–544.

Mafu, L. (2023). There is nothing un-African about being gay. Museveni's bigotry will cost lives. The *Guardian*, 15 May. https://www.theguardian.com/commentisfree/2023/may/15/our-children-gay-proudly-african-mothers-plea-uganda-president-museveni

Maguire, H., McCartan, A., Nash, C. J., & Browne, K. (2018). The enduring field: Exploring researcher emotions in covert research with antagonistic organisations. *Area, 51*(2).

Maines, D. R., Sugrue, N. M., & Katovich, M. A. (1983). The sociological import of GH Mead's theory of the past. *American Sociological Review, 48*(2), 161–173.

MAPS/Movement Advancement Project. (2023). LGTBQ curricular laws. https://www.lgbtmap.org/equality-maps/curricular_laws

March, L. (2021). Queer and trans* geographies of liminality: A literature review. *Progress in Human Geography, 45*(3), 455–471.

Margaret Fonow, M., & Cook, J. A. (2005). Feminist methodology: New applications in the academy and public policy. *Signs: Journal of Women in Culture and Society, 30*(4), 2211–2236.

Marshall, W. P. (2018). Extricating the religious exemption debate from the culture wars. *Harvard Journal of Law & Public Policy, 41*(1), 67–77.

Martin, A., & Lynch, M. (2009). Counting things and people: The practices and politics of counting. *Social Problems*, *56*(2), 243–266.

Martin, B. (1994). Sexualities without genders and other queer utopias. *Diacritics*, *24*(2/3), 104–121.

Martin, K. (2022). 'Fairness in women's sports?' *Southern Political Science Association Annual Conference*. San Antonio, TX. 13–5 January.

Martin, K., & Rahilly, E. (2023). Value frames in discourse supporting transgender athlete bans. *Discourse & Society*, *34*(6), 732–751.

Mason, R. (2017). Theresa May plans to let people change gender without medical checks. The *Guardian*, 24 August. https://www.theguardian.com/society/2017/oct/18/theresa-may-plans-to-let-people-change-gender-without-medical-checks (accessed 26 August 2023).

Mason-Schrock, D. (1996). Transsexuals' narrative construction of the 'true self'. *Social Psychology Quarterly*, *59*, 176–192.

Massie, A. (2021). Self-ID is a fantasy that hurts trans people. *The Times*, 14 December. https://www.thetimes.co.uk/article/self-id-is-a-fantasy-that-hurts-trans-people-bnpvt0h5k (accessed 26 August 2023).

Máté-Tóth, A., & Nagy, G. D. (2023). Hidden dynamics of religion and human rights in central and Eastern Europe. *Religions*, *14*(7), Article 7.

Matthews, A. (2017). Half of transgender prisoners could be sex offenders: Predatory inmates are 'falsely' defining their gender to target vulnerable women, charity warns. *Daily Mail* (online, 19 November). https://www.dailymail.co.uk/news/article-5097213/Half-trans-prisoners-sex-offenders.html (accessed 24 August 2023).

Mažylis, L., Rakutienė, S., & Unikaitė-Jakuntavičienė, I. (2014). Two competing normative trajectories in the context of the first baltic gay pride parade in Lithuania. *Baltic Journal of Law & Politics*, *7*(2), 37–76.

McCann, J. (2022). More than half of trans inmates have been convicted of a sexual offence. *Express* (Online), 23 January. https://login.ezproxy.lib.bbk.ac.uk/login?url=https://www.proquest.com/newspapers/more-than-half-trans-inmates-have-been-convicted/docview/2622097401/se-2?accountid=8629

McCartan, A. (2022). *Geographies of LGBTQ+ activisms: Ireland after marriage equality*. Doctoral Thesis. UCD School of Geography.

McCarty, N. (2019). *Polarization: What everyone needs to know?*. Oxford University Press.

McClintock, A. (1995). *Imperial leather: Race, gender, and sexuality in the colonial contest*. Routledge.

McCoy, J. (2023). Hyper-polarization and the security of democracy. In S. L. Wilson & N. A. Seltzer (Eds.), *Handbook on democracy and security* (pp. 165–187). Edward Elgar Publishing.

McCoy, J., & Somer, M. (2019). Toward a theory of pernicious polarization and how it harms democracies: Comparative evidence and possible remedies. *The Annals of the American Academy of Political and Social Science*, *681*(1), 234–271.

McCoy, J., & Somer, M. (2021). Overcoming polarization. *Journal of Democracy*, *32*(1), 6–21.

McCoy, J., Rahman, T., & Somer, M. (2018). Polarization and the global crisis of democracy: Common patterns, dynamics, and pernicious consequences for democratic polities. *American Behavioral Scientist*, *62*, 16–42.

McLaughlin, M. (2021). Campaign to ensure all rape suspects are recorded as men. *The Times*, 9 June. https://www.thetimes.com/uk/politics/article/campaign-to-ensure-all-rape-suspects-are-recorded-as-men-kggzb5w3m

McNeil-Willson, R., Gerrand, V., Scrinzi, F., & Triandafyllidou, A. (2019). *Polarisation, violent extremism and resilience in Europe today: An analytical framework*. BRaVE Project. https://hdl.handle.net/1814/65664

Mead, G. H. (1932). *The philosophy of the present*. Prometheus Books.

Meadow, T. (2018). *Trans kids: Being gendered in the twenty-first century*. University of California Press.

Melendez, R. M., & Pinto, R. (2007). 'It's really a hard life': Love, gender and HIV risk among male-to-female transgender persons. *Culture, Health & Sexuality, 9*(3), 233–245.

Michaeli, I., & Fischler, F. (2021). *The links between anti-trans feminists and Christian fundamentalists. Rights at Risk – Time for Action: Observatory on the Universality of Rights Trends Report*. Toronto: Association for Women's Rights in Development (AWID). https://www.awid.org/sites/default/files/2022-01/RightsAtRisk_TimeForAction_OURsTrendsReport2021.pdf

Mikulak, M. (2019). Godly homonormativity: Christian LGBT organizing in contemporary Poland. *Journal of Homosexuality, 66*(4), 487–509.

Ministry of Justice. (2022). *Her majesty's prison and probation service offender equalities annual report 2021 to 2022*. UK Government. https://www.gov.uk/government/statistics/hm-prison-and-probation-service-offender-equalities-annual-report-2021-to-2022 (accessed 9 January 2024).

Minow, M. (2007). Should religious groups be exempt from civil rights laws. *Boston College Law Review, 48*(4), 781–849.

Mizielińska, J. (2011). Travelling ideas, travelling times: On the temporalities of LGBT and queer politics in Poland and the 'West'. In R. Kulpa and J. Mizielińska (Eds.), *De-Centring Western sexualities* (pp. 85–106). Routledge.

Mizielińska, J. (2022). *Queer Kinship on the edge? Families of choice in Poland*. Taylor & Francis.

Mole, R. C. M. (2019). Constructing Soviet and post-Soviet sexualities. In *Soviet and post-Soviet sexualities*. Routledge.

Moller, J., Trilling, D., Helberger, N. et al. (2018). Do not blame it on the algorithm: An empirical assessment of multiple recommender systems and their impact on content diversity. *Information, Communication & Society, 21*(7), 959–977.

Moon, D., Tobin, T. W., & Sumerau, J. E. (2019). Alpha, omega, and the letters in between: LGBTQI conservative Christians undoing gender. *Gender & Society, 33*(4), 583–606.

Moraga, C. & Anzaldua, G. E. (1981). *The bridge called my back: Writings by radical women of color*. Kitchen Table: Women of Color Press.

Moraga, C., & Anzaldúa, G. (2022). *This bridge called my back: Writings by radical women of color*. Suny Press.

Moore, M. (2022). Alice Sullivan and Allison Bailey are misleading the public and the UK Government bodies about rape statistics and trans women in the criminal justice system. *Medium*, 8 January. https://chican3ry.medium.com/alice-sullivan-and-allison-bailey-are-misleading-the-public-and-uk-government-bodies-about-rape-f9a9335f5df4

Morris, B. J. (2016). *The disappearing L: Erasure of lesbian spaces and culture*. Suny Press.

Morse, B. (2023). World Athletics tightens rules on transgender women athletes. *CNN*, 24 March. https://www.cnn.com/2023/03/23/sport/world-athletics-transgender-ruling-spt-intl/index.html

Mosse, G. L., & Roberts, M. L. (2020). *Nationalism and sexuality: Middle-class morality and sexual norms in modern Europe* (1st ed.). University of Wisconsin Press.

Mouffe, C. (2007). Artistic activism and agonistic spaces. *Art & Research*, *1*(2), 1–5.
Muller-Heyndyk, R., & Ondrak, J. (2022). #KeepPrisonsSingleSex: How botnets pushed a hashtag to Westminster. *Logically.ai*. https://www.logically.ai/articles/keepprisons singlesex-pushed-by-botnet (accessed 26 August 2023).
Muñoz, J. E. (1999). *Disidentifications: Queers of color and the performance of politics*. University of Minnesota Press.
Muñoz, J. E. (2009). *Cruising Utopia the then and there of queer futurity*. New York University Press.
Murib, Z. (2022). Don't read the comments: Examining social media discourse on trans athletes. *Laws*, *11*(4), 53.
Muste, C. P. (2014). Reframing polarization: Social groups and 'culture wars'. *PS: Political Science & Politics*, *47*(02), 432–442.
Narkevičiūtė, E. (2020). Teisinis reguliavimas LGBT asmenims Lietuvoje Europos Sąjungos teisės ir vertybių kontekste [Vytautas Magnus University]. https://hdl.handle.net/20.500.12259/107359
Nash, C. J., & Browne, K. (2020). *Heteroactivism: Resisting lesbian, gay and transsexual rights and equalities*. Zed Books.
Neary, A. (2016). Civil Partnership and marriage: LGBT-Q political pragmatism and the normalization imperative. *Sexualities*, *19*(7), 757–779.
Newman, H. J. H., & Peel, E. (2022). 'An impossible dream'?: Non-binary people's perceptions of legal gender status and reform. *Psychology & Sexuality*, *13*(5), 1381–1395.
Nicholls, C. (2023). Global scientists urge Uganda's president to veto anti-LGBTQ bill. *Al-Jazeera*, 19 April. https://www.aljazeera.com/news/2023/4/20/ugandas-president-museveni-refuses-to-sign-lgbtq-bill
Nodin, N., Pestano, C., Peel, E., Tyler, A., & Rivers, I. (2023). Risk and resilience: Exploring the potential of LGBTQ third sector and academic partnership. *Community Development Journal*, *59*(3), 420–437.
Nyanzi, S. (2015). Knowledge is requisite power: Making a case for queer African scholarship. In T. Sandfort, F. Simenel, K. Mwachiro, V, R. Hivos (Eds.), *Boldly queer: African perspectives on same-sex sexuality and gender diversity* (pp. 125–136). HIVOS.
Nyanzi, S., & Karamagi, A. (2015). The social-political dynamics of the anti-homosexuality legislation in Uganda. *Agenda*, *29*(1), 24–38.
O'Brien, J. (2016). Seeing Agnes: Notes on a Transgender Biocultural Ethnomethodology. *Symbolic Interaction*, *39*(2), 306–329.
O'Brien, M. E. (2019). The influence of donors on cross class social movements: Same sex marriage and trans rights campaigns in New York State. *Social Movement Studies*, *18*(5), 586–601.
O'Dwyer, C. (2018). The benefits of Backlash: The divergent trajectories of LGBT-rights activism after communism. In *Coming out of communism* (pp. 1–32). New York University Press.
O'Hara, M. (2022). *Transgenderism and policy capture in the criminal justice system*. Policy Exchange. https://policyexchange.org.uk/wp-content/uploads/2022/07/Transgenderism-and-policy-capture-in-the-criminal-justice-system.pdf (accessed 24 August 2023).
O'Shea, S. C. (2020). 'I, Robot?'Or how transgender subjects are dehumanised. *Culture and Organization*, *26*(1), 1–13.
Office for National Statistics. (2018). *Sexual offending: Crown Prosecution Service appendix tables*. UK Government. https://www.ons.gov.uk/peoplepopulationandcommunity/crimeandjustice/datasets/sexualoffendingcrownprosecutionserviceappendixtables (accessed 24 August 2023).

Orbach, S. (2023). The contribution of psychotherapy to wider social change. *Online Events* [online seminar], 12 May. https://onlineevents.co.uk/courses/the-contribution-of-psychotherapy-to-wider-social-change-with-dr-susie-orbach/

Orosz, G., Bánki, E., Bőthe, B., Tóth-Király, I., & Tropp, L. R. (2016). Don't judge a living book by its cover: Effectiveness of the living library intervention in reducing prejudice toward Roma and LGBT people. *Journal of Applied Social Psychology*, 46(9), 510–517.

Ortega, R. (2023). World Athletics banned transgender women from competing. Does science support the rule? *Science*, 4 April. https://www.science.org/content/article/world-athletics-banned-transgender-women-competing-does-science-support-rule#:~:text=A%20rare%20performance%20study%20on,no%20advantage%20over%20cisgender%20women

Owen, G. (2021). Trans offenders are not female says Priti. *Mail on Sunday*, 24 October. https://login.ezproxy.lib.bbk.ac.uk/login?url=https://www.proquest.com/newspapers/trans-offenders-are-not-female-says-priti/docview/2584981544/se-2?accountid=8629

Pagulich, L. (2017). Queering the nation?: Analyzing the politics of the LGBT movement in Ukraine after the Maidan protests. Doctoral Thesis. Georgia State University. https://scholarworks.gsu.edu/wsi_theses/62

Palonen, E. (2009). Political polarisation and populism in contemporary hungary. *Parliamentary Affairs*, 62(2), 318–334.

Paternotte, D., & Kuhar, R. (2018). Disentangling and locating the 'global right': Anti-gender campaigns in Europe. *Politics and Governance*, 6(3), 6–19.

Patil, V. (2022). *Webbed connectivities: The imperial sociology of sex, gender, and sexuality*. University of Minnesota Press.

Pearce, R. (2021). *Reform of the gender recognition act: Corrections to oral evidence*. Written evidence to women and equalities select committee on reform of the gender recognition act. UK Parliament. https://committees.parliament.uk/writtenevidence/21023/pdf/ (accessed 26 August 2023).

Pearce, R., Erikainen, S., & Vincent, B. (2020). TERF wars: An introduction. *The Sociological Review*, 68, 677–698.

Peel, E. (2001). Mundane heterosexism: Understanding incidents of the everyday. *Women's Studies International Forum*, 24(5), 541–554.

Peel, E. (2005). Effeminate 'fudge nudgers' and tomboyish 'lettuce lickers': Language and the construction of sexualities in diversity training. *Psychology of Women Section Review*, 7(2), 22–34.

Peel, E. (2022). Resistant transition? Debating the future of legal gender. *Institute of Advanced Studies (IAS) event: Transitions – Festival of Ideas*, 20 May, Loughborough University.

Peel, E. (2023). 'Gender Debate' Discourse: Polarising, bigoted and validating [Symposium paper] *Polarising Sexual and Gendered Lives: Divisions, Differences and LGBTQI+ Equalities*, University College Dublin, 23 June.

Peel, E., & Harding, R. (2008). Editorial introduction: Recognizing and celebrating same-sex relationships: Beyond the normative debate. *Sexualities*, 11(6), 659–66.

Peel, E., & Newman, H. (2019). Engendering criticism? Reflection on feedback to our 'Attitudes to Gender' survey. *Future of Legal Gender*, 20 September. https://futureoflegalgender.kcl.ac.uk/2019/09/20/engendering-criticism-reflection-on-feedback-to-our-attitudes-to-gender-survey/

Peel, E., & Newman, H. J. H. (2020). Gender's wider stakes: Lay attitudes to legal gender reform. *feminists@law*, 10(2).

Peel, E., & Newman, H. J. H. (2023). 'I don't think that's something I've ever thought about really before': A thematic discursive analysis of lay people's talk about legal gender. *Feminist Legal Studies*, 31, 121–143.

Perkins, K. J. (2022). Willful lives: Self-determination in lesbian and trans feminisms. *Journal of Lesbian Studies*, 26(2), 194–199.

Perry, I. (2022). *South to America: A journey below the Mason-Dixon to understand the soul of a Nation*. Ecco.

Petition 1. (2021). *PE1876/A - Accurately record the sex of people charged or convicted of rape or attempted rape*. Submitted to Scottish Parliament Citizen Participation and Public Petitions Committee. https://www.parliament.scot/chamber-and-committees/committees/current-and-previous-committees/session-6-citizen-participation-and-public-petitions-committee/correspondence/2021/pe1876_a-petitioner-submission-of-7-june-2021 (accessed 24 August 2023).

Petition 2. (2021). *Legislate for the accurate recording of bio-sex of rape & other sexual offences*. Petition to UK Parliament. https://petition.parliament.uk/petitions/588634 (accessed 24 August 2023).

Petition 3. (2022) *Require sex of VATP & sexual offenders be recorded throughout justice system*, Petition to UK Parliament. https://petition.parliament.uk/petitions/590123 (accessed 24 August 2023).

Pew Research Center. (2011). Evangelical beliefs and practices. 22 June. https://www.pewresearch.org/religion/2011/06/22/global-survey-beliefs/

Phillimore, S., & Peters, A. (2022). *Transpositions: Personal journeys into gender criticism*. P&P Publishing.

Phipps, A. (2020). *Me, not you: The trouble with mainstream feminism*. Manchester University Press.

Phoenix, J. (2021a). Let me drive the point…[tweet], 27 September. https://twitter.com/JoPhoenix1/status/1442487003749175301 (accessed 23 August 2023).

Phoenix, J. (2021b). Rape charges can only…[tweet], 28 September. https://twitter.com/JoPhoenix1/status/1442733080314269698 (accessed 23 August 2023).

Plakhotnik, O. (2019). Imaginaries of sexual citizenship in post-maidan Ukraine: A queer feminist discursive investigation. Doctoral Thesis. The Open University. https://oro.open.ac.uk/62741/

Plummer, K. (1995). *Telling sexual stories: Power, intimacy and social worlds*. Routledge: London.

Plummer, K. (2010). Generational sexualities, subterranean traditions, and the hauntings of the sexual world: some preliminary remarks. *Symbolic Interaction*, 33(2), 163–190.

Plummer, K. (2019). *Narrative power: The struggle for human value*. Polity Press.

Police Scotland. (2021). Freedom of information request 2021-1394. Dalmaraock, Scotland: Information Managment (Disclosure). *Police Scotland*. https://web.archive.org/web/20221129040853/https://www.scotland.police.uk/spa-media/yeynhlst/21-1394-response.pdf (accessed 24 August 2023).

Polletta, F., & Jasper, J. M. (2001). Collective identity and social movements. *Annual Review of Sociology*, 27(1), 283–305.

Power, S. (2015). Making LGBT rights universally respected human rights. *Council for Global Equality Luncheon, United Nations*, Washington, D.C, 14 October 2015.

Proksch, S., & Slapin J. (2012). Institutional foundations of legislative speech. *American Journal of Political Science*, 56(3), 520–537.

Puar, J. K. (2007). *Terrorist assemblages: Homonationalism in queer times*. Duke University Press.

Puar, J. (2013). Rethinking homonationalism. *International Journal of Middle East Studies*, 45(2), 336–339.
Public Religion Research Institute. (2020). Americans are broadly supportive of a variety of LGBTQ rights. *Public Religion Research Institute*, 30 October. https://www.prri.org/spotlight/americans-are-broadly-supportive-of-a-variety-of-lgbtq-rights/
Public Religion Research Institute, (2021). Is religious liberty a shield of a sword? *Public Religion Research Institute*. 10 February. https://www.prri.org/research/is-religious-liberty-a-shield-or-a-sword/
Public Religion Research Institute. (2023). More acceptance but growing polarization on LGBTQ rights, 3 March. https://www.prri.org/press-release/more-acceptance-but-growing-polarization-on-lgbtq-rights-findings-from-the-2022-american-values-atlas/
Pumprickaitė, N. (2013). A. Zuokas apie gėjų eitynes: Teismui ir policijos vadovui įtaką darė politikai. [A. Zuokas about Gay Pride: The court and the head of police were under influence of politicians]. *LRT*, 14 July. https://Www.Delfi.Lt/News/Daily/Lithuania/a-Zuokas-Apie-Geju-Eitynes-Teismui-Ir-Policijos-Vadovui-Itaka-Dare-Politikai.d?Id=61854605
Rahilly, E. (2021). *Trans-affirmative parenting: Raising kids across the gender spectrum*. New York University Press.
Rahilly, E., & Tecklenburg, K. M. (2023). Talking past each other: Anti-trans and pro-trans frameworks regarding transgender athlete bans in state legislatures [Symposium paper] *Polarising Sexual and Gendered Lives: Divisions, Differences and LGBTQI+ Equalities*, University College Dublin, 23 June.
Raising Children Network. (ND). Circle of friends: personal boundaries activity for children 3-15 years. https://raisingchildren.net.au/autism/development/sexual-development/circle-of-friends-personal-boundaries-activity-children-3-15-years (accessed 28 August 2023).
Rasmussen, C. (2023). Fertile ground: The biopolitics of natalist populism. *ACME*, 22(3), 1069–1092.
Rao, R. (2014). The locations of homophobia. *London Review of International Law*, 2(2), 169–199.
Rao, R. (2015). Global homocapitalism. *Radical Philosophy*, 194, 38–49.
Rao, R. (2020). *Out of time: The queer politics of postcoloniality*. Oxford University Press.
Reid, G. (2023). It is vital for South Africa to oppose Uganda's dangerous anti-gay bill. *Human Rights Watch*, 31 March. https://www.hrw.org/news/2023/03/31/it-vital-south-africa-oppose-ugandas-dangerous-anti-gay-bill
Reidy, T. (2020). The 2018 Abortion Referendum: Over before it began! In S. Calkin & K. Browne (Eds.), *After repeal: Rethinking abortion politics* (pp. 21–35). Zed Books.
Reinsborough, P., & Canning, D. (2017). *Re: Imagining change: How to use story-based strategy to win campaigns, build movements, and change the world*. Pm Press.
Renkin, H. Z. (2009). Homophobia and queer belonging in Hungary. *Focaal*, 53, 20–38.
Reilly, M. (2009). *States Limiting Legislative Debate. Report for the Office of Legislative Research*. Connecticut General Assembly. https://www.cga.ct.gov/2009/rpt/2009-r-0249.htm
Republican National Convention. (2016). *Republican Platform 2016*. Committee on Arrangements for the 2016 Republican National Convention.
Richardson, S. (2012). Sexing the X. *Signs*, 37(4), 909–933.
Richman, Kimberly D. (2010). *Courting change: Queer parents, judges, and the transformation of American family law*. New York University Press.

Riggs, D. W., & Ciccarello, C. (2023). The challenges of online recruitment in human-animal studies: A case study of social media advertising focused on LGBTIQA people. *Animal Studies*, 8 March. https://animalsinsocietygroup.wordpress.com/2023/03/08/the-challenges-of-online-recruitment-in-human-animal-studies-a-case-study-of-social-media-advertising-focused-on-lgbtiqa-people/

Risman, B. J. (2018). *Where the Millennials will take us*. Oxford University Press.

Roberts, T., Smalley, J., & Ahrendt, D. (2021). Effect of gender-affirming hormones on athletic performance in transwomen and transmen: Implications for sporting organisations and legislators. *British Journal of Sports Medicine*, *55*(11), 577–583.

Robertson, S. (2015). Natives making space: The Softwood Lumber dispute and the legal geographies of Indigenous property rights. *Geoforum*, *61*, 138–147.

Rogers, B. A. (2023). TERFs aren't feminists: lesbians stand against trans exclusion. *Journal of Lesbian Studies*, *28*(1), 24–43.

Rollock, N. (2012). The Invisibility of Race: Intersectional Reflections on the Liminal Space of Alterity. *Race Ethnicity and Education*, *15*(1), 65–84..

Rothschild, L. (2023). New skin for an old ceremony: The gay revolution and the formation of Israeli heteroactivism. *ACME: An International Journal for Critical Geographies*, *22*(3), 1115–1140.

Rowling, J. (2022a). Only 2% of sexual offenders are female…[tweet], 16 September. https://twitter.com/jk_rowling/status/1570834805008498688 (accessed 23 August 2023).

Rowling, J. (2022b). Safeguarding exists…[tweet], 16 September. https://twitter.com/jk_rowling/status/1570749115994370048 (accessed 23 August 2023).

Rubin, D. A. (2017). *Intersex matters: Biomedical embodiment, gender regulation, and transnational activism*. SUNY Press.

Rudy, Susan. (2020). Gender's ontoformativity, or refusing to be spat out of reality: Reclaiming queer women's solidarity through experimental writing. *Feminist Theory*, *21*(3), 351–365.

Rustin, S. (2022). Trying to erase the biological definition of sex isn't just misguided – it's dangerous. *The Guardian*, 28 June. https://www.theguardian.com/commentisfree/2022/jun/28/erase-biological-definition-sex-gender-self-identification-trans-transgender-feminist-case

Ryan-Flood, R. (2024). Queer lineage: On generational sexualities, LGBTQ identity, and visibility. In R. Ryan-Flood. & A. T. Murphy (Eds.), *Queering desire: Lesbians, gender and subjectivity* (pp. 171–183). Routledge.

Rymer, S., & Cartei, V. (2015). Supporting transgender survivors of sexual violence: Learning from users' experiences. *Critical and Radical Social Work*, *3*(1), 155–164.

Sadgrove, J., Vanderbeck, R. M., Andersson, J., Valentine, G., & Ward, K. (2012). Morality plays and money matters: Towards a situated understanding of the politics of homosexuality in Uganda. *The Journal of Modern African Studies*, *50*(1), 103–129.

Sagatys, G. (2010). The concept of family in Lithuanian law. *Jurisprudencija*, *119*(1).

Saldaña, J. (2021). *The coding manual for qualitative researchers* (4th ed.). SAGE Publications, Inc.

Schulman, S. (2021). *Let the record show: A political history of ACT UP New York, 1987-1993*. Farrar, Straus and Giroux.

Schutz, A. (1970). *On phenomenology and social relations*. University of Chicago Press.

Scott, J. C. (1990). *Domination and the arts of resistance: Hidden transcripts*. (Reprint ed.). Yale University Press.

Sears, A. (2005). Queer anti-capitalism: What's left of lesbian and gay liberation? *Science & Society*, *69*(1), 92–112.

Serano, J. (2021). Transgender people, bathrooms, and sexual predators: What the data say. *Medium*, 8 June. https://juliaserano.medium.com/transgender-people-bathrooms-and-sexual-predators-what-the-data-say-2f31ae2a7c06 (accessed 26 August 2023).

Shah, S. P. (2015). Queering critiques of neoliberalism in India: Urbanism and inequality in the era of transnational 'LGBTQ' rights. *Antipode*, 47(3), 635–651.

Sharpe, A. (2018). *Sexual intimacy and gender identity 'fraud': Reframing the legal and ethical debate*. Routledge.

Sharpe, A. (2020a). Will gender self-declaration undermine women's rights and lead to an increase in harms? *The Modern Law Review*, 83(3), 539–557.

Sharpe, A. (2020b). *Women and Equalities Select Committee, UK Parliament, Transgender inquiry oral hearing 9/12/20*. Written Evidence to the Women and Equalities Committee on Reform of the Gender Recognition Act. https://committees.parliament.uk/writtenevidence/19156/pdf/ (accessed 24 August 2023).

Sharrow, E. (2021). Sports, transgender rights, and the bodily politics of cisgender supremacy. *Laws*, 10(3), 63.

Singh Dhillon, A. (2023). The culture war doesn't exist: Call it what it is: class war. *Novara Media*, 19 April. https://novaramedia.com/2023/04/19/the-culture-war-doesnt-exist/ (accessed 26 August 2023).

Skeggs, B., Moran, L., Tyrer, P., & Binnie, J. (2004). Queer as folk: Producing the real of urban space. In A. Collins (Ed.), *Cities of pleasure: Sex and the urban socialscape* (pp. 209–226). Routledge.

Shaw, A. (2023). *Uganda Anti-Homosexuality Bill of 2023: No basis in evidence*. Williams Institute (UCLA). https://williamsinstitute.law.ucla.edu/wp-content/uploads/Uganda-Anti-LGBT-Bill-Apr-2023.pdf

Slaymaker, E. (2023). Uneasy alliances: Organizing across difference to resist anti-trans legislation [Symposium paper] *Polarising Sexual and Gendered Lives: Divisions, Differences and LGBTQI+ Equalities*, University College Dublin, 23 June.

Smith, D. E. (1999). *Writing the social: Critique, theory, and iInvestigations*. University of Toronto Press.

Smith, M. (2022). Where does the British public stand on transgender rights in 2022. *YouGov*, 11 February. https://yougov.co.uk/topics/society/articles-reports/2022/07/20/where-does-british-public-stand-transgender-rights (accessed 24 August 2023).

SNP Women's Pledge. (2020). Press Release – February 2020. https://web.archive.org/web/20200918104345/http://www.snpwomenspledge.com/press-release-february-2020/ (accessed 24 August 2023).

Snyder, T. (1995). National myths and international relations: Poland and Lithuania, 1989-1994. *East European Politics and Societies*, 9(2), 317–343.

Solnit, R. (2016). *Hope in the dark: Untold histories, wild possibilities*. Haymarket Books.

Spade, D. (2015). *Normal life: Administrative violence, critical trans politics, and the limits of law*. Duke University Press.

Spišák, S. (2023). 'It's a generational thing, really'. Understandings of sexual rights in a digital age. *Sexualities*, 27(3), 13634607231160058.

Spivak, G. C. (1988). Can the subaltern speak? In C. Nelson & L. Grossberg (Eds.), *Marxism and the interpretation of culture* (pp. 271–313). University of Illinois Press.

Sremac, S., & Ganzevoort, R. R. (2015). The interplay of religious and sexual nationalisms in central and Eastern Europe. In R. Ganzevoort and S. Sremac (Eds.), *Religious and sexual nationalisms in central and Eastern Europe* (pp. 1–14). Brill.

Stewart, A. J., McCarthy, N., & Bryson, J. J. (2020). Polarization under rising inequality and economic decline. *Science Advances*, 6, eabd4201.

Stein, A. (2022). *The stranger next door: The story of a small community's battle over sex, faith, and civil rights; Or, How the right divides us.* Beacon Press.
Stock, K. (2021). *Material girls: Why reality matters for feminism.* Hachette UK.
Stokes, N. (2021). *Transgender victims' and survivors' experiences of domestic abuse.* SafeLives. https://safelives.org.uk/transgender-experiences-of-DA (accessed 24 August 2023).
Stokoe, E. (2006). On ethnomethodology, feminism, and the analysis of categorial reference to gender in talk-in-interaction. *The Sociological Review, 54*(3), 467–494.
Stone, A. L. (2009). More than adding a T: American lesbian and gay activists' attitudes towards transgender inclusion. *Sexualities, 12*(3), 334–354.
Stone, A. L. (2012). *Gay rights at the ballot box.* University of Minnesota Press.
Stone, A. L. (2017). Gender panics about transgender children in religious right discourse. *Journal of LGBT Youth, 15*(1), 1–15.
Stone, A. L. (2018). The geography of research on LGBTQ life: Why sociologists should study the South, rural queers, and ordinary cities. *Sociology Compass, 12*(11), e12638.
Stonewall. (2018). *Supporting trans women in domestic and sexual violence services.* Stonewall and nfpSynergy Report. https://www.stonewall.org.uk/system/files/stonewall_and_nfpsynergy_report.pdf (accessed 26 August 2023).
Strobel, C. (2023). [Untitled symposium paper] *Polarising Sexual and Gendered Lives: Divisions, Differences and LGBTQI+ Equalities*, University College Dublin, 23 June.
Stryker, S. (2017). *Transgender history: The roots of today's revolution.* Hachette UK.
Stryker, S., & Currah, P. (2014). Introduction. *Transgender Studies Quarterly, 1*(1–2), 1–18.
Stryker, S., & Whittle, S. (Eds.). (2013). *The transgender studies reader.* Routledge.
Stychin, C. (2003). *Governing sexuality: The changing politics of citizenship and law reform.* Hart Publishing.
Suhay, E. (2015). Explaining group influence: The role of identity and emotion in political conformity and polarization. *Political Behavior, 37*, 221–251.
Sullivan, A. (2021). *Professor Alice Sullivan submission of 27 August 2021.* Citizen Participation and Public Petitions Committee, The Scottish Parliament. https://www.parliament.scot/chamber-and-committees/committees/current-and-previous-committees/session-6-citizen-participation-and-public-petitions-committee/correspondence/2021/pe1876_h-professor-alice-sullivan-submission-of-27-august-2021 (accessed 26 August 2023).
Sullivan, M. (2022). *Lesbian death: Desire and danger between feminist and queer.* University Of Minnesota Press.
Sutherland, D. K. (2023). 'Trans enough': Examining the boundaries of transgender-identity membership. *Social Problems, 70*(1), 71–86.
Švaraitė, I. (2015). Seksualinių mažumų pateikimas Lietuvos nacionaliniuose dienraščiuose (2008–2013). *Žurnalistikos Tyrimai, 7*, 87–128.
Swerts, T. (2017). Creating space for citizenship: The liminal politics of undocumented activism. *International Journal of Urban and Regional Research, 41*(3), 379–395.
Tajfel, H., & Turner, J. C. (1986). The social identity theory of intergroup behavior. In S. Worchel & W. G. Austin (Eds.), *Psychology of intergroup relation*. Hall Publishers
Tamale, S. (2023). Homosexuality is not Un-African. *Al-Jazeera*, 26 April. https://america.aljazeera.com/opinions/2014/4/homosexuality-africamuseveniugandanigeriaethiopia.html
Tandoc, E. C. J. (2019). The facts of fake news: A research review. *Sociology Compass, 13*(9), e12724.
Tannehill, B. (2014). Myths about transition regrets. *HuffPost*, 18 November. https://www.huffpost.com/entry/myths-about-transition-regrets_b_6160626 (accessed 26 August 2023).

Taylor, V., & Whittier, N. E. (1992). Collective identity in social movement communities: Lesbian feminist mobilization. In A. D. Morris & C. M. Mueller (Eds.), *Frontiers in social movement theory* (pp. 104–129). Yale University Press.

Tereškinas, A. (2007). *'Not private enough?': Homophobic and injurious speech in the Lithuanian media*. Lithuanian Gay League. https://hdl.handle.net/20.500.12259/41633

Tereškinas, A. (2019). Precarious sexualities, alternative intimacies in postsocialist Lithuania. *Kultūra Ir Visuomenė: Socialinių Tyrimų Žurnalas, 10*(1), 11–28.

The *Guardian*. (2018). The guaridan view on the gender recognition act: Where rights collide. The *Guardian*, 17 October. https://www.theguardian.com/commentisfree/2018/oct/17/the-guardian-view-on-the-gender-recognition-act-where-rights-collide (accessed 26 August 2023).

Thurlow, C. (2022). From TERF to gender critical: A telling genealogy? *Sexualities, 27*(4), 962–978.

Thurlow, C. (2024). Sisters, it's been a while! The emotional pull of the lesbian 'gender critical' movement and a failure of solidarity. *Journal of Lesbian Studies, 28*(1), 161–174.

Travers, A. (2018). *The trans generation: How trans kids (and their parents) are creating a gender revolution*. New York University Press.

Travis, A. (2014). Police crime figures lose official status over claims of fiddling. The *Guardian*, 15 January. https://www.theguardian.com/uk-news/2014/jan/15/police-crime-figures-status-claims-fiddling (accessed 24 August 2023).

Troiden, Dr. R. R. (1989). The formation of homosexual identities. *Journal of Homosexuality, 17*(1–2), 43–74.

Tryl, L., Surmon, T., Kimaram, A., et al. (2022). *Britons and gender identity: Navigating common ground and division*. UK: More in Commmon. https://www.moreincommon.org.uk/our-work/research/britons-and-gender-identity/

Tucker, A. (2009). *Queer visibilities: Space, identity and interaction in Cape Town*. Wiley-Blackwell.

Turnbull-Dugarte, S. J., & McMillan, F. (2023). 'Protect the women!' Trans-exclusionary feminist issue framing and support for transgender rights. *Policy Studies Journal, 51*(3), 629–666.

Turner, J. (2018). Trans rapists are a danger in women's jails. *The Times* (London), 8 September. https://www.thetimes.co.uk/article/trans-rapists-are-a-danger-in-women-s-jails-5vhgh57pt (accessed 26 August 2023).

Turner, V. (1969). Liminality and communitas. In *The ritual process: Structure and anti-structure* (pp. 94–130). Alline Publishing.

UK Government Equalities Office. (2023). *Policy statement of reasons on the decision to use section 35 powers with respect to the Gender Recognition Reform (Scotland) Bill*. Equality Hub. UK Government. https://assets.publishing.service.gov.uk/government/uploads/system/uploads/attachment_data/file/1129495/policy-statement-section-35-powers-Gender-Recognition-Reform-_Scotland_-Bill.pdf (accessed 24 August 2023).

U.S. Department of State. (2015). Further US efforts to protect human rights in Uganda. *The White House*, 11 May. https://obamawhitehouse.archives.gov/blog/2014/06/19/further-us-efforts-protect-human-rights-uganda

Valentine, D. (2007). *Imagining transgender: An ethnography of a category*. Duke University Press.

Valverde, M. (2010). Practices of citizenship and scales of governance. *New Criminal Law Review, 13*(2), 216–240.

Valverde, M. (2014). The rescaling of feminist analyses of law and state power: From (Domestic) subjectivity to (Transnational) governance networks. *UC Irvine Law Review, 4*(1), 325–352.

Valverde, M. (2015). *Chronotopes of law: Jurisdiction, scale and governance*. Routledge.
Van Dyke, N., & Amos, B. (2017). Social movement coalitions: Formation, longevity, and success. *Sociology Compass, 11*(7), e12489.
Van Dyke, N., & McCammon, H. J. (2010). *Strategic alliances: Coalition building and social movements*. University of Minnesota Press.
Van Gennep, A. (1960) *The rites of passage*. University of Chicago Press.
Van Gennep, A. (2019). *The rites of passage*. University of Chicago press.
Velte, K. (2021). Free exercise and LGBTQ discrimination: The race analogy in historical perspective. *Berkley Forum*, 26 July. https://berkleycenter.georgetown.edu/responses/free-exercise-and-lgbtq-discrimination-the-race-analogy-in-historical-perspective (accessed 26 July 2021).
Vērdiņš, K., & Ozoliņš, J. (2020). The Latvian LGBT movement and narratives of normalization. In R. Buyantueva & M. Shevtsova (Eds.), *LGBTQ+ activism in central and Eastern Europe: Resistance, representation and identity* (pp. 239–264). Springer International Publishing.
Vilain, E., & Martinez-Patiño, M. (2019). Science's place in gender-based policies in athletics. *The Lancet, 393*(10180), 1504.
Wahab, A. (2016). 'Homosexuality/homophobia is Un-African'?: Un-mapping transnational discourses in the context of Uganda's anti-homosexuality bill/act. *Journal of Homosexuality, 63*(5), 685–718.
Waites, M. (2017). LGBTI organizations navigating imperial contexts: The Kaleidoscope Trust, the Commonwealth and the need for a decolonizing, intersectional politics. *The Sociological Review, 65*(4), 644–662.
Waitt, G. (2005). Sexual citizenship in Latvia: Geographies of the Latvian closet. *Social & Cultural Geography, 6*(2), 161–181.
Wakefield, J. R. H., Kalinauskaite, M., & Hopkins, N. (2016). The nation and the family: The impact of national identification and perceived importance of family values on homophobic attitudes in Lithuania and Scotland. *Sex Roles, 75*(9–10), 448–458.
Wakefield, L. (2022). Abolishing legal sex and gender comes with many, many pros, radical new report finds. *PinkNews*, 11 May. https://www.thepinknews.com/2022/05/11/legal-sex-gender-future-legal-project-research/
Wakefield, R. L., & Wakefield, K. (2022). The antecedents and consequences of intergroup affective polarisation on social media. *Information Systems Journal, 33*(3), 640–668.
Walters, S. D. (1996). From Here to Queer: Radical Feminism, Postmodernism, and the Lesbian Menace (Or, Why Can't a Woman Be More Like a Fag?) *Signs: Journal of Women in Culture and Society 21*(4), 830–69.
Ward, J. (2008). *Respectably queer: Diversity culture in LGBT activist organizations*. Vanderbilt University Press.
Warner, M. (2000). *The trouble with normal: Sex, politics, and the ethics of queer life*. Harvard University Press.
Washington, C. (2013). Fall down on me: Stories of the club from black gay men in the South. In R. U. Whitlock (Ed.), *Queer South rising: Voices of a contested place*, (pp. 73–89). Information Age Publishing.
Weber, C. (2016). *Queer international relations: Sovereignty, sexuality and the will to knowledge*. Oxford University Press.
Webster, L. (2022). 'Erase/rewind': How transgender Twitter discourses challenge and (re)politicize lesbian identities. *Journal of Lesbian Studies, 26*(2), 174–191.

Weeks, J. (2007). *The world we have won: The remaking of erotic and intimate life*. Routledge.
Weiss, Meredith L., & Bosia, M. J. (2013). *Global homophobia: States, movements, and the politics of oppression*. University of Illinois Press.
West, C., & Zimmerman, D. H. (1987). Doing gender. *Gender and Society*, *1*(2), 125–151.
Westbrook, L., & Saperstein, A. (2015). New categories are not enough: Rethinking the measurement of sex and gender in social surveys. *Gender & Society*, *29*(4), 534–560.
Westbrook, L., & Schilt, K. (2013). Doing gender, determining gender: Transgender people, gender panics, and the maintenance of the sex/gender/sexuality system. *Gender & Society*, *28*(1), 32–57.
Whitehead, A. L., & Perry, S. L. (2019). Is a 'Christian America' a more patriarchal America? Religion, politics, and traditionalist gender ideology. *Canadian Review of Sociology/Revue canadienne de sociologie*, *56*(2), 151–177.
Whitehead, A., & Perry, S. (2022). *Taking America back for god: Christian nationalism in the United States*. Oxford University Press.
White House Office of the Press Secretary. (2011). Presidential Memorandum – International Initiatives to Advance the Human Rights of Lesbian, Gay, Bisexual, and Transgender Persons. *The White House*, 6 December. https://obamawhitehouse.archives.gov/the-press-office/2011/12/06/presidential-memorandum-international-initiatives-advance-human-rights-l
Whittle, S., & Simkiss, F. (2020). *A perfect storm: The UK governments failed consultation on the Gender Recognition Act 2004. Research handbook on gender, sexuality and the law*. Edward Elgar Publishing.
Wiik, A., Lundberg, T. R., Rullman, E., Andersson, D. P., Holmberg, M., Mandić, M., Brismar, T. B., Dahlqvist Leinhard, O., Chanpen, S., Flanagan, J. N., Arver, S., & Gustafsson T. (2020). Muscle strength, size, and composition following 12 months of gender-affirming treatment in transgender individuals. *The Journal of Clinical Endocrinology & Metabolism*, *105*(3), dgz247.
Williams Institute. (2019). *Adult LGBT population in the United States*. UCLA. https://williamsinstitute.law.ucla.edu/wp-content/uploads/LGBT- PopulationEstimates-March-2019.pdf (accessed 5 November 2019).
Witcomb, G. L., & Peel, E. (Eds.). (2022). *Gender diversity and sport: Interdisciplinary perspectives on increasing inclusivity*. Routledge.
Witcomb, G. L., & Peel, E. (2022). Introduction: Situating gender diversity and sport. In *Gender diversity and sport* (pp. 1–12). Routledge.
Wilkinson, C. (2020). *LGBT rights in the former Soviet Union: The evolution of hypervisibility*. Oxford University Press. https://doi.org/10.1093/oxfordhb/9780190673741.013.12
Williams, C. (2015). Fact check: Study shows transition makes trans people suicidal. *The Trans Advocate*, 2 November. http://www.transadvocate.com/fact-check-study-shows-transition-makes-trans-people-suicidal_n_15483.htm (accessed 26 August 2023).
Women and Equalities Committee. (2020). *Oral evidence: Reform of the Gender Recognition Act, HC 884 – Wednesday 9 December 2020*. UK Parliament. https://committees.parliament.uk/oralevidence/1393/html/ (accessed 26 August 2023).
Woodell, B., Kazyak, E., & Compton, D. L. (2015). Reconciling LGB and Christian identities in the rural South. *Social Sciences*, *4*(3), 859–878.
Wynter, S. (1992). *Do not call us Negros: How 'multicultural' textbooks perpetuate racism*. Aspire Books.

Yermakova, O. (2021). PiS vs LGBT: The 'othering' of the LGBT movement as an element of populist radical right party discourse in Poland. *Sprawy Narodowościowe*, 53, 1–28.

Yip, A. K. (2012). *The Ashgate research companion to contemporary religion and sexuality*. Routledge.

York, G. (2022). How I joined feminism's undercover fightback. *Daily Mail*, 21 March. https://www.dailymail.co.uk/femail/article-10633875/Secret-group-women-resort-guerrilla-tactics-protect-single-sex-spaces.html (accessed 26 August 2023).

Zeller, M. C., & Vidra, Z. (2021). Illiberalism, polarisation, social resilience, and resistance: Concepts in dynamic tension. *Intersections: East European Journal of Society and Politics*, 7(4), 1–12.

Zerubavel, E. (1991). *The fine line: Making distinctions in everyday life*. The University of Chicago Press.

INDEX

40th annual British Social Attitudes Survey 140
303 Creative LLC v. Elenis 33
2003 *Lawrence v. Texas* decision 34
2009 Anti-Homosexuality Bill 84
2015 *Obergefell v. Hodges* decision 34
2020 *Bostock v. Clayton County* decision 34
2022 US Trans Survey 57

abortion 8, 10, 14, 140, 157–62, 164, 170, 172, 173 n.4, 176, 184
Abramowitz, A.I. 3
activism 1, 2, 5–9, 11, 36, 53, 62, 66, 67, 72–3, 75, 97–9, 107, 157, 158, 190
activist initiatives 61, 62, 73
Adiah 54, 55
advocacy organizations 94
affective 3, 71, 110, 112, 118, 139
affective polarization 2, 105, 116
Agnes 111, 112
Ahmed, Sara 149, 161
allies 19, 89, 91–5, 98, 103, 122, 123, 130, 189, 190
'Amber Heart' 65
Anghie, Anthony 78
Anglo-American critiques 177
'anti-Christian forces' 35
anti-colonialism 5
anti-EU nationalist rhetoric 63
anti-gay agenda 35
anti-gay sentiment, Uganda 85
'Anti-Homosexuality Act' (AHA) 85, 86
anti-immigrant politics 5
anti-LGBTQ 5, 12, 35, 48, 50, 68, 78, 85, 89
anti-LGBTQ+ 50, 61, 62, 64–70, 72, 73
anti-LGBTQIA+ polarisations 4–9
anti-trans 13, 22, 24, 135 n.9, 183, 184
  agenda 24
  alliances 151

bills 9, 89, 93, 95–8, 100–2
discourse 184
feminists 122
legislation 13, 50, 89–91, 93–9, 101–3
policy 89, 92, 95, 102
politics 6, 124, 137
sentiments 152
sports law 91, 92, 99, 100, 103
anti-western 5
Anzaldua, G.E. 114
artist-led workshop 162–9, 173 n.2, 185
arts-based research methods 159
asexual 1
assigned sex 25, 26
assimilationist politics 92
'Attitudes to Gender' survey 129–30
Ayoub, P.M. 5

Bailey, Allison 145, 146
Bakke, J.A. 25, 26
Ballantine, C. 11, 14, 48 n.1, 176, 181–6, 188
Baltic Pride 64, 65
Barker, M-J. 121
bathroom bills 94, 99, 103 n.1
BBC News 154 n.15
Beech, N. 53
Bennett, L. 25
Berlant, L. 182
Beyond Opposition project 14, 157–62, 172, 181, 183, 185
binaries/binary 5, 9–11, 14, 23–5, 53, 75, 78, 81, 82, 86, 106, 120, 121, 153 n.4, 176, 178, 189, 190
binaristic understandings of sex 28
binary drama 134
binary patterns 75
bio-essentialist 30
biological advantage 18, 20, 25, 30
biological sex 24, 27, 28, 30, 45, 46, 123, 133, 134, 140, 146, 147

biology-based gender ideology 50
biopolitical governance 83
bisexual 1, 37, 72, 91, 93–5, 102, 121, 138, 154 n.17, 176, 187
Black Americans 53, 56
black civil rights movement 36
black queer studies 114
Black transgender women 12, 49–59, 59 n.1, 178, 186
borrowed approximations 92, 95
Boss, Pauline 121
Bostock v. Clayton County 33
Brickell, Katherine 79
Britain 137–40, 143, 152, 153 n.4, 154 n.17
British culture 119, 154 n.11
British empire 77
British gender wars 139–40, 151, 152
British media 141
Brown, G. 72
Browne, Kath 47, 88 n.1, 118 n.1, 119, 158, 176
Browne, L. 14, 47, 88 n.1, 118 n.1, 119, 176, 181–6, 188
Brown v. Board of Education 40
Brubaker, R. 107
Bryson, J.J. 147
Burgess, Ernest W. 161
Burke, K. 14
Butler, Judith 107, 180, 184, 188

capitalist 6, 63
Castor Semenya 27, 28
Catholic Church 4
Catholic-driven society 178
CEE states 61, 63
Central Europe 11
Central European Nationhood of Lithuania 11
Centre for Crime and Justice Studies 146
centre/periphery binaries 82
Cepicky, S. 29
Christian 12, 34, 35, 37, 38, 41, 42, 47, 48
Christian nationalism 35
Christian right activism 3–5, 35
cisgender 13, 20, 46, 48, 91–5, 101, 103, 126, 127, 182

cisgender boys 46
cisgender female athletes 26
cisgender LGB activists 93, 103
cis-heteronormative system 6
civilizational binary 84
civil rights 34, 36, 41
class-based inequality 49
classist 58, 111
Clemmons, J.R. 29
click-bait-driven media 138
coalition building 89, 90, 187
coalitions 11, 13, 90–3, 95–7, 101–3, 183, 187
collective identity 90, 91, 103, 106, 112
Collins, Hill 114
colonial control 79, 82
colonialism 5, 7, 87
Colorado's nondiscrimination law 33
colour feminisms 114
coming out 94, 98, 99, 108
community 8, 12, 20, 31, 39, 44, 51, 53–6, 58, 59, 61, 63, 68, 69, 94, 97–102, 105, 116, 118, 127, 130, 134, 135, 148, 152, 183, 187
community organisation 54–8
Conover, M.D. 19
conservative 4, 17, 18, 22, 27, 29, 35, 36, 101, 138
conservative messaging 22
conservative religious ideology 4
Constitutional Court 65
'continuum' model 20, 30
Cooper, Davina 120
corporate media 152
counter-imaginary 188
court discourse 12, 47, 48
Crawley, S.L. 10, 11, 13, 178, 179, 182
creative methods 158, 160, 162, 170, 172
Crenshaw, Kimberle 111
crime statistics 141, 145–7
cross-sex hormones 29, 30
Crow, Jim 49
Crown Prosecution Service 147
culture wars 4, 8, 10, 14, 107, 119, 137, 138, 153 n.3, 154 n.11, 187
Cuomo, Dana 79
Currah, P. 111
the *Daily Mail* 142, 146

Daniels, J. 28
data gathering 171
'date rape drug' rohypnol 151
Davis, Wendy 96
'Day of Silence' 38–40
debate 1, 2, 7, 8, 15, 19, 22, 25, 26,
    29–31, 36, 46, 49, 53, 56, 58, 98,
    107, 108, 116, 121, 129, 132–4,
    137–41, 148, 150–2, 158, 160, 162,
    175, 178, 180, 190
  chamber debates 19, 21, 25
  culture war debate 14
  'gender debates' 120–3, 128, 129,
    131, 141
  ideological debates 49, 50
  International Women's Day
    debate 146
  intra-community debates 6, 8
  legal debates 85
  legislative debate 18–20, 188
  moral debates 49
  polarized debates 85, 105, 176, 183
  political debates 12, 18, 27, 29
  social debates 4
  sociopolitical debates 175
  'trans debates' 8, 121
decolonial 77
decriminalization 77
defensive postures 181
DeGeneres, Ellen 114, 115
delaney 88 n.4
democrat 3, 9, 12, 17, 19, 21, 30, 105
democratic 3, 9, 12, 17, 25, 64, 92, 187,
    188, 190
Democratic Party 19
Dentice, D. 53
Dhejne, Cecilia 144
Dietart, M. 53
Dills, S. 28
disability 6, 155 n.22
discrimination 7, 19, 23, 34, 36, 37, 47,
    48, 50, 57, 62, 65, 77, 94, 95, 143,
    144, 154 n.13
  double discrimination 185
  gender discrimination 92
  religious discrimination 37
  sexual discrimination 123
disinformation 141

diversity 7, 73, 129, 180
  gender diversity 124
division 1, 9–14, 17–19, 67, 71, 73, 78,
    89, 119, 124, 128–34, 137, 138, 152,
    157, 158, 172, 181
  homophobic divisions 176
  ideological divisions 4
  intra-community divisions 2
  intra-community LGBTQIA+/feminist
    divisions 6–9
  politicized divisions 5
  social divisions 3, 158, 159, 176
  socio-economic divisions 5
domestic violence 80
Dossett, J.A. 24, 28
double discrimination 185
Drag Queen Story Hours 95
Du Bois, W.E.B. 53
Dwyer, M. 26

Eastern Europe 5, 61
emotional investments 150–1
empathy 13, 71–3, 118, 127
Employment Division v. Smith 33
employment equalities 1
enemies of the nation 12, 63–4, 66, 71
England & Wales 140, 148
epistemic violence 87
equalities 4, 7, 8, 16 n.1, 19, 25, 38, 137
  economic inequality 3
  employment equalities 1
  gender equalities 7
  legislative equalities 5
  LGBT equalities 5
  LGBTQIA+ equalities 1, 2, 9–11, 15,
    135
  sexual equalities 8
  sexual/gendered equalities 5
Equality Texas 96, 101
equal rights 127
Establishment Clause 39
ethnography 80
European Court of Human Rights 65
Evangelical Protestant 4
Evangelical Protestantism 35
exclusion 12, 56, 69, 78, 80, 107, 127,
    137, 159
  political exclusion 55

social exclusion   52, 53, 58
extension dilemma   90
extremism   11, 121, 123, 183

Facebook   72, 97
family-related rights   35
Farmer, G.   26, 27
feminism   5, 7–9, 14, 116, 118, 121, 128, 132, 138
   colour feminisms   114
   radical feminisms   114
   trans-inclusive feminism   153
feminist legal geography   13, 75, 76, 79–81, 83
feminists   2, 6–9, 13, 15, 23, 30, 75, 79, 88, 107, 113, 114, 117–22, 124, 128, 130, 132–4, 135 n.5, 137–9, 152, 176, 178
feminist-sexual-legal geography   82
femonationalism   7
First Amendment Free Speech Clause   39, 43, 45
Fisher, Owl   155 n.21
Foucault, M.   117, 179
Free Exercise Clause   39
fringe groups   139, 149
Future of Legal Gender (FLAG) project   13, 119, 124, 129, 131–3, 135 n.1, 135 n.2, 135 n.3, 136 n.19

Garfinkel, H.   111
gay friendliness   79
gay marriage   42–5, 91
gay rights   7
Gay-Straight Alliance (GSA)   34, 38
gender-affirmative medical care   89
gender-based inequality   49
gender-based violence   51, 141, 149, 150, 152
gender binary   17, 24, 25, 30, 120, 128
gender critical   10, 121, 122, 124, 128, 131, 133, 135 n.4, 138, 147, 148, 151, 152, 154 n.19, 173 n.2
   beliefs   153 n.4
   feminists   119, 122, 123, 132, 133, 138, 152, 176
   groups   138–41, 148, 150, 154 n.10, 181

gender debate   120, 122, 123, 128, 129, 131, 141
gender-diverse   93, 120, 123, 126–8, 150
gender diversity   124
gender expression   56
gender fluidity   107
gender identifications   23
gender identity   22, 29, 33, 34, 37, 43, 45, 46, 56, 57, 75, 85, 87, 91, 107, 119, 120, 122, 130, 133, 134, 138, 139, 145, 147, 155 n.22, 177, 185
gender ideology   5, 50, 138
gender minorities   36, 85, 178, 183
gender non-conforming   19, 115, 149, 183
gender norms   63, 123, 128
gender panics   50
gender presentation   56
genderqueer   125
Gender Recognition Act 2004 (GRA)   136 n.13, 137–40, 144, 150, 159, 175
Gender Recognition Certificates   143, 153 n.2
Gender Recognition Reform Bill   140, 153 n.2
gender-segregated spaces   137
gender self-determination   137
gender transition   20
gender variance   24
gender wars   8, 10, 11, 13, 14, 119, 134, 151, 152, 175
   in Britain   137–52
Gender Wrongs   62
'Gender Wrongs' activists   68
generational polarization   106
generations   13, 17, 67, 69, 105–7, 109, 115, 116, 128, 175, 178
   political generations   116
   sexual generations   106, 108, 109
Gennep, Van   52
geopolitical binaries   77
Gidron, N.   2
Gill-Peterson, Jules   149
global approximations   92
global homocapitalism   86
global populism   105
Gloppen, Siri   84
Goffman, E.   117

González, Jessica 95
good gay 8
Greene, J. 55
group-based identity 106
groupism 10, 13, 105–9, 111, 116, 117
the *Guardian* 133, 134

Hagai, Ben 116
Halley, Janet 36
Halperin, D.M. 111
Harkins, Gillian 149
Harper, Tyler Chase 38–42
Harper v. Poway case 38–42
hegemonic masculinity 55
Hemmings, C. 105, 117, 118
Herman, D. 35
heteroactivism 5, 158
(hetero)patriarchy 7, 8
heteronormativity 5, 67, 72, 111, 135 n.7, 177
heterosexuality 61, 183
Hilliard, L. 14, 176
Home Office 147
homonationalism 7, 62, 72–5, 86
homonormativities 7, 13, 62, 68, 72–4
homophobia 75, 77, 79, 85, 86, 94, 95, 123
homosexual 37–40, 42, 64, 67, 74
homosexuality 38–40, 42–5, 70, 72, 77, 83–6
Horizon 2020 programme 173 n.1
hormone replacement therapy 23
hormones 26, 27, 147
   cross-sex hormones 29, 30
hormone therapy 23, 27
Horne, W. 2
House Bill (HB) 25 89, 92, 94, 95
Huntley, Ian 143

Iantaffi, Alex 121
identity-based movements 91
identity formation 49–53, 58, 185
ideological binaries 77
ideology 19, 110
   conservative religious ideology 4
   gender ideology 5, 50, 138
   polarizing ideology 2, 50, 57
   trans ideology 130, 139
immoral sexuality 66

imperfect utopias 187, 189
inclusion 4–8, 12, 21, 48, 49, 52, 58, 72, 74, 82, 84, 93, 102, 107, 139, 140, 158, 170, 175, 177, 178, 187
infighting 8, 90
in-group 2, 52
interactionism 109
interconnectivity 181
intergroup relations 126
international law 13, 75, 76, 78, 79, 81, 82, 84, 86, 88, 178, 179
international LGBTQ rights 76, 78
International Women's Day 146
interpretive-materialism 106
intersectionality/intersectionalities 6–8, 111, 114
intersex 27, 28, 30, 91
   athletes 27, 28
intersubjectivity 115
intra-community 1, 2, 6–9, 11, 14, 134
Irish artist-led workshop 160–1
Irish politics 159, 178
Irish Repeal Campaign 184
Išgirsti 62

Järvinen, M. 109, 110, 116
Jasper, James 90
Jenkin, Bernard 146
Jessup, Brad 82
Jjuuko, Adrian 84
Journal of Lesbian Studies 107
jurisdictional binaries 80

Kamarauskaite, R. 11, 12, 31, 177, 183, 184, 188
Kao, Y.C. 114
Kazyak, Emily 4, 10–12, 14, 88 n.1, 118 n.1, 190 n.2
Keating, A. 181
Keeling, K. 110
Keen-Minshull, Kellie-Jay 153 n.5
Keep Prisons Single Sex (KPSS) 140
#KeepPrisonsSingleSex 148
Kelley, R.D. 54
Kilkenny, K. 131
kinship 7, 55, 72
Kirt, J. 28
Kreiss, D. 90, 102, 134
Kulpa, R. 62, 72, 73

Lakeyah   55
Lalor, K.   10, 13, 178, 185
Lamble, S.   8, 10, 11, 13, 14, 178, 180, 181, 184, 185, 188
Latinx   94
law and space   77–8
Law of the Protection of Minors   65
law-space-sexuality   79
left-wing   124, 133, 138, 153 n.9
legal geographies of polarisations   76–9
legal geography   13
   queer legal geographies   75–88, 178, 179
legal sex   82, 119, 130, 133, 147
legislation   1, 4–6, 8, 17, 21–4, 26–9, 31, 35, 36, 49, 84, 101, 153 n.2, 175
   anti-LGBTQ legislation   35, 94, 178
   anti-LGBTQ+ legislations   50
   anti-trans legislation   13, 50, 89–91, 93–9, 101–3, 103 n.1
   democratic legislation   12
   discriminatory legislation   25
   in Europe   159
   LGBTQIA+ legislations   9
   in Texas   94
   Ugandan homophobic legislation   85
lesbian   6–8, 34, 35, 37, 39–41, 66, 67, 70, 72, 73, 88 n.3, 91–5, 102, 105, 107, 114–17, 122, 123, 125, 138, 139, 154 n.17, 182, 183
Levitas, R.   188
lexicons   77, 107, 111–17, 182
   'identity lexicons'   179
LGB   8, 10, 93, 94, 103, 151
LGBQ   13, 35
LGBTQ
   coalition   95, 97, 102
   inclusion   12, 48
   movements   91, 92, 94, 102
   polarisations   13, 75, 76, 78, 79, 82, 83, 86–8
   politics   3, 12, 98
   pride events   176
   rights   12, 13, 33–7, 47, 50, 75–9, 81, 82, 86–8, 175, 178, 179, 186
LGBTQIA+   1, 2, 4–9, 12, 14, 15, 16 n.1, 127
liberal democracies   5
liberalization   140, 157, 162

liminality   12, 50–3, 58, 59, 186
liminal space   51–9, 185
Lithuanian domestic activism   72–3
Lithuanian queer activists   61, 72–4
litigants   34–7
   Christian litigants   37
   public school litigants   47
   religious litigants   33, 34, 38, 44, 46–8
Lively, Scott   86
Living Library   62, 70
local politics   95, 96
Loder, K.   11, 12, 178, 185, 186
L Out UK   153 n.9
Love, H.   110, 118
Lynch, M.   108, 117

McGregor, S.C.   90, 102, 134
McIlwraith, Clare   82
Mackay, Finn   120
Maines, D.R.   109, 110, 116
male biological advantage   30
male-pattern criminality   141, 144–5
marginalisation   183, 186, 187
marginality   52, 58
margins   50, 52, 53, 69, 111
marriage equality   159, 177, 186
Martin, A.   108, 117
Martin, K.   9, 11, 12, 14
Mason's Manual   19
Massie, Alex   146
materialities   13, 83
Mead, George Herbert   106, 109, 110
media   2, 6, 8, 13, 14, 64, 67, 97, 99, 105, 119, 120, 125–9, 134, 137, 140, 141, 143, 147, 152, 157, 175, 184
   British media   141
   news media   141, 144
   online media   129
   polarising media   121–5
   social media   10, 13, 36, 100, 115–17, 119–21, 129, 130, 134, 135 n.9, 136 n.19, 137–9, 141, 142, 144–6, 148, 149, 152, 157, 184
Ministry of Justice   147, 148
Minow, M.   36
misinformation   14, 124–6, 141, 147, 149, 180, 184, 188, 189
   in the 'gender wars'   137–52

misogyny   123
Mizielińska, J.   72, 114
Moore-Ponce, Jody   14, 179–82, 187
Moraga, C.   114
morality   64, 68, 82, 114
mothers' activism   97
mothers of transgender children   95–7
Msosa, Alan   84
Muslim immigrants   7

narrative analysis   62
narrative production   105, 106, 108
narrative turn   108, 109
Nash, C.J.   47, 119, 158
nation   1, 4, 5, 12, 13, 61, 62, 67, 69, 72–4, 79, 178, 179
  Catholic nation   176
  Christian nation   35
  enemies of the nation   63–6, 71
  Lithuanian nation   61, 67
national belonging   61, 62, 64, 65, 72
national values   65
nationhood   62, 73
neoliberal   6
news media   141, 144
New Statesman   144
non-binary   20, 91, 93, 94, 101, 115, 117, 120, 121, 127–8, 151, 179
non-binary lesbian   117
nondiscrimination curriculum   42
Non-Governmental Organisations Act 2016   84
non-heterosexual sexualities   61, 87
normativities   51, 179

Office for National Statistics   155 n.24
online media   129
openness   70
opposite biological sex   46
opposition   2, 4, 10–12, 14, 18, 29, 30, 34, 38–40, 43, 45–8, 55, 63–5, 74, 84, 105, 118, 137, 158, 159, 175–7, 179, 180, 186
  binary oppositions   9, 85
oral history interviews   51
Orbach, Susie   119
organizational leadership   101
Orientalist   114
othering   82, 152

otherness   78, 81, 82, 149
out-group   2, 19, 52
overlapping approximations   92

pansexual   94
'parental rights'   47
Parents for Privacy v. Barr case   45–7
Parker v. Hurley case   42–5
patriarchy   121
Peel, E.   8, 10, 11, 13, 14, 119, 182–4
people of color   91
Perry, S.L.   24, 35
phantasmic circulation   188
Phillips, Anne   133, 134
Phipps, Alison   149
Phoenix, Jo   146
PinkNews   130–2
Plummer, K.   108, 109
polarizing media   121–5
Polarising Sexual and Gendered Lives symposium   153 n.1, 175
polarized binaries   85
polarizing ideology   2, 50, 57
polarizing media   121–5
political communication   18
political discourse   129
political homophobia   79
political polarizations   2–4, 9, 17, 18, 31, 50, 57–9, 90, 105, 129
populism   5, 105, 137
populist radical right (PRR)   2
pornography   8
predatory sex offenders   184
pre-pubertal hormone blockers   29
pre-pubertal suppressants   29
President Museveni of Uganda   77
Pride March   139
prison   141–3, 155 n.20, 155 n.22, 175
Prison Inspectorate's Annual Reports   143
production of identities   106
pronouns   120, 151
propaganda   49, 65
protecting women   23
pseudo science   124
puberty blockers   20, 29
public schools   12, 34, 35, 37–9, 41–5, 47, 48, 89

public spaces   12, 34, 36–8, 43, 45, 47, 48, 69
putative generations   106, 109, 116
putative real groups   105, 106

qualitative analysis software program   21
queer activism   6, 7, 11
   in Lithuania   61–74
queer culture   67, 107
queer historicity of sexuality   111
queer legal geography   83–7
queer lovers   7
queerness   6, 13, 66, 67, 73, 76, 81, 83, 86, 87
queer playful politics   69
queer temporalities   114
queer Ugandans   84
queer woman   107

race   7, 36, 39–41, 49, 50, 53, 54, 58, 80, 91, 92, 114
racial identity   53
racial minorities   36, 39, 41, 48
racial tension   41
racism   7, 50, 56, 123
radical feminisms   8, 114
radical feminist ('radfem')   122
'radical' queer contestations   6
Rahilly, E.   11, 12, 14, 44, 184, 187, 188
Rao, Rahul   86
rape statistics   145, 146
'Reality Check' report   142
reclaiming the past   112
'refusal to name trans'   23
relatable queerness   13, 73
relational identity   183
relationality   176, 180, 185–7, 189
religion   4, 5, 33–7, 41, 42, 45, 47, 63, 85, 86, 178
religiosity   4
religious freedom   33, 36–7
religious group   35, 46
replicability   172
republican   3, 9, 12, 17, 19, 21, 30, 89, 93, 105, 138
Republicans and Democrats   12, 17, 21
Respublika   64
Rowling, J.K.   145
Rudy, Susan   107

Rustin, S.   132–4

safety   8, 38, 76, 122, 138–40, 147–50, 152
   of LGBTQI+ Ugandans   84
   physical safety   23
   'Student Safety Plan'   45
   women's safety   24, 141, 180
same-sex couples   33
same-sex marriage   1, 6, 7, 33, 34, 47, 157, 159, 176
same-sex sexualities   34, 47, 61–7, 69–71, 73, 112
Saunders, K.L.   3
Schilt, K.   50
Schneider, M.   25
Schutz, A.   106, 115
scientific discourse   28
Scott, J.C.   53
Scottish Gender Recognition Bill   151
second-wave feminist movement   23
self-determination (self-ID)   11, 59, 137, 139, 140, 144, 151, 154 n.12
   Say No to Sex Self-ID   150
sex-based discrimination   23
sex-based record-keeping   145
sex-based rights   175
sex-change operation   111
sex classification   25, 119
sex education curriculum   95
sex essentialism   140
sex/gender binary   25, 30
sex/gender 'drama'   120
sexism   50, 92, 128
sex reassignment   26
sex-segregated   20, 92
sexual biology   17, 22, 28
sexual generations   106, 108, 109
sexualization   66
sexual legal geography   76, 79, 81–3
sexual minorities   41
sexual norms   56, 68
sexual offences   155 n.23
sexual orientation   19, 33–9, 41, 43, 50, 69, 75, 85, 116
sexual promiscuity   65, 84
sexual-spatial-legal nexus   82
sexual violence   145, 149, 150, 152
sex wars   8

sex work   6, 8
Simpson, Homer   131
Slaymaker, E.   11, 13, 31, 182–4, 188
Smith, Lorie   33
SMUG v. Lively case   86
social constructionist theory   106
social drama   34
social exclusion   52, 53, 58
social group identity   105
social justice   19, 21, 25, 159, 160
social media   10, 13, 36, 100, 115–17, 119–21, 129, 130, 134, 135 n.9, 136 n.19, 137–9, 141, 142, 144–6, 148, 149, 152, 157, 184
Social Media Induced Polarisation (SMIP)   129
social movement   4, 10, 11, 13, 90, 91, 97, 176, 177
social movement activists   36
social polarisation   159, 160, 162, 172
social stigma   50
social stratification   52
socio-legal scholarship   36
sociopolitical   12, 34, 48, 50, 55, 59, 175–7, 179, 187
sociopolitical polarisation   50
sodomy laws   34
SOGI   75, 77, 78, 80, 84, 87
Solnit, R.   188
The Souls of Black Folk (Du Bois)   53
sovereignty   13, 64, 75, 78, 81, 87, 182
spatial binaries   77, 80
spatial concepts   78
spatio-legal   76, 78–81, 83, 84, 87
    binaries   85
    lens   13, 75
    mechanisms   10, 75, 76
    polarisations   75, 76, 79, 86
    regulations   76, 82
sports   20–1
Stargel, K.   26, 27
state sovereignty   13, 75, 78
Stone, Amy   92, 94
Stone, Sandy   111
straight   127, 129
Strobel, C.   180, 185–7
Stryker, S.   111
'Student Safety Plan'   45
subjectification   6, 179

subjugation   52
Suhay, E.   52
Sullivan, Alice   145–7
the *Sunday Times*   142
Swerts, T.   53

Tatchell, Peter   130, 133, 134, 136 n.18
Tecklenburg, K.M.   184, 187, 188
temporal   7, 10, 13, 75, 117, 118, 176
temporalities   112–16, 178
TERF   107, 125
TERF wars   105
Third World Approaches to International Law (TWAIL)   79
Title IX   23, 27, 175
Title VII employment nondiscrimination protections   33
tolerance   39, 40, 44, 45, 47, 176
trans activists (TRA)   123
trans adults   91, 92, 96–8, 102
trans advocates   93, 97–103
trans debates   8, 121
trans dyke   117
trans-exclusionary radical feminists   107, 121
transfemininity   99
transgender   12, 13, 17, 19–24, 26, 27, 34, 37, 45–7, 49, 50, 53, 55, 56, 59, 89, 91, 93, 95–8, 102, 111, 112, 122, 124, 126, 134, 135 n.9, 143, 178, 186
    athlete bans   18, 19, 21
    athletes   20, 21, 24
    children   103
    communities   55
    identity   24, 46, 57, 92
    male   45
    rights   17, 18, 29–31, 35, 46, 175
    sports policies   12
    terminology   23
Transgender Advocates Knowledgeable Empowering (T.A.K.E.)   51–2, 54–8
Transgender Studies Quarterly   111
trans girls   23, 28
'trans-identifying males' (TIM)   142
trans ideology   130, 139
trans-inclusive feminism   153
transition   20, 23, 55–7, 96, 114, 144
trans kids   25, 93, 95–9, 102

transphobia 50, 124–6, 151
trans prisoners 141–4, 151, 154 n.18, 155 n.22
transsexual 91, 124
trans women 20, 23, 28, 50, 54, 57, 58, 99–102, 122, 125, 136 n.12, 140–2, 144–9, 183
trans youth 17, 25, 92, 98, 103, 103 n.2
Travis, A. 155 n.24
Trump, Donald 178
Twitter 19, 117, 119, 121, 122, 128–34, 145, 148

Ugandan Anti-Homosexuality Act (AHA) 2023 77
UK 'gender debates' 120
UK's 2004 Gender Recognition Act 137
'uneasy alliances' 183
United States
    anti-trans sports law in Texas 89–103
    'conservatives' 17
    LGBTQ rights 34–6
    'liberals' 17
    partisan politics 3
unity through diversity 91–3
Usain Bolt 22, 29
US Christian Right 4
US electoral politics 9
US Presidential Memorandum of 2011 76
US public 3, 4
US south 12, 49–51, 53, 54, 57–9, 186

us-*versus*-them 180–6
utopia 170, 186–9

Vaitiekūnas, Dominykas 62, 66, 67, 71, 72
verbal assault 41
victimisation 187
Viljoen, Frans 84
vulnerability 25, 70–1, 73, 80, 122, 150

Walke, C. 27, 28
Westbrook, L. 50
Western 1, 88, 117, 118
    culture 53
western decadence 63
Whitehead, A.L. 35
Whitmire, J. 24
Women & Equalities Committee Inquiry 144
women of color 94
women's-only spaces 175
'Women's Pledge Group' 144
women's rights 7, 8, 23, 30, 137, 140, 176
women's safety 24, 140, 141, 180
women's 'sex-based rights' 139
world-making 76, 78, 84, 85, 117
Wynter, S. 52

'zero-sum conception of rights' 137

Zerubavel, E. 107
Zuokas, Artūras 64